Course	Textbook First Year Japanese
Course Number	**JPN 101 / 102 / 103** Portland Community College

http://create.mheducation.com

ISBN-10: 1121906680   ISBN-13: 9781121906686

Contents

Credits

Yookoso! An Invitation to Contemporary Japanese, Third Edition

1

Getting Started

GETTING STARTED

In Getting Started you are going to:

■ Learn how to greet others and introduce yourself
■ Talk about your classroom
■ Learn numbers up to 10,000
■ Learn to ask and tell telephone numbers and time
■ Learn to ask what something is
■ Talk about daily activities and weekly schedules
■ Talk about past and future activities and events
■ Learn to express what you like and dislike
■ Learn to invite someone to do something
■ Learn to talk about the weather
■ Learn to ask about location, existence, and price

YOOKOSO! MULTIMEDIA

Review and practice grammar and vocabulary from this chapter and watch video clips on the *Yookoso!* Interactive CD-ROM. Visit the *Yookoso!* Online Learning Center at **www.mhhe.com/yookoso3** for additional exercises and resources.

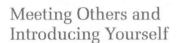

Part One

OBJECTIVES

Meeting others and introducing yourself
Everyday greetings
Classroom expressions
The Japanese writing system (1): Introduction

Meeting Others and Introducing Yourself

Dialogue 1: A Simple Introduction

Two classmates, John Kawamura and Linda Brown, are introducing themselves.

KAWAMURA: Hajimemashite. <u>Kawamura</u> desu.
BURAUN: Hajimemashite. <u>Buraun</u> desu.
KAWAMURA: Doozo yoroshiku.
BURAUN: Doozo yoroshiku.

言語ノート

LANGUAGE NOTE: Romanization

Romanization is the transcription of Japanese using **rooma-ji** (lit., *Roman letters*), or the English alphabet. In Japan the only words you see written in **rooma-ji** are station names (for the sake of foreigners), trademarks, ad catchphrases, and the like. In this textbook, romanization is used only as an aid for the beginning student. By the end of Getting Started, you should have a good working knowledge of **hiragana** and **katakana**.

The Language Notes present helpful information about the Japanese language as well as useful expressions.

Hajimemashite (literally, *it's the first time we meet*) and **doozo yoroshiku** (lit., *please regard me favorably*) are set phrases. **Desu** corresponds to the verb *to be* (*am, are, is,* etc., depending on context).

Dialogue 1   KAWAMURA: How do you do? I am <u>Kawamura</u>.   BROWN: How do you do? I am <u>Brown</u>. KAWAMURA: It's nice to meet you.   BROWN: It's nice to meet you.

Yookoso! An Invitation to Contemporary Japanese, Third Edition

3

STUDY HINT

Working in Pairs or in Groups

Because most of you do not have many opportunities to speak regularly with native or near-native speakers of Japanese, your Japanese class is the most important place to practice speaking Japanese. This textbook includes many activities in which you practice using Japanese with your classmates in pairs or in groups. Pair or group activities are indicated by a speech bubble icon throughout the book. When working in pairs or groups, first find out the objective of a given activity (getting specific information, giving information, creating a dialogue, solving a problem, etc.) and then work together to accomplish that objective by using Japanese. Try to express yourself as much as possible using what you already know. If you have any questions, ask your partner(s) or your instructor. If a partner has difficulties, help out. Pair or group activities in the classroom probably present the most important opportunities for you to practice speaking Japanese. Try to avoid chatting in English.

The Study Hints offer useful strategies for learning Japanese. Review and use these hints often to maximize your study of Japanese.

When Japanese greet each other, they bow. Nowadays, many Japanese shake hands while greeting, but they may also bow while shaking hands. How deeply and how often Japanese bow depends on such factors as their relative ages and social statuses.

ACTIVITY **1**

Using Dialogue 1 as a model, introduce yourself and meet as many classmates as you can. Circulate throughout the classroom and write down their names.

Dialogue 2: Meeting Someone and Then Introducing Yourself

Linda Brown is introducing herself to Mei Lin Chin, another classmate.

BURAUN: Sumimasen. <u>Chin-san</u> desu ka.
  CHIN: Hai, soo desu.
BURAUN: <u>Buraun</u> desu. Hajimemashite. Doozo yoroshiku.
  CHIN: <u>Chin</u> desu. Hajimemashite. Doozo yoroshiku.

Listening activities, indicated by the headphones icon, can also be found on the Textbook Audio Program.

Sumimasen is an expression of apology, corresponding to the English *I'm sorry* or *excuse me.* It is also frequently used to attract someone's attention or to express appreciation (in the latter case *thank you* is a closer English equivalent). To form a simple yes/no question in Japanese, add **ka** to the end of a statement (with a raising intonation). **Ka** takes the place of a question mark.

Dialogue 2   BROWN: Excuse me. Are you <u>Ms. Chin</u>?   CHIN: Yes, I am. (lit., *Yes, that's right.*) BROWN: I am <u>Brown</u>. How do you do? It's nice to meet you.   CHIN: I am <u>Chin</u>. How do you do? It's nice to meet you.

When Japanese give their full names, they say their family name first and given name last (Japanese do not have middle names). Japanese typically introduce themselves with their family name alone and address others (except close friends and family members) by family name followed by a respectful title. For now, the only titles you need to know are **-san** (*Mr./Ms.*) for your friends or classmates and **-sensee** (*Professor*) for your instructor. *Never attach these titles to your own name.*

Dialogue 3: Inquiring About Someone's Name

John Kawamura is looking for Masao Hayashi.

KAWAMURA: Sumimasen. Hayashi-san desu ka.
TANAKA: Iie.
KAWAMURA: Shitsuree shimashita.
TANAKA: Iie.

The Culture Notes present interesting information about Japanese culture, society, and modes of interaction.

ACTIVITY   2

Practice Dialogues 2 and 3 with several classmates using your own names. (Do you remember your classmates' names from doing Activity 1?)

Dialogue 4: Asking for Someone's Name

Linda Brown and Mei Lin Chin are getting acquainted.

BURAUN: Hajimemashite. Buraun desu. O-namae wa?
CHIN: Chin desu. Hajimemashite.

LANGUAGE NOTE: Informal Questions

Notice that the question **o-namae wa?** does not end in **ka.** In formal Japanese, questions end in **ka,** but in an informal, colloquial style of speech questions are often abbreviated. **O-namae wa?** is short for **O-namae wa nan desu ka** (lit., *As for your name, what is it?*). Here is a very literal translation of Dialogue 4.

Note that the subject may be left unexpressed in Japanese when it can be figured out from the context.

Dialogue 3   KAWAMURA: Excuse me. Are you Mr. Hayashi?   TANAKA: No.   KAWAMURA: I'm sorry. (lit., *I committed a rudeness.*)   TANAKA: Not at all.

Dialogue 4   BROWN: How do you do? I am Brown. May I have your name?   CHIN: I am Chin. How do you do?

BURAUN: **O-namae wa?**	Your name?
CHIN: **Chin desu.**	Is Chin.

Notice how Brown began the sentence and Chin finished it. This is common in Japanese conversation. Being an active listener when speaking Japanese is important.

Dialogue 5: Using a Name Card

Linda Brown is meeting her neighbor, Yooichi Takada.

BURAUN: Hajimemashite, <u>Tookyoo Daigaku no Buraun</u> desu.
TAKADA: Hajimemashite, <u>Sonii no Takada</u> desu.
BURAUN: Kore, watashi no meeshi desu.
TAKADA: Doomo arigatoo gozaimasu. Kore, watashi no meeshi desu.
BURAUN: Doomo arigatoo gozaimasu.

When you introduce yourself in Japan, it is common to state your affiliation. Japanese tend to identify strongly with the group they belong to (their "in-group") and are interested in knowing another person's affiliation and rank. You can tell a lot about someone from his/her affiliation and rank. Stating affiliation also helps get a conversation going by giving your conversational partner something more to ask you about. To clarify your affiliation, say

> (*Company/school*) no (*last name*) desu.
> *I am (name) of (institution).*
>
> Tookyoo Daigaku no Kawamura desu.
> *I am Kawamura of the University of Tokyo.*

You may also hand your name card in silence while lightly bowing.

> **J**apanese tend to stand farther apart during a conversation than North Americans do. Some Japanese also consider it rude to look directly into another person's eyes, especially if that person has a higher social status.

CULTURE NOTE: Name Cards

文化ノート

Name cards (**meeshi**) play an important role in Japan because they contain the following pieces of information essential to developing a relationship:

- company or school affiliation
- rank in the company or school
- the correct written form and pronunciation of the person's name
- address, telephone, and fax numbers, and often e-mail address

A few people also put their photographs on the card, and those who deal with international visitors usually have their information in English on the reverse side. Some Japanese personal names are written in such unusual ways that even native speakers have trouble figuring out their correct written form and pronunciation, so this notation is an important part of the **meeshi**. The information about the person's rank is significant because it helps you figure out what level of politeness you should use in speaking to him or her.

(Continues.)

Dialogue 5   BROWN: How do you do? I am <u>Brown of the University of Tokyo</u>.   TAKADA: How do you do? I am <u>Takada of Sony</u>.   BROWN: This is my name card.   TAKADA: Thank you very much. This is my name card.   BROWN: Thank you very much.

五

Since the **meeshi** represents the person, you should treat it with respect, receiving it with both hands while bowing slightly and studying it for a few moments before putting it away, preferably in a card holder, or **meeshi-ire.** (Never put it in your back pocket.) If you receive a **meeshi** during a business meeting, you may want to keep it on the table in front of you for handy reference.

山村商事
営業部

部長　山口健次

〒102–0075　東京都千代田区三番町
二一六一七山村ビル
Tel (03) 3334-4561

東京大学工学部三年

ジョン・カワムラ

〒113–0033 東京都文京区本郷三丁目 2–11
TEL (03) 3212-2118

KENJI YAMAGUCHI
General Manager
Sales and Marketing Department

YAMAMURA TRADING CO., LTD.
Yamamura Building
2-6-7, Sanbanchō, Chiyoda-ku
Tokyo 102–0075 Japan   *Telephone (03) 3334-4561*

JOHN KAWAMURA
Junior
Faculty of Engineering
University of Tokyo

2-11, Hongō 3-chōme, Bunkyō-ku
Tokyo 113–0033 Japan
TEL. (03) 3212-2118

ACTIVITY 3

Now make your own English name card including all the information discussed in Culture Note: Name Cards. Then practice Dialogue 5 with your classmates, using your name card. Be sure to offer and receive the name cards properly.

言語ノート

LANGUAGE NOTE: Expressing Gratitude

Japanese express gratitude and apologize frequently as ways of maintaining harmonious relationships. Among the many ways to express gratitude in Japanese are these common expressions, listed from formal to informal.

> **Doomo arigatoo gozaimasu.**
> **Arigatoo gozaimasu.**

> **Doomo arigatoo.**
>
> **Arigatoo.**
>
> **Doomo.**
>
> Among these, **doomo** (lit., *very*) is commonly used in everyday conversation when speaking to social equals or subordinates. Students often use **sankyuu** (from English *thank you*). Note that such an expression of apology as **(doomo) sumimasen (deshita)** is also used as a polite expresson of gratitude. When someone expresses gratitude and you would like to say *you're welcome*, say **doo itashimashite** or **iie, doo itashimashite**.

Everyday Greetings

Dialogue 6: Morning Greetings

Linda Brown runs into Professor Yokoi in the morning.

BURAUN: Yokoi-sensee, ohayoo gozaimasu.
  YOKOI: Aa, Buraun-san, ohayoo.
BURAUN: Ii o-tenki desu ne.
  YOKOI: Ee, soo desu ne.

ACTIVITY **4**

Using Dialogue 6 as a model, with a partner play the roles of student and professor greeting one another in the morning. Then exchange roles.

> **N**otice that Brown says **ohayoo gozaimasu** to her professor, who simply says **ohayoo** to her student. This is because students are expected to speak politely to their professors, while professors have the option of speaking informally to their students.

| Vocabulary: Common Greetings and Leave-Taking | |

Greetings

Ohayoo gozaimasu.	Good morning. (*formal*)
Ohayoo.	Good morning. (*informal*)
Konnichi wa.	Good afternoon.
Konban wa.	Good evening.
O-genki desu ka.	How are you?
Ee, genki desu.	(Yes,) I am fine.
Okagesama de, genki desu.	Thanks to you, I'm fine.
Ee, okagesama de...	(Yes,) thanks to you...(I'm fine). (*informal*)

(Continues.)

Dialogue 6 BROWN: Professor Yokoi, good morning. YOKOI: Ah, Ms. Brown, good morning.
BROWN: It's fine weather, isn't it? YOKOI: Yes, it is.

O-hisashiburi desu ne.	I haven't seen you for a long time.
Shibaraku desu ne.	I haven't seen you for a long time. (*informal*)

Leave-Taking

Shitsuree shimasu.	Good-bye. (lit., *Excuse me.*)
Ja (or De wa), mata.	See you later (lit., *again*).
Ja (or De wa).	See you. (*very informal*)
Sayo(o)nara.	Good-bye.
O-yasumi nasai.	Good night. (*informal*)

> **S**hitsuree shimasu is commonly used among business associates and as a polite way of taking leave of one's superior.

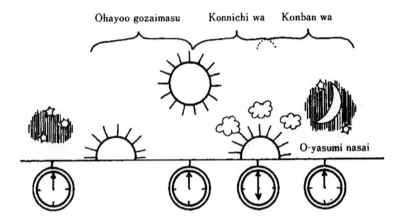

LANGUAGE NOTE: Greetings

In America, *How are you?* is not an inquiry about your health as much as an idiomatic way of saying *hello.* In Japan, commenting on the weather serves much the same function. If someone greets you with **Ii o-tenki desu ne,** do not feel compelled to give your opinion on the matter. Just be agreeable: **Soo desu ne** (*Yes, it is, isn't it*).

So what about **O-genki desu ka?** This *How are you?* really means *How have you been lately?*, so don't say it to anyone you have seen recently. If you haven't seen someone for some time, or if you are sincerely concerned about his or her health, **O-genki desu ka** is appropriate. The proper response when asked **O-genki desu ka** is **Okagesama de** (lit., *Thanks to you*). The implication is that the questioner's concern has contributed to your physical and spiritual health.

Also, be careful with **sayo(o)nara.** It has a sense of finality, so don't say it to someone you expect to see later in the day or in a couple of days in most situations. In this case, say **ja mata** or **de wa mata.** (School children say **sayo(o)nara** at the end of a day.)

ACTIVITY   **5**

Review the following greetings and phrases and then go to step 1.

1. Konnichi wa.
2. O-genki desu ka.
3. Ja, mata.
4. Konban wa.
5. Arigatoo gozaimasu.

6. Hajimemashite.
7. Shibaraku desu ne.
8. Ohayoo gozaimasu.
9. Ii o-tenki desu ne.
10. O-yasumi nasai.

Step 1 (in pairs)

Ask a classmate to respond appropriately to the ten greetings and phrases. Then, that classmate will quiz you on the same greetings and phrases. Note: there may be more than one response to a greeting or phrase. Try to say the greetings and responses from memory instead of reading them off the page.

Step 2 (instructor and students)

Your instructor will say a greeting or phrase to a selected student. That student will in turn say the same greeting or phrase to another student, who will then give the appropriate response.

Example:

    Instructor to Student 1: Hajimemashite.
      Student 1 to Student 2: Hajimemashite.
                Student 2: Hajimemashite, doozo yoroshiku.

ACTIVITY   **6**

Practice the following situations with your classmates.

1. It's 8:00 A.M. on a fine day and you see one of your friends, Mr. Sawai. Greet him.
2. It's 10:00 P.M. You see your friend Mr. Kawai, who is on his way home from work. Greet him.

ACTIVITY   **7**

Interaction: Turn to the classmate sitting next to you and do the following.

- Greet him or her appropriately.
- Ask how he or she is.
- Find out his or her name.
- Give a book to him or her.
    Useful expression: Doozo. (*Please [accept this]. or Here you are.*)

九

Classroom Expressions

ACTIVITY 8

You will have many opportunities in class to ask your instructor or a classmate how to say something in Japanese as in this example.

> Desk wa Nihongo de nan to iimasu ka.
> *How do you say desk in Japanese?*

> Tsukue to iimasu.
> (*You*) *say tsukue.*

Now practice asking your instructor to identify items in the classroom, following the example.

In informal speech, **Desk wa Nihongo de nantte iimasuka.—Tsukuette iimasu** is more common.

言語ノート

LANGUAGE NOTE: Japanese Nouns

Japanese nouns do not have different singular and plural forms. One word means both *book* and *books;* another means *person* and *people;* another, *idea* and *ideas.* Context determines which is meant. Later you will learn how to indicate a specific number of items in cases where you need to make a plural/singular distinction. Remember that although their English equivalents are given in the singular, Japanese nouns in vocabulary lists throughout this book assume the plural too, unless otherwise stated. Note, too, that unlike nouns in such languages as Spanish and French, Japanese nouns have no gender (i.e., they are not masculine or feminine). In addition, Japanese nouns keep the same form whether they are the subject or the object of a sentence.

Vocabulary: Classroom Expressions

Here are some useful expressions that you will hear and use frequently in class. Learn to understand your instructor's commands and to make the appropriate responses. Other useful expressions, which you will learn gradually as you hear them repeated, are presented in Vocabulary Library: More Classroom Expressions.

Student

Practice saying these aloud, as your instructor models them for you.

Shitsumon ga arimasu.	I have a question.
Moo ichido onegai shimasu.	Please say that again.
Wakarimasen.	I don't understand.
Wakarimashita.	I understood.
Chotto matte kudasai.	Please wait a moment.
Book wa Nihongo de nan to iimasu ka.	How do you say <u>book</u> in Japanese?
<u>Hon</u> to iimasu.	(You) say <u>hon</u>.

> **A** verb accompanied by **kudasai** is used to ask someone politely to do something.

Instructor

Listen carefully as your instructor says these expressions.

Hon o tojite kudasai.	Please close your book.
Hon o akete kudasai.	Please open your book.
Hon o mite kudasai.	Please look at your book.
Hon wa minaide kudasai.	Don't look at your book.
Kiite (ite) kudasai.	Please listen.
Mite kudasai.	Please look at (me, it, this).
Itte kudasai.	Please say it.
Moo ichido itte kudasai.	Please repeat again.
Yonde kudasai.	Please read (it).

(Continues.)

+
−

Nihongo de itte kudasai.	Please say it in Japanese.
Kurikaeshite kudasai.	Please repeat.
Kaite kudasai.	Please write.
Renshuu shite kudasai.	Please practice.
Pea o tsukutte kudasai.	Pair off with a classmate.
Nooto o dashite kudasai.	Please take out your notebook.
Nooto ni kaite kudasai.	Please write in your notebook.
Nani mo kakanaide kudasai.	Please don't write anything down.
Wakarimasu ka.	Do you understand?
Hai, wakarimasu.	Yes, I understand.
Iie, wakarimasen.	No, I don't understand.
Shitsumon ga arimasu ka.	Do you have any question(s)?
Hai, arimasu.	Yes, I do (have questions).
Iie, arimasen.	No, I don't (have any questions).

VOCABULARY LIBRARY

More Classroom Expressions

Hajimemashoo.	Let's begin.
Moo ichido.	Once again, please.
Minasan, issho ni.	Everyone (do it) together.
Ii desu ka.	Is that all right?
Ii desu ne.	That's fine.
Yoku dekimashita.	Well done.
De wa mata kono tsugi.	See you next time.

The Vocabulary Library presents additional, optional vocabulary for use in activities.

ACTIVITY 9

Close your textbook and follow the commands that your instructor gives you.

1.

2.

3.

4.

5.

6.

7.

8.

STUDY HINT

Listening

The first step in learning Japanese is to acquire good listening skills. Though it may sound like a contradiction, you have to listen to a lot of Japanese in order to speak Japanese fluently. So when you listen to your instructor, pay close attention to what is said. Try to understand the meaning based on the context. Take note of your instructor's gestures and the pictures or photos that he/she uses, and draw on your own experiences with the Japanese language. Focusing on the meaning of what you hear will help build your grammar and vocabulary knowledge base, but try not to translate in your head before responding. It is also important for you to react to what you hear and to demonstrate your understanding. In Activity 9, your instructor may ask you to follow his/her commands or to point to appropriate illustrations in order to check your understanding. Throughout this textbook many listening activities are presented in order to help you acquire good listening skills.

言語ノート

LANGUAGE NOTE: Japanese Accentuation

Japanese has pitch accent, which is very different from stress accent in English. In English, accented syllables are pronounced louder than nonaccented syllables. In Japanese, accented syllables are pronounced at a higher pitch than other syllables. In English, only one sound (or syllable) can be primarily accented but in Japanese more than one syllable in a word can be accented and pronounced at the same pitch. Generally speaking, Japanese has only two pitches—high and low.

i^{chi} (*one*)   yo_n (*four*)

Ni^{hongo} (*Japanese language*)   wa^{karima} su (*understand*)

Ichi has the accent pattern low-high, and **yon** has the accent pattern high-low. In **Nihongo,** the pitch rises after the first syllable. In **wakarimasu,** the pitch rises after the first syllable and falls after the fourth syllable. Sometimes pitch is the only way (other than context) to distinguish between two homonyms in spoken Japanese.

ha^{shi} (*bridge*)   ha_{shi} (*chopsticks*)

ha^{na} (*flower*)   ha^{na} (*nose*)

Both **hana** (*flower*) and **hana** (*nose*) have the same pitch pattern (low-high) when they are pronounced independently. However, there is a fall in pitch after **na** in **hana** (*flower*). This means that when a particle follows

(Continues.)

十
三

that word, the particle is pronounced with low pitch. In contrast, a particle following **hana** (*nose*) is pronounced with high pitch.

ha^{na} ga^{ooki}i (*the flower is big*)   ha^{na ga} ooki_i (*the nose is big*)

The primary function of Japanese accentuation is to show the unity of words in a phrase more than to distinguish the meanings of words. For this reason, no accent is indicated in the vocabulary lists in this textbook. Just listen to your instructor and the tape very carefully and try your best to mimic them. Rather than paying too much attention to the accent pattern of each word, you should accurately articulate the overall intonation of the sentence in order to communicate effectively in Japanese.

The Japanese Writing System (1)

Introduction

Modern Japanese is written by combining three different writing systems: **hiragana, katakana,** and **kanji. Hiragana** and **katakana,** like the Roman alphabet, are composed of symbols that represent sounds. **Kanji,** or Chinese characters, are ideographs that represent sound and meaning. You will study **hiragana** and **katakana** in the next parts of Getting Started. The textbook introduces only the basics of these writing systems; you will need to complete the extensive exercises in the workbook to master them.

Hiragana and **katakana** are called *syllabaries,* which means each letter represents one syllable (a vowel, a consonant, or a consonant + vowel). Native speakers of Japanese spell words in terms of syllables and describe a word's length in terms of the number of syllables it contains. For example, **sushi** is a two-syllable word (**su-shi**), **Honda** is a three-syllable word (**Ho-n-da**), and **Tookyoo** (*Tokyo*) is a four-syllable word (**To-o-kyo-o**). Each syllable is held for one beat, so **Tookyoo** (four syllables) takes twice as long to say as **sushi** (two syllables).

With the forty-six basic symbols of the **hiragana** or **katakana** syllabary and two diacritical marks, you can transcribe all standard Japanese sounds. In theory you could write Japanese using just **hiragana** or **katakana,** but in practice the result would be too hard to read and understand.

Katakana is used primarily to transcribe foreign loanwords (e.g., **hottodoggu** for English *hot dog*) and onomatopoeic words (e.g., **zaa zaa,** meaning *raining hard*).

Vocabulary 🎧

This is a list of words that you have used or heard in Part 1 of this textbook. Before beginning Part 2, make sure that you know the words listed under the categories **Greetings and Polite Expressions, Questions, Classroom,** and **Other Useful Words.** These are considered active vocabulary, which means you will need not only to recognize them when you see or hear them, but also to use them yourself.

> **F**or your reading practice this list is rendered in **hiragana** and **katakana.** In authentic writing, **kanji** would be used in many words.

Greetings and Polite Expressions

Arigatoo.	ありがとう。	Thank you.
Arigatoo gozaimasu.	ありがとうございます。	Thank you. (*formal*)
Doo itashimashite.	どういたしまして。	You are welcome.
Doomo.	どうも。	Thanks. (*very informal*)
Doomo arigatoo.	どうもありがとう。	Thank you very much.
Doomo arigatoo gozaimasu.	どうもありがとうございます。	Thank you very much. (*most formal*)
Doozo yoroshiku.	どうぞよろしく。	Nice meeting you.
Genki desu.	げんきです。	I am fine.
Hajimemashite.	はじめまして。	How do you do?
Ii o-tenki desu ne.	いいおてんきですね。	It's fine weather, isn't it?
Ja (de wa).	じゃ(では)。	See you.
Ja (de wa) mata.	じゃ(では)また。	See you. (*formal*)
Kekkoo desu.	けっこうです。	No thanks.
Konban wa.	こんばんは。	Good evening.
Konnichi wa.	こんにちは。	Good afternoon.
O-genki desu ka.	おげんきですか。	How are you?
Ohayoo.	おはよう。	Good morning. (*informal*)
Ohayoo gozaimasu.	おはようございます。	Good morning. (*formal*)
O-hisashiburi desu ne.	おひさしぶりですね。	I haven't seen you for a long time.
Okagesama de genki desu.	おかげさまでげんきです。	Thanks to you, I am fine.
O-negai shimasu.	おねがいします。	Please (give me)…
O-yasumi nasai.	おやすみなさい。	Good night.
Sayo(o)nara.	さよ(う)なら。	Good-bye. (*formal*)
Shitsuree shimasu.	しつれいします。	Good-bye.
Sumimasen.	すみません。	Excuse me, thank you.

Questions

O-namae wa.	おなまえは。	May I have your name?

Classroom

booru-pen	ボールペン	ballpoint pen
chooku	チョーク	chalk

(*Continues.*)

十
五

denki	でんき	light, lamp
doa	ドア	door
enpitsu	えんぴつ	pencil
gakusee	がくせい	student
hon	ほん	book
isu	いす	chair
jisho	じしょ	dictionary
kaaten	カーテン	curtain
kaban	かばん	bag; briefcase
kabe	かべ	wall
kami	かみ	paper
keshigomu	けしゴム	eraser
kokuban	こくばん	chalkboard
kokuban-keshi	こくばんけし	eraser (for blackboard)
kyookasho	きょうかしょ	textbook
kyooshitsu	きょうしつ	classroom
mado	まど	window
mannenhitsu	まんねんひつ	fountain pen
nooto	ノート	notebook
sensee	せんせい	teacher, professor
shaapu penshiru	シャープ・ペンシル	mechanical pencil
teeburu	テーブル	table
tenjoo	てんじょう	ceiling
tsukue	つくえ	desk
yuka	ゆか	floor

Other Nouns

daigaku	だいがく	university
meeshi	めいし	name card, business card

Other Useful Words

desu	です	to be (copula)
doozo	どうぞ	please
Hai, soo desu.	はい、そうです。	Yes, that's right.
iie	いいえ	no
ka	か	(*question marker*)
kore	これ	this (*thing*)
no	の	(*possessive marker*)
watashi	わたし	I

Part Two

OBJECTIVES

Numbers up to 20

Asking and giving telephone numbers

Asking and telling time

Asking what something is

The Japanese writing system (2):
   Hiragana (1)

Numbers up to 20

Here's how to count to 20.

0	ree, zero
1	ichi
2	ni
3	san
4	yon, shi
5	go
6	roku
7	shichi, nana
8	hachi
9	ku, kyuu
10	juu
11	juu-ichi
12	juu-ni
13	juu-san
14	juu-yon, juu-shi
15	juu-go
16	juu-roku
17	juu-shichi, juu-nana
18	juu-hachi
19	juu-ku, juu-kyuu
20	ni-juu (*i.e., 2 tens*)

There are two different ways to say zero, four, seven, and nine. As you continue studying Japanese, you will learn which forms are used in different contexts.

Two common numbers are considered unlucky by Japanese: 4 and 9.

十
七

ACTIVITY **1**

What number(s) between 0 and 20 do you associate with the following?
Answer in Japanese.

1. baseball   **5.** rectangle   **9.** lucky
2. unlucky   **6.** a week   **10.** circle
3. twin   **7.** a watch
4. rainbow   **8.** fingers

Asking and Giving Telephone Numbers

Dialogue 1: Asking for Someone's Telephone Number

Linda Brown asks her classmate, Hitomi Machida, for her telephone
number.

BURAUN: Machida-san no denwa bangoo wa?
MACHIDA: 675–8941 desu.
BURAUN: 675–8941 desu ne.
MACHIDA: Hai, soo desu.

> **H**ai, soo desu indicates the speaker's agreement or assurance.

You can ask for a telephone number by saying

> (*Place or person*) **no denwa bangoo wa?**
> *What is _____'s telephone number?*

The particle **no** in **Machida-san no denwa bangoo** denotes possession and
roughly corresponds to the English *of* or the possessive apostrophe *s*.

ACTIVITY **2**

Practice Dialogue 1 with several classmates, substituting your real names
and telephone numbers.

文化ノート

CULTURE NOTE: Telephone Numbers in Japan

Telephone numbers in Japan are usually four-digit
numbers preceded by a prefix of one to four digits. The
larger the town, the longer its prefix is. For example,
the prefixes for Tokyo, the largest city, have four digits,
but the prefix for a remote island may have only one
digit. However, cell phones are assigned their own set
of area codes, no matter what part of Japan the owner
lives in. Area codes begin with zero and have at least
two digits. When saying a telephone number out loud,
substitute the particle **no** for the hyphens. For example, the number 03-3521-0987 is read **zero-san no
san-go-ni-ichi no zero-kyuu-hachi-nana.**

十
八

Dialogue 1   BROWN: Ms. Machida, what is your telephone number?   MACHIDA: It's 675–8941.
BROWN: 675–8941, right?   MACHIDA: Yes, that's right.

Yookoso! An Invitation to Contemporary Japanese, Third Edition

19

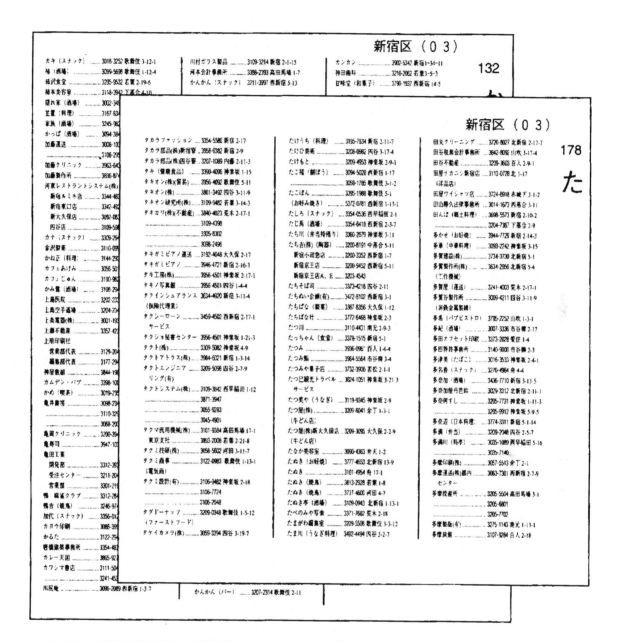

言語ノート

LANGUAGE NOTE: Sentence-Final Particle *ne*

The sentence-final particle **ne,** as in **675-8941 desu ne,** is very common in Japanese. When said with a high or rising intonation, **ne(e)** is used to ask for someone's agreement (*don't you think?*), to confirm that your knowledge is correct (*that's right, isn't it?*), and to check that the listener is following you (*you see?*). When said with a falling intonation and extended to **nee,** the particle indicates your agreement with others or your hesitation.

(Continues.)

Ne(e) is just one of a variety of sentence-final particles that reveal the speaker's emotion and introduce subtle shades of meaning to an utterance. Spoken Japanese uses many different sentence-final particles in order to express one's emotions and intentions. You will learn more such particles later.

Dialogue 2: Asking for Clarification

Practice this variation of Dialogue 1 with another student, substituting the names and places in the art that follows the dialogue for those underlined in the dialogue.

Linda Brown asks John Kawamura for Professor Toshiko Yokoi's telephone number.

BURAUN: <u>Yokoi-sensee</u> no denwa bangoo wa?
KAWAMURA: <u>0134-76-9328</u> desu.
BURAUN: <u>0134-67-9328</u> desu ne.
KAWAMURA: <u>Iie, 0134-76-9328</u> desu.

Asking and Telling Time

Dialogue 3: Asking What Time It Is

John Kawamura asks a classmate, Masao Hayashi, what time it is.

KAWAMURA: Sumimasen. Ima nan-ji desu ka.
HAYASHI: <u>Hachi-ji</u> desu.
KAWAMURA: Arigatoo gozaimasu.
HAYASHI: Doo itashimashite.

ACTIVITY **3**

Practice Dialogue 3 with your classmates by changing the underlined time.

Telling Time

To tell time, add **-ji** (*o'clock*) to the appropriate numeral.

ichi-ji	*one o'clock*
ni-ji	*two o'clock*
san-ji	*three o'clock*
yo-ji (*not* yon-ji *or* shi-ji)	*four o'clock*

Dialogue 2 BROWN: What is <u>Professor Yokoi's</u> telephone number? KAWAMURA: It's <u>0134-76-9328</u>. BROWN: It's <u>0134-67-9328</u>, right? KAWAMURA: No, it's <u>0134-76-9328</u>.
Dialogue 3 KAWAMURA: Excuse me. What time is it now? HAYASHI: It's <u>eight o'clock</u>. KAWAMURA: Thank you very much. HAYASHI: You are welcome.

go-ji	*five o'clock*
roku-ji	*six o'clock*
shichi-ji (*some people say* nana-ji)	*seven o'clock*
hachi-ji	*eight o'clock*
ku-ji (*not* kyuu-ji)	*nine o'clock*
juu-ji	*ten o'clock*
juu-ichi-ji	*eleven o'clock*
juu-ni-ji	*twelve o'clock*
ni-ji han	*2:30* (**han** means *half*)
Nan-ji desu ka.	*What time is it?*
Ni-ji han desu.	*It's 2:30.*

ACTIVITY   4

Practice this short dialogue, substituting the times that follow.

STUDENT 1:* Ima nan-ji desu ka.
STUDENT 2: _____ -ji desu.

 1.   **2.**   **3.**   **4.**

 5.   **6.**   **7.**   **8.**

Dialogue 4: Asking About the Time in Other Places

Two classmates, Takeshi Mimura and Heather Gibson, are talking about the time in the United States.

MIMURA: Ima nan-ji desu ka.
GIBUSON: <u>Juu-ji</u> desu.
MIMURA: <u>Shikago</u> wa ima nan-ji desu ka.
GIBUSON: Eeto, <u>shichi-ji</u> desu.
MIMURA: Gozen <u>shichi-ji</u> desu ka.
GIBUSON: Hai, soo desu. <u>Amerika</u> wa ima <u>asa</u> desu.

Dialogue 4   MIMURA: What time is it now?   GIBSON: It's <u>ten o'clock.</u>   MIMURA: What time is it now in <u>Chicago</u>?   GIBSON: Uh. . . it's <u>seven o'clock.</u>   MIMURA: Do you mean <u>7 A.M.</u>? (lit., *Is it 7 A.M.?*)   GIBSON: That's right. It's <u>morning in the States</u> now.

---

*In later activities, STUDENT 1 and STUDENT 2 will be abbreviated S1 and S2, respectively.

言語ノート

LANGUAGE NOTE: Speech Fillers

When English speakers are trying to think of what to say next or are stalling for time in answering a question, they use so-called speech fillers such as *uh, let me see,* or *you know.* Japanese speakers also use certain words and phrases as speech fillers. The following can be used for this purpose.

Eeto desu nee (↓)	Well, let me see. . .
Soo desu nee (↓)	Well, let me see. . .
Anoo (↓)	Well, . . .
Eeto(*o*)	Well, . . .

When you are speaking Japanese, you should avoid English speech fillers, such as *uh,* and make an effort to use the Japanese ones.

Vocabulary: Time of Day

gozen	A.M.
gogo	P.M.
asa	morning
hiru	noon, around noontime
yuugata	evening
yoru	night

ACTIVITY   **5**

Your instructor will point out a place on the map and ask you the time at that place.

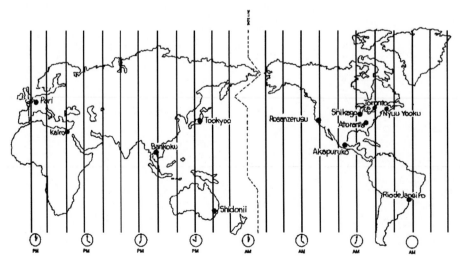

Dialogue 5: Asking When Something Is Taking Place
Two classmates, John Kawamura and Mei Lin Chin, are relaxing in the
student lounge.

KAWAMURA: Ima nan-ji desu ka?
     CHIN: Eeto, <u>ni-ji</u> desu.
KAWAMURA: <u>Miitingu</u> no jikan desu ne.
     CHIN: Ee, soo desu ne.

ACTIVITY   **6**

Step 1: Practice Dialogue 5 with another classmate, substituting times
and activities from John Kawamura's schedule in the following
illustration.

Step 2: Referring to John's schedule, ask a classmate what time each
activity occurs.

Example:

     s1: <u>Nihongo no kurasu</u> wa nan-ji desu ka.
     s2: <u>Gozen hachi-ji</u> desu.

JOHN'S SCHEDULE

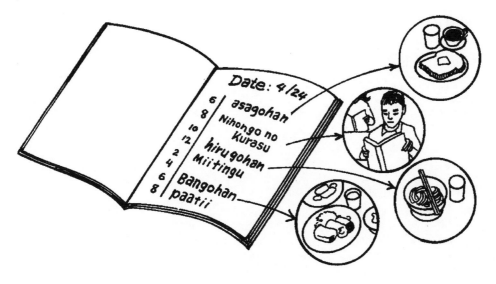

Dialogue 5   KAWAMURA: What time is it now?   CHIN: Uh…it's <u>two o'clock</u>.   KAWAMURA: It's
time for <u>the meeting</u>, isn't it?   CHIN: Yes, that's right.

Activity 6   s1: What time is <u>Japanese class</u>?   s2: It's at <u>8 A.M.</u>

Vocabulary Library

Daily Activities

asagohan	breakfast
hirugohan	lunch
bangohan	dinner, supper
kurasu	class
Nihongo no kurasu	Japanese language class
miitingu	meeting
deeto	date
eega	movie
paatii	party
kaimono/shoppingu	shopping
sanpo	a stroll, strolling
undoo	(physical) exercise
benkyoo	study, studying

> **V**ocabulary Library sections present additional vocabulary that will help you express yourself more freely. If you need a Japanese word that is not listed, ask your teacher by using _____ **wa Nihongo de nan to iimasu ka.**

Asking What Something Is

In Japan, you may encounter many things you have never seen before. Here's how to ask people what things are.

Dialogue 6: Asking for Clarification

Linda Brown is at a restaurant.

BURAUN: Sumimasen. Are wa nan desu ka.
UEETAA: <u>Soba</u> desu.
BURAUN: <u>Nihon ryoori</u> desu ka.
UEETAA: Hai, soo desu.
BURAUN: Jaa, are o onegai shimasu.

> **I**n Dialogue 6, **sumimasen** (_excuse me_) is used to attract the waiter's attention. You can also use **anoo** to attract someone's attention.

言語ノート

LANGUAGE NOTE: _Ko-so-a-do_ Words

The pronouns **kore, are,** and **sore** are used to refer to objects. They mean _this one, that one over there,_ and _that one near you,_ respectively. Thus **kore** refers to objects near the speaker, **are** to objects away from both the speaker and the hearer, and **sore** to objects near the hearer.

Kore wa soba desu.	This (near me) is soba.
Sore wa nan desu ka.	What is that (near you)?
Are wa jisho desu.	That (over there) is a dictionary.

Dialogue 6   BROWN: Excuse me. What's that?   WAITER: It's <u>soba noodles</u>.   BROWN: Is it <u>Japanese food</u>?   WAITER: Yes, it is.   BROWN: Well then, I would like some.

二十四

When you are not sure which item the speaker is referring to, you can use **dore**.

Are wa nan desu ka.	What is that (over there)?
Dore desu ka.	Which one?
Hora, are desu.	Look. That one. (*while pointing*)
Aa, are desu ka. Jisho desu yo.	Oh, that one. That's a dictionary.

ACTIVITY 7

With a classmate, play the roles of a foreign student who is in Japan for the first time and a waiter/waitress in a restaurant. When the student asks what a certain dish is, the waiter/waitress will respond using the answer in the first column. The student will then ask for more information, as indicated in the second column. Finally, the waiter/waitress must decide which of the following ways to end the exchange.

	Hai, soo desu.	*Yes, it is.*
or	Iie, chigaimasu. ____ desu.	*No, it's not. It's ____.*

Useful Word: kudamono *fruit*

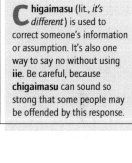

C**higaimasu** (lit., *it's different*) is used to correct someone's information or assumption. It's also one way to say no without using **iie**. Be careful, because **chigaimasu** can sound so strong that some people may be offended by this response.

WAITER/WAITRESS	STUDENT
1. sushi	Nihon ryoori desu ka.
2. marugariita	O-sake (*alcoholic beverage*) desu ka.
3. tenpura	Amerika ryoori desu ka.
4. kiui	Yasai (*vegetable*) desu ka.

言語ノート

LANGUAGE NOTE: Devoiced Vowels

When Japanese vowels [i] and [u] fall between voiceless consonants (i.e., [k], [s], [sh], [t], [ch], [ts], [h], and [p]) or when one of these vowels, preceded by one of these consonants, ends a word, it is whispered. Vowels are normally pronounced by vibrating the vocal cords but no vibration of the vocal cords accompanies pronunciation of these whispered, or devoiced, vowels. The devoiced vowels are underlined in the romanization.

すし	sushi	sushi
くつ	kutsu	shoe
えんぴつ	enpitsu	pencil
スペイン	Supein	Spain
ふたり	hutari	two people
あのひとはやま	Ano hito wa	That person is
ぐちさんです。	Yamaguchi-san desu.	Mr. Yamaguchi.

In standard, everyday Japanese spoken at a normal or fast speed, the devoicing of vowels occurs naturally in the aforementioned contexts. However, when people enunciate words slowly or emphatically or when they are under stress, they may not devoice their vowels.

The Japanese Writing System (2)

Hiragana (1)

Following is the basic **hiragana** syllabary chart. Under each symbol is the romanization used in this book to remind you of the Japanese pronunciation. Remember, you must listen closely to your instructor and the tapes to learn correct pronunciation. (Writing exercises for **hiragana** are included in your Workbook.)

二十六

あ a	い i	う u	え e	お o
か ka	き ki	く ku	け ke	こ ko
さ sa	し shi	す su	せ se	そ so
た ta	ち chi	つ tsu	て te	と to
な na	に ni	ぬ nu	ね ne	の no
は ha	ひ hi	ふ hu	へ he	ほ ho
ま ma	み mi	む mu	め me	も mo
や ya		ゆ yu		よ yo
ら ra	り ri	る ru	れ re	ろ ro
わ wa				を o
ん n				

を falls on the *w* line because historically it was pronounced **wo.**

The addition of two diacritical marks adds twenty-five more sounds (see the following list) to the basic **hiragana** chart. The ゛ (**dakuten**) turns the unvoiced consonants (*k, s, t,* and *h*) into voiced consonants (*g, z/j, d/j,* and *b,* respectively). The ゜ (**handakuten**) changes *h* to *p.*

が ga	ぎ gi	ぐ gu	げ ge	ご go
ざ za	じ ji	ず zu	ぜ ze	ぞ zo
だ da	ぢ ji	づ zu	で de	ど do
ば ba	び bi	ぶ bu	べ be	ぼ bo
ぱ pa	ぴ pi	ぷ pu	ぺ pe	ぽ po

言語ノート

LANGUAGE NOTE: *a-i-u-e-o* order

In Japanese dictionaries, words are listed in the same order as the **hiragana** syllabary: **a, i, u, e, o, ka, ki, ku, ke, ko, sa, shi,** and so on. You might think of this as the Japanese alphabetical order. Since you cannot use a Japanese dictionary without knowing it, it is important to learn the order of the **hiragana** syllables. By the way, listings in address books, encyclopedias, and the Japanese-English Glossary at the end of this book are ordered in the same way. In addition, knowing the **hiragana** syllabary makes it easier to remember Japanese verb conjugations. Note that words starting with voiced sounds (e.g., **ga, gi, gu, ge, go**) are listed along with words starting with the corresponding voiceless sounds (e.g., **ka, ki, ku, ke, ko**). The listings in telephone directories are in **a-i-u-e-o** order, but when names are homonyms, other rules governing **kanji** order come into play.

The first line of **hiragana** consists of five symbols representing the five Japanese vowels.

あ   a   pronounced roughly as in English *father*, but the mouth is not so wide open as in English

い   i   as in English *see*, but shorter

う   u   as in English *doodle*, but it is short and does not require lip rounding

え   e   as in English *egg*, but the mouth is not open so wide

お   o   as in English *comb*, but it does not require so much lip rounding

The rest of the symbols (except ん **n** and を **o**) consist of a consonant or a semivowel (**y** or **w**) followed by one of the five vowels. Most Japanese consonants are easy for English speakers to pronounce, but note the following differences.

sh in し	as in <u>she</u>, but less lip-rounding
ch in ち	as in <u>ch</u>eese, but with no lip-rounding
ts in つ	as in ca<u>ts</u>
h in は、へ、ほ	is similar to English *h*
h in ひ	as in <u>he</u>, but with friction as the air is expelled
h in ふ	articulated by bringing both lips close together without any rounding and then forcing air out between them
r in ら	Japanese **r**, very similar to the *t/d* in wa<u>t</u>er or ri<u>d</u>er, is articulated by tapping the tip of the tongue very quickly against the gum just behind the upper teeth
w in わ	as in English <u>we</u>, but with less tension
g in が	as in *gate* but some speakers pronounce this sound like *ng* in *sing* when it occurs in the middle of a word
j in じ、ぢ	as in English <u>jeep</u>

Some Japanese pronounce ひ **hi** like English *he* but shorter and with no friction.

Hu ふ is sometimes transcribed as **fu**. You will notice this especially in common words like **futon** and Japanese personal names and places that begin with the ふ syllable: **Fuji-san** (*Mt. Fuji*), **Fukushima, Fujiwara, Fukuoka,** and so on.

ん **(n)** represents a nasal sound with the length of one full syllable. (Thus, it is called syllabic nasal.) The actual sound represented by this symbol depends on the context. Before [m], [p], or [b], it is pronounced [m]; before [s], [sh], [t], [ts], [ch], [n], [r], [z], [d], or [j], it is pronounced [n]; and before vowels, before [k], [y], [w], [g], or [ng], or at the end of a word, it is pronounced [ng]. In this book, however, ん is represented as **n** regardless of where it appears.

enpitsu	えんぴつ	*pencil*
kanji	かんじ	*Chinese character*
Nihongo	にほんご	*Japanese language*
hon	ほん	*book*
kin'en	きんえん	*no smoking*
cf. kinen	きねん	*commemoration*

Note that ん can never begin a word.

言語ノート

LANGUAGE NOTE: The Origins of *Hiragana* and *Katakana*

Chinese characters (**kanji**) were imported to Japan around the fifth century A.D., before which time Japan had no writing system. The use of **kanji** to transcribe the Japanese language was inconvenient, to say the least, because **kanji** were designed to transcribe a completely different language. To remedy this problem, **hiragana** symbols were created by simplifying **kanji**.

以　以 → ﾚゝ → い
I　　　　　　　　　　i

礼　礼 → れ → れ
REE　　　　　　　re

Katakana was originally created by Japanese priests to annotate Buddhist books written in **kanji**. **Katakana** symbols were created from parts of **kanji**.

伊　伊 → イ
I　　　　　i

礼　礼 → レ
REE　　　re

Hiragana and katakana spelling does not always conform to the **rooma-ji** spelling in *Yookoso!* For example, **sensee** (*teacher*) is the **rooma-ji** spelling, but it is written with the **hiragana** letters **se-n-se-*i* せんせい**; **doozo** (*please*) is written as **do-*u*-zo どうぞ**. These and other differences are explained in Parts 3 to 5.

二十九

Vocabulary 🎧

This is a list of words that you have used or heard in Part 2 of Getting Started. Before beginning Part 3, make sure that you know the words listed under the categories **Questions, Classroom, Numbers, Time Expressions,** and **Other Useful Words.** These are considered active vocabulary.

> **F**or your reading practice this list is rendered in **hiragana** and **katakana.** In authentic writing, **kanji** would be used in many words.

Questions

Nan desu ka.	なんですか。	What is it?
Nan-ji desu ka.	なんじですか。	What time is it?
____ wa Nihongo de nan to iimasu ka.	____はにほんごでなんと いいますか。	How do you say ____ in Japanese?

Classroom

enpitsu	えんぴつ	pencil
hiragana	ひらがな	cursive syllabary
hon	ほん	book
jisho	じしょ	dictionary
katakana	かたかな	square syllabary
kanji	かんじ	Chinese characters
kurasu	クラス	class
Nihongo no kurasu	にほんごのクラス	Japanese language class
sensee	せんせい	teacher, professor

Numbers

ree, zero	れい、ゼロ	zero
ichi	いち	one
ni	に	two
san	さん	three
yon, shi	よん、し	four
go	ご	five
roku	ろく	six
shichi, nana	しち、なな	seven
hachi	はち	eight
ku, kyuu	く、きゅう	nine
juu	じゅう	ten
juu-ichi	じゅういち	eleven
juu-ni	じゅうに	twelve
juu-san	じゅうさん	thirteen
juu-yon, juu-shi	じゅうよん、じゅうし	fourteen
juu-go	じゅうご	fifteen
juu-roku	じゅうろく	sixteen
juu-shichi, juu-nana	じゅうしち、じゅうなな	seventeen

三十

juu-hachi	じゅうはち	eighteen
juu-ku, juu-kyuu	じゅうく、じゅうきゅう	nineteen
ni-juu	にじゅう	twenty

Time Expressions

ichi-ji	いちじ	one o'clock
ni-ji	にじ	two o'clock
san-ji	さんじ	three o'clock
yo-ji	よじ	four o'clock
go-ji	ごじ	five o'clock
roku-ji	ろくじ	six o'clock
shichi-ji, nana-ji	しちじ、ななじ	seven o'clock
hachi-ji	はちじ	eight o'clock
ku-ji	くじ	nine o'clock
juu-ji	じゅうじ	ten o'clock
juu-ichi-ji	じゅういちじ	eleven o'clock
juu-ni-ji	じゅうにじ	twelve o'clock
. . . han	〜はん	. . . thirty (when telling time)
ni-ji-han	にじはん	2:30
asa	あさ	morning
gogo	ごご	P.M.
gozen	ごぜん	A.M.
hiru	ひる	noontime
jikan	じかん	time
yoru	よる	night
yuugata	ゆうがた	evening

Foods/Beverages

Nihon ryoori	にほんりょうり	Japanese food
o-sake	おさけ	alcoholic beverage
soba	そば	soba, buckwheat noodles
sushi	すし	sushi

Other Nouns

asagohan	あさごはん	breakfast
bangoo	ばんごう	number (as in **denwa bangoo** [telephone number])
bangohan	ばんごはん	dinner, supper
benkyoo	べんきょう	study, studying
denwa	でんわ	telephone
eega	えいが	movie
hirugohan	ひるごはん	lunch

(Continues.)

三十一

kaimono	かいもの	shopping
sanpo	さんぽ	strolling
undoo	うんどう	exercise

Language

| Nihongo | にほんご | Japanese |

Place and Personal Names

Akapuruko (Mekishiko)	アカプルコ（メキシコ）	Acapulco (Mexico)
Atoranta (Amerika)	アトランタ（アメリカ）	Atlanta (U.S.A.)
Bankoku (Tai)	バンコク（タイ）	Bangkok (Thailand)
Kairo (Ejiputo)	カイロ（エジプト）	Cairo (Egypt)
Nyuu Yooku (Amerika)	ニューヨーク（アメリカ）	New York (U.S.A.)
Pari (Huransu)	パリ（フランス）	Paris (France)
Rosanzerusu (Amerika)	ロサンゼルス（アメリカ）	Los Angeles (U.S.A.)
Riodejaneiro (Burajiru)	リオデジャネイロ（ブラジル）	Rio de Janeiro (Brazil)
Shidonii (Oosutoraria)	シドニー（オーストラリア）	Sydney (Australia)
Shikago (Amerika)	シカゴ（アメリカ）	Chicago (U.S.A.)
Tookyoo (Nihon)	とうきょう（にほん）	Tokyo (Japan)
Toronto (Kanada)	トロント（カナダ）	Toronto (Canada)

Other Useful Words

aa	ああ	Oh
anoo	あのう	Well…
Chigaimasu.	ちがいます。	That's not right.
desu	です	to be (*copula*)
eeto	ええと	uhh, well (*used when pausing to think*)
eeto desu nee	ええとですねえ	well, let me see…
Hai, soo desu.	はい、そうです。	Yes, that's right.
Hontoo desu ka.	ほんとうですか。	Really? (lit., *Is that true?*)
hora	ほら	Look!
ima	いま	now
jaa	じゃあ	well, then
ne(e)	ね（え）	Right? (Isn't that so?)
no	の	(*possessive marker*)
wa	は	(*particle topic marker [pronounced わ]*)
yo	よ	(*emphatic sentence-final particle*)
are	あれ	that (thing over there)
kore	これ	this (thing)
sore	それ	that (thing)
dore	どれ	which (thing)

Part Three

OBJECTIVES

Talking about daily activities

Talking about future activities and events

Talking about likes and dislikes

The Japanese writing system (3):

Hiragana (2)

Talking About Daily Activities

Dialogue 1: Talking About One's Schedule

Two classmates, Masao Hayashi and Linda Brown, are talking about what time they get up in the morning.

HAYASHI: Buraun-san wa nan-ji ni okimasu ka.
BURAUN: Go-ji desu.
HAYASHI: Waa, hayai desu ne.
BURAUN: Hayashi-san wa?
HAYASHI: Ku-ji desu.

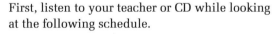 ACTIVITY **1**

First, listen to your teacher or CD while looking at the following schedule.

JOHN KAWAMURA'S DAY

6:00 A.M.	okimasu (*get up*)
7:00 A.M.	asagohan o tabemasu (*eat breakfast*)
8:00 A.M.	gakkoo e ikimasu (*go to school*)
Noon	hirugohan o tabemasu (*eat lunch*)
1:00 P.M.	koohii o nomimasu (*drink coffee*)
3:00 P.M.	toshokan e ikimasu (*go to the library*)
7:00 P.M.	bangohan o tabemasu (*eat dinner*)

Dialogue 1 HAYASHI: What time do you get up in the morning, Ms. Brown?
BROWN: Five o'clock. HAYASHI: Wow, that's early. BROWN: How about you, Mr. Hayashi?
HAYASHI: (I get up at) nine o'clock.

(Continues.)

三十三

8:00 P.M.	terebi o mimasu (*watch TV*)
9:00 P.M.	hon o yomimasu (*read a book*)
Midnight	nemasu (*go to sleep*)

Now answer the following questions in Japanese.

Useful Word: mainichi *every day*

Example:

> Kawamura-san wa mainichi nan-ji ni okimasu ka. (*What time does Mr. Kawamura get up every day?*) →
> Gozen 6-ji desu.

1. Nan-ji ni asagohan o tabemasu ka.

2. Nan-ji ni gakkoo e ikimasu ka.

3. Nan-ji ni hirugohan o tabemasu ka.

4. Nan-ji ni toshokan e ikimasu ka.

5. Nan-ji ni bangohan o tabemasu ka.

6. Nan-ji ni hon o yomimasu ka.

7. Nan-ji ni nemasu ka.

Vocabulary: Daily Activities

	(*I, you, he, she, we, they*)...
okimasu	get up/wake up
asagohan o tabemasu	eat breakfast
hirugohan (*lunch*),	
bangohan (*dinner*)	
gakkoo e ikimasu	go to school
kurasu, toshokan (*library*),	
shigoto (*work*)	
o-cha o nomimasu	drink tea
koohii, wain, koocha (*black tea*)	
uchi e kaerimasu	go back home
undoo o shimasu	(do) exercise
jogingu, earobikusu	
terebi o mimasu	watch TV
eega (*movie*), **dorama, nyuusu**	
hon o yomimasu	read a book
shinbun (*newspaper*),	
zasshi (*magazine*)	
ongaku o kikimasu	listen to music
rajio (*radio*), **shiidii** (*CD*)	
Nihongo o benkyoo shimasu	study Japanese
suugaku (*math*),	
Huransugo (*French*)	
nemasu	go to sleep; go to bed
kara... made	from, beginning at... until

There is no subject-verb agreement in Japanese. In other words, Japanese verbs take the same form irrespective of the person and number of the subject.

三十四

言語ノート

LANGUAGE NOTE: Basic Sentence Structure of Japanese

You may have already noticed that the sentence structure of Japanese is different from that of English. In English, the basic sentence structure is Subject-Verb-Object, as in *Mr. Kawamura watches TV*. In Japanese, the basic structure is Subject-Object-Verb (as in **Kawamura-san wa terebi o mimasu** (*Mr. Kawamura TV watch*). Thus, Japanese verbs (e.g., **okimasu**) come toward the end of a sentence.

In English, you can tell whether a noun is a subject or an object by its position in the sentence. If a noun comes at the beginning of a sentence, it is the subject. If it comes after a verb, it is an object. In Japanese, both the subject noun and object noun come before a verb. The roles of the nouns are differentiated by the use of particles (small words) that follow the word they mark. Notice, for instance, that the particle **o** marks the direct object. In **bangohan o tabemasu** (*I eat supper*), **o** marks **bangohan** as the object of the verb **tabemasu**.

Unlike English prepositions, Japanese particles are short words that occur after other words and thus are often called *postpositions*. Particles help identify the relationship of the word they follow to other parts of the sentence.

More Time Expressions

2:05	ni-ji go-hun
2:10	ni-ji jup-pun
	ni-ji jip-pun
2:15	ni-ji juu-go-hun
2:20	ni-ji ni-jup-pun
	ni-ji ni-jip-pun
2:25	ni-ji ni-juu-go-hun
2:30	ni-ji han
	ni-ji san-jup-pun
	ni-ji san-jip-pun
2:35	ni-ji san-juu-go-hun
2:40	ni-ji yon-jup-pun
	ni-ji yon-jip-pun
2:45	ni-ji yon-juu-go-hun
2:50	ni-ji go-jup-pun
	ni-ji go-jip-pun
2:55	ni-ji go-juu-go-hun

三十五

ACTIVITY 2

Practice this short dialogue with a classmate, substituting the times that follow.

s1: Ima nan-ji desu ka.
s2: ___ desu.

1.   **2.**   **3.**   **4.**

5.   **6.**   **7.**   **8.**

LANGUAGE NOTE: Telling Time Politely

言語ノート

Japanese people think it is more polite to express themselves vaguely rather than clearly and directly. This tendency extends to unexpected areas like telling time. When you would like to tell time politely or give an approximate time, use **goro** (*about*).

Nan-ji ni uchi o demasu ka.
What time do you leave home?

Hachi-ji goro demasu.
I leave about 8:00.

Nan-ji goro ikimasu ka.
Around what time will you go?

Ni-ji goro ikimasu.
I'll go around 2:00 (*lit.*, at about 2:00).

Note that the particle indicating a point of time, **ni,** may be dropped when **goro** is used.
    Don't be fooled by the use of **goro.** Some Japanese are extremely punctual and expect the same of others.

ACTIVITY 3

Step 1: Write down your daily schedule (choose one day of the week) in English.

Step 2: Work in pairs. Explain your schedule to your partner in Japanese.

Dialogue 2: Asking How Often Someone Does Something

Two classmates, Masao Hayashi and Heather Gibson, are talking about how often they go to the movies or watch television.

HAYASHI: Gibuson-san wa yoku eega ni ikimasu ka.
GIBUSON: Uun, amari ikimasen ne. Hayashi-san wa?
HAYASHI: Tokidoki ikimasu. Demo, terebi no eega wa yoku mimasu.
GIBUSON: Watashi wa terebi mo amari mimasen.

Mo is a particle meaning *too, either*.

言語ノート

LANGUAGE NOTE: Indicating Frequency

Yoku, tokidoki, amari, and **zenzen** are some adverbs indicating frequency.

Yoku terebi o mimasu ka?	Do you often watch TV?
Hai, yoku mimasu.	Yes, I watch it often.
Hai, tokidoki mimasu.	Yes, I watch it sometimes.
Iie, amari mimasen.	No, I don't watch it so often.
Iie, zenzen mimasen.	No, I don't watch it at all.

Amari and **zenzen** are used only in negative sentences.

言語ノート

LANGUAGE NOTE: Conjugation

Japanese verbs conjugate (change their form) based on three factors: tense, affirmative/negative, and politeness or formality of speech. Japanese has two tenses, past and nonpast. Such verb forms as **ikimasu** and **mimasu** are nonpast forms used to describe actions that you do habitually or in the future. **Ikimasen** and **mimasen** (see Dialogue 2) are nonpast forms, but they are the negative counterparts of **ikimasu** and **mimasu.** The verb forms you have been studying so far are all polite forms used to convey the speaker's politeness toward the addressee. The students in Professor Yokoi's class have just met, so they have been using polite forms. As they become more familiar with each other and their relationship gets closer, they will begin using informal forms.

Dialogue 2   HAYASHI: Ms. Gibson, do you often go to movies?   GIBSON: Well, I don't go very much. How about you, Mr. Hayashi?   HAYASHI: I go (to movies) sometimes, but I often watch movies on TV.   GIBSON: I don't watch TV very much, either.

ACTIVITY   **4**

Talk with one or more classmates about your daily schedules using the following questions.

1. ___ san wa mainichi nan-ji ni okimasu ka.
2. Nan-ji ni uchi o demasu ka.
3. Nan-ji ni uchi e kaerimasu ka.
4. Nan-ji ni yuugohan o tabemasu ka.
5. Yoku terebi o mimasu ka.
6. Yoku hon o yomimasu ka.
7. Yoku ongaku o kikimasu ka.
8. Nan-ji ni nemasu ka.

VOCABULARY LIBRARY

More Daily Activities

(I, you, he, she, we, they)...

tegami o kakimasu	write a letter
deeto (o) shimasu	go on a date
yakyuu o shimasu	play baseball
kaimono ni ikimasu	go shopping
ichinichi-juu nemasu	sleep all day
tomodachi ni aimasu	see/meet a friend
tomodachi to hanashimasu	talk with a friend
Nihongo o renshuu shimasu	practice Japanese
denwa o shimasu	make a phone call

ACTIVITY   **5**

Step 1: The purpose of this activity is to find out the habits of one of your classmates. Write five questions that will help you understand his or her habits.

Step 2: Work in pairs. Ask your partner the five questions.

Step 3: Explain your partner's habits to the class.

Talking About Future Activities and Events

Dialogue 3: Asking About Someone's Weekend Plans

Two classmates, Hitomi Machida and John Kawamura, are talking about activities for a coming weekend.

KAWAMURA: Machida-san wa konshuu no shuumatsu, nani o shimasu ka.
  MACHIDA: Tomodachi to kaimono ni ikimasu. Kawamura-san wa?
KAWAMURA: Mochiron, Nihongo o benkyoo shimasu.
  MACHIDA: Majime desu ne.

Vocabulary: Days and Weeks

kyoo	today
ashita	tomorrow
asatte	the day after tomorrow
konshuu	this week
raishuu	next week
saraishuu	the week after next
shuumatsu	weekend

ACTIVITY 6

Discuss your future activities. Ask a classmate

1. if he/she will come to school tomorrow.
2. if he/she will go to a library tomorrow.
3. if he/she will study Japanese this weekend.
4. if he/she will go shopping this weekend.
5. if he/she will see friends this weekend.
6. if he/she will exercise this weekend.

	Su	M	T	W	Th	F	Sa
konshuu				kyoo	ashita	asatte	
raishuu							
saraishuu							

Talking About Likes and Dislikes

Dialogue 4: Expressing One's Likes and Dislikes

John Kawamura and Hitomi Machida are talking in a cafeteria.

KAWAMURA: Machida-san wa sakana ga suki desu ka.
  MACHIDA: Ee, toku ni o-sashimi ga suki desu.
KAWAMURA: Watashi wa o-sashimi ga kirai desu.
  MACHIDA: Hontoo desu ka!

Dialogue 3 KAWAMURA: Ms. Machida, what are you going to do this weekend?
MACHIDA: I'm going shopping with my friends. How about you, Mr. Kawamura?
KAWAMURA: Of course, I am going to study Japanese.   MACHIDA: You sure are diligent.
Dialogue 4 KAWAMURA: Do you like fish, Ms. Machida?   MACHIDA: Yes. I especially like
raw fish.   KAWAMURA: I dislike raw fish.   MACHIDA: Really! (lit., *Is that true?*)

三十九

LANGUAGE NOTE: Talking About Likes and Dislikes

Use the following sentence structures to express likes and dislikes.

___ ga suki desu.
I (you, he, she, we, they) like ___.

___ ga kirai desu.
I (you, etc.) dislike ___.

___ ga suki ja arimasen.
I (you, etc.) don't like ___.

To ask if someone likes something, say:

___ ga suki desu ka.
Do (you, etc.) like ___?

To ask what kind of things a person likes, use this pattern:

Donna ___ ga suki desu ka.
What kind of ___ do you like?

ACTIVITY 7

Ask a classmate whether he or she likes the following things.

Examples:

> Nihongo no kurasu ga suki desu ka. → Hai, suki desu.
> Paatii ga suki desu ka. → Iie, suki ja arimasen.

1. yasai (*vegetable*[*s*]), niku (*meat*), sakana (*fish*), burokkorii, piza, aisu kuriimu
2. Nihon ryoori (*Japanese food*), Itaria ryoori, Huransu ryoori, Mekishiko ryoori
3. koohii (*coffee*), aisutii, koora, juusu
4. biiru, wain, kakuteru, uisukii
5. huttobooru, sakkaa, tenisu, supootsu
6. bokushingu, sukii, suiee (*swimming*)
7. eega (*movies*), sanpo (*strolling*), benkyoo, paatii
8. jazu, rokku, kurashikku (*classical music*), rappu
9. Madonna, Julia Roberts, Johnny Depp, Tiger Woods

Dialogue 5: Saying What Foods One Especially Likes

Hitomi Machida and Linda Brown are talking about the foods they like.

MACHIDA: Buraun-san wa donna tabemono ga suki desu ka.

BURAUN: Tabemono desu ka. Soo desu nee. Itaria ryoori ga ichiban suki desu ne.

MACHIDA: Soo desu ka.

BURAUN: Ee, toku ni pasuta ga suki desu.

> **S**oo desu nee is a speech filler (see the Part 2 Language Note on speech fillers).

言語ノート

LANGUAGE NOTE: Echo Questions

In Dialogue 5, Machida asks a question and Brown responds by repeating a part of Machida's question **(Tabemono desu ka)**. Brown's question is called an *echo question*, which consists of a noun and **desu ka**. Echo questions are used often in conversation as a strategy to confirm what the other speaker is asking about or to keep communication channels open while thinking of an answer to the question.

> **Ashita nan-ji ni gakkoo e ikimasu ka.**
> What time will you go to school tomorrow?

> **Gakkoo desu ka. 8-ji ni ikimasu.**
> You mean school? I will go at eight.

or **Ashita desu ka. 8-ji ni ikimasu.**
You mean tomorrow? I will go at eight.

> **Kawamura-san, yoku terebi o mimasu ka.**
> Mr. Kawamura, do you often watch TV?

> **Watashi desu ka. Ee, yoku mimasu.**
> You are asking me? Yes, I watch it often.

or **Terebi desu ka. Ee, yoku mimasu.**
You mean TV? Yes, I watch it often.

These echo questions, like speech fillers, are frequently used in Japanese conversations as a device to keep communication flowing smoothly. Dialogue 5 contains both an echo question and a speech filler.

Dialogue 5 MACHIDA: What kind of food do you like, Ms. Brown? BROWN: You mean food? (lit., *Is it food?*) Let's see. I like Italian food best. MACHIDA: Is that so? BROWN: Yes, I especially like pasta.

四十一

ACTIVITY **8**

Working in pairs, ask questions about the likes and dislikes of Henry Curtis and Mei Lin Chin.

Example:

s1: Chin-san wa jazu ga suki desu ka.
s2: Hai, suki desu.

1. Nihon ryoori	**2.** niku	**3.** sakana	**4.** koohii
5. jazu	**6.** koora	**7.** rokku	**8.** biiru

ACTIVITY **9**

Following the example, ask your classmates their preferences in the following areas.

Example:

> supootsu—huttobooru, sakkaa, tenisu, bareebooru →
> s1: Donna <u>supootsu</u> ga suki desu ka.
> s2: <u>Tenisu</u> ga ichiban suki desu.

1. ongaku—kurashikku (*classical music*), jazu, rokku, rappu, kantorii ando uesutan, min'yoo (*Japanese folk music*)

2. nomimono—koohii, o-cha (*green tea*), koora, wain, juusu, biiru, mizu (*water*)

3. kurasu—Nihongo no kurasu, Huransugo no kurasu, Supeingo no kurasu (*Your answer is obvious, isn't it?*)

4. tabemono—yasai, niku, sakana

5. gakki (*musical instrument*)—piano, gitaa, huruuto, doramu

The Japanese Writing System (3)

Hiragana (2)

By writing や **ya**, ゆ **yu**, or よ **yo** small after symbols ending in the vowel **i**, you can transcribe the following sounds. Each syllable is composed of a consonant + **y** + **a, u,** or **o**. (In horizontal writing the small symbols are written lower than the regular-size ones; in vertical writing they are written somewhat to the right.) This **y** is sometimes called a glide or semi-vowel.

四十二

きゃ kya	きゅ kyu	きょ kyo
しゃ sha	しゅ shu	しょ sho
ちゃ cha	ちゅ chu	ちょ cho
にゃ nya	にゅ nyu	にょ nyo
ひゃ hya	ひゅ hyu	ひょ hyo
みゃ mya	みゅ myu	みょ myo
りゃ rya	りゅ ryu	りょ ryo
ぎゃ gya	ぎゅ gyu	ぎょ gyo
じゃ ja	じゅ ju	じょ jo
びゃ bya	びゅ byu	びょ byo
ぴゃ pya	ぴゅ pyu	ぴょ pyo

Double Vowels

When two of the same vowel occur together, hold the sound twice as long as a single vowel. In writing, these double vowels are transcribed by adding a corresponding single vowel symbol.

obasan	おばさん	*aunt*
obaasan	おばあさん	*grandmother*
ie	いえ	*house*
iie	いいえ	*no*
suugaku	すうがく	*math*

A double vowel sound **ee** is in most cases written by adding い (**i**).

meeshi	めいし	*name card*
Shitsuree.	しつれい。	*Excuse me.*

(Continues.)

四
十
三

There are a few exceptions in which え (**e**) is added.

| oneesan | おねえさん | *older sister* |
| ee | ええ | *yes* |

A long vowel **oo** is in most cases written by adding う (**u**).

| Doomo arigatoo. | どうもありがとう。 | *Thank you.* |
| ryoori | りょうり | *food, cuisine* |

There are several exceptions in which お (**o**) is added.

ooi	おおい	*many*
tooi	とおい	*far*
too	とお	*ten*
ookii	おおきい	*large, big*

Cases where a double vowel sound **ee** can be indicated by え (**e**) or い (**i**) are limited to ええ／えい or ねえ／ねい. Otherwise, only い is used, as in けい, せい, へい, じい.

Cases where a double vowel sound **oo** can be indicated by お (**o**) or う (**u**) are limited to おお／おう or とお／とう. Otherwise, only う is used, as in こう, のう, ほう, ごう.

Double Consonants

Double consonants (**pp, kk,** etc.) are written using a small っ (**tsu**), which doubles the sound it precedes.

kita	きた	*north*
kitta	きった	*(I) cut*
kako	かこ	*past*
kakko	かっこ	*parenthesis*

However, double **nn** is written with ん(**n**). Note that ん must always follow a vowel sound; it can never begin a word.

| hone | ほね | *bone* |
| honne | ほんね | *true intention* |

LANGUAGE NOTE: Syllables

言語ノート

Syllables that are used in Japanese can be classified as follows:

1. syllables consisting of only one vowel: あ、い、う、え、お
2. syllables consisting of one consonant and one vowel: か、き、く、け、こ、さ、し、etc.
3. syllables consisting of one consonant, glide **y**, and one vowel: きゃ、きゅ、きょ、しゃ、しゅ、etc.
4. special syllables: ん, っ (double consonant), double vowel

In Japanese, the length of a word is usually counted by the number of syllables included in it, or, in other words, the number of **hiragana** or **katakana** required to write it.

ki	き	*tree*	one-syllable word
ai	あい	*love*	two-syllable word
asa	あさ	*morning*	two-syllable word
gogo	ごご	*P.M.*	two-syllable word
kyoka	きょか	*permission*	two-syllable word
kin	きん	*gold*	two-syllable word
kagami	かがみ	*mirror*	three-syllable word
kooka	こうか	*effect*	three-syllable word
kippu	きっぷ	*ticket*	three-syllable word
kooi	こうい	*behavior*	three-syllable word
sanpo	さんぽ	*walk*	three-syllable word
gohan	ごはん	*rice; meal*	three-syllable word
kyoomi	きょうみ	*interest*	three-syllable word
gakkoo	がっこう	*school*	four-syllable word
ginkoo	ぎんこう	*bank*	four-syllable word

It is important that each syllable, irrespective of its type (1 through 4), is pronounced in almost the same amount of time. Thus, uttering a four-syllable word basically takes twice as long as uttering a two-syllable word.

Some Notes on the Writing of Functional Words

Japanese uses several particles (small words) to indicate grammatical functions. They are written in **hiragana,** but you must be careful about how to write some of them.

- The topic particle (indicating the topic of a sentence) **wa** is written は.
- The direction particle (indicating the direction of movement) **e** is written へ.
- The direct object particle (indicating the direct object of a verb) **o** is written を.

はやしさんはまいにちカフェテリアへいきます。
Mr. Hayashi goes to the cafeteria every day.

ブラウンさんはまいあさジョギングをします。
Ms. Brown jogs (does jogging) every morning.

Vocabulary 🎧

This is a list of words that you have used or heard in Part 3 of this textbook. Before beginning Part 4, make sure that you know the words listed under the categories **Classroom, Time Expressions,** and **Other Useful Words.** These are considered active vocabulary.

> **F**or your reading practice this list is rendered in **hiragana** and **katakana.** In authentic writing, **kanji** would be used in many words.

Classroom		
suugaku	すうがく	math
tomodachi	ともだち	friend

Time Expressions		
go-hun	ごふん	five minutes
jup-pun,	じゅっぷん、	ten minutes
jip-pun	じっぷん	
juu-go-hun	じゅうごふん	fifteen minutes
ni-jup-pun,	にじゅっぷん、	twenty minutes
ni-jip-pun	にじっぷん	
ni-juu-go-hun	にじゅうごふん	twenty-five minutes
. . . han	〜はん	. . . thirty (*when telling time*)
san-jup-pun,	さんじゅっぷん、	thirty minutes
san-jip-pun	さんじっぷん	
san-juu-go-hun	さんじゅうごふん	thirty-five minutes
yon-jup-pun,	よんじゅっぷん、	forty minutes
yon-jip-pun	よんじっぷん	
yon-juu-go-hun	よんじゅうごふん	forty-five minutes
go-jup-pun,	ごじゅっぷん、	fifty minutes
go-jip-pun	ごじっぷん	
go-juu-go-hun	ごじゅうごふん	fifty-five minutes
konshuu no shuumatsu	こんしゅうのしゅうまつ	this weekend
mainichi	まいにち	every day
tokidoki	ときどき	sometimes
kyoo	きょう	today
ashita	あした	tomorrow
asatte	あさって	the day after tomorrow
konshuu	こんしゅう	this week
raishuu	らいしゅう	next week
saraishuu	さらいしゅう	the week after next
shuumatsu	しゅうまつ	weekend

Verbs		
		(*I, you, he, she, we, they*)…
benkyoo shimasu	べんきょうします	study
deeto (o) shimasu	デート(を)します	have a date

四十六

denwa (o) shimasu	でんわ(を)します	make a phone call
hanashimasu	はなします	speak
ikimasu	いきます	go
kaerimasu	かえります	return
kakimasu	かきます	write
kikimasu	ききます	listen
kimasu	きます	come
mimasu	みます	look, watch
nemasu	ねます	sleep
nomimasu	のみます	drink
okimasu	おきます	get up
renshuu shimasu	れんしゅうします	practice
shimasu	します	do
tabemasu	たべます	eat
yomimasu	よみます	read

Foods/Beverages

aisutii	アイスティー	ice tea
biiru	ビール	beer
hanbaagaa	ハンバーガー	hamburger
juusu	ジュース	juice
kakuteru	カクテル	cocktail
koocha	こうちゃ	black tea
koohii	コーヒー	coffee
koora	コーラ	cola
Nihon ryoori	にほんりょうり	Japanese food
niku	にく	meat
nomimono	のみもの	beverage
o-cha	おちゃ	green tea
o-sake	おさけ	alcoholic beverage
o-sashimi	おさしみ	raw fish, sashimi
pasuta	パスタ	pasta
sakana	さかな	fish
tabemono	たべもの	food
uisukii	ウイスキー	whiskey
wain	ワイン	wine
yasai	やさい	vegetable

Other Nouns

bokushingu	ボクシング	boxing
dorama	ドラマ	drama
doramu	ドラム	drum(s)
earobikusu	エアロビクス	aerobics
eega	えいが	movie(s)
gakki	がっき	musical instrument

(Continues.)

四十七

gakkoo	がっこう	school
gitaa	ギター	guitar
hon	ほん	book
huruuto	フルート	flute
huttobooru	フットボール	football (American)
jogingu	ジョギング	jogging
kantorii ando uesutan	カントリーアンドウエスタン	country and western
kurashikku	クラシック	classical music
nyuusu	ニュース	news
ongaku	おんがく	music
piano	ピアノ	piano
rajio	ラジオ	radio
rappu	ラップ	rap music
rokku	ロック	rock music
sakkaa	サッカー	soccer
shigoto	しごと	work
shiidii	シーディー	CD
shinbun	しんぶん	newspaper
suiee	すいえい	swimming
sukii	スキー	skiing
supootsu	スポーツ	sports
tenisu	テニス	tennis
terebi	テレビ	TV
toshokan	としょかん	library
uchi	うち	house, home
zasshi	ざっし	magazine

Countries/Languages

Huransugo	フランスご	French language
Itaria	イタリア	Italy
Nihongo	にほんご	Japanese language

Other Useful Words

amari	あまり	not very (*in a negative sentence*)
Hontoo desu ka.	ほんとうですか。	Really? (lit., *Is that true?*)
ichiban	いちばん	(the) best (lit., *number one*)
kirai	きらい	to dislike
majime	まじめ	diligent, earnest
mo	も	too, either
suki	すき	to like
toku ni	とくに	especially
yoku	よく	often
zenzen	ぜんぜん	(not) at all (*in a negative sentence*)
hima	ひま	free time
kara… made	から… まで	from, beginning at… until

Part Four

OBJECTIVES

Talking about activities and events in the past

Inviting someone to do something

Talking about weekly schedules

Talking about the weather

The Japanese writing system (4): **Katakana** (1)

Talking About Activities and Events in the Past

Dialogue 1: Saying What One Ate the Night Before

Masao Hayashi is seeing his physician, Dr. Miyai.

MIYAI: Kinoo no yoru nani o tabemashita ka.
HAYASHI: Eeto, kinoo no yoru desu ka. Sukiyaki o tabemashita.
MIYAI: Hoka ni wa.
HAYASHI: Eeto, hoka ni wa… Yakitori o tabemashita.

> **Y**akitori is bite-sized marinated pieces of chicken meat cooked like shish kebab on skewers over an open fire.

| Vocabulary: Days and Weeks (2) |

kinoo   yesterday
ototoi   the day before yesterday
senshuu   last week
sensenshuu   the week before last

	Su	M	T	W	Th	F	Sa
sensenshuu							
senshuu							
konshuu		ototoi	kinoo	kyoo	ashita	asatte	
raishuu							
saraishuu							

Dialogue 1   MIYAI: What did you eat last night?   HAYASHI: Uh, last night?… I ate sukiyaki.
MIYAI: Anything else?   HAYASHI: Hmm, anything else… I ate yakitori.

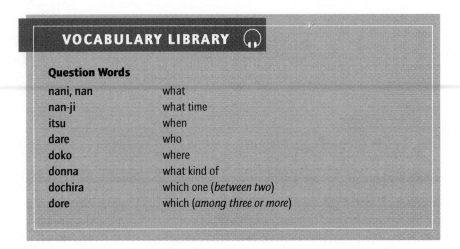

Question Words

nani, nan	what
nan-ji	what time
itsu	when
dare	who
doko	where
donna	what kind of
dochira	which one (*between two*)
dore	which (*among three or more*)

ACTIVITY   1

First, listen to your teacher or CD while looking at the following schedule, which describes what Linda Brown did yesterday.

LINDA BROWN'S SCHEDULE FOR YESTERDAY

5:00 A.M.	okimashita (*got up*)
5:30 A.M.	sanpo shimashita (*took a walk*)
6:25 A.M.	asagohan o tabemashita (*ate breakfast*)
8:00 A.M.	gakkoo e ikimashita (*went to school*)
11:50 A.M.	kafeteria de hirugohan o tabemashita (*ate lunch at a cafeteria*)
1:00 P.M.	Kawamura-san to hanashimashita (*talked with Mr. Kawamura*)
3:30 P.M.	toshokan e ikimashita (*went to the library*)
5:45 P.M.	uchi e kaerimashita (*returned home*)
6:15 P.M.	bangohan o tabemashita (*ate dinner*)
8:00 P.M.	terebi o mimashita (*watched TV*)
9:20 P.M.	hon o yomimashita (*read a book*)
11:30 P.M.	nemashita (*went to sleep*)

Can you tell the difference between verb forms expressing daily, habitual actions and those expressing past actions?

Now answer the following questions.

Example:

> Buraun-san wa kinoo nan-ji ni okimashita ka. (*What time did Ms. Brown get up yesterday?*) →
> Gozen 5-ji ni okimashita. (*At 5:00 A.M.*)

1. Gozen 5-ji han ni nani o shimashita ka. (*What did she do at 5:30 A.M.?*)
2. Nan-ji ni asagohan o tabemashita ka.
3. Nan-ji ni gakkoo e ikimashita ka.

五十

4. Nan-ji ni hirugohan o tabemashita ka.

5. Gogo 1-ji ni nani o shimashita ka.

6. Nan-ji ni uchi e kaerimashita ka.

7. Nan-ji ni bangohan o tabemashita ka.

8. Gogo 8-ji kara 9-ji nijippun made nani o mimashita ka.

9. Kinoo nan-ji goro nemashita ka.

Can you answer the following questions?

10. Gozen 6-ji 25-hun ni nani o shimashita ka.

11. Gozen 8-ji ni doko e ikimashita ka.

12. Doko de hirugohan o tabemashita ka.

13. Gogo 1-ji ni dare to hanashimashita ka.

14. Gogo 8-ji kara 9-ji nijippun made nani o shimashita ka.

15. Kinoo no yoru nani o yomimashita ka.

ACTIVITY	2	

Step 1: Write down your schedule for yesterday in English.

Step 2: Work in pairs. Explain your schedule to your partner in Japanese.

Dialogue 2: Saying What One Drank the Night Before

Dr. Miyai and Masao Hayashi continue the consultation.

MIYAI: O-sake wa nomimasu ka.

HAYASHI: Ee, chotto.

MIYAI: Kinoo wa?

HAYASHI: Zenzen nomimasen deshita.

STUDY HINT

Making a Generalization

Up to this point, you have heard many Japanese verb forms and you may have formed some of your own ideas about how Japanese verbs are conjugated. You may have already guessed the meaning of such particles as **ni, to,** and **de** or how to form question sentences using **nani, doko,** and **dare.** Reading a grammar book and memorizing grammar rules is not the only way to learn a new language. Making generalizations or guessing about grammatical rules or the meaning of vocabulary items will shorten the time it takes to acquire a new language. Don't be afraid to take risks. Don't hesitate to guess while listening or reading. Be willing to make generalizations. Risk takers are better language learners.

Dialogue 2   MIYAI: Do you drink sake?   HAYASHI: Yes, a little bit.   MIYAI: How about yesterday?   HAYASHI: I didn't drink at all.

ACTIVITY 3

Now let's talk about your life. Answer the following questions.

1. Kinoo nan-ji ni okimashita ka.

2. Kinoo asagohan o tabemashita ka. Tabemasen deshita ka.

3. Kinoo gakkoo e kimashita ka. Kimasen deshita ka.

4. Kinoo koohii o nomimashita ka. Nomimasen deshita ka.

5. Kinoo toshokan e ikimashita ka.

6. Kinoo Nihongo o benkyoo shimashita ka.

7. Senshuu kaimono ni ikimashita ka.

8. Senshuu eega o mimashita ka.

Inviting Someone to Do Something

Dialogue 3: Making Plans with Another Person

Mei Lin Chin and Masao Hayashi are making plans.

CHIN: Hayashi-san, kyoo no gogo eega ni ikimasen ka.
HAYASHI: Kyoo no gogo desu ka. Kyoo wa nan'yoobi desu ka.
CHIN: Eeto, kin'yoobi desu.
HAYASHI: Jaa, daijoobu desu yo.

An apostrophe (') indicates that the preceding **n** is pronounced ん; it is not part of the following syllable.

言語ノート

LANGUAGE NOTE: Invitation

You can invite someone to do something by using the nonpast, negative form of verbs plus **ka**, as the following sentences show.

Issho ni hirugohan o tabemasen ka.
Shall we eat lunch together?
Ashita jogingu shimasen ka.
Shall we go jogging tomorrow?
Eega o mimasen ka.
Shall we watch a movie?

When you accept an invitation, you can say:

Ee, ii desu ne.
Yes, that's good.
Ee, yorokonde.
Yes, with pleasure

Dialogue 3 CHIN: Mr. Hayashi, shall we go to a movie this afternoon (lit., *today's* P.M.)? HAYASHI: This afternoon... What day of the week is it today? CHIN: Well, it's Friday. HAYASHI: Then, it's OK.

When you politely decline an invitation, you can say

Chotto. . .
I cannot do that. (*lit.,* a little bit. . .)
Sumimasen ga, chotto. . .
I'm sorry, but I cannot. (*lit.,* I am sorry, but a little. . .)
Ee, demo chotto. . .
Yes, but I cannot do that. (*lit.,* Yes, but a little. . .)

ACTIVITY　　　**4**

Listen to your instructor or CD, and write down in English what the speaker is inviting someone else to do. Also, indicate whether or not the other speaker accepted an invitation.

Vocabulary: Days of the Week

nichiyoobi	Sunday
getsuyoobi	Monday
kayoobi	Tuesday
suiyoobi	Wednesday
mokuyoobi	Thursday
kin'yoobi	Friday
doyoobi	Saturday
konshuu no getsuyoobi	this Monday (lit., *Monday of this week*)
senshuu no kayoobi	last Tuesday (lit., *Tuesday of last week*)
raishuu no kin'yoobi	next Friday (lit., *Friday of next week*)
nan'yoobi	what day of the week?

ACTIVITY　　　**5**

Listen to your instructor or CD. On a separate sheet of paper write down what day of the week the speaker is asking someone else to do something with him or her.

1. …
2. …
3. …
4. …
5. …

予 定 メ モ

1	日 仏滅		
2	月 大安	初午	
3	火 赤口	節分 豆まき	
4	水 先勝	立春	
5	木 友引		
6	金 先負		
7	土 仏滅		
8	日 大安	針供養	
9	月 赤口		
10	火 先勝		
11	水 友引	建国記念の日	
12	木 先負		
13	金 仏滅		
14	土 大安	バレンタインデー	
15	日 赤口		
16	月 先勝		
17	火 友引	「主婦の友」3月号発売日	
18	水 先負		
19	木 仏滅	雨水	
20	金 大安		
21	土 赤口		
22	日 先勝		
23	月 友引		
24	火 先負		
25	水 仏滅		
26	木 大安		
27	金 赤口		
28	土 友引		

五十三

ACTIVITY   **6**

Work in pairs. One of you will ask the other to do the following together. The second person will accept or decline the invitation. Practice by changing roles.

1. have lunch tomorrow

2. go to the library the day after tomorrow

3. watch TV this afternoon

4. have lunch at the cafeteria

5. study Japanese next week

Talking About Weekly Schedules

Dialogue 4: Making Plans for a Dinner

Masao Hayashi and Mei Lin Chin are making arrangements to have dinner together.

HAYASHI: Chin-san, kin'yoobi issho ni yuugohan o tabemasen ka.

CHIN: Eeto, kin'yoobi desu ka. Kin'yoobi wa chotto…

HAYASHI: Sore wa zannen desu ne.

CHIN: Demo, doyoobi wa daijoobu desu yo.

ACTIVITY   **7**

Step 1: In your notebook, draw a grid and fill it in with your own activities from Sunday of last week through Saturday of next week.

Step 2: Work in pairs. Looking at your partner's grid, ask about his/her activities.

Talking About the Weather

Dialogue 5: Exchanging Greetings

Linda Brown and her landlord, Kunio Sano, run into each other in front of Linda's apartment.

BURAUN: Ohayoo gozaimasu.

SANO: Ah, Buraun-san, ohayoo gozaimasu.

BURAUN: Ii o-tenki desu ne.

SANO: Soo desu ne.

Refer to the Language Note: Greetings, on page 8.

Dialogue 4   HAYASHI: Ms. Chin, shall we have dinner together on Friday?   CHIN: Well, Friday is not good. (lit., *Is it Friday? A little bit…*)   HAYASHI: That's too bad. (lit., *That's regrettable.*) CHIN: But Saturday is OK with me.

Dialogue 5   BROWN: Good morning.   SANO: Oh, Ms. Brown. Good morning.   BROWN: It's nice weather, isn't it?   SANO: Yes, it is.

Vocabulary: Weather Expressions Often Used as Greetings

Ii o-tenki desu ne.	It's good/nice weather, isn't it?
Hidoi o-tenki desu ne.	It's terrible weather, isn't it?
Hidoi ame desu ne.	It's raining hard, isn't it?
Hidoi yuki desu ne.	It's snowing a lot, isn't it?
Kyoo wa samui desu ne.	It's cold today, isn't it?
Kyoo wa atsui desu ne.	It's hot today, isn't it?
Kyoo wa atatakai desu ne.	It's warm today, isn't it?
Kyoo wa suzushii desu ne.	It's cool today, isn't it?

ACTIVITY 8

Work in pairs. Practice greeting each other in the following situations.

1.

2.
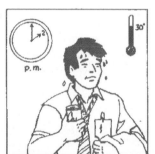

3.

4.

5.

五十五

The Japanese Writing System (4)

Katakana (1)

The second syllabary used in writing Japanese is very similar to **hiragana.** The forty-six symbols represent the same sounds and many even resemble their **hiragana** counterparts. The differences are in appearance and in use. **Katakana** are more angular than the curved, flowing **hiragana.** Generally speaking, the use of **katakana** is restricted to loanwords, onomatopoeic (sound effect) words, and words the writer wishes to emphasize. Plant and animal names are also often written in **katakana.**

Over the centuries the Japanese language has borrowed many foreign words from Chinese and Western languages, especially English, French, and German. In transcribing Western loanwords, the Japanese usually try to replicate the foreign pronunciation with **katakana.** Thus, *Porsche* becomes **porushe,** ポルシェ. Because foreign loanwords give an impression of sophistication and modernity, you will find them used frequently in fashion magazines and advertisements and among young urbanites, even when a perfectly good native Japanese word exists.

Included in the category of onomatopoeic words written with **katakana** are words expressing natural sounds (*meow, bang,* etc.) and those expressing manner (*twinkle, zigzag,* etc.). There are so many **katakana** words in Japanese that entire dictionaries are devoted just to foreign loanwords and to onomatopoeic words.

Here is the basic **katakana** syllabary.

ア a	イ i	ウ u	エ e	オ o
カ ka	キ ki	ク ku	ケ ke	コ ko
サ sa	シ shi	ス su	セ se	ソ so
タ ta	チ chi	ツ tsu	テ te	ト to
ナ na	ニ ni	ヌ nu	ネ ne	ノ no
ハ ha	ヒ hi	フ hu	ヘ he	ホ ho
マ ma	ミ mi	ム mu	メ me	モ mo
ヤ ya		ユ yu		ヨ yo
ラ ra	リ ri	ル ru	レ re	ロ ro
ワ wa				ヲ o
ン n				

Use the diacritical marks ゛ and ゜, just as you do in **hiragana.**

ガ ga	ギ gi	グ gu	ゲ ge	ゴ go
ザ za	ジ ji	ズ zu	ゼ ze	ゾ zo
ダ da	ヂ ji	ヅ zu	デ de	ド do
バ ba	ビ bi	ブ bu	ベ be	ボ bo
パ pa	ピ pi	プ pu	ペ pe	ポ po

(*Continues.*)

Similarly, add small ヤ **ya,** ユ **yu,** and ヨ **yo** just as in **hiragana.**

キャ kya	キュ kyu	キョ kyo
シャ sha	シュ shu	ショ sho
チャ cha	チュ chu	チョ cho
ニャ nya	ニュ nyu	ニョ nyo
ヒャ hya	ヒュ hyu	ヒョ hyo
ミャ mya	ミュ myu	ミョ myo
リャ rya	リュ ryu	リョ ryo
ギャ gya	ギュ gyu	ギョ gyo
ジャ ja	ジュ ju	ジョ jo
ビャ bya	ビュ byu	ビョ byo
ピャ pya	ピュ pyu	ピョ pyo

Double Vowels

In **katakana,** double vowels are written with the vowel extender ー
(choo-on kigoo).

aato	アート	*art*
kii	キー	*key*
suutsu	スーツ	*suit*
sukeeto	スケート	*skate, skating*
nooto	ノート	*notebook*

Double Consonants

As in **hiragana,** double consonants are written with a small ッ **tsu** that
doubles the following consonant.

katto	カット	*cut*
beddo	ベッド	*(Western-style) bed*

Yookoso! An Invitation to Contemporary Japanese, Third Edition

59

Vocabulary 🎧

This is a list of words that you have used or heard in Part 4 of Getting Started. Before beginning Part 5, make sure that you know the words listed under the categories **Greetings and Polite Expressions, Time Expressions,** and **Other Useful Words.** These are considered active vocabulary.

> **F**or your reading practice this list is rendered in **hiragana** and **katakana.** In authentic writing, **kanji** would be used in many words.

Greetings and Polite Expressions

yorokonde	よろこんで	with pleasure

Time Expressions

kinoo	きのう	yesterday
ototoi	おととい	the day before yesterday
senshuu	せんしゅう	last week
sensenshuu	せんせんしゅう	the week before last
mainichi	まいにち	every day

Days of the Week

nichiyoobi	にちようび	Sunday
getsuyoobi	げつようび	Monday
kayoobi	かようび	Tuesday
suiyoobi	すいようび	Wednesday
mokuyoobi	もくようび	Thursday
kin'yoobi	きんようび	Friday
doyoobi	どようび	Saturday
konshuu no getsuyoobi	こんしゅうのげつようび	this Monday (lit., *Monday of this week*)
senshuu no kayoobi	せんしゅうのかようび	last Tuesday (lit., *Tuesday of last week*)
raishuu no kin'yoobi	らいしゅうのきんようび	next Friday (lit., *Friday of next week*)
nan'yoobi	なんようび	what day of the week?

Question Words

dare	だれ	who
dochira	どちら	which (*among three or more*)
doko	どこ	where
donna	どんな	what kind of
dore	どれ	which one (*between two*)
itsu	いつ	when
nani	なに	what
nan-ji	なんじ	what time

(Continues.)

五十九

Foods/Beverages

sukiyaki	すきやき	sukiyaki
yakitori	やきとり	yakitori

Other Useful Words

atatakai	あたたかい	warm (weather)
atsui	あつい	hot (weather)
daijoobu	だいじょうぶ	OK (lit., *safe*)
hidoi	ひどい	hard, terrible, a lot
ii o-tenki	いいおてんき	nice/good weather
issho ni	いっしょに	together
samui	さむい	cold (weather)
suzushii	すずしい	cool (weather)
zannen desu ne	ざんねんですね	that's too bad (lit., *that's regrettable*)
hoka no (ni)	ほかの（に）	other (*in addition*)

Part Five

OBJECTIVES

Asking location

Numbers from 21 to 10,000

Asking about existence

Asking about price

Talking more about likes and dislikes

The Japanese writing system (5):
Katakana (2); Uses of **kanji**,
hiragana, and **katakana**;
Introduction to kanji

Asking Location

Dialogue 1: Asking Where Something Is Located

John Kawamura is at a department store.

KAWAMURA: Sumimasen. <u>Kasa</u> wa doko desu ka.
TEN'IN: Hai, <u>kasa</u> wa <u>san-kai</u> desu.
KAWAMURA: A, soo desu ka. Arigatoo gozaimasu.
TEN'IN: (*bows*).

Hai, kasa wa san-kai desu.

(*Continues.*)

Dialogue 1   KAWAMURA: Excuse me. Where are the <u>umbrellas?</u>   CLERK: (Yes.) They are on the
<u>third floor.</u>   KAWAMURA: Oh, I see. (Lit., *Oh, is that right?*) Thank you.   CLERK: (*bows*).

One way to ask the location of something is to say

_____ wa doko desu ka.   *Where is _____?*

To indicate the location of something, say

_____ wa (*place*) desu.   _____ *is at/on* (*place*).

Use the counter suffix **-kai** to name floors of a building. Add **chika** (*underground*) before the number to indicate a basement level. For example, **chika san-kai** (often written as **B3** in Japan) is three stories underground.

Floors of a Building

B1 chika ik-kai	5 go-kai	9 kyuu-kai
1 ik-kai	6 rok-kai	10 juk-kai (*or* jik-kai)
2 ni-kai	7 nana-kai	11 juu-ik-kai
3 san-kai	8 hachi-kai (*or*	
4 yon-kai	hak-kai)	

> **A**n alternate pronunciation for the third floor is **san-gai.**

11		tokee
10		kagu
9		hon
8		bunboogu
7		kamera
6		shatsu
5		seetaa
4		sokkusu
3		kasa
2		suutsu
1		kutsu
B1		

ACTIVITY 1

Ask a classmate where the following items are, referring to the store directory and using Dialogue 1 as a model.

1. kamera
2. seetaa
3. sokkusu
4. suutsu
5. kagu
6. tokee
7. shatsu
8. hon
9. kaban
10. teeburu

Dialogue 2: Asking Where Someone's Home Is

Linda Brown inquires about the location of John Kawamura's home.

BURAUN: <u>Kawamura-san</u> no <u>uchi</u> wa doko desu ka.
KAWAMURA: <u>Setagaya</u> desu.
BURAUN: <u>Chotto tooi desu ne</u>.
KAWAMURA: <u>Ee</u>.

ACTIVITY 2

Use the following map to practice Dialogue 2, making substitutions for the names and underlined parts.

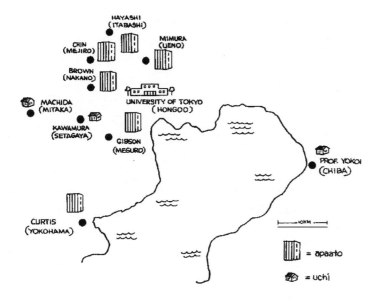

Dialogue 2 BROWN: Where is <u>your house, Mr. Kawamura</u>? KAWAMURA: It's in <u>Setagaya</u>.
BROWN: <u>That's a bit far, isn't it</u>? KAWAMURA: <u>Yes</u>.

ACTIVITY   **3**

Now ask a classmate where his or her house or apartment is. Do you think it is close to or far from your school?

Useful words:

uchi	*house, home* (informal)
apaato	*apartment*
ryoo	*dormitory*
daigaku	*university*
(Totemo) chikai desu.	*It's (very) close.*
(Totemo) tooi desu.	*It's (very) far.*

Numbers from 21 to 10,000

Large Numbers

21	ni-juu-ichi	700	nana-hyaku
29	ni-juu-kyuu, ni-juu-ku	800	hap-pyaku
30	san-juu	900	kyuu-hyaku
40	yon-juu	996	kyuu-hyaku-kyuu-juu-roku
50	go-juu	1,000	sen
60	roku-juu	2,000	ni-sen
70	nana-juu, shichi-juu	3,000	san-zen
80	hachi-juu	4,000	yon-sen
90	kyuu-juu	5,000	go-sen
99	kyuu-juu-kyuu, kyuu-juu-ku	6,000	roku-sen
100	hyaku	7,000	nana-sen
101	hyaku-ichi	8,000	has-sen
110	hyaku-juu	9,000	kyuu-sen
153	hyaku-go-juu-san	9,990	kyuu-sen-kyuu-hyaku-kyuu-juu
200	ni-hyaku		
300	san-byaku	9,999	kyuu-sen-kyuu-hyaku-kyuu-juu-ku
400	yon-hyaku		
500	go-hyaku	10,000	ichi-man
600	rop-pyaku		

ACTIVITY   **4**

Read these numbers aloud.

1. 34	**6.** 459	**11.** 2,073
2. 66	**7.** 555	**12.** 5,555
3. 87	**8.** 803	**13.** 8,906
4. 108	**9.** 1,001	**14.** 9,713
5. 196	**10.** 1,562	

Asking About Existence

Dialogue 3: Asking What's Available

John Kawamura is at the student cafeteria of the University of Tokyo.

KAWAMURA: Sumimasen. <u>Supagetti</u> wa arimasu ka.
UEETORESU: Sumimasen ga, chotto…
KAWAMURA: Ja, <u>hanbaagaa</u> wa arimasu ka.
UEETORESU: Hai, arimasu.
KAWAMURA: Ja, <u>hanbaagaa</u> o o-negai shimasu.
UEETORESU: Hai, <u>220-en</u> desu.

Arimasu is a verb meaning *to exist* or *to have*. To ask whether something exists, say:

___ wa arimasu ka.   *Is there (Do you have) ___?*

言語ノート

LANGUAGE NOTE: Saying No (Without Saying No)

Sumimasen ga, chotto. . . in Dialogue 3 literally means *I am sorry, but a little bit.* . . . In Japan it is considered clumsy and impolite to say no directly. For example, in this case, to say **lie, arimasen** (*No, we don't have any*) would be grammatically correct but socially inappropriate. There are a number of ways to indicate a negative answer indirectly. **Sumimasen ga, chotto.** . . or just **Chotto.** . . said with a trailing intonation is one of these strategies.

ACTIVITY **5**

Now practice Dialogue 3 with a classmate, using the following menu.

Tookyoo Daigaku Kafeteria menyuu			
supagetti	urikire	Nomimono	
piza	urikire	koora	¥100
suteeki	¥1100	juusu	¥180
sushi	urikire	aisu miruku	urikire
omuretsu	¥470	aisutii	¥120
raamen	¥400	koohii	¥150
Hanbaagaa		Saido Oodaa	
hanbaagaa	¥220	hurenchi hurai	¥90
chiizu baagaa	¥330	onion ringu	¥170
daburu baagaa	¥420	suupu	¥150
janbo baagaa	¥510	sarada	¥230
chikin baagaa	urikire		
fisshu baagaa	¥350		

Dialogue 3 KAWAMURA: Excuse me. Do you have <u>spaghetti</u>?   WAITRESS: I'm sorry, but…
KAWAMURA: Then, do you have <u>hamburgers</u>?   WAITRESS: Yes, we do.   KAWAMURA: Then, I would like a <u>hamburger</u>.   WAITRESS: Certainly (lit., *Yes*). That's <u>220 yen</u>.

Asking About Price

Dialogue 4: Asking How Much Something Is

Linda Brown is at the university cafeteria.

BURAUN: Sumimasen. <u>Chiizubaagaa</u> wa arimasu ka.
UEETORESU: Hai, arimasu.
BURAUN: Ikura desu ka.
UEETORESU: <u>330-en</u> desu.
BURAUN: Jaa, <u>chiizubaagaa</u> to <u>koohii</u> o o-negai shimasu.
UEETORESU: Arigatoo gozaimasu. <u>480-en</u> desu.

> **T**o is a particle meaning *and*. It can connect two or more nouns to express such meanings as *A and B* and *A, B, and* C. It cannot be used to connect two verbs.

言語ノート

LANGUAGE NOTE: Asking Price

The most common way to ask how much something costs is to say **Ikura desu ka.**

—Kore wa ikura desu ka. How much is this?
—3,000-en desu. It's 3,000 yen.
—Kono tokee wa ikura desu ka. How much is this watch?
—9,500-en desu. It's 9,500 yen.

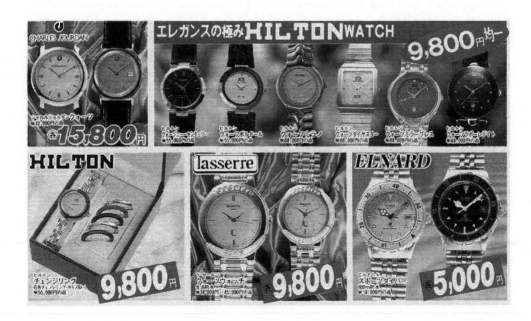

Dialogue 4 BROWN: Excuse me. Do you have <u>cheeseburgers</u>? WAITRESS: Yes, we do.
BROWN: How much are they? WAITRESS: <u>330 yen</u>. BROWN: Well then, please give me
a cheeseburger and coffee. WAITRESS: Thank you. That will be <u>480 yen</u>.

Yookoso! An Invitation to Contemporary Japanese, Third Edition

67

Dialogue 5: Ordering a Meal

Heather Gibson is at the student cafeteria.

GIBUSON: <u>Fisshubaagaa</u> wa arimasu ka.
UEETORESU: Hai, arimasu.
GIBUSON: Ikura desu ka.
UEETORESU: <u>350-en</u> desu.
GIBUSON: Ja, <u>fisshubaagaa</u> o o-negai shimasu.
UEETORESU: O-nomimono wa ikaga desu ka.
GIBUSON: Ie, kekkoo desu.

> **...wa ikaga desu ka** is commonly used to make a suggestion. More informally, **...wa doo desu ka** is used.

LANGUAGE NOTE: *Kekkoo desu*

言語ノート

Kekkoo desu can mean *It's fine* or *No, thank you*, depending on the context. In Dialogue 5, **kekkoo desu** means *No, thank you*. In the following exchange, it means *It's fine*.

—**Kore de ii desu ka.**   Is this OK?
—**Ee, kekkoo desu.**   Yes, it's fine.

Dialogue 6: Ordering Coffee

Henry Curtis is at a coffee shop.

KAATISU: <u>Koohii</u> wa arimasu ka.
UEETORESU: Hai. <u>Aisu</u> to <u>hotto</u> ga arimasu ga...
KAATISU: Soo desu ne. <u>Aisu</u> o onegai shimasu.
UEETORESU: 550-en desu.

ACTIVITY **6**

Pair up with a classmate and practice ordering at a **kissaten. Kissaten** are coffee shops where people go to talk or rendezvous with friends or business contacts, to relax, to eat, or just to kill time. Order from the coffee shop menu on page 68.

(Continues.)

Dialogue 5 GIBSON: Do you have <u>fishburgers</u>?   WAITRESS: Yes, we do.   GIBSON: How much are they?   WAITRESS: 350 yen.   GIBSON: Well then, I would like a <u>fishburger</u>.   WAITRESS: How about something to drink?   GIBSON: No, thank you.

Dialogue 6 CURTIS: Do you have <u>coffee</u>?   WAITRESS: Yes. We have <u>ice coffee</u> and <u>hot coffee</u>. CURTIS: Let me see. <u>Ice coffee</u>, please.   WAITRESS: 550 yen, please.

DRINKS
お飲物

ブレンドコーヒー ‥‥‥‥‥‥‥ ￥400	
YOKOのオリジナルの香りをお楽しみください。	
アメリカンコーヒー ‥‥‥‥‥‥ ￥400	
一日に何回も飲む人のコーヒーです。	
カフェオレ（Hot or Ice） ‥‥‥‥ ￥600	
ミルクとコーヒー2つの味の調和をお楽しみください。	
カフェウィンナー ‥‥‥‥‥‥‥ ￥600	
生クリームとコーヒーの2つの味を一度に味わってください。	
カフェカプチーノ ‥‥‥‥‥‥‥ ￥650	
シナモンの香りをお楽しみください。	
エスプレッソコーヒー ‥‥‥‥‥ ￥600	
コクと香りの世界がお楽しみいただけます。	
アイリッシュコーヒー ‥‥‥‥‥ ￥800	
アイリッシュウイスキーの入った大人のコーヒーです。	
レモンティー ‥‥‥‥‥‥‥‥‥ ￥400	
ダージリン茶を使用した香り高い紅茶です。	
ロイヤルティー ‥‥‥‥‥‥‥‥ ￥600	
本格派の紅茶。	
ロシアンティー ‥‥‥‥‥‥‥‥ ￥600	
ジャムの甘さと紅茶の香りを楽しんでください。	
フレーバーティー（アールグレ・アップル	
・ストロベリー） ‥‥‥‥‥‥ ￥500	
飲むほどに味のある紅茶です。	
ミルク（Hot or Ice） ‥‥‥‥‥‥ ￥600	

100パーセント Fresh Juice です。

オレンジジュース ‥‥‥‥‥‥‥ ￥750	
グレープフルーツジュース ‥‥‥‥ ￥800	
グレープジュース ‥‥‥‥‥‥‥ ￥800	
アップルジュース ‥‥‥‥‥‥‥ ￥650	
レモンジュース ‥‥‥‥‥‥‥‥ ￥750	
サンキストレモンを絞った生の味です。	

FOODS
お食事

サンドイッチはイギリスパンです。

ヒレカツサンドイッチ ‥‥‥‥‥ ￥1,200	
カツの厚みとイギリスパンの調和した力作です。	
フィンガーサンドイッチ ‥‥‥‥ ￥1,000	
女性にやさしい一口タイプのサンドイッチです。	
アメリカンクラブハウスサンドイッチ ‥‥ ￥1,500	
ボリュームタップリのアメリカ風サンドイッチです。	
ハンバーグサンドイッチ ‥‥‥‥ ￥1,000	
牛肉と玉子だけのYOKO自慢のサンドイッチです。	
ワッフル ‥‥‥‥‥‥‥‥‥‥‥ ￥1,000	
YOKOのオリジナルの味をお楽しみください。	

A LA CARTE
アラカルト

フルーツ（季節ごとに変わります） ‥‥ ￥1,000	
四季のバラエティーに富んだメニューです。	
フルーツクリームヨーグルト ‥‥‥‥ ￥800	
アイスクリームとフルーツを添えたヨーグルトです。	
ヨーグルトドリンク ‥‥‥‥‥‥ ￥700	
ヘルシー志向の人に最適な飲物です。	
ココア ‥‥‥‥‥‥‥‥‥‥‥‥ ￥800	
ヨーロッパスタイルのやさしい飲物です。	
ペリグリーノ ‥‥‥‥‥‥‥‥‥ ￥500	
イタリア産自然炭酸水です。	
ビール（小ビン） ‥‥‥‥‥‥‥ ￥600	

café-terrasse
yōkō
燿光

Koohii shoppu

ACTIVITY 7

Practice Dialogue 6 with your classmates, replacing the underlined parts with the following.

1. aisu kuriimu   banira   chokoreeto
2. juusu   orenji   gureepu
3. piza   peparoni   bejitarian
4. koocha   remon   miruku
5. koohii   moka   kona

Talking More About Likes and Dislikes

Dochira (*which*) is used to ask for a choice between two items. To choose among three or more items, use **dore.** Study these examples that use **dochira** to ask and answer which of two items is preferred.

> Nihon ryoori to Itaria ryoori to dochira ga suki desu ka.
> *Between Japanese food and Italian food, which do you prefer?*
>
> Nihon ryoori ga suki desu.
> *I prefer Japanese food.*
>
> Dochira mo suki desu.
> *I like both.*
>
> Dochira mo kirai desu. Huransu ryoori ga suki desu.
> *I don't like either. I prefer French food.*
>
> Saa, wakarimasen ne.
> *Well, I don't know.*
>
> Uun… Muzukashii desu ne.
> *Um, it's tough.*

ACTIVITY 8

Listen to your instructor or the CD, and on a separate piece of paper write down the items that each person likes.

ACTIVITY 9

Work in pairs. Ask your partner which of the following he or she likes more.

1. yasai   niku
2. Itarian doresshingu Hurenchi doresshingu
3. koohii   o-cha
4. tenisu   goruhu
5. jazu   kantorii ando uesutan

The Japanese Writing System (5)

Katakana (2)

In **katakana** you can use a small vowel symbol in combination with other symbols to create foreign sounds introduced into Japanese with loanwords.

イェ	ye	イェメン	yemen	*Yemen*
ウィ	wi	ウィンター	wintaa	*winter*
ウェ	we	ウェーター	weetaa	*waiter*
ウォ	wo	ウォーター	wootaa	*water*
キェ	kye	キェー	kyee	(screaming sound)
ギェ	gye	ギェー	gyee	(screaming sound)
クァ	kwa	クァトロ	kwatoro	*cuatro* (Spanish)
クィ	kwi	クィック	kwikku	*quick*
クェ	kwe	クェート	kweeto	*Kuwait*
クォ	kwo	クォーター	kwootaa	*quarter*
シェ	she	シェイプアップ	sheipuappu	*workout* (lit., *shape up*)
ジェ	je	ジェリー	jerii	*Jerry*
チェ	che	チェーン	cheen	*chain*
ツァ	tsa	ツァー	tsaa	*Tsar*
ツェ	tse	ツェッペリン	Zepperin	(*Led*) *Zeppelin*
ツォ	tso	ツォイス	tsoisu	*Zeus* (German pronunciation)
ティ	ti	ティー	tii	*tea*
ディ	di	ディーゼル	diizeru	*diesel*
デュ	dyu	プロデューサー	purodyuusaa	*producer*
トゥ	tu	トゥエンティー	tuentii	*twenty*
ドゥ	du	ドゥー	duu	*do* (*it yourself*)
ヒェ	hye	ヒェー	hyee	(screaming sound)
ファ	fa	ファッション	fasshon	*fashion*
フィ	fi	フィルム	firumu	*film*
フュ	fyu	フュージョン	fyuujon	*fusion*
フェ	fe	フェリー	ferii	*ferryboat*
フォ	fo	フォーム	foomu	*form*
ヴァ	va	ヴァイオリン	vaiorin	*violin*
ヴィ	vi	ヴィオラ	viora	*viola*
ヴ	vu	クリスマス・イヴ	kurisumasu ivu	*Christmas Eve*
ヴェ	ve	ベートーヴェン	Beetooven	*Beethoven*
ヴォ	vo	ヴォリューム	voryuumu	*volume*

Some Japanese transcribe the foreign sound [v] as ヴ, but most simply use バ、ビ、ブ、ベ、or ボ、which represent the more usual Japanese pronunciation. Note that the **katakana** spelling of foreign loanwords may differ from person to person, depending on each speaker's pronunciation.

言語ノート

LANGUAGE NOTE: Katakana Kuizu

According to one survey, about 5 percent of the vocabulary listed in a medium-size Japanese dictionary for native speakers are **katakana** loanwords from Western languages. (These **katakana** loanwords are usually called **gairaigo**.) In fact, more and more **gairaigo** are used every day in Japan, reflecting the increasing interaction of Japanese people with foreigners and foreign countries. **Gairaigo** is pervasive in Japan. Let's take a look at one typical young Japanese urbanite, Mr. Kimura. Can you guess what each **katakana** word means? (Answers are in Appendix 4.)

Mr. Kimura lives in an **apaato** in the suburbs of Kobe. He gets up with the noisy sound of an **araamu kurokku.** He shaves with a **sheebaa** and brushes his teeth with a **ha-burashi.** He eats **toosuto** with **bataa** and **jamu** and drinks **koohii** for breakfast. He goes to work in his **ootomachikku (kaa)** with **kaa sutereo, san ruuhu,** and **ea kon.** On the way to his company, he listens to **shiidii** of **popyuraa myuujikku.** He arrives at the **biru** of his company at 8:45 A.M. From underground **paakingu** he goes to his **ofisu** by **erebeetaa.** Between noon and 1 P.M. is his **ranchi taimu.** He eats lunch at a nearby **resu-toran.** He likes **karee raisu.** After lunch, he goes to the **koohii shoppu** and has **remon tii.** After work, he has a **deeto** with his **fianse,** who is a **konpyuuta puroguramaa** at the same company. He plans to marry her, so he gave her an **engeeji ringu** last month. After eating **dinaa** at a **Huransu resutoran,** they go for a **doraibu** to the top of a mountain. From there, they can see the beautiful **neon** of the city. After returning home from his **deeto,** Mr. Kimura drinks **uisukii.** He takes a **shawaa.** He sleeps in a **beddo.**

Uses of Kanji, Hiragana, and Katakana

As you now know, to write modern Japanese you need to use a combination of **kanji** (*Chinese characters*), **hiragana,** and **katakana.** The general rules of each script's use can be summarized as follows.

1. **Kanji** are usually used to represent such content words as nouns, adjective roots, adverbs, and verb roots.
2. In most cases, **hiragana** are used to represent such functional words as particles, and verb conjugational endings.
3. **Katakana** are used mainly to represent loanwords from Western languages and onomatopoeic words.

For instance,

兄	は	フランス	から	帰	りました。
kanji	hiragana	katakana	hiragana	kanji	hiragana
Ani	wa	Huransu	kara	kae	rimashita.

(Continues.)

七十一

兄	*older brother* (noun)
は	(topic particle [functional word])
フランス	*France* (loanword)
から	*from* (particle)
帰	*to return* (verb stem)
りました	(past, polite form [verb conjugational ending])

By the way, the only exception to writing with all three scripts is children's books. Young children have not studied many **kanji,** so **hiragana** are used phonetically in place of **kanji.**

言語ノート

LANGUAGE NOTE: Word Space and Punctuation

In Japanese writing, no space is used between words. An exception is books and other written materials for young children: Because they are written entirely in **hiragana** and **katakana,** they need word spaces to make them readable. The lack of word spacing in written Japanese is due to the influence of Chinese writing, which does not use spaces between words. Moreover, word boundaries are quite clear when **hiragana, katakana,** and **kanji** are intermixed. In fact, in many cases the changes in script in a sentence coincide with word boundaries.

Similarly, the co-use of the three systems makes it possible for readers to easily tell where a clause or sentence ends. For this reason, a punctuation system was not fully developed until about one hundred years ago. In modern Japanese, the following punctuation marks are used.

。	**maru**	a period, a question mark
、	**ten**	a comma
「」	**kagikakko**	quotation marks
・	**nakaten**	midpoint
…	**santen riidaa**	ellipsis points

The Japanese period is used to end a sentence, but the usage of the Japanese comma is not clear-cut. It resembles the English comma, but writers vary in how they use it. The quotation marks are used to set off quoted speech, titles of works (books, movies, etc.), and words the writer wishes to emphasize (somewhat as English writers underline words). The midpoint separates the individual words of **katakana** loanwords (e.g. トレーニング・センター), including personal names (the midpoint occurs between the first and last name; e.g. リンダ・ブラウン), or connects two nouns with the meaning *and.* Finally, as in English, Japanese ellipsis points are used to indicate missing words. You will also occasionally see question marks and exclamation points, both borrowed from Western languages.

Introduction to **Kanji**

Japan's Ministry of Education, Science, and Health requires Japanese grade schools to teach 1,006 **kanji** from grades one through six. These **kanji** are called **kyooiku kanji** (*educational Chinese characters*). By the time they graduate from high school, Japanese are expected to know a total of 1,945 **kanji.** These 1,945 **kanji** are called **jooyoo kanji** (*Chinese characters for everyday use*). Not only must students learn these **kanji,** but the Ministry of Education, Science, and Health also recommends that newspapers and magazines use only **jooyoo kanji** plus about 280 other characters used in people's names (or else provide the pronunciation for the unsanctioned **kanji**). Generally, educated Japanese know more than these required **kanji.**

　Kanji represent both sound and meaning. Most characters have more than one sound or reading. Centuries ago, when **kanji** were originally borrowed from Chinese for transcribing spoken Japanese, their Chinese pronunciations came along with them. These Chinese readings are called **on-yomi** (**on**-*readings*). When Chinese characters were used to write Japanese concepts or words, native Japanese pronunciations were also assigned to the characters. These native Japanese readings are called **kun-yomi** (**kun**-*readings*). For historical reasons, many **kanji** have more than one **on**-reading and more than one **kun**-reading. How do you know which reading applies? The answer is context. For instance, the character 人 meaning *person* is read **hito** in the phrase あの人 (*that person*), but it is read **jin** in the word アメリカ人 (*American*). In 三人 (*three people*), 人 is read **nin**. **Hito** is the **kun-yomi,** and **jin** and **nin** are the **on-yomi.** The more you practice reading Japanese and the more thoroughly you master spoken language, the more quickly and intuitively you will be able to choose the correct reading.

言語ノート

LANGUAGE NOTE: Hurigana

Because one **kanji** may have several different pronunciations (e.g., twenty for the character 生), it can be difficult even for native speakers of Japanese to remember all of them. For rarely occurring pronunciations and for rarely used **kanji** (those not included in the standard 1,945), the remedy is **hurigana.** These tiny **hiragana** or **katakana** written above the character (or to the right in vertical writing) provide the correct reading. You will see many **hurigana** in children's books, books dealing with difficult subjects, and textbooks for Japanese language students. Here is a sample of what they look like.

佐野さんの御夫婦はわたしのアパートの管理人です。
山本さんの勤める喫茶店は中野の住宅街にあります。

LANGUAGE NOTE: Vertical Writing and Horizontal Writing

Japanese can be written both vertically and horizontally. Vertical writing is commonly used in newspapers and magazines. The lines are read from right to left and from top to bottom. Literature books also follow this system. Textbooks, except Japanese language textbooks for native speakers, generally use horizontal writing, in which case you read letters from left to right. Horizontal writing is especially common in books that include many foreign words, mathematical formulas, and so on. When Japanese people write a letter, they use either vertical or horizontal writing depending on their personal preference (formal letters are usually vertically written). Young people seem to prefer using horizontal writing in letters.

再生によって古くなったり傷んだ組織を リフレッシュメントできないか

阿形清和

I. 修理と治療

「古くなったもの・悪くなったものは切って捨て、よいもの・新しいものに交換する。」不況下のリストラのパターンとして定着しつつあるが、最新メカの修理パターンでもある。研究機器が壊れて修理を頼むと、サービスマンが来て何を修理するかと思えば、ただ基板を交換して帰るだけで何万円と修理費を取られることになる。昔は、修理といえば、壊れた部品を取り出してサービスマンが念入りにチェックして修理する姿を思い浮かべたものだったが。最近は修理＝交換というパターンが定着してしまった。

人間の病気を治す場合は、修理とよばずに治療というのだが、移植による治療は上にあげた機械の修理とほぼ精神を同じくしているよう気がする。悪くなった臓器を取り出し、健常な他人の臓器を移植する。この大胆なアイデアを誰が考え、初めて実行したかは知らないが、生き物としての人間を一歩進んでロボットのようなものとして見たこの治療法は、人類史上特筆すべきものであることは間違いない。移植が行われた当初においては、悪魔の治療法だとか何やかやと騒がれたに違いないのだが、今では、脳死判定が話題になっても移植そのものが話題になることはなくなっている。それほど移植が定着し、さらに、時代は人工臓器へと移行しつつある。丸ごと交換の時代なのである。

II. 再生で細胞の リフレッシュメントはできないか

そんな時代に、再生による治療などと時代錯誤的な特集を組んだとお思いの読者も多いかもしれない。

1　コンピュータがある教室

１９８８年２月某日。

わたしは、大学の池の見える教室にいます。

教室とはいってもこの教室はふつうの教室とはちょっと違っています。教室には、黒板も教卓もありません。１６台のパソコンが向い合わせに３列ならんでいるだけです。１６台ぜんぶのパソコンの前には学生がひとりずつすわっています。

ときどき、キーボードをたたく音がします。本のページをくる音がします。

「くやしい、これが絶対正解だと思ったのに。」

「ああ、また最初からやりなおし。これで３回目だ。」

こんな声が聞こえてきます。

ここは、神戸学院大学のCAI教育施設、通称７６１教室です。CAIとは、Computer Assisted（またはAided）Instructionを省略したことばで、コンピュータを使った教育であることはごぞんじですね。

Vocabulary 🎧

This is a list of words that you have used or heard in Part 5 of Getting Started. Make sure that you know the words listed under the categories **Greetings and Polite Expressions, Classroom, Numbers,** and **Other Useful Words.** These are considered active vocabulary.

Greetings and Polite Expressions

Chotto.	ちょっと。	Well (no)… (lit., *A little…*)
Ikaga desu ka	いかがですか。	How about…
Kekkoo desu.	けっこうです。	No, thanks.

Classroom

kaban	かばん	bag
teeburu	テーブル	table

(Continues.)

七十五

Numbers

san-juu	さんじゅう	thirty
yon-juu	よんじゅう	forty
go-juu	ごじゅう	fifty
roku-juu	ろくじゅう	sixty
nana-juu, shichi-juu	ななじゅう、しちじゅう	seventy
hachi-juu	はちじゅう	eighty
kyuu-juu	きゅうじゅう	ninety
hyaku	ひゃく	one hundred
ni-hyaku	にひゃく	two hundred
san-byaku	さんびゃく	three hundred
yon-hyaku	よんひゃく	four hundred
go-hyaku	ごひゃく	five hundred
rop-pyaku	ろっぴゃく	six hundred
nana-hyaku	ななひゃく	seven hundred
hap-pyaku	はっぴゃく	eight hundred
kyuu-hyaku	きゅうひゃく	nine hundred
sen	せん	one thousand
ni-sen	にせん	two thousand
san-zen	さんぜん	three thousand
yon-sen	よんせん	four thousand
go-sen	ごせん	five thousand
roku-sen	ろくせん	six thousand
nana-sen	ななせん	seven thousand
has-sen	はっせん	eight thousand
kyuu-sen	きゅうせん	nine thousand
ichi-man	いちまん	ten thousand

Foods/Beverages

aisu	アイス	ice coffee/ice
aisukuriimu	アイスクリーム	ice cream
banira	バニラ	vanilla
bejitarian	ベジタリアン	vegetarian
chiizubaagaa	チーズバーガー	cheeseburger
chokoreeto	チョコレート	chocolate
gureepu	グレープ	grape(s)
hanbaagaa	ハンバーガー	hamburger
hotto	ホット	hot coffee
koohii	コーヒー	coffee
orenji	オレンジ	orange
peparoni	ペパロニ	pepperoni
piza	ピザ	pizza
regyuraa	レギュラー	regular (*not decaf*)
supagetti	スパゲッティ	spaghetti
yasai	やさい	vegetable

Nouns

apaato	アパート	apartment
daigaku	だいがく	university
jiinzu	ジーンズ	jeans
kagu	かぐ	furniture
kamera	カメラ	camera
kasa	かさ	umbrella
ryoo	りょう	dormitory
seetaa	セーター	sweater
shatsu	シャツ	shirt
sokkusu	ソックス	socks
suutsu	スーツ	suit
tokee	とけい	watch, clock
uchi	うち	house, home

Other Useful Words

-en	〜えん	¥___ (*counter for yen*)
-kai	〜かい	___ floor (*counter for floors of a building*)
chotto	ちょっと	a little
ikura	いくら	how much?
kono	この	this ___
tooi	とおい	far
chikai	ちかい	close, nearby

チェックリスト

Use this checklist to confirm that you can now:

- Greet others and introduce yourself
- Talk about your classroom
- Use numbers up to 10,000
- Ask and tell telephone numbers and time
- Ask what something is
- Talk about daily activities
- Talk about future activities and events
- Talk about activities and events in the past
- Express what you like and dislike
- Invite someone to do something
- Talk about weekly schedules
- Talk about the weather
- Ask about location, existence, and price

七十七

Introduction to *Yookoso!*

Now that you have finished **Getting Started,** we can say welcome (**yookoso**) to the heart of your textbook. Here you will begin studying grammar, **kanji** (*Chinese characters*), and other essentials for mastering Japanese. The rest of this book is divided into seven chapters, each of which revolves around a single theme, such as classmates, daily life, food, shopping, and so on.

When you start a chapter, take a look at the list of objectives to get a good idea of what you will learn and to focus your mind on the reasons for studying the material.

Following that list, each chapter has three parts called *Vocabulary and Grammar.* They contain two sections: **Vocabulary and Oral Activities** and **Grammar and Practice Activities.**

The **Vocabulary and Oral Activities** section introduces vocabulary relating to the chapter theme and includes one or two (or sometimes more) oral activities that will help you learn and use these new words and expressions.

The **Grammar and Practice Activities** section contains one or more grammar points. Each point begins with brief dialogues illustrating the use of the new grammar in context. These dialogues are followed by explanations of the grammar. Oral and written activities allow you to practice the new grammar using vocabulary you already know.

Language Skills is the part of the chapter where you'll put your new knowledge of vocabulary and grammar to work in more real-life situations.

The first section of this part is called **Reading and Writing.** It contains two reading selections with preparatory and follow-up activities and two writing activities. The reading materials relate to the chapter topics, and the writing focuses on the vocabulary and grammatical structures you have just studied, so it will be very useful to review the vocabulary and **kanji** lists at the end of the chapter before doing these activities.

In **Language Functions and Situations,** you will study important expressions used for functions such as apologizing, asking for directions, and keeping a conversation flowing smoothly. You'll practice how to communicate in a restaurant or a department store. Dialogues in this section are models for interaction with native speakers in many real-life situations, and activities and role playing provide you with opportunities to practice handling those situations.

The conversations and narrations you hear in the **Listening Comprehension** section will be on the now-familiar topics covered in the chapter. These activities will strengthen your ability to understand spoken Japanese.

Each chapter ends with a short section called *Vocabulary,* a summary list of words, expressions, and **kanji** that you are responsible for learning and being able to use in the chapter and in future chapters. These are the lists we suggest you review before you do the **Language Skills** part of each chapter.

After the ***Vocabulary*** and **kanji** lists is a checklist that you can use to check your progress on the chapter objectives. Additional practice and review activities are available on the *Yookoso!* Online Learning Center and on the *Yookoso!* Interactive CD-ROM.

Throughout the text you will see many more of the features you have already encountered in **Getting Started.** You will see authentic Japanese print materials that you would encounter in Japan—ads, tickets, and magazine clippings for example. You will also see many brief notes that will help you learn more about Japan and its language and people. Culture notes（文化ノート）offer useful cultural information. Linguistic notes （言語ノート）offer insights into interesting facts about the Japanese language, brief explanations of useful grammar points, and hints for communicating more effectively in Japanese.

So it's time to move ahead. Good luck and have fun!

1

Classmates

第一章 クラスメート

だいがく
大学のキャンパス

OBJECTIVES

In this lesson you are going to

- Talk about nationalities and languages
- Learn to identify things and people
- Learn to express possession
- Learn to exchange personal information
- Talk about your campus
- Learn to use personal pronouns and demonstratives
- Learn to ask questions
- Write to a pen pal
- Learn to introduce friends
- Learn to introduce yourself

YOOKOSO! MULTIMEDIA

Review and practice grammar and vocabulary from this chapter and watch video clips on the *Yookoso!* Interactive CD-ROM. Visit the *Yookoso!* Online Learning Center at **www.mhhe.com/yookoso3** for additional exercises and resources.

Vocabulary and Grammar 1A

Vocabulary and Oral Activities
Nationalities and Languages

Yokoi   Brown   Gibson   Hayashi   Curtis   Machida   Chin   Kawamura

アクティビティー **1**

ダイアログ：この人はだれですか。(*Who is this person?*)
山口さんとカワムラさんが写真を見ています。

> 山口： この人はだれですか。
> カワムラ： その人はブラウンさんです。
> 山口： 大学のクラスメートですか。
> カワムラ： はい、そうです。

Yamaguchi-san to Kawamura-san ga shashin o mite imasu.

YAMAGUCHI: Kono hito wa dare desu ka.

KAWAMURA: Sono hito wa <u>Buraun</u>-san desu.

YAMAGUCHI: Daigaku no kurasumeeto desu ka.

KAWAMURA: Hai, soo desu.

Now ask about the other people in the photograph, modeling your conversation after the dialogue. Replace the underlined words as necessary. An alternate ending to the dialogue follows.

> いいえ、違います。 _____です。(Iie, chigaimasu. _____ desu.)
> (*No, that's not right. He/She is _____.*)

Kawamura is a Japanese family name. Because John Kawamura is an American citizen, however, his name is written in **katakana**.

Mr. Yamaguchi and Mr. Kawamura are looking at a photo.   YAMAGUCHI: Who is this person?
KAWAMURA: That's Ms. <u>Brown</u>.   YAMAGUCHI: Is she (your) classmate at the university?
KAWAMURA: Yes, that's right.

STUDY HINT

This chapter continues to provide romanization, but try to refer to the Japanese writing as much as possible. From the next chapter on, you will be reading Japanese with no romanization as a crutch. Now is the time to start reading Japanese!

Vocabulary: People at School

クラスメート	**kurasumeeto**	classmate
友だち	**tomodachi**	friend
大学生	**daigakusee**	college student

Review: 学生（がくせい）、先生（せんせい）

Nationalities and Languages

Country	Nationality	Language
日本（にほん）Japan	日本人（にほんじん）	日本語（にほんご）
アメリカ U.S.	アメリカ人（じん）	英語（えいご）
イギリス England	イギリス人（じん）	英語（えいご）
イタリア Italy	イタリア人（じん）	イタリア語（ご）
カナダ Canada	カナダ人（じん）	英語（えいご）／フランス語（ご）
韓国（かんこく）South Korea	韓国人（かんこくじん）	韓国語（かんこくご）
シンガポール Singapore	シンガポール人（じん）	英語（えいご）／中国語（ちゅうごくご）
スペイン Spain	スペイン人（じん）	スペイン語（ご）
台湾（たいわん）Taiwan	台湾人（たいわんじん）	中国語（ちゅうごくご）
中国（ちゅうごく）China	中国人（ちゅうごくじん）	中国語（ちゅうごくご）
ドイツ Germany	ドイツ人（じん）	ドイツ語（ご）
ブラジル Brazil	ブラジル人（じん）	ポルトガル語（ご）
フランス France	フランス人（じん）	フランス語（ご）
香港（ほんこん）Hong Kong	香港人（ほんこんじん）	中国語（ちゅうごくご）
メキシコ Mexico	メキシコ人（じん）	スペイン語（ご）
ロシア Russia	ロシア人（じん）	ロシア語（ご）

八十三

言語ノート

Nationalities and Languages

With few exceptions, you can form the word for someone's nationality or language by attaching a suffix to the name of his or her country. Add the suffix 人（じん: *people/person*) for the nationality and 語 （ご: *language*) for the language. To ask someone's nationality or what language(s) he or she speaks, use the following expressions. Remember that since the subject isn't explicitly stated here, context will determine about whom you are talking.

お国はどちらですか。—アメリカです。

What country are (you) from?—(I) am from America.

何語を話しますか。— 英語を話します。

What language(s) do (you) speak?–I speak English.

You can also ask someone's nationality by saying 何人（なにじん）ですか. However, this question sounds very rude when asked of someone directly.

アクティビティー **2**

チンさんは中国人です。(*Ms. Chin is Chinese.*)

カワムラ： この人はチン・メイリンさんです。
山口： チンさんは中国人ですか。
カワムラ： はい、そうです。中国語を話します。

KAWAMURA: Kono hito wa <u>Chin Meirin</u>-san desu.
YAMAGUCHI: <u>Chin</u>-san wa <u>Chuugoku</u>-jin desu ka.
KAWAMURA: Hai, soo desu. <u>Chuugoku-go</u> o hanashimasu.

Practice the dialogue based on the following information.

PERSON	COUNTRY
リンダ・ブラウン	アメリカ
ホセ・ロドリゲス	メキシコ
クロード・ミレー	フランス
ハンス・シュミット	ドイツ
アナ・ラポーソ	ブラジル
キム・チョンヒ	韓国

KAWAMURA: This is Ms. <u>Mei-Lin Chin</u>.　YAMAGUCHI: Is Ms. <u>Chin Chinese</u>?　KAWAMURA: Yes, that's right. She speaks <u>Chinese</u>.

Grammar and Practice Activities
1. Identification: The Copula です

レストランで

カワムラ： すみません。あれは何ですか。

ウエーター： あれは「すきやき」です。

カワムラ： じゃ、あれをお願いします。

ブラウン： あの人は林さんではありませんか。

カワムラ： どの人ですか。

ブラウン： ほら、あの人です。

カワムラ： いいえ、林さんじゃありませんよ。

> **R**eminder: 「 and 」 are quotation marks.

1.1 To identify people and things in Japanese, you can use the following grammatical structure, where X and Y are nouns or pronouns.

X	は	Y	です。	X is Y.
これ		ペン		*This is a pen.*
わたし		ブラウン		*I am Brown.*
すきやき	は	日本料理	です。	*Sukiyaki is a Japanese dish.*
町田さん		学生		*Ms. Machida is a student.*
受付け		あそこ		*The reception desk is over there.*

This structure means *X is equivalent to Y, X is a member of the group Y,* or *X is described* (or *modified*) *by Y.*

は is usually called a *topic particle*. It indicates that the preceding noun is the topic of the sentence. For instance, in this sentence the speaker would like to talk about Mr. Takada.

高田さんはエンジニアです。
Mr. Takada is an engineer.

Usage of the topic particle will be discussed in more detail later.

(*Continues.*)

At a restaurant KAWAMURA: Excuse me. What is that? WAITER: That's sukiyaki. KAWAMURA: Then please give me that.
BROWN: Isn't that person Mr. Hayashi? KAWAMURA: Which person? BROWN: Over there. (lit., *Look.*) (I mean) that person. KAWAMURA: No, that's not Mr. Hayashi.

です is called the *copula*. It roughly corresponds to the verb *to be*. Like other Japanese verbs, です does not change form to agree with the subject of the sentence in number or person. In other words, (*I*) *am*, (*you*) *are*, (*he*) *is*, (*they*) *are*, and so on, are all expressed with the same form です. です also marks a certain level of politeness, which will be discussed later.

1.2 The negative form of です is ではありません (contracted to じゃありません in more informal speech).

X	は	Y	ではありません (じゃありません)。	X isn't Y.
これ		ペン		*This is not a pen.*
わたし		ブラウン		*I am not Brown.*
すきやき	は	中国料理	ではありません	*Sukiyaki is not a Chinese dish.*
町田さん		先生	(じゃありません)。	*Ms. Machida is not a teacher.*
受付け		ここ		*The reception desk is not here.*

1.3 Yes/No questions are formed in Japanese simply by adding か (the *interrogative* or *question particle*) to the end of a sentence. You can think of か as a verbal question mark.

あの人は町田さんです。
That person is Ms. Machida.
あの人は町田さんですか。
Is that person Ms. Machida?

あの人は町田さんではありません。
That person is not Ms. Machida.
あの人は町田さんではありませんか。
Isn't that person Ms. Machida?
(rising intonation)

Here are some typical ways to answer a yes/no question.

あの人は町田さんですか。
Is that Ms. Machida?

YES
はい、町田さんです。
Yes, it's Ms. Machida.
はい、そうです。
Yes, that's right.

With falling intonation, the last sentence can mean *Oh, I see. That person isn't Ms. Machida.*

Yookoso! An Invitation to Contemporary Japanese, Third Edition

87

NO

いいえ、町田さんではありません。
（いいえ、町田さんじゃありません。）
No, it's not Ms. Machida.
いいえ、そうではありません。
（いいえ、そうじゃありません。）
No, that's not right.
いいえ、ちがいます。
No, that's wrong (lit., *different*).

OTHER

すみません、わかりません。
I'm sorry, but I don't know.

言語ノート

Alternative Questions

To ask either/or questions, string the two alternate questions together: A ですか。B ですか (*Is it A? Is it B?* or in smoother English, *Is it A or B?*).

あれは日本料理ですか、中国料理ですか。

Is that Japanese food or Chinese food?

これは万年筆ですか、ボールペンですか。

Is this a fountain pen or a ballpoint pen?

1.4 The particle も means *too*. Substitute も for は in the X は Y です construction—X も Y です—to say that *X is a member of Y, too* (or *X, too, is described by* [or *equivalent to*] *Y*).

わたしはアメリカ人です。
I am an American.
— 本当ですか。わたしもアメリカ人です。
— *Really? I am an American, too.*

アクティビティー **3**

何人ですか。何語を話しますか。(*What is his nationality? What language does he speak?*)

(*Continues.*)

八十七

Answer these questions for each person listed below.

[例] ポール・マッカートニー →   例 *example(s)*
　　　ポール・マッカートニーはイギリス人です。英語を話します。

1. ニコール・キッドマン　　　　5. セルマ・ハヤック
2. ヴラヂイミール・プーテイン　6. デイヴィッド・ボイ
3. ジャッキー・チャン　　　　　7. 鈴木イチロー
4. ジュリア・ロバーツ

アクティビティー　4

イギリス人です。(*He's English.*)

Can you describe someone famous or anyone around you with the following traits?

[例]　イギリス人、英語
　　　→ ヒュー・グラントはイギリス人です。
　　　　　英語を話します。

1. オーストラリア人、英語
2. 日本人、日本語
3. メキシコ人、スペイン語
4. フランス人、フランス語
5. ドイツ人、ドイツ語

アクティビティー　5

スミスさんは先生です。(*Ms. Smith is a teacher.*)

Connect the appropriate words from the columns on the left and right to make ...は ...です sentences.

マドンナ	飲み物
わたし	日本人
アコード	学生
松井秀喜	アメリカ人
コーラ	コンピュータ
マッキントッシュ	ホンダの車 (car)

2. Possessive Particle の

2.1 の is a particle used to connect and relate nouns or pronouns. The result is a noun phrase. X の Y means *Y of X* in a broad sense and thus carries the meanings *Y belongs to X*, *Y is a part of X*, *Y is possessed by X*, *Y has a characteristic of X*, and so on, depending on the context.

N1	の	N2	
わたし		本	*my book*
大学	の	図書館	*the university library*
町田さん		万年筆	*Ms. Machida's fountain pen*
アメリカ		州	*a state in America*
コットン		ジーンズ	*cotton jeans*

> **T**hroughout this book, N1 stands for *a noun* and N2 stands for *another noun*, or *Noun 1* and *Noun 2*.

The particle の can connect more than two nouns or pronouns.

わたしの友だちの大学
my friend's university

三村さんのガールフレンドの家
the house of Mr. Mimura's girlfriend

2.2 When the item possessed is clear from the context, it can be omitted as shown in the following examples.

これはだれのセーターですか。—ブラウンさんのです。
Whose sweater is this? —It's Ms. Brown's.

あれもブラウンさんのセーターですか。—いいえ、町田さんのです。
Is that also Ms. Brown's sweater? —No, it's Ms. Machida's.

アクティビティー **6**

友だちの名前は...。(*My friend's name is...*)

Complete these sentences with...です.

[例] わたしは... →
わたしは東京大学の学生です。

1. わたしの日本語の先生は...。

2. わたしのクラスメートの＿＿＿さんは...。

3. わたしの先生のなまえは...。

4. トニー。ブレアは...。

5. ジョン・カワムラさんは...。

Vocabulary and Grammar 1B

Vocabulary and Oral Activities

Personal Information

Vocabulary: Personal Information

名前	**namae**	name
出身	**shusshin**	origin; hometown
専攻	**senkoo**	major
学部	**gakubu**	(academic) department
学年	**gakunen**	year in school; school year
一年生	**ichinensee**	freshman
二年生	**ninensee**	sophomore
三年生	**sannensee**	junior
四年生	**yonensee**	senior
大学院生	**daigakuinsee**	graduate student

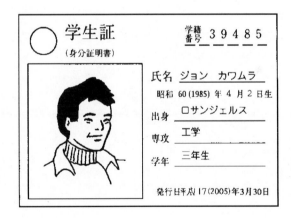

Yookoso! An Invitation to Contemporary Japanese, Third Edition

91

文化ノート

CULTURE NOTE: 出身(しゅっしん) Origins

Japanese often ask the question ご出身はどちらですか。 (*Where are you from?*) A variety of responses is possible. You can give your hometown, the place where you were born, as the answer. For example, ロサンゼルスの出身です。 (*I am from Los Angeles.*) If you moved away from your birthplace as a child and you have a stronger attachment to a different place, you can give that place as the answer. To Japanese, 出身 means the place you identify with geographically, mentally, and emotionally, so it has more meanings than *birthplace*. For example, the word is also used to indicate what school you graduated from and what social group you are from. Someone who graduated from the University of Tokyo might say 東京大学 (とうきょうだいがく) の出身です。 (*I am a graduate of* [lit., *I am from*] *the University of Tokyo.*) Or you might hear 農家 (のうか) の出身です。 (*I am from a farmer's family.*)

One of the reasons Japanese people ask this question so often is that the notions of in-group and out-group are of central importance in Japanese society. Depending on whether or not someone is a member of your group, your language, behavior, and attitude will differ. Asking this question is a way for Japanese to find out whether someone belongs to their in-group and to discover any common ground. When speaking to foreigners, Japanese will often substitute the question どちらのお国 (くに) の方 (かた) ですか or お国 (くに) はどちらですか。 (*What country are you from?*) as a means to break the ice and identify any common experience.

VOCABULARY LIBRARY 🎧

Academic Subjects and Majors

人類学	jinruigaku	anthropology
美術	bijutsu	art
生物学	seebutsugaku	biology
化学	kagaku	chemistry
コンピュータ・サイエンス	konpyuuta-saiensu	computer science
経済学	keezaigaku	economics
教育学	kyooikugaku	education
工学	koogaku	engineering
外国語	gaikokugo	foreign languages
歴史学	rekishigaku	history
法学	hoogaku	law
言語学	gengogaku	linguistics
文学	bungaku	literature
数学	suugaku	mathematics
音楽	ongaku	music
哲学	tetsugaku	philosophy
物理学	butsurigaku	physics
政治学	seejigaku	political science
社会学	shakaigaku	sociology

(Continues.)

九十一

If your major is not listed here, ask your instructor. Be aware, however, that some subjects frequently taught at North American universities are not taught at Japanese universities.

文化ノート

CULTURE NOTE: Japanese Universities and Colleges

In order to enter a Japanese university or college, you must take a nationally administered examination and/or an entrance exam specific to the school you wish to enter. These exams are usually held between January and March. (In Japan, the academic year starts in April.) The competition to enter prestigious national and private universities is severe, with medical schools and dental schools being the most difficult to get into. The extraordinarily intense pressure has led some to call this experience "examination hell." Many students who fail the entrance examination for the university of their choice decide to wait a year and retake the exam the following year, studying at a cram school or on their own in the meantime. These students are called 浪人 (ろうにん: *masterless samurai*).

When students apply to universities, they specify which department they wish to enter. During their freshman and sophomore years, however, students study a required core liberal arts curriculum consisting of 教養科目 (きょうようかもく: lit., *general education subjects*). As upperclassmen, they can study 専門科目 (せんもんかもく: *specialized subjects*).

While getting into a university can be extremely difficult, it is almost impossible to flunk out. Many students study little, treating the undergraduate years as a welcome break between the pressures of high school and the responsibilities of work and family life.

I passed the entrance exam of the University of Tokyo!

言語ノート

Academic Subjects and Departments

Most academic subjects are expressed by adding 学 (がく: [study] of) to a relevant noun. For example, 経済学 (けいざいがく: economics) is a combination of 経済 (けいざい : economy) and 学. Academic department names are formed by adding 学部 (がくぶ: academic department, faculty) to the same relevant noun. Thus, 経済 plus 学部 becomes Department of Economics, or 経済学部 (けいざいがくぶ). Similarly, 美術 (びじゅつ: fine arts) plus 学部 (academic department) becomes the Department of Fine Arts, or 美術学部 (びじゅつがくぶ). Japanese undergraduates typically identify their department as a way of stating their major.

わたしは文学部の学生です。

I am a student in the Department of Literature.

カワムラさんは工学部の三年生です。

Mr. Kawamura is a junior in the Engineering Department.

アクティビティー **7**

ダイアログ：専攻は何ですか。(*What is his/her major?*)

山口：ブラウンさんのご出身はどこですか。

ブラウン：ボストンの出身です。

山口：何年生ですか。

ブラウン：三年生です。

山口：専攻は何ですか。

ブラウン：歴史学です。

YAMAGUCHI: Buraun-san no go-shusshin wa doko desu ka.

BURAUN: Bosuton no shusshin desu.

YAMAGUCHI: Nannensee desu ka.

BURAUN: Sannensee desu.

YAMAGUCHI: Senkoo wa nan desu ka.

BURAUN: Rekishigaku desu.

(*Continues.*)

YAMAGUCHI: Where are you from, Ms. Brown?   BROWN: I'm from Boston.   YAMAGUCHI: What year student are you?   BROWN: I'm a junior.   YAMAGUCHI: What is your major?   BROWN: It's history.

Now talk about Linda Brown's classmates based on the following table.

Name なまえ 名前	Nationality こくせき 国籍	Hometown しゅっしん 出身	Year がくねん 学年	Major せんこう 専攻
ジョン・カワムラ	アメリカ	ロサンゼルス	さんねんせい 三年生	こうがく 工学
ヘザー・ギブソン	カナダ	エドモントン	にねんせい 二年生	けいざいがく 経済学
チン・メイリン	ちゅうごく 中国	ペキン	にねんせい 二年生	かがく 化学
ヘンリー・カーチス	アメリカ	アトランタ	よねんせい 四年生	コンピュータ・ サイエンス
はやしまさお 林 正男	にほん 日本	あそ 阿蘇	にねんせい 二年生	ほうがく 法学
まちだ 町田ひとみ	日本	とうきょう 東京	さんねんせい 三年生	ぶんがく フランス文学

アクティビティー **8**

インタビュー：ご出身^{しゅっしん}はどこですか。 (*Where are you from?*)

Following the example, ask your classmates questions.

STUDENT 1: ご出身^{しゅっしん}はどこですか。

STUDENT 2: シアトルです。

S1: 何年生^{なんねんせい}ですか。

S2: 二年生^{にねんせい}です。

S1: 専攻^{せんこう}は何^{なん}ですか。

S2: 生物学^{せいぶつがく}です。

S1: Go-shusshin wa doko desu ka.

S2: Shiatoru desu.

S1: Nannensee desu ka.

S2: Ninensee desu.

S1: Senkoo wa nan desu ka.

S2: Seebutsugaku desu.

---

s1: Where are you from? s2: I'm from Seattle. s1: What year are you in? s2: I'm a sophomore. s2: What is your major? s2: It's biology.

Yookoso! An Invitation to Contemporary Japanese, Third Edition

95

言語ノート

Asking for Personal Information

Here are some common ways of eliciting personal information. Note the use of the honorific prefix **o-** or **go-** when referring to someone else's name, residence, etc.; remember to drop these prefixes when talking to an out-group member about your own name, residence, and so on, or that of a member of your in-group (for example, a sister or a coworker).

お名前は（何ですか）。	O-namae wa (nan desu ka).	(What is) your name?
ご出身は（どちらですか）。	Go-shusshin wa (dochira desu ka).	Where are you from?
お国は（どちらですか）。	O-kuni wa (dochira desu ka).	What country are you from?
おすまいは（どちらですか）。	O-sumai wa (dochira desu ka).	Where do you live?
お年は（おいくつですか）。	O-toshi wa (o-ikutsu desu ka).	How old are you?
お電話番号は（何番ですか）。	O-denwa bangoo wa (nan-ban desu ka).	What is your telephone number?

In all of the above questions, you can omit the words in parentheses. Similarly, when answering these questions, you can say:

名前はジョン・カワムラです。	Namae wa Jon Kawamura desu.	My name is John Kawamura.

or simply

ジョン・カワムラです。	Jon Kawamura desu.	(My name) is John Kawamura.

Vocabulary: Age 🎧

The counter suffix **-sai** (*years old*) is used with the Sino-Japanese system of numerals to express a person's age. For ages 1 through 10, the Japanese system of numerals — 一つ、二つ、etc.—may also be used. You will study more about these two number systems in **Chapter 2.** *Twenty* has its own special word, 二十（はたち）.

	SINO-JAPANESE SYSTEM	JAPANESE SYSTEM
1 year old	is-sai 一歳	hitotsu 一つ
2 years old	ni-sai 二歳	hutatsu 二つ
3 years old	san-sai 三歳	mittsu 三つ

(Continues.)

九十五

	SINO-JAPANESE SYSTEM	JAPANESE SYSTEM
4 years old	yon-sai 四歳	yottsu 四つ
5 years old	go-sai 五歳	itsutsu 五つ
6 years old	roku-sai 六歳	muttsu 六つ
7 years old	nana-sai 七歳	nanatsu 七つ
8 years old	has-sai 八歳	yattsu 八つ
9 years old	kyuu-sai 九歳	kokonotsu 九つ
10 years old	jus-sai 十歳 jis-sai 十歳	too 十
11 years old	juu-is-sai 十一歳	
12 years old	juu-ni-sai 十二歳	
20 years old	ni-jus-sai 二十歳 ni-jis-sai 二十歳	hatachi 二十
25 years old	ni-juu-go-sai 二十五歳	
46 years old	yon-juu-roku-sai 四十六歳	
99 years old	kyuu-juu-kyuu-sai 九十九歳	
100 years old	hyaku-sai 百歳*	

To ask someone's age, use one of these expressions:

お年は（おいくつですか）。
How old are (you)?
（山口さんは）おいくつですか。
How old are (you, Mr. Yamaguchi)?
（カワムラさんは）何歳ですか。
How old are (you, Mr. Kawamura)?
—22 歳です。
—*(I am) 22 years old.*

The age of a baby under one year old is usually given with the counter
〜ケ月(months), which is read かげつ. (This counter is also written カ月
or か月.)

—7ケ月です。
—*(He or she is) seven months old.*

---

*Japanese have the longest average lifespan of the people of any nation in the world: 78.07 years for men and 84.93 years for women (in 2002). (Ministry of Health, Labor, and Welfare)

Vocabulary: Months

一月	ichi-gatsu	January	七月	shichi-gatsu	July
二月	ni-gatsu	February	八月	hachi-gatsu	August
三月	san-gatsu	March	九月	ku-gatsu	September
四月	shi-gatsu	April	十月	juu-gatsu	October
五月	go-gatsu	May	十一月	juu-ichi-gatsu	November
六月	roku-gatsu	June	十二月	juu-ni-gatsu	December

Examples of how speakers talk about months follow.

今月は何月ですか。	Kongetsu wa nan-gatsu desu ka.	What month is it this month?
－十月です。	—Juu-gatsu desu.	—It's October.
カワムラさんは何月生まれですか。	Kawamura-san wa nan-gatsu umare desu ka.	What month were you born in, Mr. Kawamura?
－四月生まれです。	—Shi-gatsu umare desu.	—I was born in April.

アクティビティー 9

本当ですか。違いますか。 (*True or False?*)

Look at the table. Are the statements below true or false?

Name	Age	Month of Birth	Hometown	Residence	Telephone Number
Masao Hayashi	19	May	Aso	Itabashi	03-3682-0961
Hitomi Machida	20	December	Tokyo	Mitaka	0422-45-4986
Kunio Sano	67	March	Yamagata	Nakano	03-3497-1276
Satomi Yamaguchi	22	May	Tokyo	Setagaya	03-5782-0876
Yuriko Yamaguchi	51	February	Fukushima	Setagaya	03-5782-0876

(*Continues.*)

1. 林さんのご出身は阿蘇です。
2. 林さんのおすまいは板橋です。
3. 町田さんは二十歳です。
4. 町田さんは十一月生まれです。
5. 佐野さんは七十六歳です。
6. 佐野さんのご出身は中野です。
7. 佐野さんのお電話番号は03-3497-1276です。
8. 山口さとみさんは二十二歳です。
9. 山口さとみさんのご出身は福島です。
10. 山口さとみさんと山口ゆり子さんのおすまいは世田谷です。
11. 山口ゆり子さんは五十一歳です。

> **R**emember that the particle と is used to connect two nouns.

文化ノート

CULTURE NOTE: Asking Personal Questions

If Japanese people sometimes seem overly curious about your age, it may be because age is one of the factors that go into determining the appropriate style and politeness level of speech. (Generally, a younger person speaks more politely to an older one.)

Similarly, don't be offended if Japanese ask lots of questions about your family. In Japan, despite weakening traditional values, the family is still the most important social unit and has much bearing on one's happiness and social standing. If your family is solid and supportive, Japanese will be happy for you. Those persistent questions arise from a desire to ascertain that you, too, have a good family you can rely on.

アクティビティー 10

学生証 (*Student ID*)

What do you think the following words mean? Look for hints on Henry Curtis' student ID.

1. 年齢
2. 生年月日
3. 出身地
4. 専攻
5. 住所
6. 国籍
7. 学部

学生証
（身分証明書）

学籍番号 １０９５７

氏名 ヘンリー・カーティス

年齢 22
生年月日 1983.7.14
国籍 アメリカ
出身地 アトランタ市
住所 横浜市西区中央2-18
学部 工学
専攻 コンピューター・サイエンス

アクティビティー **11**

何月生まれですか。(*What month was he/she born in?*)

Based on the following ID, answer the questions.

学生証
(身分証明書)
学籍番号 １０９５７

氏名 町田ひとみ

昭和 59 (1984) 年12月5日生

電話番号 0422-45-4986
東京出身
住所 三鷹市

1. 町田さんのご出身はどこですか。
2. 町田さんはおいくつですか。
3. 町田さんのおすまいは。
4. 町田さんは何月生まれですか。
5. 町田さんのお電話番号は。
6. 町田さんは何歳ですか。

アクティビティー **12**

ダイアログ：もう一度お願いします。(*Once more, please.*)
大学の事務室で

事務員：お名前は。
ブラウン：リンダ・ブラウンです。
事務員：お電話番号は。
ブラウン：すみません。もう一度お願いします。
事務員：お電話番号は。
ブラウン：03-5871-8952です。
事務員：すみません。ゆっくりお願いします。
ブラウン：03-5871-8952です。

Daigaku no jimushitsu de

JIMUIN: O-namae wa.
BURAUN: Rinda Buraun desu.
JIMUIN: O-denwa bangoo wa.
BURAUN: Sumimasen. Moo ichido o-negai-shimasu.
JIMUIN: O-denwa bangoo wa.
BURAUN: 03-5871-8952 desu.
JIMUIN: Sumimasen. Yukkuri o-negai-shimasu.
BURAUN: 03-5871-8952 desu.

At a university office   CLERK: May I have your name?   BROWN: Linda Brown.   CLERK: May I have your phone number?   BROWN: Excuse me, would you repeat that? (lit., *Excuse me. Once more, please.*) CLERK: May I have your phone number?   BROWN: 03-5871-8952. CLERK: Excuse me, would you say that slowly?   BROWN: 03-5871-8952.

九十九

お願いします。

言語ノート

お願（ねが）いします (lit., *Please do me a favor*) is a polite, infinitely useful phrase that can mean *Please (do something for me)* or *Please give me . . .* For example, when making a purchase or when ordering in a restaurant, you might say これ、お願いします (*I would like this,* or *Please give me this*). In the same situations you could use お願いします to get the clerk's or waiter's attention (*Could you help me, please?*).

In fact, anytime you would like someone to do something for you, you can simply use this expression instead of making a specific request. If you are on the receiving end of such a request, you will have to figure out from context what the speaker is asking you to do. For instance, in the preceding dialogue, もう一度（いちど）お願いします means *Please say it once more.*

アクティビティー **13**

お名前（なまえ）は。 (*May I have your name?*)

Role-play the situation in **Activity 12** using もう一度（いちど）お願（ねが）いします and ゆっくりお願（ねが）いします as necessary. Student 1 (the office clerk) should write down the information provided by Student 2.

s1: お名前（なまえ）は。
s2: ＿＿＿＿です。
s1: ご出身（しゅっしん）は。
s2: ＿＿＿＿です。
s1: 何月生（なんがつう）まれですか。
s2: ＿＿＿＿生まれです。
s1: おすまいは。
s2: ＿＿＿＿です。
s1: お電話番号（でんわばんごう）は。
s2: ＿＿＿＿です。

アクティビティー **14**

ここにサインしてください。 (*Please sign here.*)

Complete the sentences to make yes-no questions. Then ask your classmates these questions. If someone answers yes, ask for his or her signature on a separate piece of paper. Don't ask the same person more than two questions in a row.

[例]（れい） カワムラさんは (school year) ＿＿＿＿ですか。

S1: 二年生（にねんせい）ですか。
S2: はい、そうです。
S1: ここにサインしてください。

1. (*person's name*) ＿＿＿＿さんは(*nationality*)＿＿＿＿ですか。

2. (*person's name*) ＿＿＿＿さんは(*language*)＿＿＿＿を話（はな）しますか。

3. ＿＿＿＿の出身（しゅっしん）ですか。

4. ＿＿＿＿の専攻（せんこう）ですか。

5. ＿＿＿＿のクラスを取（と）っていますか。

6. (*person's name*) ＿＿＿＿さんは＿＿＿＿の学生（がくせい）ですか。

7. (*person's name*) ＿＿＿＿さんは＿＿＿＿ですか。

Grammar and Practice Activities

3. Personal Pronouns and Demonstratives 🎧

ブラウン：（写真（しゃしん）を指（さ）しながら）この人（ひと）はだれですか。

町田（まちだ）：どの人（ひと）ですか。

ブラウン：このセーターの人（ひと）です。

町田：ああ、これはわたしの友（とも）だちのジョンソンさんです。

ブラウン：高田（たかだ）さんのオフィスはどこですか。

受付（うけつ）け：3階（かい）です。

ブラウン：エレベーターはどこですか。

受付け：あちらです。

BROWN: (Pointing to someone in a photo) Who is this person? MACHIDA: Which person?
BROWN: This person wearing (lit., *of*) a sweater. MACHIDA: Oh, that (lit., *this*) is my friend
Mr. Johnson.

BROWN: Where is Mr. Takada's office? RECEPTIONIST: It is on the third floor. BROWN: Where is
the elevator? RECEPTIONIST: It's over there.

百
一

3.1 Personal pronouns are used to refer to a person without mentioning his or her name. Following are the most common personal pronouns in Japanese. Notice that this is one subject area where a singular/plural distinction is frequently made. Pronouns have varying levels of politeness and some are used only by or in reference to women or men, so you must be careful in selecting which pronoun to use.

Singular		Plural	
私 *わたし*	I	私 たち *わたし*	we
僕 *ぼく*	I (*male, informal*)	僕たち *ぼく*	we (*male, informal*)
あたし	I (*female, informal*)	あたしたち	we (*female, informal*)
あなた	you	あなたたち	you
		あなたがた	you
彼 *かれ*	he	彼ら、彼たち *かれ*	they (*male*)
彼女 *かのじょ*	she	彼女ら、彼女たち *かのじょ*	they (*female*)
あの人 *ひと*	he/she	あの人たち *ひと*	they
あの方 *かた*	he/she (*polite*)	あの方たち *かた*	they (*polite*)

Pronouns are used mostly for emphasis in Japanese and are usually omitted. In particular, **あなた** is considered an intimate pronoun—women traditionally call their husbands **あなた**—so people tend to avoid it except when talking to family members or close friends. (It is sometimes seen in impersonal writing, such as the instructions for using a product.) It is also considered rude to refer to an older person or other social superior as 彼 or 彼女. In formal situations or when talking to or about strangers or superiors, it is best to use the person's name or title.

> これは佐野さんのハンドバッグですか。
> *さの*
> *Is this your handbag, Ms. Sano?*

The first-person pronouns (*I, we*) are usually omitted, unless there is no other way to make clear what the subject of the sentence is. If a conversation or paragraph starts with a sentence that lacks a subject, you can usually assume that the underlying subject is *I* or *we*. If the first sentence is a question without a stated subject, the underlying subject is probably *you*.

> （わたしは）カワムラです。どうぞよろしく。
> *I am Kawamura. It's nice to meet you.*

> （あなたは）ブラウンさんじゃありませんか。
> *Aren't you Ms. Brown?*

3.2 Demonstrative pronouns are used to point out or to indicate a specific person, thing, place, or direction. The following chart shows the primary demonstratives in Japanese.

> あの人 literally means *that person*.
> 方 is a polite substitute for 人 *person*.

> When you talk with your classmates, try to use their real names instead of あなた. When you don't understand what other students say, try to use such phrases as
> すみません。もう一度
> *いちど*
> お願いします、ゆっくりお
> *ねが*
> 願いします、or はい in less formal situations.

百
二

	Thing	**Place**	**Direction**
こ-series	これ	ここ	こちら
そ-series	それ	そこ	そちら
あ-series	あれ	あそこ	あちら
ど-series	どれ	どこ	どちら

Each column follows the pattern of こ-そ-あ-ど (the first syllable of each word) from top to bottom. For this reason, Japanese demonstratives are often called こそあどことば or **ko-so-a-do** words.

- The こ-series is used to point out whatever is close to the speaker.
- The そ-series is used to point out whatever is close to the hearer.
- The あ-series points out whatever is some distance from both the speaker and the hearer.
- The ど-series are interrogatives used to ask which one, which place, or which direction.

これはブラウンさんの本ですか。
Is this Ms. Brown's book?
それをお願いします。
I would like that one.
図書館はあそこです。
The library is over there.
カワムラさんのコーヒーはどれですか。
Which one is Mr. Kawamura's coffee?

In most contexts, it is rude to use これ、それ、あれ、どれ to refer to people. Instead, こちら、そちら、あちら、どちら are used.

こちらは東京大学の横井先生です。
This is Professor Yokoi of the University of Tokyo.
ブラウンさんはどちらですか。
Which one of you is Ms. Brown?

Demonstrative adjectives, which modify nouns and come before them, also follow the **ko-so-a-do** pattern.

	Demonstrative Adjectives
こ-series	この
そ-series	その
あ-series	あの
ど-series	どの

この本はブラウンさんの本です。
This book is Ms. Brown's book.
あの映画は日本の映画ですか。
Is that movie a Japanese movie?

(Continues.)

百
三

どの means *which of three or more alternatives*. Similarly, どれ means *which one of three or more alternatives*.

> ブラウンさんの本はどの本ですか。
> *Which book is yours, Ms. Brown?* (out of three or more books)
> カワムラさんのかばんはどれですか。
> *Which bag is Mr. Kawamura's?* (out of three or more bags)

If the choice is between two alternatives, use どちら.

> 林さんの本はどちらですか。
> *Which one is your book, Mr. Hayashi?* (There are two books.)

言語ノート

どちらへ Where to?

When you are on the way out of the door, friends, neighbors, or colleagues may ask you どちらへ (*Where to?*) or おでかけですか (*Are you going out?*). These are not nosy questions, but rather common formulaic greetings to those who are about to go somewhere. The feeling behind these expressions is that the speaker is happy because you are healthy enough to go out, or perhaps the speaker is concerned that you have to go out so often. Whichever the sentiment, the remark conveys a wish for a safe return.

In replying, you need not be specific about where you are going. The best answer to these questions is ええ、ちょっとそこまで (*Yes, just around the corner* [lit., *Yes, just to over there*]).

アクティビティー 15

これはビールですか。 (*Is this beer?*)

Formulate questions, following the example.

[例] ラジカセ (combined radio and tape cassette player) →
これはラジカセですか。

1. 携帯電話   3. 辞書   5. ワイン
2. スーツケース   4. えんぴつ

Now answer the questions you made, following the example.

[例] これはラジカセですか。 →
いいえ、ラジカセじゃありません。CDプレーヤーです。

1. コンピュータ   3. 教科書   5. ジュース
2. かばん   4. ペン

Make dialogues following the example.

[例] これはだれのラジカセですか。町田さん →
　　　町田さんのラジカセです。

1. ブラウンさん　　　3. 横井先生　　　5. 佐野さん

2. カーティスさん　　4. 林さん

 アクティビティー **16**

友だちも二十歳です。(*My friend is 20, too.*)

Make up appropriate follow-up sentences using も.

[例] ブラウンさんはアメリカ人です。→ カワムラさんもアメリカ人です。

1. わたしの先生は45さいです。　　　5. サッカーはスポーツです。

2. わたしは学生です。　　　6. すきやきは日本料理です。

3.「アミーゴ」はスペイン語です。　　　7. パナソニックは日本のメーカーです。

4. バナナはくだものです。

> **R**emember that the particle も means *too, also.*

Vocabulary and Grammar 1C

Vocabulary and Oral Activities
Around Campus

Vocabulary: Around Campus		
事務室	**jimushitsu**	administration office (*inside a building*)
ビル	**biru**	building
実験室	**jikkenshitsu**	laboratory
寮	**ryoo**	dormitory
		(*Continues.*)

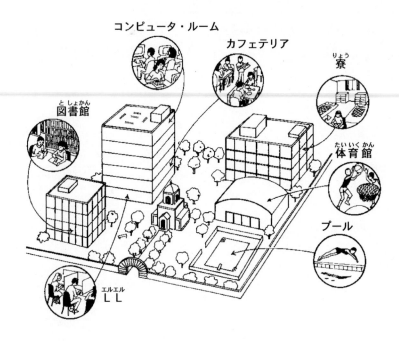

コンピュータ・ルーム

カフェテリア

寮
りょう

図書館
としょかん

体育館
たいいくかん

プール

L L
エルエル

アクティビティー **17**

ダイアログ：図書館はどこですか。(*Where is the library?*)
　　　　　としょかん

キャンパスで

ブラウン： すみません。図書館はどこですか。
　　　　　　　　　としょかん
　　学生： あそこです。
　　がくせい
ブラウン： 文学部はどこですか。
　　　　　ぶんがくぶ
　　学生： あのビルの３階です。
　　　　　　　　　　かい

Kyanpasu de

BURAUN: Sumimasen. Toshokan wa doko desu ka.
GAKUSEE: Asoko desu.
BURAUN: Bungakubu wa doko desu ka.
GAKUSEE: Ano biru no san-kai desu.

Vocabulary: Days of the Week	

日曜日	**nichiyoobi**	Sunday
月曜日	**getsuyoobi**	Monday
火曜日	**kayoobi**	Tuesday

百
六

On campus　BROWN: Excuse me. Where is the library?　STUDENT: It's over there.
BROWN: Where is the Literature Department?　STUDENT: It's on the third floor of that building.

水曜日	**suiyoobi**	Wednesday
木曜日	**mokuyoobi**	Thursday
金曜日	**kin'yoobi**	Friday
土曜日	**doyoobi**	Saturday
何曜日ですか。	**Nan'yoobi desu ka.**	What day of the week is it?

アクティビティー 18

時間 割 (Class schedules)

Answer the questions based on the schedules below.

[例] 数学のクラスは何 曜日ですか。→ 月 曜日です。

John's schedule

M	T	W	Th	F	S
math		German	physics		German
math	Japanese culture		engineering		
		computer science	engineering		
				Japanese	

Linda's schedule

M	T	W	Th	F	S
			history		
anthropology	Japanese culture	economics	history	political science	
literature			French	political science	
				Japanese	

1. 日本文化 (*Japanese culture*) のクラスは何 曜日ですか。
2. 歴史学のクラスは何 曜日ですか。
3. コンピュータのクラスは何 曜日ですか。
4. 工学のクラスは何 曜日ですか。
5. 人 類学のクラスは何 曜日ですか。
6. フランス語のクラスは何 曜日ですか。
7. 物理 学のクラスは何 曜日ですか。

Now write down your class schedule and explain it to your classmates.

百
七

アクティビティー **19**

Which of the words listed in parentheses is most closely connected to the first word given?

［例］名前（一年生、ヘザー・ギブソン、図書館、日本人）
　　　ヘザー・ギブソンです。

1. 大学（アメリカ、出身、学部、金曜日）
2. 図書館（本、ジュース、カフェテリア、教室）
3. 学生（パーティー、勉強、日曜日、友だち）
4. 専攻（ＬＬ、月曜日、日本文化、クラスメート）
5. スケジュール（水曜日、学生、友だち、事務室）

Grammar and Practice Activities

4. Asking Questions: Interrogatives

ブラウン：あれは何ですか。
町田：あれは「のり」です。

山口：あの人はだれですか。
カワムラ：クラスメートの林さんです。
山口：ご出身はどこですか。
カワムラ：九州です。
山口：あの方はどなたですか。
カワムラ：あの方は横井先生です。
山口：何の先生ですか。
カワムラ：日本文化です。

BROWN: What is that?　MACHIDA: That's seaweed.

YAMAGUCHI: Who is he?　KAWAMURA: He is Mr. Hayashi, one of my classmates.
YAMAGUCHI: Where is he from?　KAWAMURA: He's from Kyushu.　YAMAGUCHI: Who is that person?　KAWAMURA: That's Professor Yokoi.　YAMAGUCHI: …of what is she a professor?
KAWAMURA: Japanese culture.

4.1 Questions starting with *who, why, where, when, what,* or *which* are sometimes called *wh-questions* in English. In Japanese, you can make questions corresponding to wh-questions quite easily.

これは本です。   *This is a book.*

↓   ↓

これは何ですか。   *What is this?*

きょう銀座へ行きます。   *Today I'll go to Ginza.*

↓   ↓

きょうどこへ行きますか。   *Today where are you going?*

Likewise, to answer a wh-question, simply replace the question word with the answer and drop the question particle **か**.

あの人はだれですか。   *Who is that person?*

↓   ↓

（あの人は）ブラウンさんです。   *(That person)* is Ms. Brown.

4.2 Three basic interrogatives are introduced in this chapter.

1. 何（なに、なん）= *what*

When this interrogative is followed by a word starting with [d],[t],[k], or [n], it is pronounced **なん**. Otherwise, it is **なに**.

これは何ですか。
What is this?
これは何の本ですか。
What (kind of) book is this?
何を食べますか。
What are you going to eat?

When this interrogative is attached to other words, it is pronounced **なに** to mean *what* and **なん** to mean *how many* or *how much*.

あなたのセーターは何色ですか。
What color is your sweater?
カワムラさんは何歳ですか。
How old is Mr. Kawamura?

2. だれ、どなた= *who*

（**どなた** is more polite than **だれ**.）

あの人はだれですか。
Who is that person?
あの方はどなたですか。
Who is that person? (much more polite)

3. どこ= *where*

どこで昼ごはんを食べますか。
Where are you going to eat lunch?

                                                    (Continues.)

百
九

OTHER INTERROGATIVES

■ いつ ＝ *when*

いつデパートへ行きますか。
When are you going to the department store?

■ どちら、どっち ＝ *which of two; where*
(どっち is informal.)

横井先生の研究室はどちらですか。
Where is Professor Yokoi's office?

ブラウンさんの本はどっちですか。
Which one (of the two) is Ms. Brown's book?

■ どれ ＝ *which of three or more*

どれがギブソンさんの本ですか。
Which one is Ms. Gibson's book?

■ いくつ ＝ *how many, how old*

いくつりんごを食べますか。
How many apples are you going to eat?

カワムラさんはおいくつですか。
How old is Mr. Kawamura?

■ いくら ＝ *how much* (price)

この雑誌はいくらですか。
How much is this magazine?

The above interrogatives function like nouns. Connect them to other nouns with の. Remember the pattern X の Y (私の本).

これは何の教科書ですか。
What (kind of) textbook is this?

これはだれの本ですか。
Whose book is this?

どちらの本が好きですか。
Which book (of the two) do you like?

MORE INTERROGATIVES

■ どんな ＝ *what kind of*

どんな映画が好きですか。
What kind of movies do you like?

■ どう ＝ *how, how about*

これはどうですか。
How about this one?

日本語のクラスはどうですか。
How is your Japanese class?

百十

■ どうして、なぜ = *why*

どうして町田さんと話しましたか。
Why did you talk to Ms. Machida?

なぜ日本語を勉強しますか。
Why are you studying Japanese?

言語ノート

Particles は and が

Here are some general guidelines on when to use は and when to use が in the sentence construction X [は／が] Y です. You will study the difference between these particles in detail later, but for now remember the following.

1. Use が after a question word (who, where, etc.) and in the answer to a question using such a question word.

   どれがカワムラさんの本ですか。

   Which one is Mr. Kawamura's book?

   これがカワムラさんの本です。

   This is Mr. Kawamura's book.

   どの人がブラウンさんですか。

   Which person is Ms. Brown?

   あの人がブラウンさんです。

   That person is Ms. Brown.

2. Use は in statements or questions that seek to identify or describe X.

   これは本です。

   This is a book.

   あれは本ですか。

   Is that a book?

3. Use は in negative statements.

   あの人はカワムラさんではありません。

   That person is not Mr. Kawamura.

アクティビティー 20

これは町田さんのペンですか。(*Is this Ms. Machida's pen?*)

Fill in the blanks.

[例] これは（　　　）のペンですか。—それは町田さんのペンです。（だれ）

1. これは（　　　）の教科書ですか。—それは日本語の教科書です。

(*Continues.*)

2. あの人は（　　　）ですか。—わたしの日本語の先生です。

3. ブラウンさんは（　　　）のご出身ですか。—ボストンの出身です。

4. きょうは（　　　）曜日ですか。—金曜日です。

5. 図書館は（　　　）ですか。—あそこです。

6. カワムラさんの本は（　　　）ですか。—これです。

アクティビティー 21

寮はどこですか。(*Where is your dorm?*)

These are answers to questions. What do you think the questions were?
Write down possible questions.

[例]　450円です。→ この雑誌はいくらですか。

1. 横井先生です。

2. カナダです。

3. あそこです。

4. カフェテリアです。

5. 明日いきます。

6. はい、そうです。

7. あちらです。

8. 95歳です。

9. わたしのコンピュータです。

10. 午前10時です。

アクティビティー 22

大学のキャンパス (*University campus*)

Bring a map of your campus to class and practice asking a classmate the
location of several places. Pointing to the map, use あそこ、そこ、ここ、
あちら、etc. in answering.

Ask a classmate where places on campus are.

s1: ＿＿＿はどこですか。

s2: このビルの＿＿＿です。

アクティビティー **23**

ダイアログ：これはだれのボールペンですか。(*Whose ballpoint pen is this?*)

林^{はやし}：これはだれのボールペンですか。
ギブソン：わたしのです。
林^{はやし}：あれもギブソンさんのボールペンですか。
ギブソン：いいえ、あれは町田^{まちだ}さんのです。

HAYASHI: Kore wa dare no boorupen desu ka.
GIBUSON: Watashi no desu.
HAYASHI: Are mo Gibuson-san no boorupen desu ka.
GIBUSON: Iie, are wa Machida-san no desu.

アクティビティー **24**

林^{はやし} さんのです。(*It's Mr. Hayashi's.*)

s1: これはだれの本^{ほん}ですか。
s2: 林^{はやし} さんのです。

Based on the following illustration, tell who each item belongs to.

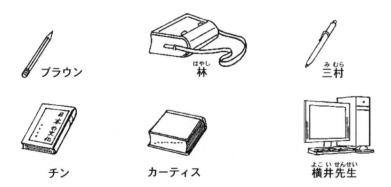

ブラウン　　　　林^{はやし}　　　　三村^{みむら}

チン　　　カーティス　　　横井先生^{よこいせんせい}

アクティビティー **25**

What do you say in the following situations? Answer in Japanese.

[例^{れい}]　You are looking at the display counter in a store selling folk crafts, and you are curious about an unfamiliar item near the salesperson.

　　→　それは何^{なん}ですか。

(*Continues.*)

HAYASHI: Whose ballpoint pen is this?　GIBSON: It's mine.　HAYASHI: Is that your ballpoint pen, too?　GIBSON: No, it's Ms. Machida's.

1. You are still in the folk craft store. You pick up an interesting object and ask the salesperson what the item in your hand is.

2. You introduce Professor Yokota, who is next to you, to one of your classmates.

3. Your friend has asked to see one of your books. Ask which one (of many books you have) he/she would like to look at.

4. There are two buildings in front of you. Ask which one the library is.

5. Someone who seems to be lost has asked you where the cafeteria (カフェテリア) is. Tell him/her the cafeteria is in that building over there.

Language Skills

Reading and Writing

Reading 1 フランス人のクラスメート

Before You Read

The following passage describes a foreign student in Japan. Your task is to retrieve the following information.

1. the name of the student
2. the name of his university
3. where he is from
4. his nationality
5. his major
6. what year student he is
7. what classes he is taking

Here are some key words that will help you locate each piece of information.

1. 名前 *name*
2. 大学 *university*
3. 出身 *hometown, origin*
4. a word ending in ～人

5. 専攻 *major*, a word ending in 学
6. a word ending in 年生
7. words ending in 学; if he is taking a language course, a word ending in 語

While reading you may want to refer to the Vocabulary Library of academic subjects and majors on page 91.

Now Read It!

Look for the preceding information while reading the passage as quickly as possible.

彼の名前はピエール・ノワールです。学生です。彼はパリの出身です。フランス人です。今、東京大学の三年生です。専攻は文学です。今、日本語、日本文学、社会学、人類学のクラスを取っています。

今 *now*

～を取っています *is taking (courses)*

After You Finish Reading

A. Using the information you retrieved, complete the ID to the right. Don't use **kanji** you haven't learned to write yet. Just use **hiragana** for now.

B. You have studied a variety of ways to elicit information from others. Here is a chance to practice what you've learned. First, with a partner write questions that ask about the listed information. Then, split up and ask the questions of one classmate you have not talked with often. Feel free to ask other questions, too.

○ 学生証
（身分証明書）

学籍
番号 ２４７８４＿＿＿＿＿

名前 ＿＿＿＿＿＿＿

国籍 ＿＿＿＿＿＿＿

大学 ＿＿＿＿＿＿＿

専攻 ＿＿＿＿＿＿＿

学年 ＿＿＿＿＿＿＿

1. name
2. age
3. where he or she lives now
4. where he or she is from
5. what year student he or she is
6. academic major
7. nationality
8. what he or she likes
9. what he or she doesn't like
10. whether he or she studies on weekends

STUDY HINT

Learning Kanji

The study of **kanji** should be approached systematically if you are to master their complexities. Each **kanji** may have several meanings. It most likely has several **on**-readings and **kun**-readings, and which reading applies depends on where it is used.

Many students make flash cards for each individual **kanji** and try to memorize the characters in that way. However, memorizing the shape of a character is only half the job, because the pronunciation of the **kanji** changes depending on the context. For example, 名 is pronounced な in the word 名まえ (*name*), and 人 is pronounced ひと in the phrase あのひと (*that person*), but 名人, a compound meaning *master, expert,* is pronounced めいじん. This is why it is a good idea to make up flash cards for the compound words as well as the individual **kanji**.

Yookoso! introduces more **kanji** than most textbooks, but it does not introduce unfamiliar compounds without indicating their pronunciations, so keep your spoken vocabulary in mind when you read. For example, if you know that the Japanese word for *Japanese person* is **Nihonjin**, you will not be tempted to pronounce 日本人 as **hi-hon-hito**.

(Continues.)

百
十
五

All in all, repetition and constant exposure are the best ways to absorb **kanji**. Read and reread your textbook. Write and rewrite sentences containing the new **kanji**. Try to find familiar **kanji** or compounds in Japanese newspapers and magazines.

Don't get discouraged. Even Japanese people require several years of study to achieve a standard level of literacy in **kanji**. And believe it or not, memorizing **kanji** actually becomes easier after the first five hundred or so!

Writing 1

Write a short profile of yourself, following the format of **Reading 1.** Start with わたしの名前は…

After you finish writing, exchange profiles with a classmate. Is there any similarity in your profiles?

Reading 2　ペンパルをさがしています！

Before You Read

Next you will read a Pen Pal Wanted ad. First, make a list of points you would mention in describing yourself if you were to place such an ad in the paper. Among those points, how many can you express in Japanese?

Now Read It!

Don't worry about the new words and **kanji** you may run across. Just read quickly and find who is looking for a pen pal.

ペンパルをさがしています！

わたしたちはアメリカ人の大学生です。トリシア、デニース、ケートです。ウエスト・コースト大学の四年生です。２２歳です。日本語のクラスのクラスメートです。トリシアとデニースは経済学の専攻です。ケートはコンピューター・サイエンスの専攻です。日本人の大学生のペンパルをさがしています。かならず返事を書きます。日本語でけっこうです。

Tricia Rosen
P.O. Box 1481
West Coast, CA 94156 U.S.A.

After You Finish Reading

Answer the following questions.

1. Who is looking for pen pals?
2. Where and what are they studying?
3. What class are they taking together?
4. What kind of pen pal are they looking for?

Guesswork

1. ペンパルをさがしています appears at the beginning and toward the end of the ad. What do you think さがしています means?

2. At the end of the ad, the word 日本語 appears in a short sentence. What do you think that sentence means?

Writing 2

1. First, write down five to ten questions in Japanese that you can use to ask a classmate for personal information.

2. Pair up and ask the questions you prepared.

3. Based on your partner's answers, write a brief profile of him or her in Japanese.

Language Functions and Situations
Introducing Friends 🎧

クラスで

ブラウン: 横井先生、ご紹介します。こちらはローラ・ヒルさんです。
　　　　　ヒルさんはアメリカの大学のクラスメートです。
横井先生: ヒルさん、はじめまして。どうぞよろしく。
　　ヒル: こちらこそ、どうぞよろしく。

Kurasu de

BURAUN: Yokoi-sensee, go-shookai shimasu. Kochira wa Roora
　　　　Hiru-san desu. Hiru-san wa Amerika no daigaku no
　　　　kurasumeeto desu.
YOKOI SENSEE: Hiru-san, hajimemashite. Doozo yoroshiku.
HIRU: Kochira koso. Doozo yoroshiku.

言語ノート

こちらこそ

こちらこそ literally means *It's this side* or *It's my side.* For example, when you meet someone and he or she says はじめまして、どうぞよろしく, you can reply with こちらこそ, meaning *I am the one* (*who's glad to meet you*). When someone bumps into you and says どうもすみません (*I am sorry*), you can say こちらこそ (*I'm the one* [*who is to blame*]). Or suppose you borrow a friend's car, notice a transmission problem, and repair it. When you return the car and thank your friend with どうもありがとうございました, he or she might say いいえ、こちらこそ (*I'm the one* [*who should say thank you*]).

(Continues.)

In class   BROWN: Professor Yokoi. Let me introduce someone to you. This is Ms. Laura Hill. Ms. Hill is my classmate at my American university.   PROFESSOR YOKOI: Ms. Hill, it's nice to meet you.   HILL: Likewise, it's nice to meet you.

カフェテリアで 🎧

ブラウン： 林_{はやし}さん、友_{とも}だちを紹介_{しょうかい}します。
　　　　　ローラ・ヒルさんです。
　　　　　アメリカの大学_{だいがく}のクラスメートです。
　　林_{はやし}： ヒルさん、はじめまして。林_{はやし}です。
　　　　　ブラウンさんからよく聞_きいています。
　　ヒル： はじめまして。ヒルです。

Kafeteria de

BURAUN: Hayashi-san, tomodachi o shookai shimasu. Roora Hiru-san desu.
　　　　Amerika no daigaku no kurasumeeto desu.
HAYASHI: Hiru-san, hajimemashite. Hayashi desu. Buraun-san kara yoku
　　　　kiite imasu.
　　HIRU: Hajimemashite. Hiru desu.

言語ノート

Introductions

Here are some common expressions used in introductions.

ご紹介_{しょうかい}します。

Let me introduce (someone to you).

こちらはギブソンさんです。

This is Ms. Gibson.

はじめまして。

How do you do? (*lit.,* This is the first time.)

どうぞよろしく。

It's nice to meet you. (*lit.,* Please be kind to me.)

Role Play

Practice the following situations with your classmates.

1. Your friend is visiting your university. Introduce him or her to one of your professors. The professor will ask several questions of the visiting friend.

At a cafeteria BROWN: Mr. Hayashi, let me introduce my friend to you. This is Laura Hill. She is my classmate at my American university. HAYASHI: Ms. Hill, nice to meet you. I am Hayashi. I've heard a lot about you from Ms. Brown. HILL: Nice to meet you. I am Hill.

2. You have brought your friend to a student lounge. Introduce him or her to one of your classmates. Those who have been introduced will ask several questions of each other.

Introducing Yourself 🎧

カワムラ：自己紹介させていただきます。東京大学のジョン・カワ
ラです。ロサンゼルスの出身です。専攻は工学です。
三年生です。どうぞよろしく。

KAWAMURA: Jikoshookai sasete itadakimasu. Tookyoo Daigaku no Jon Kawamura desu. Rosanzerusu no shusshin desu. Senkoo wa koogaku desu. Sannensee desu. Doozo yoroshiku.

Now introduce yourself to the class.

言語ノート

Self-Introductions

Self-introductions are a common occurrence at meetings and gatherings in Japan. A typical self-introduction starts this way.

自己紹介させていただきます。
Let me introduce myself.

If you want to be more humble, you can add 失礼ですが (*Excuse me but. . .*) before this expression. Then mention your name, affiliation, and so on. If you know someone who has a relationship with the person or group you are introducing yourself to, it's a good idea to mention that also.

横井先生の学生です。
I am a student of Professor Yokoi.
ブラウンさんのクラスメートです。
I am a classmate of Ms. Brown.

Conclude your self-introduction with どうぞよろしく and a polite bow.

KAWAMURA: Allow me to introduce myself. I am John Kawamura of the University of Tokyo. I am from Los Angeles. My major is engineering. I am a junior. It's nice to meet you.

百十九

Listening Comprehension 🎧

Sally MacDonald talks about five classmates in her Japanese culture class.
While listening to her descriptions, write down the name, hometown,
nationality, major, year, and age of each person. You may wish to make a
chart before you begin.

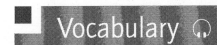

Vocabulary 🎧

Personal Information

がくねん	学年	academic year
だいがくせい	大学生	college student
いちねんせい	一年生	first-year student
にねんせい	二年生	sophomore
さんねんせい	三年生	junior
よねんせい	四年生	senior
だいがくいんせい	大学院生	graduate student
がくぶ	学部	academic department
こくせき	国籍	nationality
しゅっしん	出身	hometown; origin
せんこう	専攻	academic major
でんわばんごう	電話番号	telephone number
なまえ	名前	name

People

ともだち	友だち	friend

Loanword: クラスメート
Review: 学生、先生

Places on Campus

けんきゅうしつ	研究室	professor's office
じむしつ	事務室	administration office
たいいくかん	体育館	gym

じっけんしつ	実験室	laboratory
ビル		building
りょう	寮	dormitory

Loanwords: カフェテリア、キャンパス、プール

Review: 教室、大学、図書館

Nationalities / Languages

アメリカじん	アメリカ人	American (*person*)
イギリスじん	イギリス人	British (*person*)
イタリアじん／イタリアご	イタリア人／イタリア語	Italian (*person/language*)
えいご	英語	English (*language*)
カナダじん	カナダ人	Canadian (*person*)
かんこくじん／かんこくご	韓国人／韓国語	Korean (*person/language*)
スペインじん／スペインご	スペイン人／スペイン語	Spaniard/Spanish (*language*)
シンガポールじん	シンガポール人	Singaporean
たいわんじん	台湾人	Taiwanese (*person*)
ちゅうごくじん／ちゅうごくご	中国人／中国語	Chinese (*person/language*)
ドイツじん／ドイツご	ドイツ人／ドイツ語	German (*person/language*)
にほんじん／にほんご	日本人／日本語	Japanese (*person/language*)
ブラジルじん	ブラジル人	Brazilian (*person*)
フランスじん／フランスご	フランス人／フランス語	French (*person/language*)
ポルトガルじん／ポルトガルご	ポルトガル人／ポルトガル語	Portuguese (*person/language*)
ほんこんじん	香港人	Hong Kong native
メキシコじん	メキシコ人	Mexican (*person*)
ロシアじん／ロシアご	ロシア人／ロシア語	Russian (*person/language*)
くに	国	country

Review: 話す

Months

いちがつ	一月	January		はちがつ	八月	August
にがつ	二月	February		くがつ	九月	September
さんがつ	三月	March		じゅうがつ	十月	October
しがつ	四月	April		じゅういちがつ	十一月	November
ごがつ	五月	May		じゅうにがつ	十二月	December
ろくがつ	六月	June		なんがつ	何月	what month
しちがつ	七月	July				

(Continues.)

百二十一

Days of the Week

にちようび	日曜日	Sunday	もくようび	木曜日	Thursday
げつようび	月曜日	Monday	きんようび	金曜日	Friday
かようび	火曜日	Tuesday	どようび	土曜日	Saturday
すいようび	水曜日	Wednesday	なんようび	何曜日	what day of the week

Question Words

だれ	誰	who	なにじん	何人	what nationality
どこ		where	なんがつ	何月	what month
どちら		where (*polite*)	なんさい	何歳	how old
どなた		who (*polite*)	なんねんせい	何年生	what year (in school)
なに、なん	何	what	なんようび	何曜日	what day of the week
なにご	何語	what language			

Other Words

あそこ	that place over there	そちら		that place; there (*polite*)
あちら	that place over there (*polite*)	その		that...
あの	that...over there	それ		that thing
あれ	that thing over there	です		to be
か	(*question marker*)	ではありません		(*negative of* です)
が	(*subject marker*)	どこ		where
ここ	this place; here	どちら		where (*polite*); which (of two)
こちら	this place; here (*polite*)	どの		which... (of more than two)
この	this...	どれ		which thing (of more than two)
これ	this thing	は		(*topic marker*)
じゃありません	(*negative of* です)(*informal*)	も		too
そこ	that place; there	わたし	私	I; me

STUDY HINT

Learning New Vocabulary

Vocabulary is one of the most important tools for successful communication in a foreign language. What does it mean to know vocabulary? And what is the best way to learn vocabulary?

1. Memorization is only part of the learning process. Using new vocabulary to communicate requires practicing that vocabulary in context. What do you associate with this word? When might you want to use it? Create a context—a place, a situation, a person, or a group of people—for the vocabulary that you

want to learn, or use a context from the text. The more associations you make with the word, the easier it will be to remember. Practice useful words and phrases over and over, thinking about their meaning, until you can produce them automatically. You may find it useful to "talk to yourself," saying aloud the words you want to learn.

2. Carefully study the words in vocabulary lists and drawings. If a word is of English origin, be especially aware of its form and meaning. Sometimes the form and meaning are quite different from the original. For example, デパート came from the English phrase *department store* and has the same meaning as the English. コンセント means *plug outlet*, although it came from the English word *consent*.

3. After studying the list or illustration, cover the English and give the English equivalent of each Japanese word.

4. When you are able to translate the Japanese without hesitation and without error, reverse the procedure; cover the Japanese and give the Japanese equivalent of each English word. Write out the Japanese words in the appropriate script (but use **hiragana** if you haven't studied the appropriate **kanji** yet) once or several times and say them aloud.

5. Vocabulary lists and flash cards can be useful as a review or as a self-test.

Note that the best way to learn vocabulary is to use it as much as possible in conversation and in writing.

Kanji

Learn these **kanji:**

日	年	二	七	先
本	何	三	八	話
学	月	四	九	語
生	人	五	十	大
名	一	六	百	

Practice these **kanji** in your Workbook/ Laboratory Manual.

言語ノート

The Six Types of Kanji

Kanji (*Chinese characters*) originated in China. In China, **kanji** were categorized into one of six basic classifications depending primarily on how the character was formed. The pictograph, the most primitive type of **kanji,** was created as a representation of the physical appearance of an object. In modern Japanese there are relatively few of these characters.

Kanji of the second type represent numbers, positional relations, or abstract concepts.

Kanji in the third group are a combination of two or more of the first two types of **kanji.**

The fourth and most important type of **kanji** consists of one part that represents some aspect of its meaning and another part that suggests

(*Continues.*)

how it was pronounced in classical Chinese. For example, **aji, mi** (*flavor*) consists of a mouth (the square) and the character for *not yet* with the idea being, "This is a character that has something to do with the mouth and sounds like the word for *not yet*. More than 80 percent of the **kanji** used in modern Japanese fall into this category.

The fifth classification of **kanji** contains characters whose meanings have changed or been extended over the centuries. For example, the character whose original meaning was *to play a musical instrument* now has an additional meaning of *enjoy*.

Finally, there are **kanji** that were borrowed to express new meanings simply because of their sounds, irrespective of their meanings. For example, the Chinese took a **kanji** meaning *two people facing each other* and used it to represent *north*, which was pronounced the same.

口 ＋ 未 → 味
aji, mi   (flavor)

楽
raku (music → delight)

北
(hoku／north—originally meant people facing each other)

チェックリスト

Use this checklist to confirm that you can now:

- Talk about nationalities and languages
- Identify things and people
- Express possession
- Exchange personal information
- Talk about your campus
- Use personal pronouns and demonstratives
- Ask questions
- Write to a pen pal
- Introduce friends
- Introduce yourself

2

My Town

第二章　わたしの町
まち

とうきょう　まち
東京 の町

OBJECTIVES

In this lesson you are going to:

- Talk about commuting:
- Learn about using adjectives and adverbs
- Talk about places around town
- Learn how to express existence
- Learn how to express location
- Learn to use positional words
- Learn how to count and express numerals and counters
- Learn how to express likes and dislikes
- Talk about your hometown and neighborhood
- Learn to make sure you are communicating

YOOKOSO! MULTIMEDIA

Review and practice grammar and vocabulary from this chapter and watch video clips on the *Yookoso!* Interactive CD-ROM. Visit the *Yookoso!* Online Learning Center at **www.mhhe.com/yookoso3** for additional exercises and resources.

Vocabulary and Grammar 2A

Vocabulary and Oral Activities
Commuting

ラッシュアワー

Vocabulary: Commuting

徒歩（で）	on foot	便利（な）	convenient
...に近いです	is close to...	不便（な）	inconvenient
...から遠いです	is far from...		

便利（不便）cannot be used to mean *suited* (*not suited*) for one's schedule. Japanese say 3時はつごうがいいです (*Three o'clock is convenient for me*) and 4時はつごうがわるいです (*Four o'clock is inconvenient for me*).

アクティビティー 1

ダイアログ：地下鉄で10分ぐらいです。 (*It's about 10 minutes by subway.*)

ブラウンさんと三村さんが話しています。

ブラウン：三村さんのアパートはどこですか。

三村：上野です。

ブラウン：大学に近いですね。

三村：ええ、地下鉄で10分ぐらいです。とても便利ですよ。

X で *via, by means of X*; Y から *from Y*; とても *very*; 上野 *area of Tokyo*.

Vocabulary: Counting Minutes and Hours

To count minutes use the counter suffix, ～分 (ふん; after some sounds, ぷん) with the Sino-Japanese series of numerals. (See **Grammar 9.1**, page 154.) The counter suffix for counting hours is 時間 (じかん).

一分	いっぷん	one minute
二分	にふん	two minutes
三分	さんぷん	three minutes
四分	よんぷん、よんふん	four minutes
五分	ごふん	five minutes
六分	ろっぷん	six minutes
七分	ななふん、しちふん	seven minutes
八分	はっぷん	eight minutes
九分	きゅうふん	nine minutes
十分	じゅっぷん、じっぷん	ten minutes
一時間	いちじかん	one hour
二時間	にじかん	two hours
一時間半	いちじかんはん	one and a half hours
三時間二十五分	さんじかんにじゅうごふん	three hours twenty-five minutes

Alternatively, the counter suffix ～分間 (～ふんかん、～ぷんかん) may also be used when expressing duration of minutes: 五分話しました or 五分間話しました (*I talked for 5 minutes*). But only ～分 can name a particular minute: 一時五分に行きました (*I went at 1:05*).

Ms. Brown and Mr. Mimura are talking BROWN: Where is your apartment, Mr. Mimura? MIMURA: It's in Ueno. BROWN: It's close to the university, isn't it? MIMURA: Yes. It's about ten minutes by subway. It's very convenient.

百二十七

アクティビティー **2**

どこですか。(*Where is it?*)

Practice the dialogue in **アクティビティー 1,** substituting information from the chart below.

Useful Word: ちょっと *a bit*

Name/Type of Residence	Place	Proximity to School	Transportation Method/Time Required	Convenience
カワムラさんの うち	世田谷	ちょっと遠い	電車 50分	ちょっと不便
林 さんの アパート	板橋	近い	バス 30分	便利
横井先生の うち	千葉	遠い	車 一時間半	不便
チンさん のアパート	目白	とても近い	電車 15分	とても便利
大野先生の うち	横浜	とても遠い	電車 二時間	とても不便

Grammar and Practice Activities

5. Adjectives and Adverbs

> 林 : ブラウンさんの大学は大きいですか。
> ブラウン：いいえ、あまり大きくありません。
> 林：有名ですか。
> ブラウン：いいえ、あまり有名じゃありません。

HAYASHI: Is your university large, Ms. Brown?　BROWN: No, it's not very large.　HAYASHI: Is it famous?　BROWN: No, it's not very famous.

カワムラ：あの人はだれですか。

チン：町田さんのボーイフレンドです。

カワムラ：ハンサムな人ですね。

チン：ええ。

Useful Vocabulary: Basic Adjectives

大きい／大きな	おおきい／おおきな	big; large
小さい／小さな	ちいさい／ちいさな	small
多い	おおい	many, numerous
少ない	すくない	few, scarce
新しい	あたらしい	new
古い	ふるい	old
いい／よい		good
よくない		not good; bad
悪い	わるい	bad
静か（な）	しずか（な）	quiet; peaceful
うるさい		noisy; disturbing
きれい（な）		attractive; clean
きたない		dirty
広い	ひろい	spacious; wide
狭い	せまい	small (in area); narrow
低い	ひくい	low
高い	たかい	high; expensive
安い	やすい	inexpensive
おもしろい		interesting
有名（な）	ゆうめい（な）	famous
にぎやか（な）		lively
つまらない		boring
むずかしい		difficult
やさしい		easy; kind
長い	ながい	long
短い	みじかい	short
おいしい		delicious
まずい		bad tasting

In this textbook, adjectives are listed in their dictionary form. **Na**-adjectives are differentiated by adding **（な）** to the listed dictionary form.

The i-adjective **いい** is somewhat irregular. It is the colloquial form of **よい** and is used more commonly in informal conversation. The negative form of both **いい** and **よい** is **よくない**. (See Conjugating Adjectives, Chapter 4.)

5.1 *Adjectives* are words that modify nouns. In the phrase *a red sweater*, *red* is an adjective. In Japanese as well, the adjective precedes the noun in such a phrase: 赤いセーター (*red sweater*). This usage is called *prenominal use*, meaning *before the noun.*

Adjectives do not always precede nouns, however. In English, there are sentences such as *That sweater is red.* Likewise, in the equivalent Japanese

KAWAMURA: Who is that (person)?　CHIN: That's Ms. Machida's boyfriend.　KAWAMURA: He's nice looking. (lit., *He is a nice-looking person.*)　CHIN: Yes.

(Continues.)

sentence—あのセーターは赤いです—the adjective 赤い appears in the latter part of the sentence, which is called the predicate. (The predicate contains the verb and everything that comes after the subject.) We will call this use of an adjective the *predicate use.*

There are two types of adjectives in Japanese. We will call one type *i-adjectives* because their dictionary form (the form listed in dictionaries) always ends in the syllable い. (赤い is an **i**-adjective.) Another type of adjective is the **na**-*adjective,* named for the な that follows them in the prenominal use. These are some examples of these two types of adjectives in their dictionary form.

*I-*ADJECTIVES		*NA-*ADJECTIVES	
赤い	red	元気	healthy
あまい	sweet	静か	quiet
やさしい	gentle	きれい	pretty
暑い	hot	ハンサム	handsome
きびしい	strict	有名	famous

Note that there are several **na**-adjectives (likeきれい) whose dictionary form ends in い. You'll just have to memorize those. Note, however, that no **i**-adjectives end in **-ei.**

I-adjectives are of Japanese origin, while most **na**-adjectives are of foreign origin (from Chinese or Western languages).

5.2 The prenominal and predicate uses of **i**-adjectives and **na**-adjectives are summarized in the following chart.

*i-*Adjective	
prenominal use	おもしろい本 (*interesting book*)
predicate use (affirmative)	あの本はおもしろいです。 *That book is interesting.*
predicate use (negative)	あの本はおもしろくありません or あの本はおもしろくないです。 *That book is not interesting.*

*na-*Adjective	
prenominal use	静かな町　(*quiet town*)
predicate use (affirmative)	あの町は静かです。 *That town is quiet.*
predicate use (negative)	あの町は静かではありません or あの町は静かじゃないです。 *That town is not quiet.*

The affirmative of either type of adjective in the predicate use is formed by adding です to the dictionary form. To form the negative predicate use, you must distinguish between **i-adjectives** and **na-adjectives**. In the case of **na**-adjectives, simply change です to its negative form ではありません (or the colloquial contraction じゃありません or じゃないです). For **i**-adjectives, however, you must change the ending of the adjective. This process is called *conjugation.* Notice that the dictionary form of all **i**-adjectives ends in い. This い is actually an ending attached to the root of the adjective. To make a negative, simply replace this final い with く and add ありません or ないです. These two negative forms are identical in meaning and politeness level.

おもしろ|い|　です.　　　　　　　　　*It's interesting.*
↓
おもしろ|く|　{ ありません.　　　　　*It's not interesting.*
　　　　　　　ないです.

Some adjectives have alternate conjugations in the prenominal use.

1. 大きい (*large*) and 小さい (*small*) may take な prenominally even though they are **i**-adjectives. In this usage the final い is dropped.

大きい人　　　　大きな人　　　　*large person*
小さい人　　　　小さな人　　　　*small person*

2. Some adjectives take the ～くの form in front of a noun. Change the final い to く and add の.

近い　*near*　　　　近くの大学　*nearby university*
遠い　*far*　　　　　遠くの大学　*faraway university*

5.3 *Adverbs* modify adjectives, verbs, and other adverbs and are usually positioned before the word they modify.

とてもきれいな女の人
*a **very** pretty woman*
わたしは肉をたくさん食べました。
*I ate a **lot of** meat.*
その大学はあまり有名ではありません。
*That university is not **very** famous.*

Both とても and あまり mean *very, so,* or *extremely.* But あまり is used only in negative sentences. In conversation あんまり, a variant of あまり, is often used instead.

百三十一

ア ク テ ィ ビ テ ィ ー **3**

この大学は新しいです。 （*This university is new.*）

Practice the following as shown in the example.

［例］　この大学は古いですか。（新しい）
　　　　→ いいえ、この大学は古くありません。
　　　　新しいです。

Useful Vocabulary:　きびしい *strict,* 重い *heavy,* 軽い *lightweight,*
長い *long,* 短い *short,* 厚い *thick,* うすい *thin,* おいしい *delicious*

1. そのビルは高いですか。（低い）
2. この本はおもしろいですか。（つまらない）
3. この肉はおいしいですか。（まずい）
4. あの先生はきびしいですか。（やさしい）
5. このスーツは高いですか。（安い）
6. このテレビは重いですか。（軽い）
7. 日本語はむずかしいですか。（やさしい）
8. 山口さんのスピーチは長いですか。（短い）
9. その本は厚いですか。（うすい）
10. あなたのうちは広いですか。（せまい）

ア ク テ ィ ビ テ ィ ー **4**

あのまるいものは何ですか。 （*What is that round thing?*）

Practice, following the example.

［例］　古い、ビル → あの古いビルは何ですか。
　　　　ハンサム、人 → あのハンサムな人はだれですか。

Useful Vocabulary:　きかい *machine,* まじめ（な）*serious,* もの *thing; item,*
まるい *round,* 親切（な）*kind,* 器用（な）*skillful,* へん（な）*strange*

1. おもしろい、人
2. きれい、女の人
3. 大きい、きかい
4. きたない、もの
5. 静か、人
6. 親切、男の人

7. やさしい、男の人
8. へん、もの
9. まじめ、男の人
10. 便利、きかい
11. まるい、もの
12. 器用、女の人

百三十二

アクティビティー 5

その話はおかしいです。(*That story is funny!*)

Change affirmative sentences to negative, and negative sentences to affirmative.

[例] このアパートはとても便利です。 →
このアパートはあまり便利ではありません。
その人はあまりきびしくありません。 →
その人はとてもきびしいです。

Useful Vocabulary: 若い *young,* 安全(な) *safe,* 話 *tale; story,* 元気(な) *healthy,* おかしい *funny; strange,* 近所 *neighborhood,* 町 *town*

1. この近所はとても静かです。
2. あの男の人はあまり若くありません。
3. その大学はとても古いです。
4. この車はあまり安全じゃありません。
5. この町はとてもにぎやかです。
6. この話はとてもおかしいです。
7. カーティスさんはとても元気です。
8. あの人はあまりエレガントではありません。
9. このバナナはあまりおいしくありません。
10. このドレスはあまり安くありません。

アクティビティー 6

その先生は有名な人です。 (*That teacher is a famous person.*)

Rewrite these sentences following the examples.

[例] あれはつまらない本です。 → あの本はつまらないです。

Useful Word: はで(な) *gaudy; bright-colored*

1. これは安い時計です。
2. あれはとても静かな村です。
3. この町はとても小さいです。
4. これは古いカーテンです。
5. このネクタイははでです。
6. あの町はにぎやかです。
7. あれはとても有名なビルです。

アクティビティー 7

おもしろいですか、つまらないですか。 (*Is it interesting or boring?*)

Choose one adjective that best fits the given noun and make a sentence. Translate the sentence into English.

[例] 日本語のクラスやさしい、おもしろい、むずかしい、つまらない
→日本語のクラスはつまらないです。(*Japanese class is boring.*)

1. わたし
静か、にぎやか、元気、まじめ、ハンサム、きれい

2. わたしの日本語の先生
きれい、うつくしい (*beautiful*)、ハンサム、やさしい、エレガント、若い

3. アーノルド・シュワルツネーガー
タフ、やさしい、若い、静か、いそがしい、ハンサム

4. エディー・マーフィー
元気、やさしい、いそがしい、おもしろい、ハンサム

5. わたしの大学
有名、大きい、むずかしい、やさしい、いい

6. わたしのうち
大きい、小さい、きれい、ひろい、せまい、きたない

7. わたしのとなりの人 (*the person next to me*)
うるさい、きれい、ハンサム、やさしい、へん (*strange*)、静か

8. この練習 (*exercise*)
むずかしい、やさしい、つまらない、長い

STUDY HINT

Learning Grammar

Learning a language is similar to learning any other skill; knowing about it is only part of what is involved. Consider swimming, for example. Through books you could become an expert in talking about swimming; but until you actually got into a pool and practiced swimming, you would probably not swim very well. In much the same way, if you memorize all the grammar rules but spend little time practicing them, you will not be able to communicate very well in Japanese.

Since the best way to learn grammar is to use grammatical structures in actual contexts, the first few exercises in each section of the chapter are designed to let you practice the new structures and vocabulary in communicative situations. You may be able to pick up the new structures almost without thinking as you imitate the models in the communicative activities.

Accompanying each set of communicative activities is an explanation of the grammar you have been practicing. First read the explanations, asking your instructor about any parts that you don't understand, and analyze the sample sentences. Then begin to practice. Do the activities that follow the explanation, and then check your answers. When you are certain that your answers are correct, practice doing each exercise several times until you can do them automatically. As you do the exercises, pay attention to spelling and pronunciation and think about how you would use the forms in real life.

Always remember that language learning is cumulative. When you move on to the next chapter, you can't forget or ignore what you learned in this chapter any more than you can forget your arithmetic when you start learning algebra. A few minutes spent each day reviewing "old" topics will increase your confidence and success in communicating in Japanese.

アクティビティー **8**

インタビュー：大学に近いですか。 (*Is it close to the university?*)

Pair up and ask each other the following questions.

s1: ＿＿＿さんのうちはどこですか。
s2: ＿＿＿です。
s1: 大学に近いですか。
s2: はい、近いです。＿＿＿で＿＿＿分です。
    (いいえ、遠いです。＿＿＿で＿＿＿分です。) *or*
    (いいえ、遠いです。＿＿＿で＿＿＿時間です。)
s1: 便利ですね。(不便ですね。)

文化ノート

CULTURE NOTE: Long Commutes

According to one recent survey, the average commuting time of workers living in the greater Tokyo area is one hour thirty-five minutes—each way! What's more, 20 percent of the surveyed workers spend over two hours getting to (or from) work. Because affordable housing is scarce in central Tokyo where many of the jobs are, the majority of workers have to live in outlying suburbs and cities some distance from the city center. Because the train and subway systems are so well-developed in Tokyo—they are extensive networks of punctual, frequent trains—about 50 percent of commuters use trains and/or subways, while only 25 percent use cars.

(Continues.)

とうきょうえき　でんしゃ　に じ かん
東 京 駅：電車で二時間
　　　　　　　　　とお
です。一遠いですね。

Vocabulary and Grammar 2B

Vocabulary and Oral Activities

Cities and Neighborhoods

Vocabulary: Cities and Towns

近所	きんじょ	neighborhood
区	く	ward of a city
郊外	こうがい	suburbs
市	し	city
人口	じんこう	population
所	ところ	place
町	まち	town
村	むら	village

…町 (lit., *town;* pronounced まち or ちょう) are usually subdivided into numbered districts called …丁目 (ちょうめ).

アクティビティー　**9**　

ダイアログ：どんなところですか。(*What kind of place is it?*)

カワムラ：林さんのご出身はどこですか。

林：九州の阿蘇です。

カワムラ：どんなところですか。

林：小さい町です。

カワムラ：きれいな町ですか。

林：ええ。

Now practice the dialogue replacing the underlined parts with the following words.

1. 大きい、古い　　　　　　　　**3.** 古い、小さい

2. きれいな、静かな

アクティビティー　**10**　

古山さんのうちはどこですか。(*Where is Mr. Huruyama's house?*)

Talk about the commute experience and neighborhood of each student listed below. Pair up and use the model dialogue as a guide.

[例]　s1: 古山さんのうちはどこですか。

s2: 横浜の郊外です。

s1: 大学に近いですか。

s2: いいえ、電車で1時間20分です。

s1: どんなところですか。

s2: 静かなところです。

Name	Residence	Commutes...	Neighborhood
Mikawa	house in Koohu	2 hours by train	inconvenient
Hanada	apartment in Choohu	55 minutes by car	beautiful
Kanai	house in Shibuya	30 minutes by subway	convenient
Nomura	apartment in Ueno	5 minutes by bus	lively

KAWAMURA: Where are you from, Mr. Hayashi?　　HAYASHI: I am from Aso, Kyushu.
KAWAMURA: What kind of place is it?　　HAYASHI: It's a small town.　　KAWAMURA: Is it an attractive town?　　HAYASHI: Yes.

s1: Where is Mr. Huruyama's house?　　s2: It's in the suburbs of Yokohama.　　s1: Is it close to the university?　　s2: No, it's an hour and twenty minutes away by train.　　s1: What kind of place is it?　　s2: It's a quiet place.

Grammar and Practice Activities

6. Expressing Existence: The Verbs あります and います

レストランで

  カワムラ ：すみません。ドイツのビールはありますか。

  ウエイター ：すみません。ありません。でも、オランダのビールは
           あります。

  カワムラ ：そうですか。じゃ、オランダのビールをお願いします。

  ブラウン ：すみません。電話はありますか。

    林 ：ええ、そこにあります。

  ギブソン ：林さんはいますか。

  カワムラ ：いいえ。

  ブラウン ：あっ、林さんはカフェテリアにいますよ。

  ギブソン ：本当ですか。林さんはいつもカフェテリアにいますね。

6.1 To express existence in Japanese, you can use the verbs あります (dictionary form ある) and います (dictionary form いる). あります is used to denote the existence of inanimate objects and abstract concepts (e.g., notebooks, coffee, dead bodies, flowers, air, love, and ideas), while います is used to express the existence of living things (e.g., people, animals, and insects, but not plant life).

> ある and いる are the plain forms of あります and います, respectively. (See 言語ノート.)

言語ノート

Polite Form Versus Plain Form

Japanese has two different speech styles, the plain and the polite. The polite form is used when speaking to people outside your own group or to people within your group who rank above you. The plain form is used when speaking to close friends, family members, children, animals, and people who rank below you. The overall politeness of a sentence is determined by the last verb, because certain grammatical structures within the sentence—you will learn them later—require the plain form even when you are speaking politely.

At a restaurant   KAWAMURA: Excuse me, do you have German beer?   WAITER: I'm sorry, we don't. But we have Dutch beer.   KAWAMURA: I see. Then, I would like Dutch beer.

BROWN: Excuse me. Is there a phone (I could use)?   HAYASHI: Yes, there's one there.

GIBSON: Is Mr. Hayashi here?   KAWAMURA: No.   BROWN: Oh, he's in the cafeteria.
GIBSON: Really? He's always in the cafeteria.

The beginning of this textbook focuses on the polite forms. These are the forms most commonly used when talking to people you don't know very well, and you will not accidentally offend anyone by using them. Besides, the polite forms are completely regular and easier to memorize than the plain forms!

6.2 This is the simplest way to say *X exists* or *there is/are X.*

Existent	Particle	Verb (Affirmative)
N (inanimate)	が	ある（あります）
N (animate)	が	いる（います）

N stands for noun.

There is _____ ; There are _____ .

6.3 The nonexistence of something is expressed by the negative forms of the same verbs.

Existent	Particle	Verb (Negative)
N (inanimate)	が	ない（ありません）
N (animate)	が	いない（いません）

ない and いない are the plain forms of ありません and いません, respectively.

There isn't _____ ; There aren't _____ .

6.4 The location or position where something or someone exists usually occurs at the beginning of the above sentence structures and is marked with the particle に.

Location に	Particle	Existent	Particle が	Verb
N1	に	N2 (inanimate)	が	ある（あります）
N1	に	N2 (animate)	が	いる（います）

There is/are _____ at/in _____ .

ここに本があります。
There are books here.
ここに辞書はありません。
There are no dictionaries here.
そこにペンはありますか。
Is there a pen over there?
公園に何がありますか。
What is there in the park?
うちに犬がいます。
There is a dog at my house.

Note that the particle は is used in negative and yes/no questions instead of が.

(Continues.)

百三十九

<ruby>教<rt>きょう</rt></ruby><ruby>室<rt>しつ</rt></ruby>に<ruby>三<rt>み</rt></ruby><ruby>村<rt>むら</rt></ruby>さんはいません。
Mr. Mimura is not in the classroom.
そこにカワムラさんはいますか。
Is Mr. Kawamura there?
<ruby>今<rt>いま</rt></ruby>、<ruby>教<rt>きょう</rt></ruby><ruby>室<rt>しつ</rt></ruby>にだれがいますか。
Who is in the classroom now?

6.5 When you would like to say how many or how much of something exists, a phrase denoting quantity comes just before the verb of existence.

Location	Particle に	Existent	Particle が	Quantity	Verb
N1	に	N2 (inanimate)	が		ある(あります)
N1	に	N2 (animate)	が		いる(います)

There is one _____ at/in _____ .
There are (number) _____ s at/in _____ .

> *N1* and *N2* stand for two different nouns.

ここにチョコレートがひとつあります。
Here is one piece of chocolate.
あそこに<ruby>学<rt>がく</rt></ruby><ruby>生<rt>せい</rt></ruby>が<ruby>三<rt>さん</rt></ruby><ruby>人<rt>にん</rt></ruby>います。
There are three students.
ここにアメリカ<ruby>人<rt>じん</rt></ruby>は<ruby>何<rt>なん</rt></ruby><ruby>人<rt>にん</rt></ruby>いますか。
How many Americans are here?

アクティビティー **11**

<ruby>父<rt>ちち</rt></ruby>は<ruby>家<rt>いえ</rt></ruby>にいます。 (*Father is in the house.*)

Make sentences using あります or います based on the information provided.

1. (in this class) (chalkboard)
2. (in my room) (computer)
3. (in the cafeteria) (classmates)
4. (in Nakano) (Ms. Brown's apartment)
5. (in this class) (students)
6. (at home) (my bicycle)
7. (at the library) (books)

アクティビティー **12**

ここに<ruby>何<rt>なに</rt></ruby>がありますか。 (*What is there here?*)

1. Make five existential sentences based on inanimate and living things around you.
2. Make five existential sentences based on people and things in your classroom.

Yookoso! An Invitation to Contemporary Japanese, Third Edition

141

Vocabulary and Grammar 2C

Vocabulary and Oral Activities
Buildings and Places Around Town

Vocabulary: Places Around Town	

道	みち	street; road
通り	とおり	avenue; street
建物	たてもの	building
家	いえ	house
うち		house; home; family
公園	こうえん	park
学校	がっこう	school
病院	びょういん	hospital
映画館	えいがかん	movie theater
銀行	ぎんこう	bank

Both 家 (いえ) and うち mean *house*, but the nuances are different. 家 usually refers to a private house in contrast to a company building, government office, or store. On the other hand, うち refers to the place where one leads one's life or where a family resides—in other words, a *home*. うち is sometimes used to mean the people who live in one house, or a *family*.

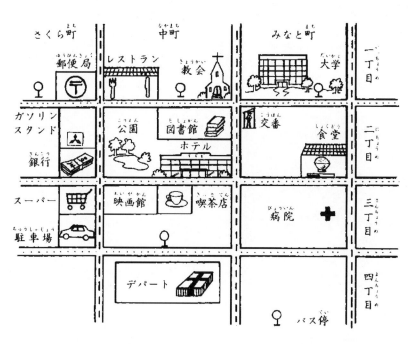

(Continues.)

郵便局	ゆうびんきょく	post office
交番	こうばん	police box
喫茶店	きっさてん	coffee (lit., *tea*) shop
ホテル		hotel
(お)寺	(お)てら	Buddhist temple
神社	じんじゃ	Shinto shrine
教会	きょうかい	church
レストラン		restaurant
食堂	しょくどう	dining hall; informal restaurant
スーパー		supermarket
デパート		department store
ガソリン・スタンド		gas station
駐車場	ちゅうしゃじょう	parking lot
バス停	バスてい	bus stop

Review: 大学、図書館、ビル

CULTURE NOTE: 交番 *Police Boxes*

文化ノート

In Japan, you will see a *police box* or 交番 in almost every neighborhood of a city. The "box" may be a tiny freestanding structure or an office open to the street in a larger building. The policemen (おまわりさん) stationed at each police box patrol the neighborhood (often on bicycles) to help prevent crime, but probably their most frequently performed service is to give directions to people who are lost or don't know how to get to their destination. The boxes are usually open twenty-four hours a day, so citizens always know they can go there for help. It is said that the presence of these police boxes contributes, to a great extent, to the low crime rate in Japan.

プリンスホテルはどこですか。

アクティビティー **13**

どこにありますか。 (*Where is it?*)

Work in pairs. Look at the preceding map and tell where each place is.

[例] 銀行(ぎんこう)はどこにありますか。
さくら町(まち)2丁目(ちょうめ)にあります。

文化ノート

CULTURE NOTE: Japanese Addresses

Japanese addresses are structured very differently from addresses in most parts of the world. Only the main streets in the cities have names, and individual buildings may not have numbers. Large cities such as Tokyo and Osaka are divided into 区（く）or wards; the 区 are divided into 町（ちょう）, which are towns or neighborhoods; the 町 are divided into 丁目（ちょうめ）; and the blocks (番地 [ばんち]) within each 丁目 are numbered, as are the individual "lots" within each block.

A typical address is 東京都 中野区 野方 2-1-5 or, Tokyo metropolitan area, Nakano ward,

Nagata-choo, second choome, first block, fifth "lot." Note that the address narrows the location down from the largest area to the smallest.

People customarily navigate by landmarks, such as stores or schools, rather than streets or intersections. Stores often include maps in their advertisements, giving directions from the nearest station or bus stop, and Japanese people are accustomed to drawing informal maps to help others get around. When all else fails, there's always the **kooban,** where the police consult their detailed neighborhood maps to guide confused pedestrians and drivers to their destinations.

アクティビティー **14**

どこにいますか。 (*Where is he/she?*)

The following company message board shows where each employee has gone. Practice asking where each person is with your classmates.

[例] 山田(やまだ)さんは今(いま)どこにいますか。—高田(たかだ)さんのオフィスにいます。

Name	Went to	Will be Back
Yamada	Mr. Takada's office	3 P.M.
Tanaka	restaurant	2 P.M.
Yoshida	New York	tomorrow
Saitoo	library	4:30 P.M.
Sawai	Hiroshima	next Monday

Grammar and Practice Activities

7. Indicating Location 🎧

ブラウン：すみません。カフェテリアはどこにありますか。

学生（がくせい）：あのビルの一階（いっかい）にあります。

ブラウン：どうもありがとうございます。

学生（がくせい）：どういたしまして。

カワムラ：町田（まちだ）さんはどこにいますか。

チン：今（いま）、横井先生（よこいせんせい）の研究室（けんきゅうしつ）にいます。

カワムラ：横井先生（よこいせんせい）の研究室（けんきゅうしつ）はどこですか。

チン：このビルの三階（さんかい）です。

7.1 The simplest way to indicate the location of something or someone is to use the sentence structure N1 は N2 です, where N1 is a noun indicating a specific thing or person and N2 is a noun representing a place.

N1	は	N2	です
Thing Person	は	place	です

銀行（ぎんこう）はどこですか。—銀行（ぎんこう）はあそこです。
Where is the bank? —The bank is over there.

ブラウンさんはどこですか。—ブラウンさんは図書館（としょかん）です。
Where is Ms. Brown? —Ms. Brown is at the library.

BROWN: Excuse me. Where is the cafeteria?　STUDENT: It's on the first floor of that building.
BROWN: Thank you very much.　STUDENT: You're welcome.

KAWAMURA: Where is Ms. Machida?　CHIN: Right now she is in Professor Yokoi's office.
KAWAMURA: Where is Professor Yokoi's office?　CHIN: It's on the third floor of this building.

7.2 In addition, you can use the following structures.

Existent	Particle は	Location	Particle に	Quantity	Verb
N1 (inanimate)	は	N2	に		ある(あります)
N1 (animate)	は	N2	に		いる(います)

(*number*) _____ *is/are at/in* _____ .

銀行<ruby>ぎんこう</ruby>はどこにありますか。—銀行<ruby>ぎんこう</ruby>はあそこにあります。
Where is the bank? —It (*the bank*) *is over there.*
カワムラさんはカフェテリアにいますか。
Is Mr. Kawamura in the cafeteria?
学生<ruby>がくせい</ruby>はここに三人<ruby>さんにん</ruby>います。
There are three students here.

　　Note the differences between these structures and those expressing existence that are presented in **Grammar 6.5**. These structures require は instead of が, and the location + に comes immediately before the verb. The structure presented in **Grammar 6.5** is used to state ***whether or not people or things exist at a certain place,*** whereas the structures presented here are used to state ***where*** *people or things exist.*

8. Positional Words 🎧

かワムラ：机<ruby>つくえ</ruby>の下<ruby>した</ruby>にかばんがありますよ。

ブラウン：だれのカバンですか。

カワムラ：さあ…かばんの中<ruby>なか</ruby>にペンとノートと財布<ruby>さいふ</ruby>がありますよ。

ブラウン：財布<ruby>さいふ</ruby>の中<ruby>なか</ruby>には何<ruby>なに</ruby>がありますか。

カワムラ：お金<ruby>かね</ruby>とクレジット・カードがあります。

カワムラ：ブラウンさんはどこにいますか。

町田<ruby>まちだ</ruby>：あの部屋<ruby>へや</ruby>の中<ruby>なか</ruby>にいます。

カワムラ：あの赤<ruby>あか</ruby>いドアの部屋<ruby>へや</ruby>ですか。

町田：ええ、そうです。

KAWAMURA: There is a bag under the desk (you know). BROWN: Whose bag is it?
KAWAMURA: I wonder. . . There are pens, notebooks, and a wallet inside it. BROWN: What's inside the wallet? KAWAMURA: There is money and credit cards.

KAWAMURA: Where is Ms. Brown? MACHIDA: She's in that room. KAWAMURA: You mean that room with the red door? MACHIDA: Yes, that's right.

8.1 Such phrases as *in front of* and *to the left of* are expressed in Japanese with the following structure.

N	Possessive Particle の	Positional Word	
<ruby>机<rt>つくえ</rt></ruby>	の	<ruby>上<rt>うえ</rt></ruby>	*on (top of) the desk*
ブラウンさん	の	<ruby>右<rt>みぎ</rt></ruby>	*to the right of Ms. Brown*
<ruby>東京大学<rt>とうきょうだいがく</rt></ruby>	の	そば	*near the University of Tokyo* (lit., *in the vicinity of the University of Tokyo*)

These locational phrases can modify nouns, in which case they precede the noun and are linked to it with the possessive particle の (*of*).

<ruby>机<rt>つくえ</rt></ruby> の<ruby>上<rt>うえ</rt></ruby>の<ruby>本<rt>ほん</rt></ruby>
the book on the desk (lit., *the desk's top's book*)

ギブソンさんの<ruby>右<rt>みぎ</rt></ruby>の<ruby>人<rt>ひと</rt></ruby>
the person on Ms. Gibson's right (lit., *Ms. Gibson's right side's person*)

8.2 When these locational phrases are used as the location with existential verbs, they are followed by the particle に, as discussed in **Grammar 6.4** and **7.2**.

<ruby>机<rt>つくえ</rt></ruby> の<ruby>上<rt>うえ</rt></ruby>に<ruby>何<rt>なに</rt></ruby>がありますか。—<ruby>机<rt>つくえ</rt></ruby> の<ruby>上<rt>うえ</rt></ruby>に<ruby>本<rt>ほん</rt></ruby>があります。
What is on the desk? —There is a book on the desk.

ブラウンさんの<ruby>右<rt>みぎ</rt></ruby>にだれがいますか。—ブラウンさんの<ruby>右<rt>みぎ</rt></ruby>にカワムラさんがいます。
Who is to the right of Ms. Brown? —Mr. Kawamura is on the right side of Ms. Brown.

Vocabulary: Positional Words

上	うえ	on; above; up	後ろ	うしろ	back; behind
下	した	under; below; down	間	あいだ	between
			向かい	むかい	facing; across from
左	ひだり	left			
右	みぎ	right	隣	となり	next to; next door
中	なか	in; inside			
外	そと	outside; out	そば		nearby
前	まえ	front	回り	まわり	around
			横	よこ	side

For a list of other important positional words, see page 150 of this chapter.

ＡとＢの間 *between A and B*

 アクティビティー 15

どこにありますか。 (*Where is it?*)

Make dialogues following the example.

［例］ s1:（レストラン） s2:（映画館のとなり）→
s1: レストランはどこにありますか。
s2: 映画館のとなりにあります。

1. s1:（カーティスさん） s2:（図書館の前）
2. s1:（交番） s2:（銀行とスーパーの間 ）
3. s1:（駐車場 ） s2:（公園の後ろ）
4. s1:（林さん） s2:（ギブソンさんの右 ）
5. s1:（喫茶店） s2:（ホテルの中）

アクティビティー 16

本の上に何がありますか。 (*What is on the book?*)

Answer the following questions, using this illustration.

1. 机の上に何がありますか。
2. 箱の中に何がありますか。
3. 本の上に何がありますか。
4. かばんはどこにありますか。

(*Continues.*)

5. カレンダーはどこにありますか。

6. ブラウンさんの後ろに何がありますか。

7. カワムラさんはどこにいますか。

8. ギブソンさんはどこにいますか。

アクティビティー **17**

どこにいますか。   (*Where is everybody?*)

Answer the following questions, using the illustration. (Everybody's names are on page 153.)

Useful Vocabulary: ベンチ *bench,* 鳥 *bird,* 犬 *dog,* 木 *tree*

1. ギブソンさんはどこにいますか。

2. ギブソンさんの右にだれがいますか。

3. ベンチの下に何がいますか。

4. ベンチの横にだれがいますか。

5. 町田さんはどこにいますか。

6. 木の上に何がいますか。

7. 車の中にだれがいますか。

8. 車の後ろにだれがいますか。

アクティビティー **18**

ダイアログ：スーパーはどこにありますか。(*Where is the supermarket?*)
道_{みち}で

s1: すみません。このへんにスーパーはありますか。

s2: ええ、駅_{えき}の前_{まえ}にありますよ。

s1: どんな建物_{たてもの}ですか。

s2: 白_{しろ}い、大_{おお}きな建物_{たてもの}ですよ。　　　　　　　白い *white*

s1: どうもありがとうございました。

s2: どういたしまして。

As you have seen, **すみません** can be used in a variety of contexts. You have used it to convey an apology (*I'm sorry*) or your gratitude, especially when someone has gone out of their way for you (*thank you*). In this dialogue, **すみません** is used to get someone's attention in order to ask for help (*excuse me*).

Practice the dialogue, substituting the following words and expressions for the underlined portions.

1. レストラン
銀行_{ぎんこう}のとなり
グリーンのビル

2. 郵便局_{ゆうびんきょく}
映画館_{えいがかん}と病院_{びょういん}の間_{あいだ}
赤_{あか}い、小_{ちい}さな建物_{たてもの}

3. 病院_{びょういん}
公園_{こうえん}のそば
白_{しろ}い、きれいな建物_{たてもの}

4. 食堂_{しょくどう}
図書館_{としょかん}の前_{まえ}
古_{ふる}い建物_{たてもの}

5. ホテル
映画館_{えいがかん}の右_{みぎ}
グレーのビル

Sentence-Final よ

The sentence-final particle よ is used by a speaker to indicate strong conviction about a statement or to indicate that he or she is giving new information to the listener; that is, information that the speaker thinks he or she, but not the listener, knows.

カフェテリアはどこですか。
Where is the cafeteria?

(*Continues.*)

On the street　A: Excuse me. Is there a supermarket around here?　B: Yes, there's one in front of the station.　A: What kind of building is it?　B: It's a large, white building. A: Thank you very much.　B: You're welcome.

あそこですよ。

It's over there.

わかりますか。

Do you understand?

ええ、もちろんわかりますよ。

Yes, of course, I understand.

Note that, in general, sentence-final よ is not appropriate when speaking to a superior, because it can sound too direct or abrupt.

VOCABULARY LIBRARY

More Positional Words

真ん中	まんなか	middle
はじ		edge
北	きた	north
南	みなみ	south
東	ひがし	east
西	にし	west
こちら側	こちらがわ	this side
向こう側	むこうがわ	the other side

アクティビティー **19**

ボールは箱の上にあります。(*The ball is on the box.*)

What relation does the ball(s) have to the box in the following illustrations?

Useful Word: 箱 *box*

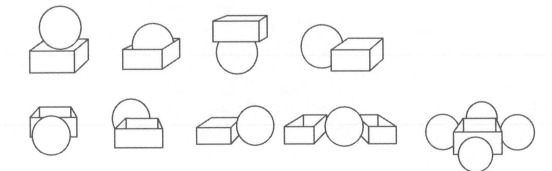

アクティビティー **20**

どこにありますか。(*Where is it?*)

Look at the picture and answer the following questions.

1. スーパーはどこにありますか。
2. 郵便局（ゆうびんきょく）はどこにありますか。
3. レストラン「フラミンゴ」はどこにありますか。
4. 学校（がっこう）はどこにありますか。
5. 駐車場（ちゅうしゃじょう）はどこにありますか。
6. デパートはどこにありますか。
7. 地下鉄（ちかてつ）の駅（えき）はどこにありますか。
8. 喫茶店（きっさてん）のとなりに何（なに）がありますか。

Make your own questions to ask your classmates.

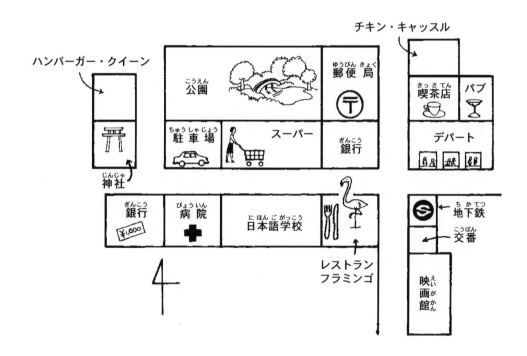

アクティビティー 21

ダイアログ：いいレストランはありますか (*Is there a good restaurant?*)

カワムラさんと町田さんが話しています。

カワムラ：この近所にいいレストランはありますか。

町田：ええ、ありますよ。となりのビルの4階にあります。

カワムラ：名前は。

町田：「ナポレオン」です。

Using the dialogue as a guide, ask your classmates whether each of the following things exists near their house or apartment. If yes, ask specifically where it is (e.g., *Is it next to a shopping mall?*). In addition, ask what it's called.

1. bank
2. good restaurant
3. convenience store （コンビニ）
4. beautiful park
5. movie theater
6. good hotel
7. hospital
8. large supermarket
9. tall building
10. famous school

アクティビティー 22

どこにいますか。(*Where is he?*)

Based on the illustration, answer the following questions.

1. チンさんはどこにいますか。
2. 町田さんはどこにいますか。
3. カーティスさんはどこにいますか。
4. 林さんはどこにいますか。
5. ギブソンさんはどこにいますか。
6. カワムラさんの右にだれがいますか。
7. 横井先生の前にだれがいますか。
8. 横井先生の後ろにだれがいますか。

Mr. Kawamura and Ms. Machida are talking. KAWAMURA: Is there a good restaurant in this neighborhood? MACHIDA: Yes, there is. There is one on the fourth floor of the building next door. KAWAMURA: What's it called? MACHIDA: "Napoleon."

9. Numerals and Counters

カワムラ：すみません。佐藤さんのうちはどこでしょうか。

おまわりさん：このへんに佐藤さんは三軒あります。

　　　　　　　どの佐藤さんですか。

カワムラ：佐藤 良男さんです。

おまわりさん：佐藤 良男さんも二人います。

ブラウン：この家には部屋がいくつありますか。

不動産屋：五つあります。

ブラウン：トイレはいくつありますか。

不動産屋：二つあります。一階に一つ、二階に一つです。

KAWAMURA: Excuse me. Where is Mr. Satoo's residence?　POLICEMAN: There are three Satoo residences in this neighborhood.　Which Mr. Satoo do you mean?　KAWAMURA: Mr. Yoshio Satoo.
POLICEMAN: There are two Yoshio Satoos.

BROWN: How many rooms does this house have?　REAL ESTATE AGENT: It has five.
BROWN: How many bathrooms does it have?　REAL ESTATE AGENT: It has two. There is one on the first floor and another on the second floor.

9.1 There are two numerical systems in Japanese: the Japanese system and the Sino-Japanese system. In the Japanese system, which covers only from one to ten, つ is the general counter. After 11, there is only one system: the Sino-Japanese system.

Refer to Appendix 3.

Numbers 1 through 10

	JAPANESE SYSTEM	SINO-JAPANESE SYSTEM		JAPANESE SYSTEM	SINO-JAPANESE SYSTEM
1	ひとつ (一つ)	いち (一)	6	むっつ (六つ)	ろく (六)
2	ふたつ (二つ)	に (二)	7	ななつ (七つ)	しち／なな (七)
3	みっつ (三つ)	さん (三)	8	やっつ (八つ)	はち (八)
4	よっつ (四つ)	し／よん (四)	9	ここのつ (九つ)	きゅう／く (九)
5	いつつ (五つ)	ご (五)	10	とお (十)	じゅう (十)

9.2 Large numbers are expressed in units of 10,000 (万), 100,000,000 (億; *100 million*), and 1,000,000,000,000 (兆; *1 trillion*).

0 (zero) is read as ゼロ or 零 (れい)。

Large Numbers

10	じゅう (十)
100	ひゃく (百)
1,000	(いっ) せん ([一] 千)
10,000	いちまん (一万)
100,000	じゅうまん (十万)
1,000,000	ひゃくまん (百万)
10,000,000	(いっ) せんまん ([一] 千万)
100,000,000	いちおく (一億)

Notice these phonological (sound) changes when 1, 3, 6, 8, and 10 appear before 百、千、or 兆.

1	一千 (いっせん)、一兆 (いっちょう)
3	三百 (さんびゃく)、三千 (さんぜん)
6	六百 (ろっぴゃく)
8	八百 (はっぴゃく)
10	十兆 (じゅっちょう *or* じっちょう)

Since the Japanese number system goes from thousands to ten thousands instead of from thousands to millions, English-speakers sometimes have trouble reading large numbers aloud.

A handy way to avoid confusion is to imagine that the number has a comma every four places from the right. The four digits to the left of the comma are read as multiples of 万, and the next four digits beyond that are read as multiples of 億.

22,000 → 2,2000 or 二万二千

600,000 → 60,0000 or 六十万

1,000,000 → 100,0000 or 百万

250,000,000 → 2,5000,0000 or 二億五千万

In real life, of course, Japanese people write large numbers with commas every three places.

9.3 When you count objects, you have to attach counter suffixes (a suffix is an element attached to the end of another element) to numbers. Which counter you use depends on the classification of what you count. Although there are many counters in Japanese (there is a dictionary just of counters), the number of commonly used counters is limited.

Bold characters indicate counters already introduced. You should know these.

Some Important Counters

a.	〜人 (にん)	people
b.	〜ヶ月 (かげつ)	number of months
c.	〜台 (だい)	heavy machinery, vehicles, office equipment, etc.
d.	〜番 (ばん)	number of order (No. 1, No. 2, etc.)
e.	〜度 (ど)	. . . times (occurrences, repetitions); degrees (temperature)
f.	〜時間 (じかん)	number of hours
g.	〜枚 (まい)	thin, flat items (paper, bedsheets, floppy disks, toast, etc.)
h.	〜着 (ちゃく)	clothes
i.	〜課 (か)	lessons
j.	〜歳 (さい)	age
k.	〜冊 (さつ)	books, notebooks, boundvolumes
l.	〜頭 (とう)	large animals (elephants, whales, horses, etc.)
m.	〜分 (ふん)	minutes
n.	〜杯 (はい)	cupfuls or glassfuls
o.	〜本 (ほん)	long, thin items (pencils, bananas, legs, trees, roads, tapes, etc.)
p.	〜階 (かい)	floors of a building
q.	〜足 (そく)	shoes, socks, footwear
r.	〜匹 (ひき)	small animals (dogs, cats, etc.)
s.	〜羽 (わ)	birds
t.	〜軒 (けん)	houses, buildings
u.	〜倍 (ばい)	. . . times (magnification)
v.	〜回 (かい)	. . . times (occurrences)
w.	〜個 (こ)	round or square objects (pears, bars of soap, boxes, etc.)

(Continues.)

山口<ruby>やまぐち</ruby>さんのうちには車<ruby>くるま</ruby>が二台<ruby>にだい</ruby>あります。
There are two cars at Mr. Yamaguchi's house.
カウンターの上<ruby>うえ</ruby>にブラウスが三枚<ruby>さんまい</ruby>あります。
There are three blouses on the counter.
テーブルの上<ruby>うえ</ruby>にバナナが五本<ruby>ごほん</ruby>あります。
There are five bananas on the table.

Depending on the numbers that come before the counters, some counters show phonological changes. Notice the exception for counting people (人). *One* and *two* use the Japanese system, while the rest use the Sino-Japanese system.

Blouses and sweaters are counted with 〜枚. Pants are counted with 〜本.

Refer to Appendix 4.

	〜人 (にん)	〜台 (だい)	〜個 (こ)	〜分 (ふん)	〜軒 (けん)
1	ひとり	いちだい	いっこ	いっぷん	いっけん
2	ふたり	にだい	にこ	にふん	にけん
3	さんにん	さんだい	さんこ	さんぷん	さんけん
					さんげん
4	よにん	よんだい	よんこ	よんぷん	よんけん
5	ごにん	ごだい	ごこ	ごふん	ごけん
6	ろくにん	ろくだい	ろっこ	ろっぷん	ろっけん
7	ななにん	ななだい	ななこ	ななふん	ななけん
	しちにん	しちだい	しちこ	しちふん	しちけん
8	はちにん	はちだい	はっこ	はっぷん	はっけん
			はちこ	はちふん	はちけん
9	きゅうにん	きゅうだい	きゅうこ	きゅうふん	きゅうけん
	くにん				
10	じゅうにん	じゅうだい	じゅっこ	じゅっぷん	じゅっけん
			じっこ	じっぷん	じっけん

9.4 When you would like to ask *how many,* attach 何 (なん) before these counters. The interrogative corresponding to the general counter 〜つ is いくつ.

このクラスに学生<ruby>がくせい</ruby>は何<ruby>なん</ruby>人<ruby>にん</ruby>いますか。
How many students are there in this class?
ここに本<ruby>ほん</ruby>が何<ruby>なん</ruby>冊<ruby>さつ</ruby>ありますか。
How many books are here?
まどはいくつありますか。
How many windows are there?

After 何, some counters undergo a sound change.

何杯 (なんばい)
何本 (なんぼん)
何匹 (なんびき)

アクティビティー 23

なんぼん
何本 ありますか。 (*How many* [*long, thin objects*] *are there?*)

What counter do you think is used to count the following? Refer to the preceding list of counters.

1. socks
2. fingers
3. computers
4. horses

5. jackets
6. envelopes
7. movie theaters
8. streets

9. parks
10. goldfish

アクティビティー 24

くるま　いちだい
車 が一台あります。 (*There's one car.*)

These are answers. What are the questions in Japanese?

1. There are five pencils on the desk.
2. There are three cars at home.
3. There are two windows in the classroom.
4. There is one person to the left of Mr. Yamada.
5. There are ten books in my bag.
6. There are six coffee shops in this town.
7. There are eight books over there.
8. There are three bananas on the table.
9. There are three parks in this neighborhood.

アクティビティー 25

たか
高いですね。 (*It's expensive, isn't it!*)

[例]　—The average starting salary in your future career
よんまん
　　　—四万ドルです。

1. How many dollars (**ドル**) are each of these?
   a. a year's tuition, room, and board for an on-campus student at your college or university
   b. the price of the car you hope to own some day
   c. the average price of a house in your community
   d. the value of ¥1,000,000 in your country's currency (Check the business section of your local newspaper if you don't know the current exchange rate.)

(Continues.)

百五十七

e. the current jackpot in your state or province's lottery

f. the annual salary of your favorite sports star

g. the price of the computer you hope to own some day

2. As you plan your trip to Japan on a moderate budget, you decide that you can spend $75 per night for a hotel, $25 a day for meals, and $25 a day for incidentals. (Your Japan Rail Pass will take care of most of your transportation needs.) How many yen will you need each day? (Use the exchange rate you looked up earlier.)

アクティビティー **26**

銀行は何軒ありますか。(*How many banks are there?*)

カワムラ：銀行はこの近所に何軒ありますか。
山口：三軒あります。

Ask a classmate how many gas stations, movie theaters, and other establishments there are in the neighborhood.

中野中央商店街

銀行
三井銀行
トマト銀行
東京銀行

レストラン
日本レストラン・竹田
ポパイ・サンドイッチ
松すし
マクドナルド
スキヤキ・ハウス

スーパー
ラッキー マート

デパート
丸井デパート

映画館
シネマ中野
中野日活

喫茶店
コーヒ・パレス
モーツァルト
ブルー・ムーン
オアシス
やすらぎ

ガソリン・スタンド
モービル
日本石油

図書館
中野中央図書館

アクティビティー **27**

ダイアログ：学生は何人いますか。(*How many students are there?*)

町田さんとブラウンさんが話しています。

　　町田：ブラウンさんの日本語のクラスに学生は何人いますか。
ブラウン：ええと、全部で15人ぐらいいます。
　　町田：全部アメリカ人ですか。
ブラウン：いいえ、中国人が五人とカナダ人が二人います。

KAWAMURA: How many banks are there in this neighborhood?   YAMAGUCHI: There are three.

Ms. Machida and Ms. Brown are talking   MACHIDA: How many students are in your Japanese class, Ms. Brown?   BROWN: Uh…there are a total of fifteen students.   MACHIDA: Are they all Americans?   BROWN: No, there are five Chinese and two Canadians.

Vocabulary: Counting People

一人	ひとり	one person	八人	はちにん	eight people
二人	ふたり	two people	九人	きゅうにん、くにん	nine people
三人	さんにん	three people	十人	じゅうにん	ten people
四人	よにん	four people	十一人	じゅういちにん	eleven people
五人	ごにん	five people	百人	ひゃくにん	one hundred people
六人	ろくにん	six people	何人	なんにん	how many people
七人	しちにん	seven people			
	ななにん				

アクティビティー **28**

^{なん}何 ^{にん}人いますか。(*How many people are there?*)

Answer these questions about your class.

1. このクラスに^{がくせい}学生は^{なんにん}何人いますか。
2. ^{せんせい}先生は^{なんにん}何人いますか。
3. ^{おとこ}男 (*male*) の^{がくせい}学生は^{なんにん}何人いますか。
4. ^{おんな}女 (*female*) の^{がくせい}学生は^{なんにん}何人いますか。
5. ^{にほんじん}日本人は^{なんにん}何人いますか。
6. アメリカ^{じん}人は^{なんにん}何人いますか。

10. Expressing Likes and Dislikes: 好き and きらい

^{まちだ}町田：ブラウンさんはどんな^{がっか}学科が^す好きですか。

ブラウン：^{れきしがく}歴史学が^す好きです。

^{まちだ}町田：きらいな^{がっか}学科はありますか。

ブラウン：ええ、^{すうがく}数学が^{だい}大きらいです。

^{はやし}林：ブラウンさんはお^{さけ}酒が^す好きですか。

ブラウン：あまり^す好きではありません。

林さんは。

^{はやし}林：^{だいす}大好きです。

MACHIDA: What academic subject do you like, Ms. Brown? BROWN: I like history. MACHIDA: Is there any subject that you don't like? BROWN: Yes, I hate math.

HAYASHI: Do you like sake, (Ms. Brown)? BROWN: I don't like it very much. How about you, (Mr. Hayashi)? HAYASHI: I love it.

(Continues.)

Such meanings as *I like* and *I dislike* are expressed by na-adjectives 好き and きらい, respectively. You can use these adjectives both prenominally and predicatively.

わたしの好きな町
a town I like; a favorite town of mine
わたしのきらいなところ
a place I dislike
山口さんはあの喫茶店が好きです。
Mr. Yamaguchi likes that coffee shop.
チンさんは大きい町がきらいです。
Ms. Chin doesn't like large cities.

Note that the object of liking and disliking (*coffee shops* and *cities* in the above examples) is marked with the particle が.

言語ノート

Different Degrees of Liking and Disliking

野菜が好きですか。	Do you like vegetables?
―はい、大好きです。	―Yes, I like them very much.
―はい、好きです。	―Yes, I like them.
―まあまあです。	―They're okay. (*lit.,* So-so.)
―あまり好きではありません。	―I don't like them very much.
―いいえ、きらいです。	―No, I dislike them.
―いいえ、大きらいです。	―No, I hate them.

アクティビティー 29

好きですか；きらいですか。(*Do you like or dislike it?*)

What's your Japanese-language and culture interest quotient? Ask a classmate the following questions. What's the score?

(5 points)	(4)	(3)	(2)	(1)	(0)
大好き	好き	まあまあ	きらい	大きらい	わかりません
					(*I'm unfamiliar with it.*)

1. てんぷらが好きですか。

2. すしが好きですか。

3. ひらがなが好きですか。

4. カタカナが好きですか。

5. 漢字が好きですか。

Total points: _____ 点

6. 日本語のクラスが好きですか。

7. 日本語の先生が好きですか。

   (Be careful!)

8. 歌舞伎が好きですか。

9. すもうが好きですか。

> 点 is a counter for points.

アクティビティー 30

大きい町が好きですか、小さい町が好きですか。(*Do you like big towns or little towns?*)

Answer the following questions.

1. 大きい町が好きですか、小さい町が好きですか。

2. 静かなところが好きですか、にぎやかなところが好きですか。

3. 新しい町が好きですか、古い町が好きですか。

4. どんな映画が好きですか。

   Useful words:　アクション映画、SF映画、コメディー、ロマンス、ドラマ

5. どんな音楽が好きですか。

   Useful words:　クラシック、ロック、ラップ、カントリーアンドウエスタン、ゴスペル

6. どんな食べ物が好きですか。

7. どんな食べ物がきらいですか。

8. どんなスポーツが好きですか。

9. どんな学科 (*academic subject*) が好きですか。

アクティビティー 31

大きい町が好きですか。 (*Do you like large towns?*)

Answer these questions.

1. 日本料理が好きですか。

2. 勉強が好きですか。

3. どんなスポーツが好きですか。

4. どんな音楽が好きですか。

5. 静かなところが好きですか、にぎやかなところが好きですか。

(Continues.)

6. 大きい町が好きですか、小さい町が好きですか。

7. どんな料理が好きですか。

8. どんな食べ物 (*food*) がきらいですか。

アクティビティー 32

この町が好きな人は何人いますか。(*How many people like this town?*)

Choose one question from the following list and ask it of ten classmates.
Then report to the class how many people answered yes.

[例] 肉が好きですか。

—はい、好きです。

—いいえ、きらいです。

肉が好きな人は八人います。

肉がきらいな人は二人います。

1. 魚が好きですか。

2. サラダが好きですか。

3. 日本料理が好きですか。

4. パーティーが好きですか。

5. この大学が好きですか。

6. この町が好きですか。

7. スポーツが好きですか。

8. お酒 (*sake*)が好きですか。

9. バナナが好きですか。

10. 日本語のクラスが好きですか。

アクティビティー 33

With a classmate, explore general preferences in at least two of the
following three topics by asking and answering questions. Get as much
information as you can about each area, and keep track of what you learn
from your partner.

Form your questions with expressions like 〜が好きですか。〜がきらい
ですか, etc.

1. クラス： やさしいクラス、むずかしいクラス、大きいクラス、
小さいクラス、午前のクラス、午後のクラス、やさしい先生のクラス、
きびしい先生のクラス

2. 町： 大きい町、小さい町、静かな町、にぎやかな町、便利な町、
きれいな町、山に近い町、海に近い町

3. 飲み物： コーヒー、お茶、ミルク、コカ・コーラ、
ダイエット・コーク、ワイン、ビール、ウイスキー

Then report some of your findings to the class.

Language Skills

Reading and Writing

Reading 1 ブラウンさんのアパートの近所

Before You Read

Linda Brown lives in an apartment in Nakano. The following passage describes her apartment and neighborhood. Before reading it, look at the map. Can you remember what the place labels mean? If not, go to the **Vocabulary** section and find them.

Do you remember these words indicating positions?

回り	となり	上
右	前	間
左	向こう側	後ろ

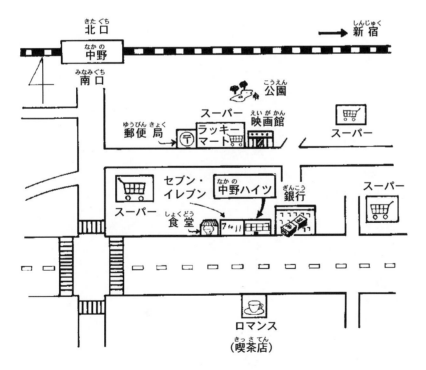

新宿 *a major commercial area of Tokyo*
北口 *north entrance*
南口 *south entrance*

Now Read It!

ブラウンさんのアパートは東京の中野にあります。中野は電車で新宿から10分ぐらいです。ブラウンさんのアパートは駅から徒歩で5分です。東京大学まで地下鉄で30分です。とても便利です。

ブラウンさんのアパートの名前は「中野ハイツ」です。3階建てです。

ブラウンさんのアパートは2階にあります。

アパートの回りにはいろいろなものがあります。アパートの右には銀行があります。アパートの左にはセブンイレブンがあります。セブンイレブンのとなりに食堂があります。とても小さな食堂です。でも、とてもおいしいです。ですから、いつもお客さんがたくさんいます。ブラウンさんはその食堂のカレーライスが大好きです。

アパートの前には広い道があります。道の向こう側に喫茶店があります。名前は「ロマンス」です。「ロマンス」にはウエートレスが3人います。ウエートレスの山本さゆりさんはブラウンさんのいい友だちです。

「ロマンス」の上にパブがあります。

ブラウンさんのアパートの近所にはスーパーが4軒あります。ブラウンさんは「ラッキーマート」が好きです。このスーパーは郵便局と映画館の間にあります。小さなスーパーです。とても安いです。

スーパーの後ろに小さな公園があります。

ブラウンさんは中野が大好きです。

中野 *Nakano (a place in Tokyo)*

から *from*

まで *(up) to*

中野ハイツ *Nakano Heights (name of an apartment building)* / 3 階建て *three-story (building)*

いろいろ(な) *various* / もの *things*

でも *however; but* / おいしい *delicious*

ですから *therefore* / いつも *always* / お客さん *customer*

パブ *pub*

After You Finish Reading

Answer these questions in English.

1. How long does it take to go from Shinjuku to Nakano by train?
2. How many minutes does it take to walk from Nakano Station to Linda's apartment?
3. How many floors does Linda's apartment building have?
4. What is to the left of Linda's apartment?
5. What is to the left of that?
6. Why does the small restaurant have many customers?
7. What does Linda like to eat there?
8. What is across the street from the apartment?
9. Where is the pub?
10. How many supermarkets are there in Linda's neighborhood?
11. Where is Lucky Mart?
12. What is behind Lucky Mart?

Fill in the blanks.

1. ブラウンさんのアパートから東京大学まで地下鉄で（　　）ぐらいです。

2. ブラウンさんのアパートは「中野ハイツ」の（　　）にあります。

3. アパートの（　　）にはいろいろなものがあります。

4. アパートの（　　）には銀行があります。

5. セブンイレブンのとなりの小さな食堂はとても（　　）です。

6. アパートの（　　）に広い道があります。

7. 「ロマンス」にはウエートレスが（　　）います。

8. 「ロマンス」の（　　）にパブがあります。

9. 「ラッキーマート」は郵便局と映画館の（　　）にあります。

10. 公園は「ラッキーマート」の（　　）にあります。

Writing 1

Imagine you live in the apartment marked with ● on the map below. Write a paragraph describing your neighborhood. Start with わたしのアパートのとなりにスーパーがあります.

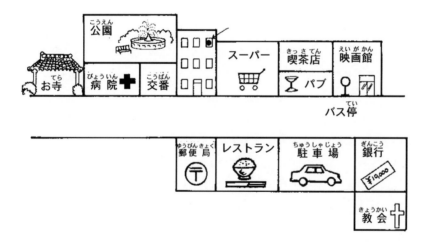

Reading 2　林さんのふるさと

ふるさと *hometown*

Before You Read

Pair up with a classmate. Discuss which of the following you can find in large cities, in very small towns, or in both.

(*Continues.*)

1. 電車の駅
2. 地下鉄の駅
3. 大学
4. バス停
5. 病院
6. 映画館
7. ホテル

8. 銀行
9. 喫茶店
10. デパート
11. スーパー
12. レストラン
13. 交番

What is the counter for each of the following?

1. 人
2. ベンチ
3. 家

4. 犬
5. 道

Now Read It!

This passage is a description of Mr. Hayashi's hometown village. What things listed in the first prereading activity can be found in his hometown? (Some may not be mentioned.)

カワムラさんのクラスメートの林さんは九州の小さい村の出身です。人口は八百人ぐらいです。家が百五十軒あります。病院はありません。

ホテルもありません。デパートもありません。レストランもありません。村は九州の真ん中にあります。村の回りに高い山がたくさんあります。山の向こうに大きい町があります。村と町の間には道が一本あります。町からバスで一時間です。電車はありません。

村にバス停が一つあります。バス停は小さいスーパーの前にあります。バス停の横に古いベンチが一つあります。ベンチの回りにいつも村の人がいます。スーパーのとなりに交番があります。交番の向かいに林さんの家があります。

九州 *Kyushu* (large island in southern Japan)

山 *mountain*

向こう *over, beyond*

バス停 (*bus stop*)

After You Finish Reading

1. What things listed in the first prereading activity exist in Mr. Hayashi's village?

2. Tell whether each of the following is true or false.

   a. Mr. Hayashi's village has a population of about 600.

   b. His village has 150 houses.

   c. His village is in the middle of Kyushu.

   d. His village is surrounded by mountains.

  e. There are two roads connecting his village and the next town.

  f. It takes two hours to travel by bus from his village to the next town.

  g. There is a bus stop in front of a small supermarket.

  h. The bench is new.

  i. There is a police box next to the supermarket.

  j. Mr. Hayashi's house is across the street from the police box.

3. Ask a classmate five questions in Japanese about the passage.

Writing 2

Write a short paragraph describing your neighborhood. Try to use **あります** and positional words.

Language Functions and Situations
Making Communication Work 🎧

Here are some useful techniques for making sure you're communicating effectively.

1. Ask someone to repeat something.

  A: スーパーは銀行の前にあります。

  B: すみません。もう一度ゆっくりお願いします。

  A: スーパーは銀行の前にあります。

2. Check that you have understood.

  A: スーパーは銀行の前にあります。

  B: 銀行の前ですね。

  A: はい、そうです。

  A: 学生は26人います。

  B: 25人ですか。

  A: いいえ、26人です。

3. Say you have understood.

  A: ギブソンさんは図書館にいます。

  B: はい、わかりました。

4. Say you didn't understand.

  A: スーパーはあの映画館のとなりにあります。

  B: すみません。わかりません。

  A: じゃ、つれていってあげましょう。(*Then I'll take you there.*)

(Continues.)

5. Show you are listening.

A: あそこに銀行がありますね。

B: ええ。

A: そのとなりにレストランがありますね。

B: はい。

A: 喫茶店はあのレストランの上にあります。

あいづち (Yes, I'm following you...)

言語ノート

One of the first things you notice when talking with Japanese people is that they frequently nod or interject はい、ええ、ああ、そうですか、うんうん, and so on after each phrase you utter. This is not a sign of impatience, boredom, or rudeness. Rather, they are engaging in the participatory style of communication that characterizes spoken Japanese. With these short interjections called あいづち, the listener is letting you know that he or she is still following you: "Yes, I'm following you, so please continue." (Even though はい [yes] is one of these **aizuchi**, it doesn't necessarily mean *yes, I agree*.)

If the listener does *not* show any reaction a Japanese speaker may feel so uneasy that he will stop and ask わかりますか (*Do you understand?*) or start over at the beginning of the conversation, perhaps speaking more deliberately, on the assumption that the listener didn't understand. This happens frequently in telephone conversations; if the listener misses too many あいづち, the speaker will start over with もしもし (*Hello?*). Mastering the correct use of あいづち will go a long way toward enhancing your fluency.

Showing Location on a Map 🎧

道で

A: すみません。赤坂ホテルはどこですか。

B: 赤坂ホテルですか。ここに地図がありますから、見てください。

A: どうもすみません。

B: 今ここにいます。赤坂ホテルはここです。
となりに映画館と銀行があります。大きな白いビルです。

On the street　A: Excuse me. Where is Akasaka Hotel?　B: Akasaka Hotel? Here is a map, so please take a look.　A: Thank you for taking the trouble.　B: (pointing to a spot on the map) We are here (now). (pointing to a different spot) Akasaka Hotel is here. Next to it are a movie theater and a bank. It is a large, white building.

A: ここから何分ぐらいですか。

B: そうですね。10分ぐらいですね。

A: どうもありがとうございました。

B: どういたしまして。

Role Play

Use the map here to practice showing location or giving directions to a classmate. Assume that you are standing in front of the station. Try to use some of the phrases you learned in **Making Communication Work.** Use your imagination to describe the building and how long it takes to get there.

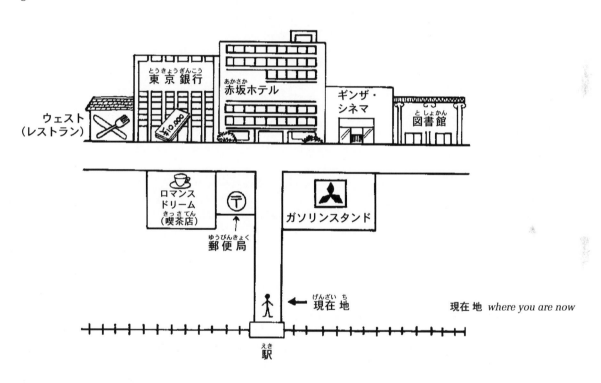

A: Approximately how many minutes is it from here?　　B: Let me see...it's about ten minutes.
A: Thank you very much.　　B: You're welcome.

Listening Comprehension

While listening to your instructor, draw the items mentioned at the appropriate places in the picture.

Vocabulary

Transportation

ジェイアール	JR	JR (Japan Railways)	ちかてつ	地下鉄	subway
くるま	車	car	でんしゃ	電車	electric train
じてんしゃ	自転車	bicycle	とほ	徒歩	walking; on foot

Loanwords: **タクシー、バス**

Places

いえ	家	house	きんじょ	近所	neighborhood
うち		house; (my) home	こうえん	公園	park
えいがかん	映画館	movie theater	こうがい	郊外	suburbs
えき	駅	station	こうばん	交番	police box
(お)てら	(お)寺	(Buddhist) temple	し	市	city
きっさてん	喫茶店	coffee (lit., *tea*) shop	しょくどう	食堂	dining hall; informal restaurant
きょうかい	教会	church			
ぎんこう	銀行	bank	じんじゃ	神社	(Shinto) shrine

たてもの	建物	building		びょういん	病院	hospital
ちゅうしゃじょう	駐車場	parking lot		まち	町	town
とおり	通り	avenue; street		みち	道	street
ところ	所	place		むら	村	village
としょかん	図書館	library		ゆうびんきょく	郵便局	post office
バスてい	バス停	bus stop				

Loanwords: ホテル、レストラン、ガソリンスタンド、スーパー、デパート

Review: 学校（がっこう）、大学（だいがく）、ビル

Nouns

じんこう	人口	population
たべもの	食べ物	food

Adjectives

あかい	赤い	red
あたらしい	新しい	new
あつい	暑い	hot
あつい	厚い	thick
あまい		sweet
いい		good
うすい		thin
うるさい		noisy; annoying
おおい	多い	many; much
おおきい／おおきな	大きい／大きな	large; big
おもい	重い	heavy
おもしろい		interesting, funny
かるい	軽い	light
きたない	汚い	dirty
きびしい		strict
きれい（な）		attractive; pretty; clean
げんき（な）	元気（な）	healthy; energetic
しずか（な）	静か（な）	quiet; peaceful
しろい	白い	white
しんせつ（な）		kind
すくない	少ない	few
せまい	狭い	small in area; narrow
だいきらい（な）	大嫌い（な）	hated
だいすき（な）	大好き（な）	favorite; very well-liked
たかい	高い	high; expensive
ちいさい／ちいさな	小さい／小さな	small

(Continues.)

百七十一

ちかい	近い	near; close
つまらない		boring; dull
とおい	遠い	far
ながい	長い	long
にぎやか (な)		lively
ひくい	低い	low
ひろい	広い	spacious; wide
ふべん (な)	不便 (な)	inconvenient
ふるい	古い	old
べんり (な)	便利 (な)	convenient
みじかい	短い	short
まずい		bad tasting
まじめ		serious
むずかしい		difficult
やさしい		easy; lenient; nice
やすい	安い	inexpensive; cheap
ゆうめい (な)	有名 (な)	famous
わかい	若い	young
わるい	悪い	bad

Loanwords: ハンサム (な)、エレガント (な)、タフ (な)

Review: 好き (な)、嫌い (な)

Adverbs

あ(ん)まり	(+ *negative*) not so much
たくさん	a lot
まあまあ	so-so, passable
Review: とても	

Verbs

| ある | there is/are (*inanimate things*) |
| いる | there is/are (*people, animals*) |

Counting Time

いっぷん	一分	one minute	ろっぷん	六分	six minutes
にふん	二分	two minutes	ななふん、	七分	seven minutes
さんぷん	三分	three minutes	しちふん		
よんぷん、	四分	four minutes	はっぷん	八分	eight minutes
よんふん			きゅうふん	九分	nine minutes
ごふん	五分	five minutes			

| じゅっぷん、
じっぷん | 十分 | ten minutes | いちじかんはん | 一時間半 | one and a
half hours |
| いちじかん | 一時間 | one hour | にじかん | 二時間 | two hours |

Counting People

ひとり	一人	one person	しちにん	七人	seven people
ふたり	二人	two people	はちにん	八人	eight people
さんにん	三人	three people	きゅうにん、くにん	九人	nine people
よにん	四人	four people	じゅうにん	十人	ten people
ごにん	五人	five people	じゅういちにん	十一人	eleven people
ろくにん	六人	six people	ひゃくにん	百人	hundred people

Large Numbers

じゅう	十	ten	いっせんまん	一千万	ten million
ひゃく	百	hundred	いちおく	一億	hundred million
せん	千	thousand	じゅうおく	十億	billion
いちまん	一万	ten thousand	ひゃくおく	百億	ten billion
じゅうまん	十万	hundred thousand	いっせんおく	一千億	hundred billion
ひゃくまん	百万	million	いっちょう	一兆	trillion

Counters

かい	～階	(counter for floors of a building)
けん	～軒	(counter for houses)
さい	～歳	(counter for age)
じかん	～時間	(counter for hours)
にん	～人	(counter for people)
ほん	～本	(counter for long [often cylindrical] items)

Review: 分 (ふん)

Positional Words

あいだ	間	between
うえ	上	on; over; up
うしろ	後ろ	behind; back
した	下	below; under; down
そと	外	outside
そば		near

(*Continues.*)

百七十三

となり	隣	next to
なか	中	inside
ひだり	左	left
まえ	前	front
まわり	回り	around
まんなか		right in the middle
みぎ	右	right
むかい	向かい	across from; facing
よこ	横	side

Kanji

Learn these **kanji:**

間	右	方
半	中	近
上	外	遠
下	前	有
分	後	
小	時	
好	山	
町	口	
田	千	
左	万	

チェックリスト

Use this checklist to confirm that you can now:

- Talk about commuting
- Use adjectives and adverbs
- Talk about places around town
- Express existence
- Express location
- Use positional words
- Count and use numerals and counters
- Express likes and dislikes
- Talk about hometown and neighborhood
- Make sure you are communicating

3

Everyday Life

第
三
章

日
常
生
活

にちじょうせいかつ

きょう　ばん
今日の晩ごはんはすきやきです。

OBJECTIVES

In this lesson you are going to:

- Talk about schedules
- Learn about the basic structure of verbs
- Talk about daily activities
- Learn to use past, polite verb forms
- Learn more about particles showing grammatical relationships
- Talk about weekends and holidays
- Learn a new way to make suggestions
- Practice making phone calls
- Learn how to extend an invitation

YOOKOSO! MULTIMEDIA

Review and practice grammar and vocabulary from this chapter and watch video clips on the *Yookoso!* Interactive CD-ROM. Visit the *Yookoso!* Online Learning Center at **www.mhhe.com/yookoso3** for additional exercises and resources.

Vocabulary and Grammar 3A

Vocabulary and Oral Activities
Schedules

Vocabulary: Days and Times of Day

今日	きょう	today
明日	あした	tomorrow
昨日	きのう	yesterday
あさって		the day after tomorrow
おととい		the day before yesterday
今朝	けさ	this morning
今日の午後	きょうのごご	this afternoon
今晩	こんばん	tonight

Review: 午前(ごぜん)、午後(ごご)、朝(あさ)、昼(ひる)、夕方(ゆうがた)、夜(よる)

アクティビティー **1**

ダイアログ：いつも忙(いそが)しいですね。(*You are always busy, aren't you!*)

ブラウン：三村(みむら)さん、明日(あした)の午後(ごご)はひまですか。
　三村(みむら)：残念(ざんねん)ですが、アルバイトがあります。
ブラウン：じゃあ、あさっての午後(ごご)はどうですか。
　三村：ううん。あさってはクラブのミーティングがあります。
ブラウン：三村(みむら)さんはいつも忙(いそが)しいですね。

Now practice the dialogue substituting different times and activities.

BROWN: Mr. Mimura, are you free tomorrow afternoon?　MIMURA: I'm sorry, but I have a part-time job.　BROWN: Then, how about the afternoon of the day after tomorrow?
MIMURA: Well, I have a club meeting the day after tomorrow.　BROWN: You are always busy, aren't you!

Yookoso! An Invitation to Contemporary Japanese, Third Edition

177

言語ノート

Asking If Someone Has Free Time

These are common ways to ask if someone has free time and some ways to respond to the questions.

<ruby>明日<rt>あした</rt></ruby>、ひまですか。

Are you free tomorrow?

ええ、ひまですが...

Yes, I'm free, but... (what do you have in mind?)

ちょっと<ruby>用事<rt>ようじ</rt></ruby>があります。

I have some things to attend to.

<ruby>明日<rt>あした</rt></ruby>、<ruby>時間<rt>じかん</rt></ruby>がありますか。

Do you have any (free) time tomorrow?

はい、ありますよ。

Yes, I do.

ちょっと<ruby>忙<rt>いそが</rt></ruby>しいです。

I'm (a bit) busy.

<ruby>明日<rt>あした</rt></ruby>、<ruby>忙<rt>いそが</rt></ruby>しいですか。

Are you busy tomorrow?

ええ、ちょっと...

Yes, (sorry, but I'm) a bit (busy).

いいえ、ひまですよ。

No, I have no plans. (*lit.,* I'm free.)

文化ノート

CULTURE NOTE: Part-Time Jobs for College Students

In Japanese, part-time jobs are commonly called アルバイト, or バイト for short, from the German word *arbeit* meaning *work*. Part-time workers are called アルバイター, or recently パート（タイマー）(from English *part-timer*). Many Japanese college students have part-time jobs, most commonly as tutors (家庭教師 [かていきょうし]) for elementary and secondary school children. Others work as waiters, waitresses, delivery workers, or shop clerks. The student affairs office of any university has a bulletin board posting job opportunities, but the most popular sources of information are the daily and weekly magazines devoted to part-time job listings, such as とらばーゆ and 求人（きゅうじん）パートバイト情報（じょうほう）.

(*Continues.*)

百七十七

アルバイト・マガジン：いいアルバイトは
ありませんか。

Vocabulary: Days of the Month

一日	ついたち	the first	十五日	じゅうごにち	the fifteenth
二日	ふつか	the second	十六日	じゅうろくにち	the sixteenth
三日	みっか	the third	十七日	じゅうしちにち	the seventeenth
四日	よっか	the fourth	十八日	じゅうはちにち	the eighteenth
五日	いつか	the fifth	十九日	じゅうくにち	the nineteenth
六日	むいか	the sixth	二十日	はつか	the twentieth
七日	なのか	the seventh	二十四日	にじゅうよっか	the twenty-fourth
八日	ようか	the eighth	二十五日	にじゅうごにち	the twenty-fifth
九日	ここのか	the ninth	二十六日	にじゅうろくにち	the twenty-sixth
十日	とおか	the tenth	二十七日	にじゅうしちにち	the twenty-seventh
十一日	じゅういちにち	the eleventh	二十八日	にじゅうはちにち	the twenty-eighth
十二日	じゅうににち	the twelfth	二十九日	にじゅうくにち	the twenty-ninth
十三日	じゅうさんにち	the thirteenth	三十日	さんじゅうにち	the thirtieth
十四日	じゅうよっか	the fourteenth	三十一日	さんじゅういちにち	the thirty-first

Note that from the second through the tenth, Japanese numbers are used and that the first, fourteenth, twentieth, and twenty-fourth are irregular.

アクティビティー **2**

ダイアログ：何日ですか。(*What is the date?*)

　　林：ギブソンさん、来週の金曜日はひまですか。

ギブソン：来週の金曜日...何日ですか。

　　林：ええと、14日です。

ギブソン：残念ですが、試験があります。

Practice this dialogue based on the following schedule.

S	M	T	W	Th	F	S
			January			1
ski club 2	3	4	today 5	part-time job 6	7	8
9	10	11	12	part-time job 13	exam 14	party 15
ski club 16	17	exam 18	19	part-time job 20	21	22
23	24	25	exam 26	part-time job 27	28	29
30	31					

Vocabulary: Weeks, Months, and Years

今週	こんしゅう	this week	何日	なんにち	what day
来週	らいしゅう	next week	何月	なんがつ	what month
先週	せんしゅう	last week	何年	なんねん	what year
			何曜日	なんようび	what day of the week
今月	こんげつ	this month	何年何月何日ですか。		What is the date
来月	らいげつ	next month			(lit., *year, month,*
先月	せんげつ	last month			*and day*)?
今年	ことし	this year			
来年	らいねん	next year			
去年	きょねん	last year			
昨年	さくねん	last year			

去年 sounds more informal than 昨年.

HAYASHI: Ms. Gibson, are you free next Friday?　　GIBSON: Next Friday... What's the date?
HAYASHI: Uh... it is the fourteenth.　　GIBSON: I'm sorry, but I have an exam.

Vocabulary and Grammar 3A

文化ノート

CULTURE NOTE: 年号（ねんごう）

The Western system of counting years (2005, 2006, etc.) is commonly used in Japan, but the traditional Japanese system, based on the reigns of emperors, is still a part of everyday life. In the past, the reign of a single emperor might encompass several eras, but since 1868, the accession of each new emperor has marked the beginning of a new era. Within each era the years are numbered starting with one. The emperor chooses an auspicious name, or 年号（ねんごう）, for his era, and after he dies he is known by that name. For example, the emperor who reigned from 1868 to 1912 chose the name 明治（めいじ）or "bright rule" for his era, and he has been known posthumously as 明治天皇（めいじてんのう）, or Emperor Meiji. The subsequent 年号 are: 大正（たいしょう）"great righteousness" (1912–late 1926); 昭和（しょうわ）"shining peace" (late 1926–early 1989); 平成（へいせい）"peace growing" (1989–).

The first year of the 年号 is called 元年（がんねん）, and the subsequent ones are simply numbered: 二年, 三年, etc. If you ever live in Japan you will need to know this system, because many forms and documents require you to state dates in that way. A good way to become familiar with the system is to determine what your birth year is and then work forward or backward to figure out other years. For example, if you were born in 1985, you would put down 昭和 60 年 as the year of your birth.

昭和60年生まれです。
I was born in **Showa** *(year) 60.*
昭和60年5月8日生まれです。
I was born on May 8, **Showa** *(year) 60.*
今日は平成18年7月5日です。
Today is July 5, 2006.

Note that dates are expressed in the order year-month-day whether the Western or Japanese system is used.

アクティビティー **3**

らい しゅう すいようび なん にち
来 週 の水曜日は何 日ですか。(*What day is next Wednesday?*)

Ask your partner the following questions. Consult a calendar if necessary.

Review the words for months and days of the week.

らいしゅう すいようび なん にち
1. 来 週 の水曜日は何 日ですか。
らいしゅう げつようび なん にち
2. 来 週 の月曜日は何 日ですか。
らいげつ みっか なんようび
3. 来月の三日は何曜日ですか。
らいげつ なんがつ
4. 来月は何月ですか。
らいげつ じゅうよっか なんようび
5. 来月の十 四日は何曜日ですか。
らいしゅう きんようび なんがつ なん にち
6. 来 週 の金曜日は何月 何 日ですか。
たんじょう び なんがつ なん にち
7. 誕 生 日(*birthday*)は何月 何 日ですか。
なんねん う
8. 何年生まれですか。(*What year were you born?*) (Can you answer using

both the Western system and the 年号 system?)

百八十

アクティビティー **4**

誕生日は何月何日ですか。(*What day is your birthday?*)

Walk around the classroom and ask your classmates when their birthdays are. For each month, have one person write his or her birth date and signature on your paper. Can you collect twelve signatures, one for each month? Do any two people in your class have the same birthday?

[例] s1: 誕生日は何月何日ですか。
     s2: 四月一日です。
     s1: ここにサインしてください。

Grammar and Practice Activities

11. The Basic Structure of Japanese Verbs

11.1 In Chapter 2, you learned how to conjugate (change the form of) adjectives to form the negative (e.g., 大きい→大きくない). Japanese verbs also change form, or conjugate, to express a variety of meanings.

    You have already studied several Japanese verbs, including 洗(あら)います [*I*] *wash*, 聞(き)きます [*I*] *listen*, 話(はな)します [*I*] *speak*, 立(た)ちます [*I*] *stand up*, 読(よ)みます [*I*] *read*, あります [*there*] *exists*, 泳(およ)ぎます [*I*] *swim*, 食(た)べます [*I*] *eat*, 寝(ね)ます [*I*] *go to bed* and 見(み)ます [*I*] *see, watch.* The verbs all end in ます because these are the polite forms of these verbs. In order to look up any of these verbs in a Japanese dictionary, you need to know the verb's dictionary form, which is listed in the following chart. Each dictionary form consists of two parts, a root and an ending.

Dictionary Form	Meaning	Root	Ending
Class 1 Verbs			
洗(あら)う	to wash	洗	う
聞(き)く	to listen	聞	く
話(はな)す	to speak	話	す
立(た)つ	to stand up	立	つ
読(よ)む	to read	読	む
ある	to exist	あ	る
泳(およ)ぐ	to swim	泳	ぐ

(Continues.)

百八十一

Class 2 Verbs			
た 食べる	to eat	食べ	る
ね 寝る	to go to sleep	寝	る
み 見る	to see	見	る
き 着る	to wear	着	る

Notice the different endings between the two groupings of verbs. The ending of the first group is variable, while that of the second group is always る. In this textbook, the first group of verbs are called *Class 1* verbs, while the second group of verbs are called *Class 2* verbs. The simple (but not foolproof) rule for distinguishing between these two classes is this: if the root of a verb ends with a syllable from the **i**-column (い、き、し、ち、etc.) or the **e**-column (え、け、せ、て、etc.) of the **hiragana** syllabary ＋る, it is a Class 2 verb. Otherwise it is a Class 1 verb.

CLASS 2 VERBS					
	-a	-i	-u	-e	-o	
た 食				べ ね 寝		＋る ＋る
		み 見 き 着				＋る ＋る

The dictionary form of all Class 1 verbs ends in one of the syllables in the **u**-column of the **hiragana** syllabary. (Note that ある ends in る, but its root does not end in a syllable from the **i**-column or the **e**-column, so it is not a Class 2 verb.)

CLASS 1 VERBS						
	-a	-i	-u	-e	-o	
あら 洗			う			(あ row)
か 書			く			(か row)
はな 話			す			(さ row)
た 立			つ			(た row)
よ 読			む			(み row)
あ			る			(ら row)
およ 泳			ぐ			(が row)

Class 1 and Class 2 verbs conjugate in different but regular ways.

In addition, there are two irregular verbs in Japanese: 来（く）る (*to come*) and する (*to do*). In this textbook these irregular verbs are called *Class 3* verbs. You will have to memorize the conjugation of these verbs individually. All compound verbs with する belong to Class 3: 勉強（べんきょう）する (*to study*), 運動 （うんどう）する (*to exercise*), 電話 （でんわ）する (*to call*), and so on.

> **Y**ou will learn more about these compound verbs with する (called nominal verbs) later on.

Here are how some common verbs are classified.

CLASS **1** VERBS		CLASS **2** VERBS		CLASS **3** VERBS	
洗う （あら）	to wash	食べる （た）	to eat	する	to do
行く （い）	to go	起きる （お）	to get up	来る （く）	to come
聞く （き）	to listen	出かける （で）	to go out		
話す （はな）	to speak	出る （で）	to leave		
飲む （の）	to drink	変える （か）	to change		
働く （はたら）	to work	見る （み）	to see; watch		
休む （やす）	to take a rest	着る （き）	to wear; put on		
乗る （の）	to ride				

11.2 The three primary meanings expressed in every Japanese verb form are tense, politeness, and affirmation/negation.

There are two basic tenses in Japanese: *past* and *nonpast.* The past tense is used to express past actions and events (*I played baseball, he remained in the hospital,* etc.). The nonpast tense is used to express present, habitual, and future actions and events (*I get up at 6:00 every morning, I will go to school later, I'm going to study tomorrow,* etc.).

> **J**apanese verbs do not conjugate in terms of the person and number of the subject.

Japanese verbs also take different forms depending on the degree of politeness the speaker or writer wishes to show the listener or reader. As you learned in Chapter 2, the *plain form* is used when speakers address very familiar people on the same social level, such as close friends. It is also used in diaries and in newspaper articles. And as you will see later, verbs in certain positions in a sentence must be in the plain form. On the other hand, the *polite form* is used, for instance, to address people with whom one is not well acquainted or to speak impersonally with in-group people (such as one's superior). In addition, it is used to address most out-group people, in personal letters, TV news, and most public speeches. The polite form is the appropriate speech register among adult speakers who are getting to know each other.

In Japanese, verbs take different endings depending on whether they are *affirmative* or *negative.*

In addition, different grammatical elements are added to the end of verb forms to express such meanings as ability and probability. The resultant forms consisting of verbs and grammatical elements also conjugate in terms of the three primary meanings.

11.3 The dictionary form of Japanese verbs is actually the *nonpast, plain, affirmative form;* for example, 書(か)く (*to write*) and 食(た)べる (*to eat*). When you look up a verb in the dictionary, this is the form you will find. The plain form can be considered a basis for conjugating the polite form.

    The nonpast, plain, negative form is made as follows.

CLASS 1 VERBS

Root + the **a**-column **hiragana** corresponding to the dictionary form ending + ない

Dictionary Form Root + Ending	Nonpast, Plain, Negative Form
書(か) + く	書(か) + か + ない
話(はな) + す	話(はな) + さ + ない
立(た) + つ	立(た) + た + ない
読(よ) + む	読(よ) + ま + ない
泳(およ) + ぐ	泳(およ) + が + ない

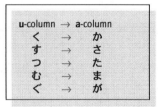

u-column	→	a-column
く	→	か
す	→	さ
つ	→	た
む	→	ま
ぐ	→	が

When the dictionary form ending of a Class 1 verb is う—for example, 洗(あら)う (*to wash*), 買(か)う (*to buy*) —わ is inserted between the root and ない to form the nonpast, plain, negative.

Dictionary Form Root + Ending	Nonpast, Plain, Negative Form
洗(あら) + う	洗(あら) + わ + ない
買(か) + う	買(か) + わ + ない

Although such verbs as 切(き)る (*to cut*), 知(し)る (*to know*), 帰(かえ)る (*to go back*), 走(はし)る (*to run*), and 入(はい)る (*to enter*) look like Class 2 verbs and satisfy the (not foolproof) rule for identifying Class 2 verbs, they belong to Class 1 and conjugate as such. Thus, their nonpast, plain, negative form is made following the same rule presented above. Note that their -ます forms all end in -ります。

Dictionary Form Root + Ending	Nonpast, Plain, Negative Form
切(き) + る	切(き) + ら + ない
知(し) + る	知(し) + ら + ない
帰(かえ) + る	帰(かえ) + ら + ない
走(はし) + る	走(はし) + ら + ない
入(はい) + る	入(はい) + ら + ない

Note that the nonpast, plain, negative form of **ある** (*to exist*) (see **Grammar 6,** Chapter 2) is simply **ない**. **ない** is an **i**-adjective representing negativity.

CLASS 2 VERBS

Root ＋ **ない**

Dictionary Form Root ＋ Ending	Nonpast, Plain, Negative Form
食^たべ ＋ る 見^み ＋ る 着^き ＋ る	食^たべ ＋ ない 見^み ＋ ない 着^き ＋ ない

CLASS 3 VERBS

Dictionary Form	Nonpast, Plain, Negative Form
する 来^くる	し ＋ ない 来^こ ＋ ない

アクティビティー 5

よく見^みてください。(*Please look carefully.*)

Are these verbs Class 1, Class 2, or Class 3? Each is cited in its dictionary form.

> **Y**ou are not expected to learn all of these verbs now. Just concentrate on their forms for the time being.

ある *to exist*

いる *to exist*

できる *to be able to do*

使^{つか}う *to use*

作^{つく}る *to make*

笑^{わら}う *to laugh*

歩^{ある}く *to walk*

走^{はし}る *to run*

踊^{おど}る *to dance*

歌^{うた}う *to sing*

泳^{およ}ぐ *to swim*

待^まつ *to wait*

泣^なく *to cry*

教^{おし}える *to teach*

見^みせる *to show*

休^{やす}む *to take a rest*

料^{りょう}理^りする *to cook*

飛^とぶ *to fly*

考^{かんが}える *to think*

会^あう *to meet*

住^すむ *to live*

わかる *to understand*

やめる *to quit*

アクティビティー 6

<ruby>林<rt>はやし</rt></ruby> さんは<ruby>起<rt>お</rt></ruby>きない。(*Hayashi-san won't get up.*)

Write the nonpast, plain, negative form of these verbs. Use **hiragana** for **kanji** you have not yet studied.

<ruby>起<rt>お</rt></ruby>きる *to get up*

<ruby>食<rt>た</rt></ruby>べる *to eat*

みがく *to brush* (*teeth*)

<ruby>洗<rt>あら</rt></ruby>う *to wash*

<ruby>出<rt>で</rt></ruby>かける *to go out*

<ruby>行<rt>い</rt></ruby>く *to go*

<ruby>飲<rt>の</rt></ruby>む *to drink*

<ruby>勉<rt>べん</rt></ruby><ruby>強<rt>きょう</rt></ruby>する *to study*

<ruby>見<rt>み</rt></ruby>る *to see*

<ruby>寝<rt>ね</rt></ruby>る *to go to bed*

<ruby>着<rt>き</rt></ruby>る *to put on* (*clothes*)

<ruby>浴<rt>あ</rt></ruby>びる *to take* (*a shower*)

<ruby>入<rt>はい</rt></ruby>る *to enter*

<ruby>言<rt>い</rt></ruby>う *to say*

<ruby>歌<rt>うた</rt></ruby>う *to sing*

いる *to exist*

<ruby>使<rt>つか</rt></ruby>う *to use*

<ruby>話<rt>はな</rt></ruby>す *to speak*

<ruby>乗<rt>の</rt></ruby>る *to ride*

<ruby>働<rt>はたら</rt></ruby>く *to work*

<ruby>休<rt>やす</rt></ruby>む *to rest*

<ruby>眠<rt>ねむ</rt></ruby>る *to sleep*

<ruby>会<rt>あ</rt></ruby>う *to meet*

<ruby>洗濯<rt>せんたく</rt></ruby>する *to do laundry*

<ruby>死<rt>し</rt></ruby>ぬ *to die*

とかす *to comb*

> **O**nce again, you do not have to memorize all of these verbs.

Vocabulary and Grammar 3B

Vocabulary and Oral Activities
Daily Activities

Vocabulary: Everyday Activities 1 🎧

夕ごはんを食べる	ゆうごはんをたべる	to eat dinner, supper
出かける	でかける	to step out; to leave for
買い物に出かける	かいものにでかける	to go out shopping

Review: <ruby>朝<rt>あさ</rt></ruby>ごはん（<ruby>昼<rt>ひる</rt></ruby>ごはん、<ruby>晩<rt>ばん</rt></ruby>ごはん）を<ruby>食<rt>た</rt></ruby>べる、テレビを<ruby>見<rt>み</rt></ruby>る、コーヒーを<ruby>飲<rt>の</rt></ruby>む、<ruby>仕事<rt>しごと</rt></ruby>をする

> <ruby>晩<rt>ばん</rt></ruby>ごはん, which you studied in **Getting Started**, and 夕ごはん are identical in meaning.

1. 起きる

2. 寝る

3. 新聞を読む

4. 昼ごはんを食べる

5. お茶を飲む

6. 勉強する

 アクティビティー **7**

ダイアログ：毎日何時に起きますか。(*What time do you get up every day?*)

カワムラさんと町田さんが話しています。

カワムラ：町田さんは、毎日何時に起きますか。
町田：5時です。
カワムラ：わあ、はやいですね。
町田：ええ、5時半から6時までジョギングをします。

With a classmate, practice the dialogue, substituting various activities from the vocabulary and the six illustrations above. Choose new times suitable for each activity.

Mr. Kawamura and Ms. Machida are talking.   KAWAMURA: What time do you get up every day, (Ms. Machida)?   MACHIDA: I get up at 5:00.   KAWAMURA: Wow, that's early!   MACHIDA: Yes, I go jogging from 5:30 to 6:00.

言語ノート

Expressions of Surprise

Here are some common ways to express surprise.

わあ。	Wow!
本当（ですか）。	Really? (*lit.*, Is that true?)
うそ。	You're kidding. (*lit.*, That's a lie.) (frequently used by young women; very colloquial)
まさか。	Impossible! That can't be! No way!
何ですって。	What! (*lit.*, What did you say?)
信じられない。	Incredible! (*lit.*, I can't believe it.)

Grammar and Practice Activities

12. The Nonpast, Polite Form of Verbs

ブラウン：三村さんは毎日何時に起きますか。

三村：六時半に起きます。

ブラウン：毎日 朝ごはんを食べますか。

三村：いいえ、朝ごはんは食べません。

ブラウン：なぜですか。

三村：朝は時間がありませんから...

チン：明日のパーティーに行きますか。

町田：いいえ、行きません。

チン：なぜですか。

町田：夜、友だちが来ますから...

The nonpast, polite, affirmative and negative form of Class 1 and Class 2 verbs are made as follows.

BROWN: What time do you get up every day?　MIMURA: I get up at 6:30.　BROWN: Do you eat breakfast every day?　MIMURA: No, I don't eat breakfast. BROWN: Why not?　MIMURA: Because I don't have time in the morning.

CHIN: Are you going to tomorrow's party?　MACHIDA: No, I'm not going.　CHIN: Why not?
MACHIDA: Because I have friends coming over (lit., *Because friends are coming*) in the evening.

CLASS 1 VERBS

Take the last hiragana of the dictionary form and change it to its corresponding **-i** syllable. This gives you the conjunctive form. Then add ます for the affirmative or ません for the negative.

EXAMPLE:

わかる *understand*
Change the る to り: わかり
Add ます: わかります
　　　ません: わかりません

Other Class 1 verbs follow the same pattern.

Dictionary Form Root + Ending	Affirmative Form	Negative Form
洗^{あら} ＋ う	洗 ＋ い ＋ ます	洗 ＋ い ＋ ません
書^か ＋ く	書 ＋ き ＋ ます	書 ＋ き ＋ ません
話^{はな} ＋ す	話 ＋ し ＋ ます	話 ＋ し ＋ ません
立^た ＋ つ	立 ＋ ち ＋ ます	立 ＋ ち ＋ ません
読^よ ＋ む	読 ＋ み ＋ ます	読 ＋ み ＋ ません
あ ＋ る	あ ＋ り ＋ ます	あ ＋ り ＋ ません
泳^{およ} ＋ ぐ	泳 ＋ ぎ ＋ ます	泳 ＋ ぎ ＋ ません

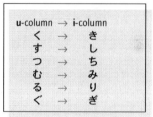

u-column	→	i-column
く	→	き
す	→	し
つ	→	ち
む	→	み
る	→	り
ぐ	→	ぎ

CLASS 2 VERBS

Take the る off the plain form. This gives you the conjunctive form. Then add ます for the affirmative or ません for the negative.

Dictionary Form Root + Ending	Affirmative Form	Negative Form
食^たべ ＋ る	食べ ＋ ます	食べ ＋ ません
見^み ＋ る	見 ＋ ます	見 ＋ ません
着^き ＋ る	着 ＋ ます	着 ＋ ません

CLASS 3 VERBS

Dictionary Form	Affirmative Form	Negative Form
する	し ＋ ます	し ＋ ません
来^くる	来^き ＋ ます	来^き ＋ ません

(*Continues.*)

To summarize, the nonpast, polite, affirmative and negative forms of verbs are formed by adding ます and ません to the conjunctive form.

言語ノート

送り仮名(おくりがな)

Most verbs and adjectives are written in a combination of **kanji** and **hiragana**. Usually the **kanji** in a word represents the root, and the **hiragana** represent the grammatical endings, although there may be some overlap, especially in Class 2 verbs. The **hiragana** used to write the endings are called **okurigana** ("send-off" kana).

Here are some examples of verbs and adjectives with **okurigana**.

大_{おお}きい　　　　　　大きくないです

食_たべます　　　　　　食べません

Always memorize the **kun** reading of a **kanji** with the **okurigana** of its dictionary form. If you memorize 見 simply as み, you risk getting it mixed up with all the other **kanji** that are pronounced that way.

アクティビティー 8

わかります、わかりません *(understand, don't understand)*

Write the nonpast, formal, affirmative and negative forms of these verbs.

1.	起きる	*to get up*	12.	会う	*to meet*
2.	洗う	*to wash*	13.	見る	*to see*
3.	みがく	*to brush* (teeth)	14.	泳ぐ	*to swim*
4.	走る	*to run*	15.	する	*to do*
5.	食べる	*to eat*	16.	帰る	*to return*
6.	飲む	*to drink*	17.	休む	*to rest*
7.	出かける	*to go out*	18.	入る	*to enter*
8.	待つ	*to wait*	19.	読む	*to read*
9.	行く	*to go*	20.	寝る	*to sleep*
10.	乗る	*to ride*	21.	来る	*to come*
11.	着く	*to arrive*	22.	話す	*to speak*

アクティビティー 9

スミスさんは来ません。(*Mr. Smith isn't coming.*)

Transform plain verbs into polite verbs and vice versa.

[例] チンさんは毎日6時に起きる。→
　　　チンさんは毎日6時に起きます。

1. ビールを飲みます。
2. 明日、ロサンゼルスへ行く。
3. 今日の午後、山田さんに会います。
4. ブラウンさんは来週、アメリカから帰る。
5. 毎日、運動します。
6. あなたは何を食べるか。
7. パーティーへ来るか。
8. わたしはテレビを見ない。
9. 町田さんを待ちますか。
10. シュミットさんは日本語を話さない。

アクティビティー 10

まりこさんは大学へ行きます。(*Mariko is going to the university.*)

Make sentences using the words provided. (Change the verbs to their polite forms.)

[例] (6時)(毎日)(起きる) → わたしは毎日6時に起きます。

1. (7時)(いつも)(朝ごはんを食べる)
2. (7時半)(毎朝)(大学へ行く)
3. (8時)(毎日)(クラスが始まる)
4. (12時)(毎日)(昼ごはんを食べる)
5. (3時)(いつも)(クラスが終わる)
6. (4時)(毎日)(図書館へ行く)
7. (5時)(いつも)(大学から帰る)
8. (6時)(毎日)(夕ごはんを食べる)
9. (7時)(いつも)(テレビを見る)

Useful words: 始まる *begin*, 終わる *end*

(*Continues.*)

10. (9時)(毎日)(日本語を勉強する)
11. (11時)(毎晩)(寝る)

アクティビティー **11**

いいえ、食べません。(*No, we won't eat.*)

Make dialogues following the example.

[例]（明日）（大学へ行く）（いいえ）→
　　—明日大学へ行きますか。
　　—いいえ、行きません。

1. (毎朝)(運動する)(いいえ)
2. (いつも)(コーヒーを飲む)(はい)
3. (よく)(町田さんに会う)(はい)
4. (毎日)(テレビを見る)(いいえ)
5. (毎晩)(レストランで食べる)(いいえ)

アクティビティー **12**

毎晩早く寝ます。(*I go to sleep early every night.*)

Complete the following sentences. Your sentences must include the polite form of a verb.

[例]　毎朝6時に... → 毎朝6時にシャワーを浴びます。

1. 日曜日の朝...
2. 毎日午前8時に...
3. わたしは毎日...
4. 日本語のクラスは...
5. わたしとガールフレンドはいつも...
6. わたしは来週の月曜日...
7. 土曜日の午後...
8. わたしは来年...

アクティビティー **13**

今日はクラスに行きません。(*I'm not going to class today.*)

Rewrite the following paragraph, substituting polite verb forms.

Useful Vocabulary: 始^{はじ}まる *to start,* 終^おわる *to finish*

わたしは毎日^{まいにち}午前^{ごぜん}五時^じに起^おきる。それから、家^{いえ}の回^{まわ}りを散歩^{さんぽ}する。午前^{ごぜん}六時^じにコーヒーを飲^のむ。朝^{あさ}ごはんは食^たべない。午前^{ごぜん}七時^じに家^{いえ}を出^でる。午前^{ごぜん}七時^じのバスに乗^のる。午前^{ごぜん}八時^じに大学^{だいがく}のクラスが始^{はじ}まる。十二時にカフェテリアで昼^{ひる}ごはんを食^たべる。午後^{ごご}一時^じにクラスへ行^いく。クラスは午後^{ごご}三時^じに終^おわる。わたしの友^{とも}だちは図書館^{としょかん}へ行^いく。でも、わたしは行^いかない。午後^{ごご}四時^じに家^{いえ}に帰^{かえ}る。それから、六時^じまで勉強^{べんきょう}する。六時^じに夕^{ゆう}ごはんを食^たべる。そのあと、テレビを見^みる。午後^{ごご}十時^じにいつも寝^ねる。

アクティビティー **14**

カワムラさんのスケジュール　(*Mr. Kawamura's schedule*)

Use the table to answer the questions that follow it.

JOHN KAWAMURA'S DAILY SCHEDULE	
6:00	get up
6:30	breakfast
8:30	Japanese class
12:00	lunch
1:30	study at the library
3:00	coffee break
4:00	return home
until 6:00	read (books)
6:15	dinner
7:00	watch TV
9:00	study Japanese
11:45	go to bed

1. カワムラさんは午前何時^{ごぜんなんじ}に起^おきますか。
2. 午前^{ごぜん}6時半^{じはん}に何^{なん}をしますか。
3. 何時^{なんじ}に昼^{ひる}ごはんを食^たべますか。
4. 午後^{ごご}1時半^{じはん}に何^{なに}をしますか。
5. 何時^{なんじ}にコーヒーを飲^のみますか。
6. 何時^{なんじ}に家^{いえ}へ帰^{かえ}りますか。
7. 何時^{なんじ}に夕^{ゆう}ごはんを食^たべますか。

(*Continues.*)

8. 午後7時から9時まで何をしますか。

9. 午後9時から何を勉強しますか。

10. カワムラさんは何時に寝ますか。、

11. カワムラさんは何時間 (*how many hours*) ぐらい寝ますか。

アクティビティー **15**

ダイアログ：そのあとは。(*What about after that?*)

林さんとギブソンさんが話しています。

林：ギブソンさん、今日の午後は忙しいですか。

ギブソン：ええ、とても。1時に日本語のクラスがあります。
それから、図書館で勉強します。

林：じゃあ、そのあとは。

ギブソン：そのあと、友だちに会います。

林：そうですか。

Describe Mr. Kawamura's schedule from アクティビティー 14 using the conjunctions presented in the following **Language Note.**

言語ノート

Connecting Sequential Actions

Here are some conjunctions commonly used to connect sentences expressing sequential actions or events.

それから	and then... (*lit.,* from that)
そして	and (then)... (*lit.,* so doing)
そのあと	after that...

7時に朝ごはんを食べます。それから、新聞を読みます。

I eat breakfast at 7:00. And then I read the newspaper.

図書館に行きました。そして、本を読みました。

I went to the library. And (then) I read some books.

レストランで夕ごはんを食べます。そのあと、映画を見ます。それから、ディスコへ行きます。

**I'll eat dinner at a restaurant. After that, I'll see a movie.
And then, I'll go to a disco.**

Mr. Hayashi and Ms. Gibson are talking   HAYASHI: Ms. Gibson, are you busy this afternoon? GIBSON: Yes, very. I have a Japanese class at one o'clock. And then I'm going to study at the library.   HAYASHI: Well, how about after that?   GIBSON: After that, I'm meeting a friend. HAYASHI: I see.

> The verb 会う *to meet with, see* (a person) takes the particle に or と to indicate the person met.

アクティビティー 16

あなたのスケジュールは。(*What about your schedule?*)

Working in pairs, ask your partner questions about his or her daily
schedule. Use the answers you get to write a schedule.

[例]　s1: 何時に起きますか。

　　　s2: ＿＿＿時に起きます。

　　　s1: それから、何をしますか。

　　　s2: ＿＿＿。

Vocabulary: Everyday Activities 2

シャワーを浴びる	シャワーをあびる	to take a shower
うちを出る	うちをでる	to leave home
(お)風呂に入る	(お)ふろにはいる	to take (lit., *enter*) a bath
歯を磨く	はをみがく	to brush one's teeth
顔を洗う	かおをあらう	to wash one's face
服を着る	ふくをきる	to put on clothes
～に乗る	～にのる	to ride or get on… (*a vehicle—train, bus, car, etc.*)
働く	はたらく	to work
休む	やすむ	to take a rest; to take time off

Review: 電話 (を)する、買い物 (を)する

寝坊する

料理する

音楽を聞く

運動する

百九十五

13. The Past, Polite Form of Verbs 🎧

林：昨日は何時に家に帰りましたか。

ブラウン：午後6時ごろです。

林：夕ごはんに何を食べましたか。

ブラウン：ステーキを食べました。

ブラウン：今何時ですか。

チン：10時15分です。

ブラウン：もうカワムラさんに電話をしましたか。

チン：いいえ、まだです。10時半にかけます。

The past, polite forms of verbs are formed as follows.

Affirmative   the conjunctive form ＋ました
Negative   the conjunctive form ＋ませんでした

Dictionary Form	Conjunctive Form	Past, Polite, Affirmative Form	Past, Polite, Negative Form
Class 1 Verbs 洗う 立つ	洗い 立ち	洗いました 立ちました	洗いませんでした 立ちませんでした
Class 2 Verbs 食べる 見る	食べ 見	食べました 見ました	食べませんでした 見ませんでした
Class 3 Verbs する 来る	し 来	しました 来ました	しませんでした 来ませんでした

HAYASHI: What time did you return home yesterday?   BROWN: About 6:00 P.M.
HAYASHI: What did you eat for dinner?   BROWN: I ate steak.

BROWN: What time is it now?   CHIN: It's 10:15.   BROWN: Have you already called Mr. Kawamura?   CHIN: No, not yet. I'll call him at 10:30.

アクティビティー **17** 🎧 💬

ダイアログ：寝坊しました。(*I overslept.*)

ブラウンさんと林さんが話しています。

ブラウン：今日は日本文化のクラスへ行きましたか。

林 ：ええ。ブラウンさん、クラスに来ませんでしたね。

ブラウン：ええ、今朝、寝坊しました。

林 ：そうですか。

アクティビティー **18**

たくさん書きました。(*I wrote a lot.*)

Write the affirmative and negative past, polite forms of the verbs listed in
アクティビティー 8.

アクティビティー **19**

ビールを飲みましたか。(*Did you drink beer?*)

Give affirmative and negative answers to the following questions.

[例]　昨日、ビールを飲みましたか。→
　　　はい、飲みました。
　　　いいえ、飲みませんでした。

1. 先週、映画を見ましたか。
2. 昨日、日本語を勉強しましたか。
3. おととい、本を読みましたか。
4. 昨日はうちにいましたか。
5. 今日、朝ごはんを食べましたか。
6. 昨日、日本語のクラスがありましたか。
7. 去年、高田さんはアメリカへ行きましたか。
8. 昨日、たくさんテレビを見ましたか。
9. おととい、スポーツをしましたか。
10. 昨日、お風呂に入りましたか。

Ms. Brown and Mr. Hayashi are talking　BROWN: Did you go to Japanese culture class today?
HAYASHI: Yes. You weren't in class, were you?　BROWN: No. I overslept this morning.
HAYASHI: I see.

<u>アクティビティー</u> **20**

何時に学校から帰りましたか。(*What time did you come home from the university?*)

Make dialogues following the example. Use the past, polite form of verbs.

[例]　(起きる) → —(*partner's name*) は昨日何時に起きましたか。

　　　　　　　　—6時に起きました。

Useful words:　お茶 *tea,* 手紙 *letter*

　1.（朝ごはんを食べる）
　2.（学校へ行く）
　3.（お茶を飲む）
　4.（図書館で勉強する）
　5.（散歩をする）
　6.（電話をかける）
　7.（音楽を聞く）
　8.（友だちと話す）
　9.（手紙を書く）
　10.（寝る）

<u>アクティビティー</u> **21**

4時半にコーヒーを飲みました。(*I drank coffee at 4:30.*)

Make up dialogues based on the example below.

[例]　get up, 5:30 → —昨日何時に起きましたか。

　　　　　　　　— 5時半に起きました。

1. get up, 5:30	9. go to the library, 1:20
2. go jogging, 6:00	10. exercise, 3:40
3. eat breakfast, 6:30	11. go home, 5:30
4. leave home, 7:00	12. watch TV, 6:00
5. board a train, 7:15	13. eat dinner, 7:15
6. go to class, 8:00	14. study Japanese, 8:45
7. eat lunch, 12:20	15. listen to music, 10:40
8. drink coffee, 1:00	16. go to bed, 11:30

アクティビティー 22

昨日は何をしましたか。(*What did you do yesterday?*)

Complete these sentences. Use the past, polite form of verbs.

1. わたしは去年...
2. 田中さんは昨日の夜...
3. わたしと山口さんは先週、...
4. 昨日は...
5. 今日の朝、...

6. 先週の土曜日、...
7. いつもうちで...
8. 昨日、6時から10時まで...
9. うちの前に...
10. 大学からうちまで...

アクティビティー 23

林 さんのスケジュール　(*Mr. Hayashi's schedule*)

Here is what Mr. Hayashi did yesterday. Describe his day in Japanese, or ask your classmates about his schedule.

Useful word: 法学 (*study of*) *law*

6:00	got up	1:00	studied at the library
6:15	took a shower	3:00	exercised
6:30	drank coffee	5:00	returned home
6:35	read the newspaper	6:00	cooked dinner
6:45	ate breakfast	7:30	ate dinner
7:15	watched TV	8:30	called a friend
8:00	left home	9:00	listened to the stereo
9:00	went to his English class	9:30	studied law
10:30	went to his law class	10:30	took a bath
12:00	ate lunch with classmates	11:00	went to bed

アクティビティー 24

昨日____しましたか。(*Did you do _____ yesterday?*)

Ask a classmate if he or she did the following yesterday. If the answer is yes, ask related questions such as *What time did you do that?*

1. oversleep
2. take a shower
3. drink tea
4. exercise

5. read the newspaper
6. call a friend
7. listen to music
8. take a bath

9. go to a library
10. watch TV

Vocabulary: Expressions of Frequency

〜回	〜かい	...times (*counter for occurrences*)
A に B 回	A に B かい	B times per A
一日に何回	いちにちになんかい	how many times a day
一週間に二回	いっしゅうかんににかい	two times a week
一ヶ月に四回	いっかげつによんかい	four times a month
毎日	まいにち	every day
毎週	まいしゅう	every week
毎月	まいつき	every month
毎朝	まいあさ	every morning
毎晩	まいばん	every night
いつも		all the time
よく		often, a lot
時々	ときどき	sometimes
たまに		once in a while
あまり		(*with negative*) not very much; not very often
ほとんど		(*with negative*) hardly; almost never
全然	ぜんぜん	(*with negative*) not at all

> ...週間 and ...ヶ月 are counters for the duration of weeks and months, respectively.

> The **kanji** 々 is used to repeat the preceding **kanji**.

アクティビティー **25**

ダイアログ：一日に三回歯を磨きます。(*I brush my teeth three times a day.*)
林さんとブラウンさんが話しています。

　　　林：ブラウンさんは歯がきれいですね。
ブラウン：一日に三回磨きます。林さんは。
　　　林：あまり磨きません。
ブラウン：一日に一回ですか。
　　　林：いいえ、一週間に一回です。
ブラウン：うそ！

Mr. Hayashi and Ms. Brown are talking.　HAYASHI: Ms. Brown, you have such nice teeth (lit., *your teeth are pretty, aren't they*).　BROWN: I brush them three times a day. How about you?　HAYASHI: I don't brush them much.　BROWN: Do you mean (lit., *is it*) once a day? HAYASHI: No, once a week.　BROWN: You're kidding!

言語ノート

Adverbs Used in Negative Sentences

Some adverbs are used primarily in negative sentences. Two examples are あまり (*not very much, not very often*) and 全然 (*not at all*).

わたしはあまり映画へ行きません。

I don't go to the movies very often.

わたしの父は全然テレビを見ません。

My father doesn't watch TV at all.

ほとんど can be used in affirmative or negative sentences, but its meaning changes in these different contexts. In the affirmative it means *almost*, while in the negative it means *almost never* or *hardly ever.*

山田さんはほとんど毎日シャワーを浴びます。

Mr. Yamada takes a shower almost every day.

山田さんはほとんどお風呂に入りません。

Mr. Yamada hardly ever takes a bath.

VOCABULARY LIBRARY

Everyday Activities 3

髪をとかす	かみをとかす	to comb one's hair
ひげをそる		to shave one's facial hair (lit., *beard*)
服を脱ぐ	ふくをぬぐ	to take off clothes
服を着替える	ふくをきがえる	to change clothes
運転（を）する	うんてん（を）する	to drive (*vehicles*)
散歩（を）する	さんぽ（を）する	to take a walk, stroll
洗濯（を）する	せんたく（を）する	to do laundry
掃除（を）する	そうじ（を）する	to clean (*house, a room, etc.*)
眠る	ねむる	to fall asleep

アクティビティー 26

よくしますか。(*Do you do that often?*)

Tell how often you do the following, selecting from the following degrees of frequency (ordered from most frequent to least frequent).

1 = 毎日	3 = よく	5 = あまりしない
2 = ほとんど毎日	4 = 時々	6 = 全然しない

(*Continues.*)

二百一

a. 歯を磨く

b. シャワーを浴びる

c. お風呂に入る

d. 朝ごはんを食べる

e. コーヒーを飲む

f. 部屋 (*room*) を掃除する

g. 料理をする

h. 買い物をする

i. 新聞を読む

j. 映画を見る

k. ラジオを聞く

l. テレビを見る

m. お酒を飲む

n. 運動する

o. デートをする

p. 勉強する

q. 電話する

14. Particles Showing Grammatical Relationships

In Japanese, the grammatical roles of some words in a sentence—subject, direct object, and so on—are identified by particles, also known as postpositions. These short words indicate the grammatical function of the word or phrase preceding them. They are a key element of Japanese grammar.

The following explanation provides an overview of various particles. It is not a complete explanation by any means, but it should give you a good idea of why you have been using certain particles in particular situations, and prepare you for new usages you will encounter from now on.

14.1 が and は were explained briefly in Chapter 1. が is a *subject particle*. It marks a word or phrase that is the subject of a sentence. は (pronounced **wa**) is called the *topic particle* because it is often used to mark a word or phrase that tells what the sentence is about.

Because topics and subjects are sometimes hard to distinguish, in many cases either は or が would be grammatically acceptable, though not interchangeable. For example

1. わたしはアメリカ人です。   *I am American.*

2. わたしがアメリカ人です。   *I am American.*

Both sentences are grammatically correct. However, if someone asks だれが アメリカ人ですか (*Who is American?*) sentence 2 is the only appropriate answer. On the other hand, if you were introducing yourself, sentence 1 is the only appropriate answer. You will learn the use of and differences between は and が as you progress through this textbook. For now, it may help to think of は as being used to introduce a general topic (as in 1.) or to refer to a topic already in discussion, whereas が shifts emphasis to the subject it follows (***I** am American*).

14.2 The particle を has several uses.

1. を marks (follows) a direct object. (A direct object is something or someone directly affected by the action of a verb.) The direct objects are underlined in the following examples.

わたしは<u>朝ごはん</u>を食べます。
I will eat <u>breakfast</u>.

> **Y**ou do not have to memorize the uses of all the particles presented here at this time. You will learn them gradually as you work through this textbook.

昨日スーパーでコーラを買いました。
I bought <u>cola</u> at the supermarket yesterday.

何を着ますか。
<u>What</u> are you going to wear?

Caution: Just because a word is a direct object in an English sentence doesn't mean its counterpart in the Japanese equivalent is also a direct object. Many Japanese verbs require に (*to*) where you might expect を. Here are some constructions to watch out for.

バスに乗りました。
I rode <u>a bus</u>. (lit., I got onto a bus.)

ブラウンさんは高田さんに会いました。
Ms. Brown met <u>Mr. Takada</u>.

日本が好きです。
I like <u>Japan</u>.

パーティーに出ました。
I attended <u>the party</u>.

2. を is also used to indicate a place or object from which something or someone leaves. In this usage, it carries the sense of *from* or *out of*.

午前8時に家を出ます。
I leave home at 8:00 A.M.

3. を is further used to indicate a place that something moves over, along, or through.

橋を渡りました。
I crossed the bridge.

道を歩きます。
I walk down the street.

14.3 に is one of the most versatile particles. Here are some of its many uses.

1. Point in time (*at, on, in*)

カワムラさんは7時に朝ごはんを食べます。
Mr. Kawamura eats breakfast at seven o'clock.

月曜日にロサンゼルスへ行きました。
I went to Los Angeles on Monday.

1975年に生まれました。
I was born in 1975.

Only time words with a specific name or number (Tuesday, October 31, six o'clock, etc.) take に. Words indicating relative time (today,

(Continues.)

tomorrow, next year) and those indicating duration (thirty minutes, five days) do not take に.

ギブソンさんは今日、東京へ来ます。
Ms. Gibson will come to Tokyo underline{today}.

来週忙しいです。
I will be busy underline{next week}.

毎日、ジョギングします。
I jog underline{every day}.

2. Location or existence

そこに銀行があります。
There is a bank there (lit., *in that place*).

高田さんはどこにいますか。
Where is Mr. Takada?

3. Purpose (*for, in order to*) when the verb is 行く or 来る.

昨日デパートへ買い物に行きました。
Yesterday I went shopping at the department store. (lit., *Yesterday I went to the department store for shopping.*)

4. Direction of an action

山口さんは毎日 お風呂に入ります。
Mr. Yamaguchi takes a bath every day. (lit., *Mr. Yamaguchi enters a bath every day.*)

林さんは8時の電車に乗りました。
Mr. Hayashi got on the eight o'clock train.

14.4 The particle へ also marks the direction toward which an action moves. While に marks movement toward a specific place, へ indicates motion in a general direction. However, the difference is unimportant in many cases, and the two particles are often interchangeable. Unlike に, へ is not used with time words or to indicate location.

明日 京都へ行きます。	*I will go to Kyoto tomorrow.*
チンさんはここへ来ますか。	*Is Ms. Chin coming here?*
いつ家へ帰りますか。	*When will you return home?*

14.5 で has three major uses. で marks the location where an action takes place.

カーティスさんはいつもここで昼ごはんを食べます。
Mr. Curtis always eats lunch here.

図書館で勉強します。
I will study at the library.

It also marks the instrument used to carry out an action.

ナイフでりんごを切りました。 *I cut the apple with a knife.*

電車で学校へ来ます。 *I come to school by train.*

The particle で also marks the reason or cause of an action. This usage corresponds to the English *because of* or *for*. You will use it later on.

昨日、病気で学校を休みました。
Yesterday I was absent from school because of illness.

今、ビジネスでロサンゼルスにいます。
I am in Los Angeles now for business.

14.6 The particle から (*from*) is used to express the starting point in space or time of an action, and the particle まで (*[up] to, until*) is used to represent its ending point.

東京から京都まで新幹線で行きます。
I will go from Tokyo to Kyoto via Shinkansen (the bullet train).

わたしは1時から3時まで図書館にいます。
I will be at the library from 1:00 to 3:00.

14.7 In Getting Started and Chapter 1, you learned that the particle も means *too* or *as much as*. When placed after a regular noun or pronoun, it usually means *too*. Be careful where you place も, because you can change the meaning of the sentence. In Chapter 5 we will see how it is used to mean *as much (many) as* and *both*.

わたしもアイスクリームが好きです。
I also like ice cream (in addition to someone else).

わたしはアイスクリームも好きです。
I also like ice cream (in addition to something else).

去年、ローマへも行きました。
Last year, I went to Rome too (in addition to some other place).

アメリカからも学生が来ました。
Students came from the United States, too.

When this particle is used in the subject or direct object position, it replaces は, が, or を. But it follows other particles, resulting in such combinations as にも, からも, までも, でも, and へも.

その本は図書館にあります。 *That book is at the library.*

その本はわたしのうちにもあります。 *That book is at my home too.*

デパートへ行きます。 *I will go to a department store.*

スーパーへも行きます。 *I will go to a supermarket too.*

(*Continues.*)

Here is a summary of these combinations and replacements of particles.

が → も
は → も
を → も
に → にも
へ → へも
で → でも

14.8 The particle と means *together with.*

ブラウンさんと映画へ行きました。
I went to the movies with Ms. Brown.

三村さんと会いましたか。
Did you meet with Mr. Mimura?

As you have already studied, this particle is also used to connect two or more nouns or pronouns in the sense of *and.*

アイスクリームとチョコレートが好きです。
I like ice cream and chocolate.

Remember: You cannot use と to connect adjectives, adverbs, verbs, or sentences.

14.9 Japanese is sometimes called a "word order-free" language because its word order is not so strictly fixed as in English. A verb or a predicate comes in the sentence-final position, but other elements can be ordered more freely. This is possible because particles indicate the grammatical function of a word or a phrase. Therefore, even if you move a word or a phrase around, as long as it is followed by a particle you can tell its grammatical function. In English, however, the grammatical function of a word or phrase is often determined by word order.

Nevertheless, a natural word order does exist in Japanese, as shown here.

N は／が (time) (place) (indirect object) (direct object) V

わたしは明日ロサンゼルスから東京へ発ちます。
I will leave Los Angeles for Tokyo tomorrow.

わたしの妹は明日、デパートでくつを買います。
My sister will buy shoes at a department store tomorrow.

アクティビティー 27

机 の上に何がありますか。(*What's on the desk?*)

Fill in the blanks.

[例] 7時(に)起きます。

1. 机 (　　) 上 (　　) 本があります。

2. テレビ (　　) 見ます。

3. 毎晩、8時 (　　) 家 (　　) 帰ります。

4. 時々、ラジオ (　　) 音楽(*music*) (　　) 聞きます。

5. 来週東京 (　　) 行きます。東京 (　　) ブラウンさん (　　) 会います。
　来月東京 (　　) 帰ります。

6. そのアメリカ人はフォーク (　　) てんぷらを食べました。

7. わたしはうち (　　) 大学 (　　) 電車で行きます。

8. 昨日カーティスさんはだれ (　　) 話しましたか。

9. デパートへ買い物 (　　) 行きました。

10. どんな本 (　　) 好きですか。

アクティビティー 28

何時にどこへ行きましたか。(*Where did you go; what time?*)

Fill in the blanks.

今日の朝、わたしは6時半 (　　) 起きました。そして、顔 (　　) 洗いました。7時 (　　) 7時半 (　　) 公園 (　　) 散歩しました。8時 (　　) 大学 (　　) 行きました。9時 (　　) 12時 (　　) クラス (　　) ありました。昼ごはんはカフェテリア (　　) ハンバーガー (　　) 食べました。ミルク (　　) 飲みました。3時 (　　) 町田さん (　　) としょかん (　　) 行きました。5時 (　　) 家 (　　) 帰りました。6時 (　　) 夕ごはん (　　) 食べました。それから、ラジオ (　　) 音楽 (　　) 聞きました。十時 (　　)、友だち (　　) 電話しました。11時 (　　) シャワー (　　) 浴びました。11時半 (　　) 寝ました。

アクティビティー **29**

いつも家で夕ごはんを食べます。(*I always eat supper at home.*)

Make a dialogue using the words given in parentheses. Use the correct particles.

[例] s1: 町田さんは先週デパートへ行きましたか。
s2: (はい) → はい、行きました。

s1: (いつ買い物に行く)
s2: (先週の土曜日)

s1: (だれと)
s2: (山口さん)

s1: (何) (買う)

s2: (ブラウス) (買う)
s1: 町田さんはよくレストランへ行きますか。

s2: (あまり)
s1: いつも家で夕ごはんを食べますか。

s2: (いつも)
s1: (昨日) (何) (食べる)

s2: (ステーキ) (食べる)
s1: (どんな) (食べ物) (好きです)

s2: (ほとんど) (何でも *everything*)

Vocabulary and Grammar 3C

Vocabulary and Oral Activities
Weekends and Holidays

Vocabulary: Holidays and Vacations

平日	へいじつ	weekday
週末	しゅうまつ	weekend
休みの日	やすみのひ	day off; holiday

休む	やすむ	to take time off; take a rest
祝日	しゅくじつ	national holiday
夏休み	なつやすみ	summer vacation
冬休み	ふゆやすみ	winter vacation
休暇	きゅうか	vacation
休暇を取る	きゅうかをとる	to take a vacation

アクティビティー **30**

<ruby>週<rt>しゅう</rt></ruby><ruby>末<rt>まつ</rt></ruby>はひまです。(*I am free on weekends.*)

How do you spend your weekends? Did you do any of these activities last weekend?

1. <ruby>部屋<rt>へや</rt></ruby>を<ruby>掃除<rt>そうじ</rt></ruby>する

2. <ruby>遅<rt>おそ</rt></ruby>くまでテレビを<ruby>見<rt>み</rt></ruby>る

3. デートをする

4. <ruby>働<rt>はたら</rt></ruby>く

5. 10<ruby>時<rt>じ</rt></ruby>まで<ruby>寝<rt>ね</rt></ruby>る

6. <ruby>勉強<rt>べんきょう</rt></ruby>する

7. <ruby>映画<rt>えいが</rt></ruby>を<ruby>見<rt>み</rt></ruby>る

8. <ruby>図書館<rt>としょかん</rt></ruby>に<ruby>行<rt>い</rt></ruby>く

9. <ruby>散歩<rt>さんぽ</rt></ruby>する

10. スポーツをする

11. <ruby>洗濯<rt>せんたく</rt></ruby>する (*do laundry*)

12. <ruby>何<rt>なに</rt></ruby>もしない (*not do anything*)

二百九

アクティビティー **31**

ウィークデーと 週末（しゅうまつ）(*Weekdays and weekends*)

Here are the weekday and weekend schedules of Mr. Takada, Linda Brown's next-door neighbor. Answer the questions below.

Useful Vocabulary: ブランチ *brunch*, 会社（かいしゃ）*company*, ウィークデー *weekday*, 週末（しゅうまつ）*weekend*

> There are two terms that mean *weekday*, ウィークデー and 平日（へいじつ）. The first is customarily used in ordinary conversation, while 平日 is used on more formal occasions, such as an interview, and in writing.

月曜日（げつようび）〜金曜日（きんようび）＝ウィークデー

6:00	get up
6:05	take a shower
6:15	eat breakfast
6:45	leave home
7:00	get on the bus
8:00	start work
9:00	attend a meeting
10:30	drink coffee
12:00	eat lunch
1:00	drink coffee
2:00	meet with clients
4:45	leave the company
6:00	arrive home
6:30	cook dinner
7:30	eat dinner
8:00	watch TV
10:00	take a bath
11:00	go to bed

土曜日（どようび）〜日曜日（にちようび）＝ 週末（しゅうまつ）

9:00	get up
9:30	drink coffee
9:45	read the newspaper
10:15	watch TV
11:00	eat brunch
12:00	clean the apartment
1:00	go shopping
2:30	do laundry
5:00	go to a restaurant
7:00	listen to the stereo
8:00	read a book
9:30	eat a snack
11:00	watch TV
12:30	go to bed

1. 高田（たかだ）さんは、ウィークデー、何時（なんじ）に起（お）きますか。週末（しゅうまつ）、何時（なんじ）に起（お）きますか。
2. 高田さんは、週末（しゅうまつ）、会社（かいしゃ）へ行（い）きますか。
3. 高田さんは、ウィークデー、何時（なんじ）と何時にコーヒーを飲（の）みますか。 高田さんは、週末（しゅうまつ）、何時（なんじ）にコーヒーを飲（の）みますか。
4. 高田さんは、ウィークデー、洗濯（せんたく）をしますか。
5. 高田さんは、週末（しゅうまつ）、朝（あさ）ごはんを食（た）べますか。
6. 高田さんは、ウィークデーも週末（しゅうまつ）もテレビを見（み）ますか。
7. 高田さんは、ウィークデーも週末（しゅうまつ）も夕ごはんを作（つく）りますか。 （作（つく）る*make, cook*）

Make your own questions to ask your classmates.

言語ノート

Connecting Disjunctive Sentences

Disjunctive conjunctions are words used to link two sentences that express contrasting ideas. A disjunctive conjunction frequently used in conversation is でも (*but, even so*). This conjunction begins the second sentence of the contrasting pair.

ウィークデー、午前6時に起きます。でも、
週末、午前10時に起きます。

**I get up at 6:00 A.M. on weekdays. But I get up at 10:00 A.M.
on weekends.**

In written discourse, the conjunction しかし (*however*) is often used.

平日は会社へ行く。しかし、週末は行かない。

**I go to the office (*lit.,* company) on weekdays. However, I don't go
there on weekends.**

A disjunctive conjunction is also a word joining two contrasting independent clauses (that is, complete sentences) into a single compound sentence. One used very frequently in conversation is が (*but*). Unlike the English position of *but* at the beginning of the second clause, が attaches to the end of the first clause; the pause in speech and the comma in writing fall *after* が.

ウィークデーは午前6時に起きますが、週末は午前10時に起
きます。

**I get up at 6:00 A.M. on weekdays, but I get up at 10:00 A.M.
on weekends.**

Japanese often end sentences with this が and a trailing intonation, expecting the listener to know what the rest of the compound sentence would be from context.

すみませんが...

I'm sorry, but . . . (we don't have any; I can't do it this time; etc.)

Excuse me, but . . . (could you help me?; I have a question; etc.)

アクティビティー **32**

ウィークデー は早く起きます。(*On weekdays I get up early.*)

Add a contrasting clause to complete the following sentences comparing weekday and weekend schedules.

(*Continues.*)

二百十一

Useful word: 遅_{おそ}く *late* (adverb)

1. ウィークデー の朝_{あさ}はシャワーを浴_あびます。でも、＿＿＿

2. 週_{しゅう}末_{まつ} はテニスをしますが、＿＿＿

3. 先_{せん}週_{しゅう} のウィークデー は毎_{まい}日_{にち}勉_{べん} 強_{きょう}しました。でも、＿＿＿

4. ウィークデー は毎日図_と書_{しょ}館_{かん}へ行_いきます。でも、＿＿＿

5. ウィークデー はカフェテリアで昼_{ひる}ごはんを食_たべますが、＿＿＿

6. ウィークデー は夜_{よる}新_{しん}聞_{ぶん}を読_よみます。でも、＿＿＿

7. ウィークデー は早_{はや}く(*early*)寝_ねますが、＿＿＿

文化ノート

CULTURE NOTE: 国民の祝日 *National Holidays*

The following are national holidays in Japan.

1 月 1 日	元日_{がんじつ}	*New Year's Day*
1 月 第2月曜 (*variable*)	成人_{せいじん}の日_ひ	*Coming-of-Age Day*
2 月 11 日	建国_{けんこく}記念_{きねん}の日_ひ	*National Foundation Day*
3 月 21 日 (*variable*)	春分_{しゅんぶん}の日_ひ	*Vernal Equinox Day*
4 月 29 日	緑_{みどり}の日_ひ	*Greenery Day*
5 月 3 日	憲法_{けんぽう}記念_{きねん}日_び	*Constitution Day*
5 月 4 日	国民_{こくみん}の日_ひ	*People's Day*
5 月 5 日	子供_{こども}の日_ひ	*Children's Day*
7 月 20 日	海_{うみ}の日_ひ	*Marine Day*
9 月 15 日	敬老_{けいろう}の日_ひ	*Respect-for-the-Aged Day*
9 月 23 日 (*variable*)	秋分_{しゅうぶん}の日_ひ	*Autumnal Equinox Day*
10 月 第 2 月曜 (*variable*)	体育_{たいいく}の日_ひ	*Health-Sports Day*
11 月 3 日	文化_{ぶんか}の日_ひ	*Culture Day*
11 月 23 日	勤労感謝_{きんろうかんしゃ}の日_ひ	*Labor Thanksgiving Day*
12 月 23 日	天皇誕生_{てんのうたんじょう}日_び	*Emperor's Birthday*

成人の日—on this holiday, the Japanese celebrate those who turned 20 years old in the preceding year. Twenty is the age of legal adulthood in Japan, and city governments hold ceremonies to recognize the new adults.

憲法記念日 is the day commemorating the promulgation of the Constitution that was drafted after World War II.

文化の日 is the day celebrating the development of culture and the proclamation of the new Constitution. On this day, those who have contributed to the enhancement of culture, technology, and community are awarded medals.

In recent years, the dates of some holidays, such as 成人の日, have been changed so that they always fall on a Monday.

成人の日：わたしたちは二十歳です。

Grammar and Practice Activities

15. Making Suggestions: 〜ましょう

カワムラ：林さん、おそいですね。

ブラウン：ええ、どうしましょうか。

カワムラ：もう少し待ちましょう。

ブラウン：でも、もう9時ですよ。出かけましょうか。

カワムラ：ええ、そうしましょう。

林　：チンさんがいませんね。

カワムラ：ええ。

林：チンさん、病気ですか。

カワムラ：さあ。

林：ぼくが家に電話しましょうか。

KAWAMURA: Mr. Hayashi is late, isn't he?　BROWN: Yes. What shall we do?　KAWAMURA: Let's wait for him a little longer.　BROWN: But it's already nine o'clock. Shall we leave (now)? KAWAMURA: Yes, let's do that.

HAYASHI: Ms. Chin isn't here, is she?　KAWAMURA: That's right. (lit., *Yes.*)　HAYASHI: Is she sick?　KAWAMURA: I don't know.　HAYASHI: Shall I call her at home?

15.1 The ましょう form, or the polite, volitional form of a verb, is made by adding ましょう to the conjunctive form. Here are some examples.

Dictionary Form	Conjunctive Form	ましょう Form
Class 1 Verbs あら 洗う た 立つ	あら 洗い た 立ち	あら 洗いましょう た 立ちましょう
Class 2 Verbs た 食べる み 見る	た 食べ み 見	た 食べましょう み 見ましょう
Class 3 Verbs する く 来る	し き 来	しましょう き 来ましょう

15.2 The ましょう form is used to suggest, propose, or invite (*Let's…* or *Shall we…?*).

いっしょ　べんきょう
一緒に勉強しましょうか。
Shall we study together?

ひる　　　　　た
昼ごはんを食べましょう。
Let's eat lunch.

でんしゃ　い　　　　　　　　　　　　　　　い
電車で行きましょうか。タクシーで行きましょうか。
Shall we go by train or taxi?

Because the ましょう form expresses the speaker's volition, without consideration to the hearer's preferences, it tends to sound somewhat pushy and forceful. It is politer to use the nonpast, polite, negative form of a verb ＋か when inviting someone to do something together or when making a suggestion.

いっしょ　ゆう　　　　た
一緒に夕ごはんを食べませんか。
Shall we eat dinner together?
Would you like to eat dinner together? (lit., *Won't you eat dinner together [with me]?*)

らいしゅう　　　　　　　　　　い
来週、デパートへ行きませんか。
Shall we go to a department store next week?
Would you like to go to a department store next week?
　　(lit., *Won't you go to a department store next week?*)

When you already know that the hearer is willing to do something together, the use of the ましょう form does not sound pushy. For example,

レストランへ行きませんか。
Shall we go to a restaurant?
ええ、いいですね。
Yes, that sounds nice.
どこへ行きましょうか。
Where shall we go?

or

のどがかわきましたね。
I am thirsty, aren't you?
ええ、とても。
Yes, very much.
ジュースを飲みましょうか。
Shall we drink juice?

15.3 The ましょう form is also used when offering to do something for someone or when expressing one's own volition.

わたしがブラウンさんに話しましょう。
I will talk to Ms. Brown.
わたしがワインを買いましょうか。
Shall I buy wine?

When the first person subject is expressed explicitly as in the preceding examples, it implies that "I but not anyone else" will do something. When the first person subject is not expressed, it simply expresses the speaker's volition without such an implication.

さあ、勉強しましょう。
Well, I guess I will start studying.
Well, I'm going to study now.

Accepting and Declining Offers

To accept an offer, say

はい、お願いします。
Yes, please.
どうもありがとうございます。
Thank you very much.
どうもすみません。

Thank you for your trouble. (*lit.,* I'm sorry for your trouble.)

To turn down an offer, say

いいえ、けっこうです。
No, thank you.
(*lit.,* No, I'm fine.)

アクティビティー 33

さあ、泳ぎましょう。(*Let's go swimming now.*)

Rewrite each sentence using the ましょう form.

[例]　コーラを飲む → コーラを飲みましょう。

1. 映画を見る
2. コンサートへ行く
3. ケーキを食べる
4. ジョギングする
5. 本を読む
6. 買物に出かける
7. プールで泳ぐ
8. 日本語で話す

アクティビティー 34

あとで話しましょうか。(*Let's talk later.*)

Complete the following dialogues using the ましょう form.

[例]　（ブラウンさんに電話する）(*accept*) →
　　　—わたしがブラウンさんに電話しましょうか。
　　　—ええ、お願いします。
　　　（掃除する）(*decline*) →
　　　—わたしが掃除しましょうか。
　　　—いいえ、けっこうです。

1. （山口さんに聞く）(*accept*)
2. （洗濯をする）(*decline*)
3. （横井先生の研究室に行く）(*accept*)
4. （その本を読む）(*accept*)
5. （料理する）(*decline*)

アクティビティー 35

ダイアログ：何を見ましょうか。(*What shall we see?*)
林さんとギブソンさんが話しています。

林：ギブソンさん、今 週 の土曜日、一緒に映画を見ませんか。

ギブソン：ええ。何を見ましょうか。

林：ラスト・サムライはどうですか。

ギブソン：いいですね。

Practice the preceding dialogue, substituting the following activities for the first and second underlined phrases. (Use the appropriate form.) Make up your own substitution for the third underlined phrase.

Useful word: プール *swimming pool*

1. 買物に行く、どこへ行く

2. ジョギングをする、どこでする

3. 夕ごはんを食べる、どこで食べる

4. ドライブする (*to go on a drive*)、どこへ行く

5. 泳ぐ (*to swim*)、どこで泳ぐ

言語ノート

Making a Suggestion

In the preceding dialogue, the phrase . . . はどうですか is used to make a suggestion.

東 急 デパートはどうですか。

How about Tookyuu Department Store? (*e.g., as a possible place to do shopping*)

大学のプールはどうですか。

How about the college swimming pool? (*e.g., as a possible place to swim*)

The phrase . . . はいかがですか is a more formal equivalent of . . . はどうですか. A shop clerk at a department store might say the following while showing a pen to a customer.

このペンはいかがですか。

How about this pen? (*as the one to buy*)

Mr. Hayashi and Ms. Gibson are talking. HAYASHI: Ms. Gibson, <u>would you like to (lit., *won't you*) see a movie</u> together this Saturday? GIBSON: Yes, <u>what shall we see</u>? HAYASHI: How about *The Last Samurai*? GIBSON: That sounds good. (lit., *That's good.*)

アクティビティー **36**

休^{やす}みましょうか。(*Shall we take a break?*)

Following the example, complete these conversations using 〜ましょう.

[例] 疲^{つか}れましたね。(*I'm tired, aren't you?*) →
　　 ええ、休^{やす}みましょうか。(*Yes, shall we take a break?*)

Useful Vocabulary: 食^たべる、飲^のむ、家^{いえ}に帰^{かえ}る、図書館^{としょかん}で勉強^{べんきょう}する、
先生^{せんせい}に聞^きく

1. おなかがすきましたね。(*I am hungry, aren't you?*)

2. のどがかわきましたね。(*I am thirsty, aren't you?*)

3. もう6時^じですね。

4. ここはうるさいですね。(*It is noisy here, isn't it?*)

5. この問題^{もんだい}、むずかしいですね。(*This problem is difficult, isn't it?*)

アクティビティー **37**

ダイアログ：ぼくが電話^{でんわ}しましょう。(*I will make the phone call.*)

カワムラさんと林^{はやし}さんが話^{はな}しています。

カワムラ：今^{いま}、何時^{なんじ}ですか。
　　林^{はやし}：ええと、2時半^{じはん}です。ブラウンさん、おそいですね。
カワムラ：ええ。ブラウンさんに電話^{でんわ}しませんか。
　　林^{はやし}：ええ、ぼくが電話^{でんわ}しましょう。
カワムラ：お願^{ねが}いします。

Mr. Kawamura and Mr. Hayashi are talking　KAWAMURA: What time is it now?　HAYASHI: Uh,
it's 2:30. Ms. Brown is late, isn't she?　KAWAMURA: Yes, shouldn't we call her (lit.,
Ms. Brown)?　HAYASHI: Yes. I will make the call.　KAWAMURA: Thank you. (lit., *Please do it
for me.*)

16. Conjoining Nouns: と and や 🎧

カワムラ：横井先生の研究室にだれがいますか。

町田：横井先生とブラウンさんがいます。

カワムラ：チンさんは。

町田：研究室の外にいます。

ブラウン：事務室にだれがいますか。

町田：カワムラさんや林さんがいます。

ブラウン：カーティスさんは。

町田：ええ、カーティスさんもいます。

You can join nouns together with と or や. と (*and*) is used to enumerate *all* objects that exist in a certain place or *all* objects that belong to a certain category, while や (*and things like that*) is used to list only representative objects. Thus, と is exhaustive, and や is not. You may conjoin as many nouns as you like with these particles. Remember: you cannot use these particles to connect adjectives, verbs, or sentences.

アクティビティー **38**

だれが来ましたか。(*Who came?*)

Answer each question two ways, first using と and then や.

1. 昨日、だれが来ましたか。 (*Hayashi, Chin, and Gibson*)
2. 夕ごはんに何を食べましたか。(*steak, salad, and fruit*)
3. そこにだれがいますか。(*Brown, Kawamura, Curtis, and Chin*)
4. どんなコンピュータがありますか。(*IBM, Apple, NEC, and Toshiba*)
5. どんなスポーツが好きですか。(*basketball, football, and tennis*)

KAWAMURA: Who is in Professor Yokoi's office?   MACHIDA: Professor Yokoi and Ms. Brown.
KAWAMURA: How about Ms. Chin?   MACHIDA: She is outside the office.
BROWN: Who is in the administrative office?   MACHIDA: Mr. Kawamura, Mr. Hayashi, and others.   BROWN: How about Mr. Curtis?   MACHIDA: Yes, he's there, too.

Language Skills

Reading and Writing

Reading 1 ブラウンさんの日常生活

Before You Read

The following passage describes Linda Brown's daily life. Before reading it, work with a partner to arrange the following activities in the order you think average students perform them.

_____ 夕ごはんを食べる   _____ 家に帰る

_____ 大学へ行く   _____ クラスに出る

_____ 起きる   _____ 昼ごはんを食べる

_____ 朝ごはんを食べる   _____ 寝る

Work in pairs. Which of the following activities do both you and your partner do every morning? Which do neither of you do?

_____ 歯を磨く   _____ 顔を洗う

_____ ラジオを聞く   _____ 服を着る

_____ シャワーを浴びる   _____ 電車に乗る

_____ 朝ごはんを食べる   _____ 新聞を読む

_____ コーヒーを飲む   _____ ジョギングをする

_____ テレビを見る

Now Read It!

わたしは毎朝6時に起きます。まず、顔を洗います。そして、歯を磨きます。それから、ジョギングをします。7時ごろ朝ごはんを食べます。7時半にうちを出ます。わたしのアパートは中野駅のそばにあります。アパートから駅まで五分歩きます。そして、地下鉄で大学へ行きます。アパートから大学まで30分ぐらいかかります。

まず *first of all*

駅 *station* ／ 歩く *to walk*

かかる *to take*

　　　クラスは8時に始まります。わたしの専攻は日本文化です。毎日、日本文化、日本語のクラスに出ます。午前のクラスは12時に終わります。いつも大学のカフェテリアで昼ごはんを食べます。午後のクラスは1時から始まります。そして、4時に終わります。クラスの後、時々、図書館へ行きます。月曜日と水曜日と金曜日は友だちとエアロビクスのレッスンに行きます。

　　　いつもアパートに5時か6時に帰ります。夕ごはんは7時半ごろ食べます。時々、アパートのそばの食堂へ行きます。

　　　夜は日本語の勉強します。本もよく読みます。ミステリーが好きです。テレビはあまり見ません。カセットやCDで音楽をよく聞きます。毎日、12時ごろ寝ます。

始まる *to start*

終わる *to finish*

…の後 *after…*

五時か六時 *five o'clock or six o'clock*

か *or*

言語ノート

Approximate Numbers

These words, when appended to quantities or points in time, make the numerical entities approximate.

1. ごろ (*around*) is used to express an approximate point in time, such as a day, month, or hour.

   毎日 5時ごろ起きます。

   I get up around 5:00 every day.

2. ぐらい or くらい (*about*) is used to express an approximate quantity. くらい and ぐらい are interchangeable.

   日本語のクラスには三十人ぐらいの学生がいます。

   There are about thirty students in the Japanese language class.

   東京から京都まで3時間ぐらいかかります。

   It takes about three hours from Tokyo to Kyoto.

   その本は二千円くらいです。

   That book costs (*lit.*, is) about 2,000 yen.

3. ほど (*about*) is also used to express approximate quantity. ほど is used in the sense of *as much as* with all but small numbers.

   レタスを二つほどください。

   Let me have two heads of lettuce.

   ここから15分ほどかかります。

   It takes (as much as) about fifteen minutes from here.

After You Finish Reading

1. Based on information provided in the passage, write up a detailed daily schedule for Linda Brown, indicating her activities from 6:00 A.M. to midnight. Indicate A.M. and P.M. with 午前 and 午後.

2. Now look at the second paragraph carefully. Identify all the particles in the paragraph and explain how each is used.

Writing 1

Write a short paragraph about your daily life. Use this beginning.

わたしは毎朝 _____ 時に起きます。それから...

Reading 2 ブラウンさんの週末

Before You Read

The following passage describes what Linda Brown did last weekend. Which of the following do you usually do on weekdays and which do you usually do on weekends?

_____ 寝坊する   _____ 映画を見る
_____ 勉強する   _____ 友だちと電話で話す
_____ 買い物をする   _____ 大学へ行く
_____ 掃除をする   _____ レコードを聞く
_____ 洗濯をする   _____ レストランへ行く
_____ 図書館へ行く

Match items in the first column to related items in the second column.

1. 誕生日   a. 日曜日
2. コインランドリー   b. ギフト
3. パーティー   c. デパート
4. 週末   d. ワイン
5. 買い物   e. 洗濯

Now Read It!

土曜日と日曜日は大学が休みです。土曜日は午前9時ごろ起きます。土曜日の朝はいつもアパートの前の喫茶店に行きます。この喫茶店のコーヒーはとてもおいしいです。お昼まで喫茶店でコーヒーを飲みます。土曜日の午後はアパートの掃除をします。夜はクラスメートと外に出かけます。先週の土曜日はカワムラさんと映画を見ました。今週の土曜日は町田さんと買い物に行きます。土曜日はいつも午後11時か12時ごろアパートに帰ります。

日曜日はいつも、お昼ごろ起きます。午後は近くのコイン・ランドリーで洗濯をします。夜、ちょっと勉強します。来週の日曜日はカワムラさんの誕生日です。カワムラさんは二十一歳になります。町田さんの家でパーティーがあります。来週の日曜日は朝早く起きます。町田さんの家で、パーティーの準備を手伝います。町田さんと一緒にケーキやごちそうを作ります。

昨日、カワムラさんのバースデー・プレゼントを買いました。カワムラさんはコンピュータが好きです。それで、コンピュータのソフトウェアを買いました。

おいしい delicious / お昼 noontime

コイン・ランドリー laundromat

...になる to become

準備 preparation / 手伝う to help; to assist / 一緒に together / ごちそう delicious food
作る to make; to cook

それで therefore

After You Finish Reading

1. Tell whether each of the following is true or false.

   a. Linda drinks coffee at a coffee shop until noon on Saturdays.
   b. Linda went out with Hitomi Machida last Saturday.
   c. Linda goes to bed at 11:00 P.M. or 12:00 midnight on Saturdays.
   d. Linda cleans her apartment and does her laundry on Sundays.
   e. Next Sunday is John Kawamura's twenty-first birthday.
   f. Hitomi Machida will come to Linda's apartment next Sunday to help Linda prepare for the party.
   g. Linda will buy computer software for John Kawamura.

2. Arrange the following activities in the order Linda Brown does them on Saturday. Create a narrative using appropriate conjunctions.

   ____ アパートに帰る　　　　　____ コーヒーを飲む
   ____ 喫茶店へ行く　　　　　　____ 午前9時ごろ起きる
   ____ 掃除をする　　　　　　　____ 友だちと出かける

Writing 2

Drawing from the journal notations on the following page, write a short paragraph about what John Kawamura did last weekend.

(*Continues.*)

```
DIARY •••••••••••••••••••••••••••••••

Sat                              Sun

10:00  got up              9:30   got up
       read paper          10:00  took shower
11:00  watched TV          11:00  listened to
12:00  ate lunch                  music
1:00   did laundry         12:00  called Linda
2:00   cleaned house              Brown
4:00   went to movie       2:00   went shopping
7:00   ate at a                   with Linda
       tempura restaurant  5:00   went to
10:00  went to pub                McDonald's
12:00  returned home       7:00   came home
       and went to bed     8:00   studied
                                  Japanese
                           10:30  went to bed
```

Language Functions and Situations
Making a Phone Call 🎧

山口：もしもし、山口です。

ブラウン：もしもし、ブラウンです。カワムラさんをお願いします。

山口：ちょっとお待ちください。

カワムラ：もしもし、カワムラです。

ブラウン：ブラウンです。

田中：もしもし。

ブラウン：もしもし、山口さんですか。

田中：いいえ、違います。

ブラウン：3567-3981ですか。

田中：いいえ、3567-3891です。

ブラウン：あっ、どうもすみません。間違えました。

田中：いいえ。

YAMAGUCHI: Hello. This is Yamaguchi speaking.　　BROWN: Hello. This is Brown. May I speak to Mr. Kawamura? (lit., *Please give me Mr. Kawamura*.)　　YAMAGUCHI: Wait a moment, please. KAWAMURA: Hello. This is Kawamura speaking.　　BROWN: This is Brown.

TANAKA: Hello.　　BROWN: Hello. Is this Mr. Yamaguchi?　　TANAKA: No, it isn't. (lit., *No, it's different*.)　　BROWN: Is this 3567-3981?　　TANAKA: No, this is 3567-3891.　　BROWN: Oh, I'm very sorry. I must have made an error. (lit., *I made a mistake*.)　　TANAKA: That's OK. (lit., *Not at all*.)

山口：もしもし、山口です。

ブラウン：もしもし、ブラウンです。カワムラさんをお願いします。

山口：カワムラさんは大学へ行きましたよ。

ブラウン：そうですか。では、また電話します。じゃ、失礼します。

山口：失礼します。

山口：もしもし、山口です。

ブラウン：もしもし、カワムラさんはいますか。

山口：今、いませんよ。

ブラウン：そうですか。ブラウンですが、電話をお願いします。

山口：電話番号をお願いします。

ブラウン：3965-9133です。

言語ノート

Talking on the Telephone

もしもし。

Hello.

林です。

This is Hayashi speaking./This is the Hayashi residence.
(*lit.*, This is Hayashi.)

チンさんをお願いします。

May I speak to Ms. Chin? (*lit.*, Please give me Ms. Chin.)

間違い電話です。

You've dialed the wrong number. (*lit.*, This is the wrong number.)

間違えました。

I made a mistake.

また電話します。

I will call back.

伝言をお願いします。

May I leave a message?

YAMAGUCHI: Hello. This is the Yamaguchi residence.   BROWN: Hello. This is Brown. May I speak to Mr. Kawamura?   YAMAGUCHI: Mr. Kawamura went to the university.   BROWN: I see. Then, I will call him back. Goodbye.   YAMAGUCHI: Goodbye.

YAMAGUCHI: Hello. This is the Yamaguchi residence.   BROWN: Hello. Is Mr. Kawamura there? YAMAGUCHI: Mr. Kawamura is not here now.   BROWN: I see. This is Brown. Can you ask him to call me?   YAMAGUCHI: May I have (lit., *Please give me*) your phone number?   BROWN: 3965-9113.

CULTURE NOTE: 携帯電話 *Cell (Mobile) Phones*
けいたいでんわ

As of December 2003, nearly 80 million cell phones were in use in Japan. Japanese cell phone companies have long offered services beyond ordinary voice calls, and Japanese people were using their phones to send and receive e-mail, take photos, and browse websites years before these options were common in North America. Young people have become adept at tapping out e-mail messages at incredible speeds, and they are particularly fond of doing so on commuter trains, where it is forbidden to make or receive voice calls.

Many companies and public institutions have special cell phone versions of their websites, which allow customers to make restaurant or travel reservations, shop, or obtain information about sports, entertainment, or business.

Neither North American nor European cell phones, not even so-called "international" models, work in Japan, which uses its own unique communication standard, but cell phones are such an important part of modern Japanese life that tourists and business travelers arriving at Japan's international airports can rent handsets and make temporary contracts with one of the country's service providers.

はい、わかりました。すぐ行きます。

Role Play

Working with a partner, practice the following situations.

1. Call the Yamamoto residence and ask for Ms. Moore, who is boarding there.

2. You have received a call, but it is the wrong number.

3. Call the Muranaka residence. You learn that Mr. Muranaka is not there and say that you will call back later.

4. Call the Sano residence. Ms. Sano is not there. Say that you would like her to call you back.

Extending an Invitation 🎧

大学で

　　　　林 ：ギブソンさん、今日の午後、ひまですか。

ギブソン：ええ。

　　　　林 ：一緒に夕ごはんを食べませんか。

ギブソン：ええ、もちろん。どこがいいですか。

　　　　林 ：「さくらレストラン」はどうですか。

ギブソン：ええ、それはいいですね。

大学で

　　　チン：今日は何時にクラスが終わりますか。

カーティス：3時です。

　　　チン：映画に行きませんか。

カーティス：ええ、いいですね。

　　　チン：どの映画がいいですか。

カーティス：「ニンジャ」はどうですか。

　　　チン：ええ、いいですね。

カーティス：どこで会いましょうか。

　　　チン：図書館の前はどうですか。

カーティス：ええ、いいですよ。

　　　三村 ：ギブソンさん、明日コンサートに行きませんか。

ギブソン：すみません。明日はちょっと仕事があります。

　　　三村 ：そうですか。残念ですね。

At the university　HAYASHI: Ms. Gibson, are you free this afternoon?　GIBSON: Yes.　HAYASHI: Shall we have dinner together?　GIBSON: Yes, certainly (lit., *of course*). Where shall we go? (lit., *Where is good?*)　HAYASHI: How about the Sakura Restaurant?　GIBSON: Yes, that sounds good.

At the university　CHIN: What time is your class over today?　CURTIS: At three o'clock. CHIN: Shall we go to the movies?　CURTIS: Yes, that would be good.　CHIN: Which movie shall we see? (lit., *Which movie is good?*)　CURTIS: How about *Ninja*?　CHIN: Yes, that would be good.　CURTIS: Where shall we meet?　CHIN: How about in front of the library? CURTIS: (Yes) That would be fine.

MIMURA: Ms. Gibson, would you like to go to a concert tomorrow?　GIBSON: I'm sorry. I have (lit., *a little*) work tomorrow.　MIMURA: I see. That's too bad.

Let's Do Something Together

言語ノート

The ましょう form or the nonpast, negative form of a verb is commonly used to suggest doing something together. (See **Grammar 15** for more about the ましょう form.)

一緒に夕ごはんを食べましょう。

Let's have dinner together.

一緒に夕ごはんを食べませんか。

Would you like to have dinner together?

(*lit.*, Won't you have dinner together [with me]?)

To agree, say

ええ、いいですね。

Yes, that sounds good.

To decline, say

すみません。またこの次。

I'm sorry, but (let's do it) next time.

いいですね。でも、また今度。

That would be nice, but (let's make it) next time.

どうもありがとうございます。でも、今はちょっと...。

Thank you very much. But I am afraid now is a bit . . . (inconvenient).

林さんへ

来週の土曜日、わたしのアパートに来ませんか。
アメリカのビデオを見ます。
カーティスさんも来ます。

ブラウン
2月 24 日

Role Play

Practice the following situations with your classmates.

1. Ask one of your classmates when his or her classes are over today, and issue an invitation to do the following.

    a. jog with you after class

    b. drink beer with you after class

    c. eat pizza with you after class

    d. go shopping with you after class

2. Invite a classmate to have lunch with you next Monday. Suggest eating at your favorite restaurant near the university. If your classmate is busy next Monday, ask when he or she is free. Remember that it is rude to say no directly in Japanese; if you are busy next Monday use one of the responses you learned in the previous Language Note, **Let's Do Something Together.**

3. Call one of your classmates and invite him or her to your home this Saturday. Give simple directions and use descriptions of your house and neighborhood.

Listening Comprehension 🎧

1. Mr. Kunio Hasegawa, one of the richest Japanese who ever lived, was murdered in the British-style garden of his large mansion in Kamakura last night. You are the police chief in Kamakura. One of your detectives, Nobuo Maruyama, interviewed six suspects about their activities last night. Listen to his report. Then list what each suspect did throughout the evening and at what time. The six suspects are Mr. Hasegawa's wife, Tamako; his daughter, Sawako; his son, Muneo; his mistress, Junko Suzuki; his chauffeur, Kazuo Morimoto; and his brother-in-law, Haruki Kameda. Who is the most likely culprit?

2. Listen to the results of a survey on the lifestyles of Japanese people. Complete the following table by filling in the appropriate numbers.

Japanese who get up before 6:30 A.M.	%
Japanese who eat breakfast	%
Japanese who start work before 8:30 A.M.	%
Japanese who eat lunch between noon and 1:00 P.M.	%
Japanese workers who return home before 7:00 P.M.	%
Japanese workers who go drinking after work	%
Japanese who watch TV every night	%
Japanese who go to bed before 11:00 P.M.	%

Vocabulary 🎧

Time Expressions

あさって		the day after tomorrow	こんばん	今晩	tonight
あした	明日	tomorrow	せんげつ	先月	last month
おととい		the day before yesterday	せんしゅう	先週	last week
きのう	昨日	yesterday	なんじかん	何時間	how many hours
きょう	今日	today	なんにち	何日	what day
きょねん	去年	last year	なんねん	何年	what year
けさ	今朝	this morning	らいげつ	来月	next month
ことし	今年	this year	らいしゅう	来週	next week
こんげつ	今月	this month	らいねん	来年	next year
こんしゅう	今週	this week			

Review: 朝、午前、午後、時間、何月、何曜日、昼、夕方、夜、夕辺

(Continues.)

二百二十九

Everyday Activities

いえをでる	家を出る	to leave home
うんどうする	運動する	to exercise
おふろにはいる	お風呂に入る	to take a bath
かおをあらう	顔を洗う	to wash one's face
シャワーをあびる	シャワーを浴びる	to take a shower
しょくじ (を)する	食事(を)する	to have a meal
つかれる	疲れる	to become tired
でかける	出かける	to go out
でんわ (を)する	電話(を)する	to make a telephone call
ねぼうする	寝坊する	to oversleep
のる	乗る	to ride (a vehicle)
はたらく	働く	to work
はをみがく	歯を磨く	to brush one's teeth
ふくをきる	服を着る	to put on clothes
やすむ	休む	to take a rest; to take time off
ゆうごはんをたべる	夕ごはんを食べる	to have dinner; to have supper
りょうり (を)する	料理(を)する	to cook

Review: 朝ごはん、行く、起きる、買い物 (を)する、帰る、聞く、仕事をする、
食べる、寝る、飲む、話す、晩ごはん、昼ごはん、勉 強する、見る、読む

Days of the Month

ついたち	一日	the first	じゅうににち	十二日	the twelfth
ふつか	二日	the second	じゅうさんにち	十三日	the thirteenth
みっか	三日	the third	じゅうよっか	十四日	the fourteenth
よっか	四日	the fourth	じゅうごにち	十五日	the fifteenth
いつか	五日	the fifth	じゅうろくにち	十六日	the sixteenth
むいか	六日	the sixth	じゅうしちにち	十七日	the seventeenth
なのか	七日	the seventh	じゅうはちにち	十八日	the eighteenth
ようか	八日	the eighth	じゅうくにち	十九日	the nineteenth
ここのか	九日	the ninth	はつか	二十日	the twentieth
とおか	十日	the tenth	にじゅうよっか	二十四日	the twenty-fourth
じゅういちにち	十一日	the eleventh			

Frequency

あまり		(*with negative*) not very much	たまに		once in a while
いつも		always	ときどき	時々	sometimes
～かい	~回	...times (*counter for occurrences*)	ほとんど		almost
ぜんぜん	全然	(*with negative*) not at all			

二百三十

ほとんど〜		(*with negative*) almost never; hardly
まいあさ	毎朝	every morning
まいしゅう	毎週	every week
まいつき	毎月	every month

まいにち	毎日	every day
まいばん	毎晩	every night
よく		often

Conjunctions

そして	and then
そのあと	after that
それから	and then

Particles

が	(*subject particle*)
から	from
で	at; by means of
と	with
に	(*indirect object particle*)

は	(*topic particle*)
へ	(*direction particle*)
まで	up to; until
も	too
を	(*direct object particle*)

Nouns

ウィークデー		weekday
へいじつ	平日	weekday
しゅうまつ	週末	weekend
やすみのひ	休みの日	day off; holiday

なつやすみ	夏休み	summer vacation
ふゆやすみ	冬休み	winter vacation

Adjectives

いそがしい	忙しい	busy
ひま(な)	暇(な)	free (*not busy*)

Verb Endings

〜ましょう	let's...
〜ます	(*nonpast, polite, affirmative*)
〜ません	(*nonpast, polite, negative*)

〜ました	(*past, polite, affirmative*)
〜ませんでした	(*past, polite, negative*)

(*Continues.*)

二百三十一

Kanji
Learn these **kanji**:

朝	飲	見
明	入	起
午	休	読
昼	夕	火
来	今	水
行	週	木
聞	曜	金
食	毎	土
出	回	会

チェックリスト

Use this checklist to confirm that you can now:

- Talk about schedules
- Understand the basic structure of verbs
- Talk about daily activities
- Use past, polite verb forms
- Use particles showing grammatical relationships
- Talk about weekends and holidays
- Make suggestions in a new way
- Make phone calls
- Extend an invitation

Weather and Climate

第四章　天気・気候
てん　き　き　こう

今日は雨です。
きょう　　あめ

OBJECTIVES

In this lesson you are going to:

- Talk about weather reports
- Talk about the four seasons
- Talk about forecasting
- Learn how to conjugate adjectives
- Learn to use comparatives and superlatives
- Learn how to express plain, nonpast negative and plain past
- Learn how to explain a reason using 〜ので
- Study the **te**-form of adjectives and verbs
- Learn how to express possibility
- Learn how to ask questions about the Japanese language

YOOKOSO! MULTIMEDIA

Review and practice grammar and vocabulary from this chapter and watch video clips on the *Yookoso!* Interactive CD-ROM. Visit the *Yookoso!* Online Learning Center at **www.mhhe.com/yookoso3** for additional exercises and resources.

Vocabulary and Grammar 4A

Vocabulary and Oral Activities

Today's Weather
今日のお天気

暑いです

寒いです

雨です

晴れです

くもりです

雪です

風が強いです

言語ノート

Talking About the Weather

Discussing the weather is a ritual of daily conversation in many cultures, and Japan is no exception. In Japanese, a reference to the weather—
いいお天気ですね (*It's fine weather, isn't it?*)—can serve as a greeting, a substitute for *Hello, how are you?* This is partly because in former times Japan's economy was based on agriculture, especially rice cultivation; many people were concerned about the weather because it affected their livelihoods. In Japan today the weather is a neutral, impersonal topic for everyday conversations with new or old acquaintances. As you will see in **Reading 1** of this chapter, a reference to the weather or season is also a standard opening line for a personal letter.

Vocabulary: Weather and Climate

（お）天気	（お）てんき	weather
気候	きこう	climate
天気予報	てんきよほう	weather forecast
天気図	てんきず	weather map
いい天気	いいてんき	good weather
悪い天気	わるいてんき	bad weather
晴れる	はれる	to clear up
くもる		to become cloudy; to be cloudy
雨が降る	あめがふる	to rain (lit., *rain falls*)
雪が降る	ゆきがふる	to snow (lit., *snow falls*)
気温	きおん	(air) temperature
…度	…ど	…degrees (*counter*)
暖かい	あたたかい	warm
涼しい	すずしい	cool
むし暑い	むしあつい	sultry; hot and humid
風が吹く	かぜがふく	The wind blows.
風が弱い	かぜがよわい	There is a slight breeze. (lit., *The wind is weak.*)
台風	たいふう	typhoon
零下…	れいか…	…below zero

Review: 高<ruby>い<rt>たか</rt></ruby>、低<ruby>い<rt>ひく</rt></ruby>

> 寒<ruby><rt>さむ</rt></ruby>い and 冷<ruby><rt>つめ</rt></ruby>たい both translate as *cold* in English. 寒<ruby><rt>さむ</rt></ruby>い is used to refer to seasons, climates, or the atmosphere, while 冷<ruby><rt>つめ</rt></ruby>たい refers to a cold object that a person can touch or sense directly. Therefore, 寒<ruby><rt>さむ</rt></ruby>い気候<ruby><rt>きこう</rt></ruby> *cold climate*, but 冷<ruby><rt>つめ</rt></ruby>たい飲<ruby><rt>の</rt></ruby>み物<ruby><rt>もの</rt></ruby> *a cold drink*, 冷<ruby><rt>つめ</rt></ruby>たい風<ruby><rt>かぜ</rt></ruby> *a cold wind*, and 冷<ruby><rt>つめ</rt></ruby>たい人 *a cold (-hearted) person*. The parallel terms for *hot* are both pronounced あつい. The difference is apparent only when writing: 暑<ruby><rt>あつ</rt></ruby>い refers to seasons, climates, etc. while 熱<ruby><rt>あつ</rt></ruby>い refers to other things, such as 熱<ruby><rt>あつ</rt></ruby>いコーヒー *hot coffee*.

アクティビティー **1**

ダイアログ：今日<ruby><rt>きょう</rt></ruby>はどんなお天気<ruby><rt>てんき</rt></ruby>ですか。(*What is the weather like today?*)

電話<ruby><rt>でんわ</rt></ruby>で

ブラウン：長野<ruby><rt>ながの</rt></ruby>は今日<ruby><rt>きょう</rt></ruby>、どんなお天気<ruby><rt>てんき</rt></ruby>ですか。

友だち：晴<ruby>れ<rt>は</rt></ruby>ですよ。

ブラウン：気温<ruby><rt>きおん</rt></ruby>は何度<ruby><rt>なんど</rt></ruby>ぐらいですか。

友だち：10度<ruby><rt>ど</rt></ruby>ぐらいです。とても涼<ruby><rt>すず</rt></ruby>しいです。

ブラウン：風<ruby><rt>かぜ</rt></ruby>はありますか。

友だち：いいえ、ありません。

Practice this dialogue, drawing on information in the following table.

(Temperatures are in degrees Celsius. See the **Culture Note** following the table.)

On the phone   BROWN: What is the weather like in Nagano today?   FRIEND: It's sunny and clear.   BROWN: (About) what is the temperature?   FRIEND: It's about 10 degrees. It's quite cool. BROWN: Is there a breeze (lit., *wind*)?   FRIEND: No, there isn't.

(Continues.)

二百三十五

Place	Weather	Temperature	Wind
Nara	Rainy	18 degrees, warm	Weak wind
Kumamoto	Cloudy	25 degrees, warm	Weak wind
Yamagata	Snow	0 degrees, cold	Strong wind
Kanazawa	Cloudy	5 degrees, cool	No wind
Naha	Clear	30 degrees, hot	Weak wind

文化ノート

CULTURE NOTE: °C

When Japanese say 20 度 (*20 degrees*), they mean *20 degrees Celsius*. In Japan only the Celsius (centigrade) system is used to measure temperature. To specify which system you are using, you can say 摂氏 20度 (*20°C*) or 華氏 68度 (*68°F*), but don't expect Japanese to know the Fahrenheit (**華氏**) system. If you are good at calculating in your head, the formula for converting °C to °F is (°C × 9/5) + 32. Otherwise, you might want to start learning the system by remembering a few benchmark equivalents: the Celsius freezing point is 0 degrees, the boiling point is 100 degrees, and so on (see the scale below for more guideposts). One way or another, you will have to get used to the metric system in order to function freely in Japan.

Celsius	−20	−10	0	10	20	30	40
Fahrenheit	−4	14	32	50	68	86	104

アクティビティー **2**

雨がよく降りますか。(*Does it rain often?*)

Ask your partner what the weather is like in January where he or she grew up. Complete the table following the example of Tokyo.

For words expressing frequency, review Chapter 3.

	東京	Your Hometown	Your Partner's Hometown
晴れる	よく晴れます。		
くもる	時々くもります。		
雨	時々 降ります。		
雪	ほとんど降りません。		
気温	5度ぐらいです。		
風	時々 強い風が吹きます。		

Grammar and Practice Activities

17. Conjugating Adjectives 🎧

ブラウン：昨日寒かったですね。

林：ええ、本当に。

ブラウン：わたしのアパートには、ストーブがまだありませんから、

こまりました。

林：それはたいへんでしたね。

町田：プールはどうでしたか。

チン：人がとても多かったです。

町田：水はきれいでしたか。

チン：いいえ、あまりきれいではありませんでした。

町田：それはよくありませんでしたね。

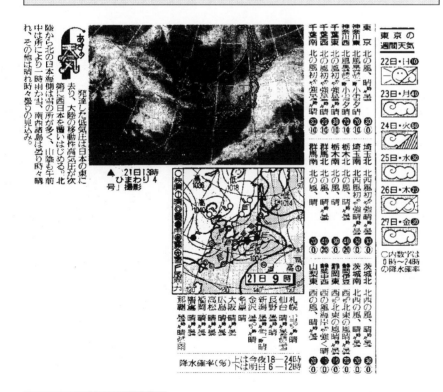

BROWN: It was cold yesterday, wasn't it?   HAYASHI: Yes, really.   BROWN: I had a hard time because there isn't a heater in my apartment yet.   HAYASHI: That must have been awful! (lit., *That was awful, wasn't it?*)

MACHIDA: How was the swimming pool?   CHIN: There were a lot of people.   MACHIDA: Was the water clean?   CHIN: No, it wasn't very clean.   MACHIDA: That's not good. (lit., *That wasn't good.*)

17.1 You have already studied the two types of Japanese adjectives, **i-**adjectives and **na-**adjectives. Both types of adjectives, like verbs, conjugate in terms of tense, politeness, and affirmation/negation and have at least eight basic conjugated forms when used as predicates (that is, when not in prenominal position).

17.2 You encountered the nonpast forms of **i-** and **na-**adjectives in Chapter 2, **Adjectives and Adverbs.** They are formed as follows.

*i-*Adjectives: 寒(さむ)い *(Cold)*		
Nonpast	**Plain**	**Polite**
Affirmative	Root + い (i.e., dictionary form) = 寒(さむ)い	Dictionary form + です = 寒(さむ)いです
Negative	Root + く + ない = 寒(さむ)くない	Root + く + ない + です = 寒(さむ)くないです or Root + く + ありません = 寒(さむ)くありません

> ないです expresses a stronger level of negation than ありません.

*na-*Adjectives: 静(しず)か *(Quiet)*		
Nonpast	**Plain**	**Polite**
Affirmative	Dictionary form + だ = 静(しず)かだ	Dictionary form + です = 静(しず)かです
Negative	Dictionary form + ではない or じゃない = 静(しず)かではない or 静(しず)かじゃない	Dictionary form + ではありません or じゃありません = 静(しず)かではありません or 静(しず)かじゃありません

> だ is the plain, nonpast, affirmative form of the copula です.

> じゃ is a contraction of では and is somewhat less formal and more colloquial than では.

Notice that **na-**adjectives themselves do not conjugate. Rather, the conjugated forms of the copula です (see **Grammar 1**) are appended to the dictionary form of a **na-**adjective.

17.3 The past forms of **i**-adjectives are formed as follows.

i-Adjectives: 寒い (*Cold*)		
Past	**Plain**	**Polite**
Affirmative	Root + かった = 寒かった	Plain, past + です = 寒かったです
Negative	Root + く + なかった = 寒くなかった	Root + く + なかったです = 寒くなかったです or Root + く + ありませんでした = 寒くありませんでした

大野先生はとてもきびしかったです。
Professor Oono was very strict.
その問題はあまりむずかしくありませんでした。
That problem wasn't very difficult.
その映画はぜんぜんおもしろくなかった。
That movie wasn't at all interesting.

The past forms of **na**-adjectives are formed by adding the conjugated forms of the copula です to their dictionary form.

na-Adjectives: 静か (*Quiet*)		
Past	**Plain**	**Polite**
Affirmative	静かだった	静かでした
Negative	静かではなかった or 静かじゃなかった	静かではあり ませんでした or 静かじゃあり ませんでした

その公園は静かでした。
That park was quiet.
チンさんはあまり元気ではありませんでした。
Ms. Chin wasn't feeling very well (lit., *wasn't very healthy*).
空がとてもきれいだった。
The sky was quite lovely.
あの人はあまり親切じゃなかった。
That person was not very kind.

二百三十九

17.4 よい (or **いい**) meaning *good* shows some irregularity, although it is an **i**-adjective.

Nonpast	Plain	Polite
Affirmative	よい or いい	いいです
Negative	よくない	よくありません or よくないです

Past	Plain	Polite
Affirmative	よかった	よかったです
Negative	よくなかった	よくありませんでした or よくなかったです

いい and **いいです** are colloquial forms of **よい** and **よいです**. These colloquial forms are more commonly used than **よい（です）** in informal conversations.

あの辞書はよくなかった。
That dictionary wasn't good.

アクティビティー **3**

忙しかったですか。(*Was he busy?*)

Disagree with these statements, using the model as a guide.

[例] ボストンは寒かったですか。（暑い）→
いいえ、寒くなかったです（寒くありませんでした）。暑かったです。

1. お天気は悪かったですか。（いい）
2. 東京は涼しかったですか。（暖かい）
3. その本はおもしろかったですか。（つまらない）
4. そこはきれいでしたか。（きたない）
5. そのレストランは静かでしたか。（うるさい）
6. 東京の冬は長かったですか。（短い）
7. まゆみさんは忙しかったですか。（ひま）
8. その先生はきびしかったですか。（やさしい）
9. その山 (*mountain*) は高かったですか。（低い）
10. その学生はまじめ (*serious*) でしたか。（ふまじめ *lazy, not serious*）

アクティビティー **4**

映画はおもしろくなかった。(*The movie wasn't good.*)

Change these sentences to the past tense, preserving the politeness level, as shown in the example.

[例] あの映画はおもしろくない。 → あの映画はおもしろくなかった。

1. アラスカはいつも寒いです。
2. 日本の夏はむし暑い。
3. 4月は毎日暖かい。
4. 今年の夏は涼しい。
5. ブラウンさんは元気じゃありません。
6. あの本はよくない。
7. 天気がいつも悪い。
8. カワムラさんはハンサムだ。
9. ギブソンさんはエレガントです。
10. この大学は有名ではない。

アクティビティー **5**

先生は昨日は元気でしたが... (*The teacher was fine yesterday, but...*)

Complete the following sentences by filling in each blank with the past form of an adjective.

[例] あの人は昨日は（　　　）が、今日は病気です。 →
　　　あの人は昨日は元気でしたが、今日は病気です。

1. わたしは昨日は（　　）が、今日はひまです。
2. 昨日は（　　）が、今日は暑いです。
3. 東京は昨日は気温が（　　）が、今日は低い。
4. そのショッピングセンターは昨日は人が（　　）が、今日は少ない。
5. 図書館は昨日は（　　）が、今日はうるさい。
6. 昨日は風が（　　）が、今日は弱いです。
7. 昨日は天気が（　　）が、今日は悪い。
8. 「ジョーズ I」は（　　）が、「ジョーズ IV」はつまらないです。

> The plain form + が is common in writing but in speech is usually used by male speakers. Females tend to use the plain form + けれども (けど).

二百四十一

アクティビティー **6**

昨日は月曜日でした。(*Yesterday was Monday.*)

Substituting 昨日 for 今日, change each predicate in the following passage to the corresponding past form.

今日は1月23日です。朝からとても寒いです。でも、お天気は
とてもいいです。空がとてもきれいです。風がありますが、あまり
強くありません。今日は土曜日ですから、クラスがありません。宿題
(*homework*) もありません。だから (*because of that*)、わたしはひまです。
今日は部屋 (*room*) を掃除します。わたしの部屋はとてもきたないです。
それから、洗濯もします。わたしのルームメートは病気です。部屋に
います。

アクティビティー **7**

昨日はどんなお天気でしたか。(*What was the weather like yesterday?*)

Use this summary of yesterday's weather in five Japanese cities to answer the questions that follow.

Place	Weather	Temperature	Wind
Sapporo	Snow	−5 degrees, cold	Strong wind
Sendai	Cloudy	7 degrees, cool	No wind
Maebashi	Rain	9 degrees, cool	Strong wind
Hiroshima	Clear	15 degrees, warm	No wind
Kagoshima	Clear	27 degrees, hot	Weak wind

1. 昨日、札幌はどんなお天気でしたか。寒かったですか。暑かったです
   か。風はありましたか。
2. 仙台はどんなお天気でしたか。気温は何度でしたか。風は
   ありましたか。
3. 前橋はどんなお天気でしたか。涼しかったですか。暖かかったですか。
   風は強かったですか。弱かったですか。

4. 広島のお天気はよかったですか。涼しかったですか。暖かかったです
か。

5. 鹿児島のお天気はよかったですか、悪かったですか。寒かったですか。
暑かったですか。気温は何度でしたか。

Now talk about yesterday's weather in your town with your classmates.

18. Comparatives and Superlatives 🎧

林：ロサンゼルスはマイアミより暑いですか。

カワムラ：いいえ、マイアミのほうが暑いです。

林：では、ロサンゼルスとマイアミとどちらのほうがたくさん雨が
降りますか。

カワムラ：マイアミのほうがたくさん降ります。

チン：札幌と仙台と東京の中でどこが一番寒いですか。

町田：札幌です。

チン：その三の中でどこが一番北にありますか。

町田：札幌が一番北にあります。

チン：なるほど。

ブラウン：仙台と山形とどちらのほうが寒いですか。

三村：山形のほうが寒いです。

ブラウン：じゃ、どちらのほうが雪がたくさん降りますか。

三村：やはり、山形のほうですね。1メートル*ぐらい降ります。

18.1 A sentence that compares *two* quantities or qualities, such as *John is taller than Mary* or *John ate more than Mary,* is called a *comparative sentence.* A Japanese comparative sentence takes one of two forms, as follows. Y より means *more than Y* or *compared to Y.*

> **N**ote that unlike English, adjectives in Japanese do not have comparative or superlative forms.

HAYASHI: Is it hotter in Los Angeles than in Miami?   KAWAMURA: No, it's hotter in Miami.
HAYASHI: Well, which has more rain—Los Angeles or Miami?   KAWAMURA: It rains more in Miami.
CHIN: Which is coldest—Sapporo, Sendai, or Tokyo?   MACHIDA: Sapporo.   CHIN: Among them, which is farthest north?   MACHIDA: Sapporo is farthest north.   CHIN: I see.
BROWN: Which is colder, Sendai or Yamagata?   MIMURA: Yamagata is colder.   BROWN: Then, which has more snow?   MIMURA: As you might expect, Yamagata. It snows about one meter.

---

*One meter is about 3.3 feet. Some people say メーター instead of メートル.

(Continues.)

```
X  は  Y  より      adjective
```

X is more…than Y. (lit., *More than Y, X is…*)

とうきょう　おおさか
東京は大阪より大きい。
Tokyo is larger than Osaka. (lit., *More than Osaka, Tokyo is large.*)

はやし　　　　みむら
林さんは三村さんよりまじめですか。
Is Mr. Hayashi more serious than Mr. Mimura? (lit., *More than Mr. Mimura, is Mr. Hayashi serious?*)

```
X  は  Y  より      adverb + verb
```

X does…more (…) than Y. (lit., *More than Y, X does…*)

ことし　ふゆ　きょねん　　　　　　あめ　　　　　　　　　ふ
今年の冬は去年の冬より雨がたくさん降りました。
It rained more this winter than last winter.

はや　お
ブラウンさんはギブソンさんより早く起きました。
Ms. Brown got up earlier than Ms. Gibson.

18.2 To ask a comparative question, use the following construction, which means *Of X and Y, which (alternative) is/does (more)…*

```
X  と  Y  と  どちら（のほう）が    adjective or       か
                                    adverb + verb
```

Which (alternative) is more…—X or Y?
Which (alternative) does…more (…) —X or Y?

The answer to this question takes the following form, meaning *The (alternative of) X is (more)…*

```
X （のほう）が      adjective or
                    adverb + verb
```

X is more…
X does (something) more…

横井先生と大野先生とどちら（のほう）がきびしいですか。

Who is stricter—Professor Yokoi or Professor Oono? (lit., *Of Professor Yokoi and Professor Oono, which* [alternative] *is strict?*)

大野先生のほうがきびしいです。

Professor Oono is stricter. (lit., *The alternative of Professor Oono is strict.*)

ブラウンさんとギブソンさんとどちら（のほう）が早く起きますか。

Who gets up earlier—Ms. Brown or Ms. Gibson? (lit., *Of Ms. Brown and Ms. Gibson, which* [alternative] *gets up early?*)

ブラウンさんのほうが早く起きます。

Ms. Brown gets up earlier. (lit., *The alternative of Ms. Brown gets up early.*)

> **N**otice that when はやい is used in its temporal meaning of *early*, the character 早い is used. When はやい means fast or quick, use the character 速い.

言語ノート

Adverbs Used with Comparatives

The following adverbs expressing degree are often used in comparative sentences.

ずっと	by far
もっと	more
少し or ちょっと	a little

この大学はあの大学よりずっと大きい。

This university is far bigger than that university.

アンカレッジはバンクーバーよりもっと寒いです。

Anchorage is colder (*lit.*, more cold) than Vancouver.

山口さんは高田さんより少し（ちょっと）若い。

Mr. Yamaguchi is a bit younger than Mr. Takada.

The counter . . . 倍 (*times*, as in magnification) or a specific number (plus the appropriate counter, if necessary) specifies the extent of the difference in comparisons. These expressions come before adjectives or adverbs.

この電車はあの電車より3倍速い。

This train is three times faster than that train.

カプチーノはカフェオレより200円高いです。

Cappuccino costs 200 yen more than cafe au lait.

18.3 A *superlative sentence* is one that compares the quality or quantity of *three or more* entities and specifies which entity has most of that quality or quantity. For instance, *Who is the most popular actress in the United States—Julia Roberts, Angelina Jolie, or Nicole Kidman?*

A Japanese superlative sentence takes one of the following forms. (一番 [lit., *number one*] means *most*.)

X とYとZ	の中で or のうちで	X が (or other particle)	一番	adjective or adverb + verb

> *X is the most…among X, Y, and Z.*
> *X does…the most (…) among X, Y, and Z.*

ロンドンとパリとモスクワの中で、モスクワが一番寒い。
Among London, Paris, and Moscow, Moscow is the coldest.

あの四人のうちで、ギブソンさんが一番速く走ります。
Among those four people, Ms. Gibson runs fastest.

ビール、ジュース、コーラの中でコーラを一番よく飲みます。
Among beer, juice, and cola, I drink cola most often.

18.4 An *equative sentence* is one that equates two entities. For example, *He is as tall as I am.* Equative sentences in Japanese are expressed as follows.

X は Y と 同じぐらい	adjective or adverb + verb

As you remember, 同じ means *same* and ぐらい means *about*. The phrase 同じぐらい means *to (about) the same extent* or *to (about) the same degree.* This sentence means *X is about the same as Y with regard to…*

広島の三月は鹿児島の三月と同じぐらい暖かいです。
March in Hiroshima is about as warm as March in Kagoshima.

町田さんは林さんと同じぐらいよくここに来ます。
Ms. Machida comes here about as often as Mr. Hayashi.

A negative equative sentence such as *A is not as… as B* is expressed with this structure. (ほど means *as much as.*)

X は Y ほど	negative form of adjective or adverb + negative form of verb

X is/does not…as much as Y.

<ruby>春<rt>はる</rt></ruby>の<ruby>夜<rt>よる</rt></ruby>は<ruby>秋<rt>あき</rt></ruby>の<ruby>夜<rt>よる</rt></ruby>ほど<ruby>寒<rt>さむ</rt></ruby>くない。
Spring evenings aren't as cold as fall evenings.

あの人はチンさんほど<ruby>速<rt>はや</rt></ruby>く<ruby>話<rt>はな</rt></ruby>しません。
That person doesn't talk as fast as Ms. Chin.

アクティビティー **8**

この<ruby>大学<rt>だいがく</rt></ruby>のほうが大きいです。 (*This university is bigger.*)

Make dialogues, following the pattern of the example.

[例] （この<ruby>大学<rt>だいがく</rt></ruby>）（あの大学）（大きい）→
　　　—この<ruby>大学<rt>だいがく</rt></ruby>とあの大学とどちらが大きいですか。
　　　—この<ruby>大学<rt>だいがく</rt></ruby>のほうが大きいです or この大学です。

1. （この<ruby>町<rt>まち</rt></ruby>）（フローレンス）（きれい）
2. （ペプシ）（コーク）（おいしい）
3. （日本の<ruby>車<rt>くるま</rt></ruby>）（アメリカの<ruby>車<rt>くるま</rt></ruby>）（<ruby>安<rt>やす</rt></ruby>い）
4. （フロリダ）（ネバダ）（<ruby>雨<rt>あめ</rt></ruby>がたくさん<ruby>降<rt>ふ</rt></ruby>る）
5. （<ruby>去年<rt>きょねん</rt></ruby>の<ruby>夏<rt>なつ</rt></ruby>）（<ruby>今年<rt>ことし</rt></ruby>の<ruby>夏<rt>なつ</rt></ruby>）（<ruby>暑<rt>あつ</rt></ruby>い）
6. （トロント）（エドモントン）（<ruby>雪<rt>ゆき</rt></ruby>が<ruby>多<rt>おお</rt></ruby>い）
7. （<ruby>昨日<rt>きのう</rt></ruby>）（<ruby>今日<rt>きょう</rt></ruby>）（<ruby>涼<rt>すず</rt></ruby>しい）
8. （<ruby>南日本<rt>みなみにほん</rt></ruby>）（<ruby>北日本<rt>きたにほん</rt></ruby>）（<ruby>台風<rt>たいふう</rt></ruby>がたくさん<ruby>来<rt>く</rt></ruby>る）

アクティビティー **9**

あなたはわたしより<ruby>速<rt>はや</rt></ruby>いです。(*You are quicker than I am.*)

Fill in the blanks to complete the sentences.

[例] このセーターはあのセーターより（<ruby>高<rt>たか</rt></ruby>いです）。

1. <ruby>東京<rt>とうきょう</rt></ruby>はニューヨークより（　　）。
2. アメリカは日本より<ruby>人口<rt>じんこう</rt></ruby>が（　　）。

(*Continues.*)

3. アメリカ人は日本人より（　　）。

4. 日本はメキシコより（　　）。

5. わたしはカワムラさんより（　　）。

6. わたしの日本語の先生は横井_{よこい}先生より（　　）。

7. 日本語はラテン語より（　　）。

8. この本はあの本より（　　）。

―― アクティビティー 10

わたしはあなたほど速_{はや}くありません。(*I'm not as quick as you.*)

Change the following into negative sentences.

［例］ この大学_{だいがく}はあの大学より大きいです。 →
あの大学_{だいがく}はこの大学ほど大きくありません。

1. 林_{はやし}さんはカワムラさんよりたくさん食_たべます。

2. 京都_{きょうと}は東京_{とうきょう}より古_{ふる}いです。

3. 昨日_{きのう}は今日_{きょう}よりむし暑_{あつ}かった。

4. 林_{はやし}さんは三村_{みむら}さんよりお酒_{さけ}が好_すきだ。

5. チンさんはシュミットさんより日本語をじょうずに (*skillfully, well*) 話す。

6. 札幌_{さっぽろ}は秋田_{あきた}より雪_{ゆき}が多_{おお}く (*a lot*) 降_ふります。

7. 町田_{まちだ}さんは本田_{ほんだ}さんよりキュートです。

8. この映画_{えいが}はあの映画_{えいが}よりおもしろかった。

―― アクティビティー 11

誰_{だれ}が一番_{いちばん}速_{はや}いですか。 (*Who is the quickest?*)

Using the words provided, make dialogues as shown in the example.

［例］ （ヘミングウェー）（ホーソン）（クラベル）（有名_{ゆうめい}）→
—ヘミングウェーとホーソンとクラベルの中で誰_{だれ}が一番_{いちばん}有名_{ゆうめい}ですか。
—ヘミングウェーが一番_{いちばん}有名_{ゆうめい}です。

Use the interrogative だれ (*who*) when asking about people, どれ (*which one*) when asking about things, concepts, and events, and どこ (*where*) when asking about places.

1. （日本語）（ロシア語）（アラビア語）（むずかしい）
2. （プレリュード）（ミヤタ）（アクラ・レジェンド）（高い）
3. （シカゴ）（ロサンジェルス）（ダラス）（風が強い）
4. （ミシガン）（フロリダ）（アイダホ）（暖かい）
5. （バス）（車）（電車）（便利）
6. （スーパー）（デパート）（セブン・イレブン）（安い）
7. （ビール）（お茶）（コーヒー）（よく飲む）

ア ク テ ィ ビ テ ィ ー　12

どの名前が 一番 好きですか。 *(What name do you like best?)*

Answer the following questions in Japanese.

1. アメリカで一番 大きい都市 *(city)* はどこですか。
2. アメリカで一番 古い都市はどこですか。
3. 世界 *(world)* で一番 高い建物は何ですか。
4. アメリカで一番 きれいな都市はどこですか。
5. アメリカで一番 有名な日本人はだれですか。
6. 日本の食べ物の中で何が一番 好きですか。
7. 一年 中 で何月が一番 暑いですか。
8. 一年 中 で何月が一番 寒いですか。
9. 一年 中 で何月が一番 忙 しいですか。
10. スポーツの中で何が一番 おもしろいですか。
11. 日本語の中でどのことば *(word)* が一番 好きですか。

ア ク テ ィ ビ テ ィ ー　13

どちらのほうが 暖かいですか。*(Which place is warmer?)*

Look at the following table of Japanese cities (arranged in order of northernmost to southernmost) while your instructor describes the weather for tomorrow.

(Continues.)

Tomorrow's Weather				
City	Weather	Temperature	Wind	Notes
Sapporo	Snow (30 cm)	−15°C	North, 20 km/h	Heavy snowfall
Aomori	Clear	−12°C	West, 5 km/h	Foggy
Niigata	Snow (10 cm)	−11°C	North, 30 km/h	Snowstorm
Tokyo	Cloudy	5°C	No wind	Rain in the afternoon
Shizuoka	Cloudy	14°C	South, 5 km/h	Storm at night
Nagoya	Rain (5 mm)	18°C	No wind	Cloudy in the afternoon
Osaka	Clear	9°C	East, 5 km/h	Clear until Saturday
Hiroshima	Rain (15 mm)	17°C	South, 5 km/h	Cloudy in the afternoon
Kagoshima	Rain (40 mm)	21°C	West, 50 km/h	Typhoon No. 2 Thursday
Naha	Clear	30°C	No wind	Sultry

Now look at the preceding table and describe the weather in several cities to a classmate.

[例] s1: 東京は、どんなお天気ですか。

s2: くもりです。午後は雨です。気温は5度ぐらいです。風はありません。

Answer the following questions.

1. 札幌と青森とどちらのほうが寒いですか。
2. 札幌と新潟とどちらのほうが雪がたくさん降りますか。
3. 青森と札幌と新潟の中でどこが一番寒いですか。
4. 静岡と大阪とどちらのほうが暖かいですか。
5. 大阪と那覇とどちらのほうが暑いですか。
6. 広島と名古屋と鹿児島の中でどこが一番雨が降りますか。
7. 新潟と札幌とどちらのほうが風が強いですか。
8. どこが一番風が強いですか。
9. どこが一番寒いですか。
10. どこが一番暑いですか。

km = kilometer (⅝ of a mile)
...km/h is read 時速 /
...キロ（メートル）

Although typhoons are designated by name in the Western world, the Japanese identify them by number, starting with 1 each year. The counter ...号 [number] is used with typhoons.

VOCABULARY LIBRARY 🎧

Precipitation and Other Weather Terms

湿度	しつど	humidity
気圧	きあつ	air pressure
小雨	こさめ	light rain
にわか雨	にわかあめ	shower
どしゃぶり		downpour (*of rain*)
梅雨	つゆ	rainy season
		(*in June and July*)
降水量	こうすいりょう	precipitation
嵐	あらし	storm
あられ		hail

文化ノート

CULTURE NOTE: Types of Rain

Rain has exerted a strong influence on Japanese life and culture since ancient times. For centuries the majority of Japanese people made their living in agriculture, for which rainfall is crucial. The amount and type of rain determined success or failure for a farmer's crop. Over the years, the Japanese coined many words to distinguish different types of rain. Among them are さみだれ (*early summer rain*), しぐれ (*drizzle*), にわかあめ (*shower*), はるさめ (*spring rain*), あきさめ (*autumn rain*), and

今日は雨がシトシト降ります。

(Continues.)

二百五十一

むらさめ (*passing rain*). There are also numerous ways to describe the manner of the rain's fall with onomatopoeia. (The Japanese language includes so many onomatopoeia that entire dictionaries are devoted to them.)

雨^{あめ}がザーザー降^ふります。
It rains cats and dogs. (lit., *It rains "zaa zaa."*)

雨がシトシト降ります。
It drizzles. (lit., *It rains "shito shito."*)

雨がポツポツ降ります。
It rains in big scattered drops. (lit., *It rains "potsu potsu."*)

Although a greater volume of rain falls in the autumn, Japan has a rainy season—called 梅雨(つゆ)—that consists of more or less constant drizzle for a month or so starting in mid-June. While the rainy season is uncomfortably cold and damp or hot and humid, it is, as the Japanese frequently remind themselves, good for the farmers.

アクティビティー **14**

何月^{なんがつ}が一番寒^{いちばんさむ}いですか。 (*Which month is coldest?*)

Using this table of actual average temperatures and rainfall in Tokyo, answer the questions that follow.

東京^{とうきょう}

Month	1	2	3	4	5	6	7	8	9	10	11	12
Temp. (°C)	5	6	8	14	18	22	25	27	23	17	12	7
Precip. (mm)	54	63	102	128	148	181	125	137	193	181	93	56

1. 東京^{とうきょう}は7月と8月とどちらが暑^{あつ}いですか。
2. 何月^{なんがつ}が一番寒^{いちばんさむ}いですか。
3. 4月と5月とどちらのほうがたくさん雨^{あめ}が降^ふりますか。
4. 1月と2月と3月の中で何月^{なんがつ}が一番^{いちばん}雨^{あめ}が多^{おお}いですか。
5. 何月^{なんがつ}が一番^{いちばん}雨^{あめ}が多^{おお}いですか。

Now, look at these statistics about the climate in five international cities and answer the questions. (Temperature is in degrees centigrade, and precipitation is in millimeters.)

Month	1	2	3	4	5	6	7	8	9	10	11	12
LONDON												
Temperature	4	4	7	9	12	16	18	17	15	11	7	5
Precipitation	53	40	37	38	46	46	56	59	50	57	64	48

Month	1	2	3	4	5	6	7	8	9	10	11	12
PARIS												
Temperature	3	4	7	10	14	17	19	18	16	11	7	4
Precipitation	54	43	32	38	52	50	55	62	51	49	50	49
SYDNEY												
Temperature	22	22	21	18	16	13	12	13	15	18	19	21
Precipitation	104	125	129	101	115	141	94	83	72	80	77	86
MOSCOW												
Temperature	−10	−9	−4	5	12	17	19	17	11	4	−2	−7
Precipitation	31	28	33	35	52	67	74	74	58	51	36	36
BUENOS AIRES												
Temperature	24	23	20	17	13	11	10	11	14	16	20	22
Precipitation	92	84	122	87	78	55	42	58	88	100	79	90

1. ロンドンでは何月が一番気温が高いですか。何月が一番気温が低いですか。
2. ロンドンでは何月が一番降水量 (precipitation) が多いですか。何月が一番降水量が少ないですか。
3. シドニーとブエノスアイレスとどちらが1月の気温が高いですか。
4. シドニーとブエノスアイレスとどちらが7月の降水量が多いですか。
5. ロンドンとパリとモスクワの中でどこが8月の気温が一番高いですか。

Make up similar questions about the table to ask your classmates.

19. The Past, Plain Forms of Verbs

さとみ：昨日、映画に行ったの。
大助：うん。
さとみ：何を見たの。
大助：「ニンジャ」。おもしろかったよ。

Note that plain forms of verbs and adjectives are used in these conversations between family members (between brother and sister in the first dialogue and between mother and daughter in the second). As discussed in **Grammar 11**, Chapter 3, plain forms are common in conversations among members of the same in-group.

SATOMI: Did you go to the movies yesterday?　DAISUKE: Yeah.　SATOMI: What did you see? DAISUKE: *Ninja*. It was good. (lit., *It was interesting.*)

(*Continues.*)

ゆり子：さとみ、昼ごはんを食べたの。

さとみ：ええ、カワムラさんと「ユアーズ」で食べたわ。

ゆり子：「ユアーズ」...どこにあるの。

さとみ：先月、駅の前にできたのよ。
　　　　知らないの?

19.1 You have studied the past, polite forms of the three classes of verbs. The formation of the past, plain forms of Class 2 verbs is very simple.

> For the definition of *past, plain,* and the three classes of verbs, review **Grammar 11** in Chapter 3. For the sake of explanation, we will start with Class 2 verbs here.

Affirmative:	Root + た	Negative:	Root + なかった

Dictionary Form	Root	Past, Plain, Affirmative	Past, Plain, Negative
食べる to eat	食べ	食べた	食べなかった
見る to see	見	見た	見なかった
着る to wear	着	着た	着なかった
変える to change	変え	変えた	変えなかった

19.2 The past, plain forms of Class 3 verbs (the irregular verbs する and くる) are as follows.

Dictionary Form	Past, Plain, Affirmative	Past, Plain, Negative
する to do	した	しなかった
来る to come	来た	来なかった

19.3 The past, plain, negative form of Class 1 verbs is formed on the same stem as the plain, nonpast negative, but the ending is なかった instead of ない.

YURIKO: Satomi, did you eat lunch?　SATOMI: Yes, I ate with Mr. Kawamura at Yours. YURIKO: Yours? Where is it?　SATOMI: It opened in front of the station last month. Don't you know (about it)?

Dictionary Form Root + Ending	Nonpast, Plain, Negative Form	Past, Plain, Negative Form
書か + く	書か + か + ない	書か + か + なかった
話は + す	話は + さ + ない	話は + さ + なかった
立た + つ	立た + た + ない	立た + た + なかった
死し + ぬ	死し + な + ない	死し + な + なかった
読よ + む	読よ + ま + ない	読よ + ま + なかった
乗の + る	乗の + ら + ない	乗の + ら + なかった
泳およ + ぐ	泳およ + が + ない	泳およ + が + なかった
洗あら + う	洗あら + わ + ない	洗あら + わ + なかった

u-column	→	a-column
く	→	か
す	→	さ
つ	→	た
ぬ	→	な
む	→	ま
る	→	ら
ぐ	→	が

The past, plain, negative form of **ある** *to exist* is simply **なかった**.

Remember that this rule applies to the formation of the nonpast, plain, negative form of these verbs: **洗わない, 言わない**.

The past, plain, affirmative form of Class 1 verbs depends on the dictionary form ending.

1. When the dictionary ending is **く**

   Rule: Change it to **いた**.

   書か く → 書か いた (*wrote*)

   There is only one exception to this rule: 行く (*to go*).

   行い く → 行い った (*went*)

2. When the dictionary ending is **ぐ**

   Rule: Change it to **いだ**.

   泳およ ぐ → 泳およ いだ (*swam*)

3. When the dictionary ending is **う, つ,** or **る**

   Rule: Change it to **った**.

   買か う → 買か った (*bought*)
   立た つ → 立た った (*stood*)
   乗の る → 乗の った (*rode*)

4. When the dictionary ending is **ぬ, む,** or **ぶ**

   Rule: Change it to **んだ**.

   死し ぬ → 死し んだ (*died*)
   読よ む → 読よ んだ (*read* [*past*])
   呼よ ぶ → 呼よ んだ (*called*)

As mentioned in **Grammar 11,** Chapter 3, **ない** in 書かない, 食べない, しない, etc. (the nonpast, plain, negative form) is an adjective expressing negativity. It is an **i**-adjective and conjugates as such. In this chapter, you have already studied how to form the past, plain forms of **i**-adjectives. In the past, plain, negative forms 書かなかった, 食べなかった, しなかった, etc., なかった is the past, plain form of **ない**.

Note that the past, plain, affirmative forms of 読よむ and 呼よぶ happen to have the same sound sequence: よんだ. Their accent patterns, however, are different.

(*Continues.*)

5. When the word ending is **す**

    Rule: Change it to **した**.

      話<ruby>話<rt>はな</rt></ruby>す → 話<ruby>話<rt>はな</rt></ruby>した (*spoke*)

The conjugations of the past, plain, affirmative form of Class 1 verbs are summarized in the following table.

Dictionary Ending	Past, Plain, Affirmative Ending	Examples
く	→いた	書<ruby>書<rt>か</rt></ruby>く→書<ruby>書<rt>か</rt></ruby>いた exception 行<ruby>行<rt>い</rt></ruby>く→行<ruby>行<rt>い</rt></ruby>った
ぐ	→いだ	泳<ruby>泳<rt>およ</rt></ruby>ぐ→泳<ruby>泳<rt>およ</rt></ruby>いだ
う、つ、る	→った	買<ruby>買<rt>か</rt></ruby>う→買<ruby>買<rt>か</rt></ruby>った 立<ruby>立<rt>た</rt></ruby>つ→立<ruby>立<rt>た</rt></ruby>った 乗<ruby>乗<rt>の</rt></ruby>る→乗<ruby>乗<rt>の</rt></ruby>った
ぬ、む、ぶ	→んだ	死<ruby>死<rt>し</rt></ruby>ぬ→死<ruby>死<rt>し</rt></ruby>んだ 読<ruby>読<rt>よ</rt></ruby>む→読<ruby>読<rt>よ</rt></ruby>んだ 呼<ruby>呼<rt>よ</rt></ruby>ぶ→呼<ruby>呼<rt>よ</rt></ruby>んだ
す	→した	話<ruby>話<rt>はな</rt></ruby>す→話<ruby>話<rt>はな</rt></ruby>した

Here are some sample sentences using the past, plain form of verbs.

昨日<ruby>昨日<rt>きのう</rt></ruby>の夜<ruby>夜<rt>よる</rt></ruby>、雨<ruby>雨<rt>あめ</rt></ruby>がたくさん降<ruby>降<rt>ふ</rt></ruby>った。
It rained a lot last night.
強<ruby>強<rt>つよ</rt></ruby>い風<ruby>風<rt>かぜ</rt></ruby>が一日中<ruby>一日中<rt>いちにちじゅう</rt></ruby>吹<ruby>吹<rt>ふ</rt></ruby>いた。
A strong wind blew all day.
山田<ruby>山田<rt>やまだ</rt></ruby>さんはアメリカへ行<ruby>行<rt>い</rt></ruby>ったけど、わたしは行かなかった。
Mr. Yamada went to America, but I didn't.
昨日<ruby>昨日<rt>きのう</rt></ruby>は8時から10時までテレビを見<ruby>見<rt>み</rt></ruby>た。その後<ruby>後<rt>あと</rt></ruby>、ラジオを聞<ruby>聞<rt>き</rt></ruby>いた。
I watched TV from 8:00 to 10:00 yesterday. After that, I listened to the radio.
かれは夕<ruby>夕<rt>ゆう</rt></ruby>ごはんをぜんぜん食<ruby>食<rt>た</rt></ruby>べなかった。
He didn't eat any dinner at all.

The past, plain, affirmative form of a verb is used to express a past action or event in an informal context. It is also used as a component of several other grammatical structures you will study later on. These other significant grammatical structures require the ability to conjugate this verb form, so it is important that you master this form now.

In most cases, the past, plain, affirmative form of a verb ends in **-ta,** so we will refer to this form as the **ta-**form.

> The past, plain, affirmative form of an adjective is also called the **ta-**form of an adjective.

アクティビティー 15

8時に出^でかけました。(*I went out at 8:00.*)

Put these sentences into the past tense, maintaining the plain form of the verb.

[例]　チンさんは中国語^{ちゅうごくご}で話す。→ チンさんは中国語で話した。

1. ブラウンさんは5時半に起^おきる。
2. 歯^はを一日^{かいみが}に3回 磨く。
3. 毎日^{まいにち}10キロ走^{はし}る。
4. オレンジ・ジュースを飲^のむ。
5. 高田^{たかだ}さんは7時に出^でかける。
6. デパートの前でギブソンさんを待^まつ (*wait*)。
7. 毎日^{まいにち}クラスへ行^いく。
8. 家^{いえ}から大学までバスに乗^のる。
9. 図書館^{としょかん}でチンさんに会^あう。
10. テレビでニュースを見^みる。
11. 午後^{ごご}プール で 泳^{およ}ぐ。
12. フランス語を勉強^{べんきょう}する。
13. 土曜日^{どようび}は家^{いえ}で休^{やす}む。
14. お風呂^{ふろ}に入^{はい}る。
15. 12時に寝^ねる。
16. いつもパーティーに来^くる。

アクティビティー 16

チンさんは 出^でかけた。　(*Ms. Chin went out.*)

Rewrite the following sentences changing the verb form from polite to plain.

[例]　昨日東京^{きのうとうきょう}へ来^きました。→ 昨日東京へ来た。

1. 先週^{せんしゅう}は雨^{あめ}がたくさん降^ふりました。
2. デパートでプレゼントを買^かいました。
3. パーティーでは山田^{やまだ}さんに会^あいませんでした。

(*Continues.*)

4. 高田さんは昨日、ワシントンから帰りました。

5. わたしはぜんぜん勉強しませんでした。

6. 昨日、ブラウンさんと話しませんでした。

7. かれのおじいさん (*grandfather*) は去年死にました。
   (死ぬ: *to die*)

8. 今朝、歯を磨きませんでした。

9. 昨日はお酒を飲みましたか。

10. 昨日、顔を洗いませんでした。

11. もうテレビのニュースは見ましたか。

12. ここに何時に着きました (*arrived*) か。

13. 昨晩はあまり寝ませんでした。

14. ディズニーランドでコーヒーカップに乗りました (*rode*)。

15. 林さんはもう出かけましたか。

16. 高田さんはスーパーへ行きました。

17. 一週間お風呂に入りませんでした。

18. シャワーは浴びましたか。

20. Explaining a Reason: …のだ 🎧

林：昨日はクラスに来ませんでしたね。

三村：ええ、アルバイトがあったんです。

林：今日はクラスに出るんですか。

三村：ええ、雨が降ったから、テニスの練習がないです。

ブラウン：林さんは何を笑っているのですか。

町田：さあ、わかりません。

ブラウン：林さん、何がおかしいんですか。

林：今、漫画を読んでいるんです。ハハハ…

HAYASHI: You didn't come to class yesterday, did you? MIMURA: No (lit., *Yes*), because I had (to go to) my part-time job. HAYASHI: Are you going to attend class today? MIMURA: Yes. Because it rained, I don't have (lit., *there isn't*) tennis practice.

BROWN: What is Mr. Hayashi laughing at? MACHIDA: I don't know. BROWN: Mr. Hayashi, what's so funny? HAYASHI: I'm reading a comic book (now). Ha, ha, ha…

カーティス：ストーブはどこですか。

チン：寒^{さむ}いんですか。

カーティス：風邪^{かぜ}をひいたんです。

チン：いつからですか。

カーティス：昨日^{きのう}からです。

林^{はやし}：北海道^{ほっかいどう}は寒^{さむ}かったんじゃありませんか。

ギブソン：はい、とても寒^{さむ}かったです。

林：雪^{ゆき}はたくさんありましたか。

ギブソン：いいえ、ぜんぜんなかったんです。

林：ぜんぜんなかったんですか。

ギブソン：はい、ぜんぜん。

Sentences ending in のだ (polite form のです) explain the reason for some event or information known to both speaker and hearer. In colloquial speech んだ (polite form んです) commonly replaces のだ (のです).

Consider these two sentences, for example.

寒^{さむ}いですか。

寒^{さむ}いんですか。

In the first sentence, the speaker has no idea whether or not the person addressed feels cold. Therefore, it is simply a straightforward question: *Are you cold?* In the second, the speaker assumes that the person addressed feels cold because, say, he is shivering or wearing a thick sweater. The second sentence, then, asks for an explanation: *Is it that you're cold?*

Similarly, if you see a friend getting ready to do something, it would be odd to say

何^{なに}をしますか。
What are you going to do?

CURTIS: Where is the heater?　CHIN: Are you cold?　CURTIS: (It's that) I've caught a cold.
CHIN: Since when?　CURTIS: Since yesterday.

HAYASHI: Wasn't it cold in Hokkaido?　GIBSON: Yes, it was very cold.　HAYASHI: Was there a lot of snow?　GIBSON: No, there wasn't any at all.　HAYASHI: There wasn't any at all?
GIBSON: That's right, (lit., *Yes*) none at all.

(*Continues.*)

because you have actually seen his or her preparations and know that he or she is about to do something. This information is shared between the two of you, so it's more appropriate to say

何をするんですか。

What are you going to do? (lit., *What is it that you are going to do?*)

Verbs, adjectives, and nouns may precede のです（んです）. In the case of verbs, the plain form is used.

チンさんにもう言ったんですか。

Did you already tell Ms. Chin? (lit., *Is it that you already told Ms. Chin?*)

林さんに電話しないのですか。

Aren't you going to call Mr. Hayashi?

The plain form of **i**-adjectives may also precede のです.

なぜ顔が赤いんですか。

Why is your face red?

夏でしたが、あまり暑くなかったんです。

It was summer, but it wasn't very hot.

When the nonpast, affirmative form of **na**-adjectives or nouns is used, な precedes のです（んです）.

三村さんはどうして有名なんですか。

Why is Mr. Mimura famous?

林さんは学生ではないんですか。

Isn't Mr. Hayashi a student?

チンさんは元気だったんですか。

Was Ms. Chin well?

言語ノート

Answering Negative Questions

In English, you answer in the same way whether you are asked a question affirmatively or negatively. Thus, whether you are asked, "Will you attend today's class?" or "Won't you attend today's class?" you would say "Yes, I will attend" or "No, I won't attend."

In Japanese, the way you answer a negative question depends on the addressee's presupposition or previous knowledge. In the dialogue on p. 259, Hayashi asks 北海道は寒かったんじゃありませんか

(*Wasn't it cold in Hokkaido?*), assuming that it must have been cold in Hokkaido around that time. In this case, you would answer

はい、寒^{さむ}かったです。

Yes, it was cold.

いいえ、寒^{さむ}くありませんでした。

No, it wasn't cold.

On the other hand, when he asks the question ぜんぜんなかったんですか (*Wasn't there snow at all?*), Hayashi already knows that there was no snow at all. In this case, you would answer

はい、ぜんぜんありませんでした。

lit., **Yes, there wasn't any at all.**

いいえ、たくさんありました。

lit., **No, there was a lot.**

Let's consider another example. Someone asks you クラスへ行^いかないんですか. (*Aren't you going to class?*) If you think the questioner assumes you won't go to class, you would respond

はい、行きません。

lit., **Yes, I won't go.**

いいえ、行きます。

lit., **No, I will go.**

If you think the questioner assumes you *will* go to class, you would respond

はい、行きます。

Yes, I will go.

いいえ、行きません。

No, I won't go.

You have to decide how to answer based on your guess about the questioner's knowledge, his or her facial expression, and other contextual factors. In addition, the intonation pattern of the question differs depending on the assumption. For example,

クラスへ行かないんですか。   assumes that you will go

クラスへ行かないんですか。   assumes that you won't go

アクティビティー **17**

くつを買（か）うんです。 (*Yes, I'm going to buy shoes.*)

Complete these dialogues using the cue in parentheses and んです.

［例］ デパートへ行（い）くんですか。（ブラウスを買（か）います。）→
　　　 はい、ブラウスを買（か）うんです。

1. 林（はやし）さん、たくさん飲（の）みますね。（お酒（さけ）が好（す）きです。）
2. 映画（えいが）に行（い）かないんですか。（明日（あした）、試験（しけん）[*exam*]です。）
3. スキーへ行（い）くんですか。（雪（ゆき）がたくさん降（ふ）りました。）
4. セーターを買（か）ったんですか。（とても寒（さむ）いです。）
5. この問題（もんだい）はわかりませんか。（先週（せんしゅう）、休（やす）みました。）
6. 昨日（きのう）学校（がっこう）へ来（き）ませんでしたね。（アルバイトがありました。）
7. 明日家（あしたいえ）にいないんですか。（スケートに行（い）きます。）
8. アパートは便利（べんり）なんですか。（駅（えき）にとても近（ちか）いです。）
9. 学校（がっこう）へ行（い）かないんですか。（今（いま）、休（やす）みです。）

アクティビティー **18**

なぜですか。(*Why?*)

Make up dialogues, using the model as an example.

［例］ パーティーに行（い）かない →
　　　 s1: パーティーに行（い）かなかったんですか。
　　　 s2: ええ、病気（びょうき）(*sick*) だったんです。

Useful Vocabulary (reasons): 雪（ゆき）が降（ふ）る、ひま（な）、天気（てんき）がいい、週末（しゅうまつ）、
暑（あつ）い、時間（じかん）がある、雨（あめ）が降（ふ）る、寒（さむ）い、きたない、誕生日（たんじょうび）、病気（びょうき）、仕事（しごと）が
ある

1. スキーに行（い）く
2. 家（いえ）にいた
3. レストランで
　 夕（ゆう）ごはんを食（た）べる
4. 映画（えいが）を見（み）る
5. クラスに行（い）かない
6. 掃除（そうじ）する
7. 10時に起（お）きる
8. プールで泳（およ）ぐ
9. 12時まで勉強（べんきょう）する

言語ノート

Asking and Answering *Why?*

Two interrogative pronouns are used to ask why: なぜ and どうして. In very informal speech, either can be used alone to mean *Why?* Otherwise follow the examples of usage below.

なぜですか。

Why (is that)?

どうしてですか。

Why (is that)?

なぜピクニックに行きませんでしたか。

Why didn't you come to the picnic?

どうしてクラスを休みましたか。

Why did you miss class?

To answer why or to give a reason, use the conjunction から (*because*) or ので (*because; it being that. . .*).

雨が降ったから、行きませんでした。

Because it rained, I didn't go.

病気だったので、休みました。

Because I was sick, I took the day off.

Or you can simply say

雨が降ったからです。

(It's) Because it rained.

病気だったのです or 病気だったんです。

It's that I was sick.

アクティビティー **19**

暑いから、海へ行きましょう。 (*Because it's hot, let's go to the ocean.*)

Complete the following sentences. How many different sentences can you make?

[例] 暑いから、... →
　　暑いから、海へ行きましょう。
　　暑いから、アイスクリームを食べます。
　　暑いから、クーラーを買います。

1. 昨日はとても寒かったので、
2. 台風が来たので、
3. 今日は暖かいから、

4. 風がとても強いので、
5. 天気がいいから、
6. 雪がたくさん降ったから、

二百六十三

Vocabulary and Grammar 4B

Vocabulary and Oral Activities

Enjoying the Four Seasons

Vocabulary: Seasons and Seasonal Activities

季節	きせつ	season
四季	しき	four seasons
カレンダー		calendar
泳ぐ	およぐ	to swim
スキーをする		to ski
スケートをする		to skate
山登りをする	やまのぼりをする	to climb mountains
釣りをする	つりをする	to fish
キャンプ（に行く）	キャンプ（にいく）	(to go) camping
ハイキング（に行く）	ハイキング（にいく）	(to go) hiking
花見（に行く）	はなみ（にいく）	(to go) cherry blossom viewing

アクティビティー **20**

どの季節が一番好きですか。(*Which season do you like best?*)

Answer the following questions.

1. 春は何月から何月までですか。
2. 夏は何月から何月までですか。
3. 秋は何月から何月までですか。
4. 冬は何月から何月までですか。
5. シドニーの8月はどんな季節ですか。
6. ニューヨークの8月はどんな季節ですか。

7. シドニーの1月はどんな季節ですか。

8. ニューヨークの1月はどんな季節ですか。

9. どの季節が一番暑いですか。

10. どの季節が一番寒いですか。

11. どの季節が一番雨が降りますか。

12. どの季節が一番好きですか。

クラスメートと花見に来ました。

 アクティビティー **21**

どの季節にしますか。   (*In what season do you do that?*)

In what season(s) do you do these activities? Ask your partner, following the example.

［例］　スキーをする →
　　　s1: どの季節にスキーをしますか。
　　　s2: 冬です。

1. 海で泳ぐ
2. ピクニックに行く
3. スケートをする
4. 山登りをする
5. キャンプに行く
6. 釣りをする
7. ゴルフをする
8. 花見に行く

What activities do you do in each of the four seasons? Discuss in class. Are there any activities you can do only in a specific season?

> **D**o you remember? The interrogative どの asks which one of three or more alternatives. To ask which one of two, use どちら. Review **Grammar 4**, Chapter 1.

アクティビティー **22**

<ruby>今年<rt>ことし</rt></ruby>の<ruby>夏<rt>なつ</rt></ruby>は<ruby>暖<rt>あたた</rt></ruby>かいですけれども...   (*This summer is warm but...*)

Complete the sentences, using the model as an example.

[例] <ruby>今年<rt>ことし</rt></ruby>の<ruby>夏<rt>なつ</rt></ruby>は<ruby>暖<rt>あたた</rt></ruby>かいですけれども、<ruby>去年<rt>きょねん</rt></ruby>の夏は... →
      <ruby>今年<rt>ことし</rt></ruby>の<ruby>夏<rt>なつ</rt></ruby>は<ruby>暖<rt>あたた</rt></ruby>かいですけれども、<ruby>去年<rt>きょねん</rt></ruby>の夏は<ruby>涼<rt>すず</rt></ruby>しかったです。

1. <ruby>今年<rt>ことし</rt></ruby>の<ruby>夏<rt>なつ</rt></ruby>は<ruby>雨<rt>あめ</rt></ruby>が<ruby>多<rt>おお</rt></ruby>いですが、<ruby>去年<rt>きょねん</rt></ruby>の夏は...
2. <ruby>夏<rt>なつ</rt></ruby>は<ruby>雨<rt>あめ</rt></ruby>がたくさん<ruby>降<rt>ふ</rt></ruby>りますが、<ruby>冬<rt>ふゆ</rt></ruby>は...
3. <ruby>今年<rt>ことし</rt></ruby>の<ruby>冬<rt>ふゆ</rt></ruby>は<ruby>暖<rt>あたた</rt></ruby>かいですけれども、<ruby>去年<rt>きょねん</rt></ruby>の冬は...
4. おととしの<ruby>冬<rt>ふゆ</rt></ruby>は<ruby>雪<rt>ゆき</rt></ruby>がたくさん<ruby>降<rt>ふ</rt></ruby>りましたが、<ruby>去年<rt>きょねん</rt></ruby>の冬は...
5. <ruby>夏<rt>なつ</rt></ruby>は<ruby>台風<rt>たいふう</rt></ruby>がたくさん<ruby>来<rt>き</rt></ruby>ますが、<ruby>冬<rt>ふゆ</rt></ruby>は...
6. <ruby>今週<rt>こんしゅう</rt></ruby>は<ruby>暑<rt>あつ</rt></ruby>いですけれども、<ruby>先週<rt>せんしゅう</rt></ruby>は...
7. <ruby>今年<rt>ことし</rt></ruby>は<ruby>雨<rt>あめ</rt></ruby>が<ruby>多<rt>おお</rt></ruby>いですけれども、<ruby>去年<rt>きょねん</rt></ruby>は...
8. <ruby>今日<rt>きょう</rt></ruby>は<ruby>風<rt>かぜ</rt></ruby>が<ruby>弱<rt>よわ</rt></ruby>いですが、<ruby>昨日<rt>きのう</rt></ruby>は...
9. <ruby>今月<rt>こんげつ</rt></ruby>は<ruby>気温<rt>きおん</rt></ruby>が<ruby>高<rt>たか</rt></ruby>いですけれども、<ruby>先月<rt>せんげつ</rt></ruby>は...

言語ノート

Linking Disjunctive Clauses with けれども

You've already learned several ways to link disjunctive or contrasting ideas, including が (*but*), でも (*but*), and しかし (*however*). Another common connector is けれども. Unlike those you have studied so far, けれども can be used either as a conjunction (i.e., to join two independent clauses into one sentence) or as a transitional phrase at the beginning of the second of two contrasting sentences. It is roughly equivalent to *although* or *however*.

ここは<ruby>冬<rt>ふゆ</rt></ruby>は<ruby>寒<rt>さむ</rt></ruby>いですけれども、<ruby>雪<rt>ゆき</rt></ruby>はあまり<ruby>降<rt>ふ</rt></ruby>りません。

Although winters are cold here, it doesn't snow much.

ここは冬は寒いです。けれども、雪はあまり降りません。

Winters are cold here. **Nevertheless**, it doesn't snow much.

Of the linking words mentioned in this note, が is most common and expresses the least contrast. でも is common in informal conversation, while しかし tends to sound bookish or formal. けれども may be shortened to けども in informai conversation, and も is often dropped (yielding けれど or けど) to express a lesser degree of contrast.

As shown in the preceding examples, the particle は often marks items being compared or contrasted, regardless of which conjunction or transition is used.

You should also be aware that in general ...ですけれども is limited to conversation. In writing, you will find that ...ですが or ...です けれども～ are more commonly used.

Grammar and Practice Activities

21. The **te**-Form of Adjectives and the Copula

カワムラ：町田さんの家のそばにスーパーはありますか。

町田：ええ。

カワムラ：どんなスーパーですか。

町田：大きくて、安いスーパーです。

カワムラ：町田さんはいつもそのスーパーで買い物するんですか。

町田：ええ、近くて、便利ですから。

チン：山田さんのガールフレンドはどんな人ですか。

林：とてもきれいで、やさしい人ですよ。

チン：本当ですか。山田さんはけちで、いじわるでしょう。

　　　なぜ、そんないいガールフレンドがいるんですか。

林：さあ、わかりませんね。

KAWAMURA: Is there a supermarket near your house Mr. Machida?　MACHIDA: Yes.
KAWAMURA: What kind of supermarket is it?　MACHIDA: It is a big and inexpensive supermarket.　KAWAMURA: Do you always shop there?　MACHIDA: Yes, because it is nearby and convenient.

CHIN: What kind of person is Mr. Yamada's girlfriend?　HAYASHI: Yes, she's a very pretty, sweet person.　CHIN: Really? Mr. Yamada is miserly and mean. Why does he have such a nice girlfriend?　HAYASHI: Hmm, I don't know.

21.1 An important conjugated form of adjectives and verbs is what we shall call the *te-form*. In **Grammar 21** and **22,** you will study the **te-**form of adjectives, the copula, and verbs.

21.2 The **te-**form of adjectives may be used to link together adjectives or whole clauses in a sentence, as *and* is used in English. The **te-**form can be used only when adjectives are in a nonfinal position in a sentence.

Create the **te-**form of **i-**adjectives by adding くて to the root.

Dictionary Form	Root	*te-*Form
赤い *red*	赤	赤くて
おいしい *tasty*	おいし	おいしくて
寒い *cold*	寒	寒くて
いい（よい）*good*	よ	よくて (irregular)

21.3 The **te-**form of **na-**adjectives is formed by adding で to the dictionary form.

Dictionary Form	*te-*Form
きれい *pretty*	きれいで
静か *quiet*	静かで
便利 *convenient*	便利で
ハンサム *handsome*	ハンサムで

21.4 Study these sample sentences.

彼女は若くて、きれいだ。
She is young and pretty.

静かで、便利なところが好きです。
I like quiet, convenient places.

In the following examples, the clause ending in the **te-**form adjective indicates a reason or cause for the following clause.

この辞書は重くて、不便です。
This dictionary is heavy and (therefore it's) inconvenient.

父はお酒が大好きで、いつもたくさん飲みます。
My father loves sake and always drinks a lot.

日本語のクラスが好きで、日本語をたくさん勉強する。
I like my Japanese class, and (that's why) I study Japanese a lot.

When you conjoin two or more adjectives this way, they must be all favorable or all unfavorable in meaning. For instance, the following sentence sounds unnatural.

> あのスーパーはきれいで、高いです。
> *That supermarket is clean and expensive.*

In such a case, you must use a conjunction for joining contrasting or contradictory statements.

> あのスーパーはきれいですが、高いです。
> あのスーパーはきれいだけど、高いです。
> *That supermarket is clean, but it's expensive.*

21.5 The **te**-form of the copula です (plain form だ) is で. It is used to conjoin nouns.

> 町田さんは日本人で、東京の出身です。
> *Ms. Machida is a Japanese national and is from Tokyo.*
> カワムラさんは東京大学の学生で、専攻は工学です。
> *Mr. Kawamura is a student at the University of Tokyo, and his major is engineering.*

A clause ending in a noun ＋で can explain a reason or cause for what follows.

> 病気で、クラスを休みました。
> *I was sick and (so I) missed class.*

> **Y**ou can use either the plain or polite form in front of けど.

アクティビティー **23**

高くて、まずいです。(*It's expensive and not good.*)

Make sentences by combining the words and phrases provided.

[例] （あのレストラン）（高い）（まずい）→
　　　あのレストランは高くて、まずいです。もう行きません！

1. （あの人のスピーチ）（長い）（つまらない）
2. （日本語の先生）（やさしい）（親切 [kind]）
3. （このケーキ）（あまい）（おいしい）
4. （このラップトップ・コンピュータ）（重い）（不便）
5. （カナダの冬）（寒い）（長い）
6. （わたしの大学）（大きい）（有名）
7. （山口さん）（エレガント）（きれい）

(Continues.)

8. （カワムラさん）（ハンサム）（やさしい）
9. （高田<ruby>高<rt>たか</rt></ruby><ruby>田<rt>だ</rt></ruby>さん）（26歳<ruby>歳<rt>さい</rt></ruby>）（サラリーマン）
10. （チンさん）（<ruby>中国人<rt>ちゅうごくじん</rt></ruby>）（ペキンの<ruby>出身<rt>しゅっしん</rt></ruby>）

アクティビティー **24**

うるさくて、きたないところです。(*It's a noisy, dirty place.*)

Answer the following questions using two adjectives.

[例] あの<ruby>町<rt>まち</rt></ruby>は<ruby>静<rt>しず</rt></ruby>かですか。 →
　　ええ、<ruby>静<rt>しず</rt></ruby>かで、いいところです。(*or* いいえ、<ruby>車<rt>くるま</rt></ruby>が<ruby>多<rt>おお</rt></ruby>くて、うるさい
　　[*noisy*] です。)

Useful Vocabulary: うるさい *noisy*, <ruby>遠<rt>とお</rt></ruby>い *far*, たいへん *terrible, awful*

1. あなたの<ruby>近所<rt>きんじょ</rt></ruby>は<ruby>便利<rt>べんり</rt></ruby>ですか。
2. 12月は<ruby>雪<rt>ゆき</rt></ruby>が<ruby>多<rt>おお</rt></ruby>いですか。
3. 日本の<ruby>夏<rt>なつ</rt></ruby>は<ruby>暑<rt>あつ</rt></ruby>いですか。
4. あなたのアパートは<ruby>駅<rt>えき</rt></ruby>から<ruby>近<rt>ちか</rt></ruby>いですか。
5. ボーイフレンドはハンサムですか。
6. <ruby>大野<rt>おおの</rt></ruby>先生のクラスは<ruby>好<rt>す</rt></ruby>きですか。

アクティビティー **25**

日本語のクラスはむずかしくて、つまらない。(*Japanese class is hard and boring.*)

Make sentences about each topic, combining as many appropriate adjectives as possible from those listed.

[例] 日本語のクラス
　　（やさしい、おもしろい、むずかしい、つまらない） →
　　日本語のクラスはやさしくて、おもしろいです。(*or* 日本語のクラス
　　はやさしいですが、つまらないです。)

1. わたし
　　（<ruby>静<rt>しず</rt></ruby>か、にぎやか、<ruby>元気<rt>げんき</rt></ruby>、いんき [*gloomy*]、ようき [*cheerful*]）

2. ジュリア・ロバーツ
　　（エレガント、<ruby>若<rt>わか</rt></ruby>い [*young*]、きれい、ほそい [*slim*]、<ruby>元気<rt>げんき</rt></ruby>、
　　やさしい、ようき、いんき）

3. アーノルド・シュワルツネーガー

（タフ、やさしい、元気、若い、いんき、静か、強い）

4. エディー・マーフィー

（元気、いんき、きびしい、若い、やさしい、忙しい、おもしろい）

5. わたしの学校

（大きい、むずかしい、やさしい、いい、静か、有名）

6. わたしの家

（大きい、小さい、きれい、広い [spacious]、せまい [small in area]、
きたない）

7. わたしのとなりの人 (the person next to me)

（うるさい、きれい、ハンサム、いんき、ようき、若い、やさしい、
へん [strange]、まじめ）

8. この練習 (exercise)

（むずかしい、やさしい、つまらない、長い、短かい、
おもしろい）

22. The te-Form of Verbs

> 林：新しいDVDがあるんですよ。うちに来て、見ませんか。
>
> ギブソン：ええ、ぜひ。
>
> 林：じゃ、明日5時ごろにうちに来てください。
>
> ギブソン：はい、じゃあ、明日。
>
> 高田：明日は何をするんですか。
>
> ギブソン：部屋を掃除して、洗濯をします。高田さんは。
>
> 高田：会社へ行って、仕事をします。
>
> ギブソン：明日は日曜日ですよ！

HAYASHI: I have a new DVD. Won't you come over (lit., *to my home*) and watch it?
GIBSON: Yes, by all means.   HAYASHI: Then please come over (lit., *to my home*) around
5:00 tomorrow.   GIBSON: Yes. See you tomorrow.

TAKADA: What are you going to do tomorrow?   GIBSON: I'm going to clean my room and
do some laundry. How about you?   TAKADA: I'll go to my company and work.
GIBSON: Tomorrow is Sunday, you know!

22.1 If you have mastered formation of the past, plain, affirmative form of verbs (that is, the **ta**-form), you can master the **te**-form very easily. Observe the following examples.

	ta-Form	*te*-Form
Class 1		
書く	書いた	書いて
行く	行った	行って
泳ぐ	泳いだ	泳いで
買う	買った	買って
呼ぶ	呼んだ	呼んで
Class 2		
食べる	食べた	食べて
見る	見た	見て
Class 3		
する	した	して
来る	来た	来て

As you can see, the **te**-form of verbs is formed by changing the た to て or だ to で.

22.2 The **te**-form of verbs is usually combined with other components to form grammatical constructions. For instance, the **te**-form of a verb +ください (*please give me*) is used to ask someone to do something for you. It literally means *Please give me your doing of* (*something*), in other words, *Please do…*

> ここに名前を書いてください。
> *Please write your name here.*
> 日本語で話してください。
> *Please speak in Japanese.*

どうぞ (*Please, go ahead*) is often added to the beginning of these request sentences to make your request sound politer.

> どうぞたくさん食べてください。
> *Please eat as much as you want.* (lit., *Please eat a lot.*)

22.3 You can express a succession of actions or events simply by connecting clauses that end in the **te**-form of a verb. For example,

> スーパーに行って、アイスクリームを買う。
> *I will go to the supermarket and buy ice cream.*
> わたしは六時に起きて、歯を磨いて、顔を洗いました。
> *I got up at 6:00, brushed my teeth, and washed my face.*

This is a fairly direct way to make a request and should therefore be used with caution, especially when speaking with superiors or strangers.

There is no grammatical limit on the number of verb clauses you can string together with this construction. The actions or events must usually take place within a short period of time and be related to one another in some sense. In most cases, they also should be listed in the same order in which the events occurred.

The tense and the speaker's attitude are expressed in the sentence-final verb—in the examples above, 買 (か) う and 洗 (あら) いました. All the preceding **te-**forms of verbs assume the same tense and other attributes of the sentence-final verb. Therefore, since 洗いました is past tense, you know that the first two actions—getting up and brushing teeth—also took place in the past. Because of the politeness level of 洗いました, you can tell that the speaker is speaking politely. In the first example, by the plain form of the final verb you can tell that the speaker is conveying information informally.

To summarize, you cannot know the tense and the speaker's attitude or emotion until you hear the last verb.

言語ノート

Conjoining Sequential Actions

You already studied how to express sequential actions and events using the transitions そして、それから、and そのあと (Chapter 3). In addition to these transitions and the **te-**form of verbs, you can also link sequential actions with a **te-**form of a verb ＋から. This pattern adds a temporal emphasis: A から, B (after A, B).

夕 (ゆう) ごはんを食 (た) べて新聞 (しんぶん) を読 (よ) んでから、日本語を勉 強 (べんきょう) しました。

After eating dinner and reading the newspaper, I studied Japanese.

ブラウンさんに会 (あ) ってから、話しましょう。

Let's talk about it after we meet Ms. Brown.

22.4 The **te-**form of verbs can be used to express a cause-and-effect relationship where the first clause explains a reason for the second. You will have to determine from context whether a causal connection is intended. For example,

寝坊 (ねぼう) して、学校 (がっこう) におくれた。
I overslept and (so) I was late for school.

古 (ふる) いケーキを食 (た) べて、病 気 (びょうき) になりました。
I ate some old cake, and (because of that) I got sick.

アクティビティー **26**

すこ やす
少し休んでください。(*Please take a short break.*)

Change each verb to its **te**-form ＋ください.

[例]　ギブソンさんと話す → ギブソンさんと話してください。

1. 早く起きる
2. 車を洗う
3. 夕ごはんを食べる
4. くすり (*medicine*) を飲む
5. 大学の前で待つ
6. スーパーへ行く

7. タクシーに乗る
8. ブラウンさんに会う
9. このかばんを見る
10. 今日の新聞を読む
11. 中に入る (*to enter*)
12. 4時にここに来る

アクティビティー **27**

すこ やす
少し休んで、テレビを見ました。(*I took a rest and watched TV.*)

Using **te**-forms, combine the sentences provided into one past tense
sentence.

[例]　(朝起きる) (コーヒーを飲む) → 朝起きて、コーヒーを飲んだ。

1. (お風呂から出る) (ビールを飲む)
2. (バスに乗る) (デパートへ行く) (セーターを買う)
3. (シャワーを浴びる) (ひげをそる)
4. (ドレスを着る) (デートに出かける)
5. (夕ごはんを食べる) (日本語を勉強する)
6. (カワムラさんの家へ行く) (話す)
7. (家に帰る) (寝る)
8. (コンピュータを使う [*to use a computer*]) (手紙 [*letter*] を書く)

アクティビティー **28**

毎日のこと (*Everyday things*)

Complete the following sentences based on your own experience.

[例]　朝起きて、 → 朝起きて、トイレに行きます。

Useful word: はく *to wear* (*shoes, socks, etc.*)

1. 日本語のクラスへ行って、

2. カフェテリアへ行って、

3. 昼ごはんを食べて、

4. バスに乗って、

5. スニーカーをはいて、

6. セーターを着て、

7. 本を読んで、

8. うちに帰って、

アクティビティー **29**

夏、何をしましたか。(*What did he do in the summer?*)

Using the information provided, tell what the person did in each sentence.

[例] —カワムラさんは夏、何をしましたか。
　　—アメリカに帰って、友だちに会いました。

1. winter, go to the mountains, ski

2. spring, go to a park, view cherry blossoms

3. fall, go to Nagano, hike

4. summer, go to the ocean, swim

Vocabulary and Grammar 4C

Vocabulary and Oral Activities

Forecasting

Vocabulary: Forecasting		
空	そら	sky
霧	きり	fog
洪水	こうずい	flood
日照り	ひでり	drought

Rain and Other Precipitation

夕立	ゆうだち	evening shower
大雨	おおあめ	heavy rain
雷	かみなり	thunder
稲妻	いなずま	lightning
吹雪	ふぶき	snowstorm
大雪	おおゆき	heavy snow

(*Continues.*)

みぞれ		sleet
霜	しも	frost
露	つゆ	dew

アクティビティー **30**

ダイアログ：冬^{ふゆ}はどんな気候^{きこう}ですか。 (*What is the climate like in winter?*)

　　林^{はやし}：エドモントンの冬^{ふゆ}はどんな気候^{きこう}ですか。

ギブソン：雪^{ゆき}がたくさん降^ふって、とても寒^{さむ}いです。

　　林^{はやし}：夏^{なつ}はどうですか。

ギブソン：夏^{なつ}は涼^{すず}しくて、おだやかな気候^{きこう}です。

Practice the dialogue, using the following pattern and information.

―(place) の (season) はどんな気候^{きこう}ですか。

―＿＿＿＿＿。

1. ―New York, winter
   ―rainy and cold
2. ―Seattle, fall
   ―clear and warm
3. ―Sapporo, spring
   ―cloudy and cool
4. ―Tokyo, summer
   ―clear and sultry

アクティビティー **31**

Odd Man Out

In each of the following groups of words, one word does not belong to the same category as the others. Identify it and tell why it is different.

1. 暑^{あつ}い、いい、寒^{さむ}い、涼^{すず}しい、暖^{あたた}かい
2. 晴^はれ、くもり、雨^{あめ}、高^{たか}い、雪^{ゆき}
3. 北^{きた}、南^{みなみ}、風^{かぜ}、東^{ひがし}、西^{にし}
4. 春^{はる}、冬^{ふゆ}、夏^{なつ}、海^{うみ}、秋^{あき}
5. 雨^{あめ}、雪^{ゆき}、雲^{くも}、くもり、晴^はれ
6. 吹雪^{ふぶき}、霜^{しも}、みぞれ、小雨^{こさめ}
7. 洪水^{こうずい}、晴^はれ、日照^{ひで}り、台風^{たいふう}
8. 露^{つゆ}、霧^{きり}、空^{そら}、にわか雨^{あめ}

HAYASHI: What is the climate like in Edmonton in winter?　GIBSON: It snows a lot, and it's very cold.　HAYASHI: What about summer?　GIBSON: Summers are cool, and the weather is mild.

Grammar and Practice Activities

23. Expressing Probability and Conjecture

ブラウン：林^{はやし}さんは来^くるでしょうか。

町田^{まちだ}：さあ、どうでしょうか。

ブラウン：来^こないかもしれませんね。

町田：さあ、わかりませんね。

ブラウン：昨日^{きのう}のパーティーはどうでしたか。おもしろかったでしょう。*

町田^{まちだ}：ええ、とてもおもしろかったです。

ブラウン：ギブソンさんはパーティーにいましたか。

町田：ええと、いたかもしれません。いや、いなかったかもしれません。

23.1 There are a variety of ways to express conjecture or uncertainty in Japanese. Two of the most commonly used expressions are でしょう (plain form だろう) meaning *probably* and かもしれません (plain form かもしれない) meaning *may* or *maybe*. The major difference between these two expressions is that かもしれません expresses a greater degree of uncertainty.

> ジョンソンさんは日本語がわかるでしょう。
> *Ms. Johnson probably understands Japanese.*
> ジョンソンさんは日本語がわかるかもしれません。
> *Ms. Johnson may understand Japanese.*

Nouns, adjectives, and verbs precede these expressions. When the speaker is guessing what will happen in the present or future, the following forms are used.

> When making a conjecture relating to yourself, かもしれない—not だろう—is used.

noun i-adjective (nonpast, plain) na-adjective (dictionary form) verb (nonpast, plain form)	でしょう（だろう） *or* かもしれません（かもしれない）

BROWN: Do you suppose Mr. Hayashi will come?   MACHIDA: Hmm, I wonder.   BROWN: He may not come, isn't that right?   MACHIDA: Hmm, I don't know.

BROWN: How was the party yesterday? It must have been fun, huh?   MACHIDA: Yes, it was great fun.   BROWN: Was Ms. Gibson there?   MACHIDA: Uhh, she may have been. No, maybe she wasn't.

---

* In the second dialogue, おもしろかったでしょう ends in a rising intonation.

(Continues.)

When the preceding nouns, adjectives, and verbs are negative, they take the following forms.

```
noun + で(は)ない
i-adjective (nonpast, plain, negative)
na-adjective (dictionary form +
    で[は]ない)
verb (nonpast, plain, negative form)
```
} +
でしょう (だろう)
or
かもしれません
（かもしれない）

明日^{あした}は雨^{あめ}でしょう。
It probably will rain tomorrow.
あの人は学生ではないでしょう。
That person probably is not a student.
明日^{あした}は暑^{あつ}いでしょう。
It probably will be hot tomorrow.
明日^{あした}は寒^{さむ}くないでしょう。
It probably won't be cold tomorrow.
あの人はまじめかもしれません。
That person may be serious.
明日^{あした}は雪^{ゆき}が降^ふるかもしれません。
It might snow tomorrow.
明日^{あした}はここに来^こないかもしれません。
I might not come here tomorrow.

To express a conjecture or to guess about what happened in the past, use these forms.

```
noun だった
i-adjective ( past, plain)
na-adjective (past, plain)
verb (past, plain)
```
} +
でしょう （だろう）
or
かもしれません（かもしれない）

When the elements that precede a conjecture about the past are negative, the following forms are used.

```
noun ではなかった （じゃなかった）
i-adjective (past, plain, negative)
na-adjective (past, plain, negative)
verb (past, plain, negative)
```
} +
でしょう （だろう）
or
かもしれません
（かもしれない）

昨日東京は雨だったでしょう。
It probably rained in Tokyo yesterday.
あの人は先生ではなかったでしょう。
That person probably wasn't a teacher.
昨日東京は寒かったでしょう。
It probably was cold in Tokyo yesterday.
昨日大阪は暑くなかったでしょう。
It probably wasn't hot in Osaka yesterday.
あの学生はまじめだったかもしれません。
That student may have been serious. Maybe that student was serious.
あの町はきれいではなかったかもしれません。
That town may not have been clean.
ブラウンさんはあそこに行ったかもしれません。
Ms. Brown may have gone there.
高田さんはあそこに行かなかったかもしれません。
Mr. Takada may not have gone there.

23.2 でしょう is often accompanied by adverbs expressing degrees of certainty, such as the following (listed in order of increasing certainty).

多分   *probably*
おそらく   *possibly, in all likelihood*
きっと   *certainly, surely*

Because of the strong probability expressed by きっと, it cannot be used with かもしれません.

かれは多分来るでしょう。
He will probably come.
かれはおそらく山下さんに電話をかけるでしょう。
Most likely he will call Mr. Yamashita.
あの学生はきっと日本語を勉強しているでしょう。
That student surely must be studying Japanese.

でしょう is often used to ask an indirect question, in which case the question particle か is pronounced with a falling intonation. As you might have guessed, this is a somewhat more formal way to ask a question.

かれはもう起きましたか。
Did he get up already?
かれはもう起きたでしょうか。
Do you suppose he already got up? I wonder if he already got up.

でしょう pronounced with a rising intonation asks for the hearer's confirmation—*isn't it? aren't you? don't you agree?*

あなたも来るでしょう。↑
You're coming too, aren't you?
その映画はおもしろかったでしょう。↑
That movie was interesting, don't you think?

アクティビティー **32**

これがわかるでしょう。(*You probably understand this.*)

Respond to the following questions using でしょう or かもしれません.

1. あの人はどこの国の人ですか。

2. あの人は何歳ですか。

3. 明日はどんなお天気でしょうか。

4. あの人は昨日どこへ行きましたか。

5. あのセーターは安いですか。
    高いですか。

6. 今、東京は暑いですか。

7. あの人はどんな人ですか。

8. 12月はニューヨークとワシントン
    とどちらが寒いですか。

9. ここから一番近い駅まで
    何分かかりますか。

10. あの人は昨日何をしましたか。

アクティビティー **33**

あなたはどう思いますか。(*What do you think?*)

What can you guess about each of these pictures? State your conjectures.

1. 明日はどんなお
天気ですか。

2. 林さんは大丈
夫ですか。

3. あのレストランは
おいしいですか。

4. ジョンソンさんは
日本語がわかりますか。

5. 台風は来ますか。

アクティビティー 34

ダイアログ：雨が降るかもしれません。(*It might rain.*)

ブラウン：いやなお天気ですね。

　　　林：ええ、空が暗いですね。

ブラウン：午後は雨が降るでしょうか。

　　　林：ええ、嵐が来るかもしれません。

アクティビティー 35

明日はどんなお天気でしょうか。(*What will the weather be like tomorrow?*)

While looking at the following table, listen to your instructor forecast tomorrow's weather.

［例］　函館は雪が降るでしょう。

Useful Vocabulary: 東 *east,* 西 *west,* 南 *south,* 北 *north*

City	Weather	Temperature	Wind
Hakodate	Cloudy, P.M. snow	−3, cold	North, strong
Fukushima	Clear, occasionally cloudy	−1, cold	West, weak
Gihu	Rain	8, cool	East, weak
Kobe	Cloudy, occasionally clear	17, warm	South, weak
Kochi	Rain	27, hot	No wind
Yakushima	Clear	30, hot	South, weak

BROWN: The weather is unpleasant, isn't it?　HAYASHI: Yes. The sky is dark (isn't it?).
BROWN: I wonder if it will rain this afternoon.　HAYASHI: Yes. It just might storm. (lit., *A storm might come.*)

アクティビティー **36**

明日は雨が降るでしょう。 (*It will rain tomorrow.*)

You are a TV meteorologist. Using the following data, give a weather forecast. Don't forget to use でしょう or かもしれません.

Kushiro	cloudy, occasional snow, very cold
	−15 degrees, very strong north wind
Okayama	sunny, very good weather
	20 degrees, warm, no wind
Nara	cloudy in the morning, rain in the afternoon
	a little cold, 5 degrees, light westerly breeze
Miyazaki	cloudy, occasional rain in the morning
	foggy in the morning, warm, 22 degrees, no wind

アクティビティー **37**

明日のお天気は？ (*What about tomorrow's weather?*)

Working with a partner, draw a map of your town or region. One of you will play a TV meteorologist predicting tomorrow's weather. As you make your predictions, draw appropriate weather symbols and temperatures on the map. The second person will play a TV anchor asking the meteorologist questions about the weather. Be creative.

Language Skills

Reading and Writing
Reading 1 ブラウンさんへの手紙

Before You Read

You are writing a letter in English to a friend, telling her about your ski vacation. How do you start your letter? What are the standard elements of an English personal letter (e.g., date, your name, etc.)? Where do you place them in a letter?

Japanese letters usually start with 拝啓, which roughly corresponds to *Dear Sir* or *Dear Madam*. This introductory greeting is generally followed by a reference to the weather or season. In what season do you think each of the following phrases would be used in a Japanese letter?

1. 毎日 暑いです。
2. 最近雪が多くて、たいへんです。
3. そちらは梅雨の季節でしょうか。ここは毎日雨が降ります。
4. さくら (cherry blossoms) がとてもきれいです。
5. 北風が吹いて、寒いです。
6. 台風の季節 に入りました。
7. 南 風が吹いて、とても暖かいです。

Now Read It!

Yooichi Takada wrote this letter to Linda Brown from Hokkaido, where he has been vacationing.

拝啓
ブラウンさん、お元気ですか。私は元気です。こちらは寒くて、たいへんですが、東京はどうですか。
さて、私は先週の土曜日に北海道に着きました。日曜日に雪がたくさん降りました。私の家の近くに山があります。月曜日に友だちとその山へ行って、スキーをしました。月曜日はいいお天気で、朝から夕方までスキーをしました。
火曜日は私の誕生日でした。家のそばの喫茶店でバースデー・パーティーがありました。友だちがたくさん来ました。
あさって、東京に帰ります。おみやげを買って、帰りますので、楽しみにしてください。
今日はこれで失礼します。寒いですから、お体に気をつけてください。

敬具

二月十五日

リンダ・ブラウン様

高田洋一

After You Finish Reading

1. Find the following information in the letter.

Date	Inquiry about addressee's
Sender's name	health
Addressee's name	Reference to sender's health
Reference to weather or season	Closing remarks
	Closing (e.g., Sincerely)

2. In English, discuss in class the differences between English letters and Japanese letters.

3. How many details did you understand? Answer the following to test yourself.

   a. What is the weather like in Hokkaido?

   b. When did Mr. Takada go to Hokkaido?

   c. When did it snow?

   d. When did Mr. Takada go skiing?

   e. What was the weather like the day he went skiing?

   f. When was Mr. Takada's birthday?

   g. What did he do on his birthday?

   h. When is Mr. Takada returning to Tokyo?

   i. When did Mr. Takada write this letter?

文化ノート

CULTURE NOTE: How to Write a Letter in Japanese

Here is the standard format of a Japanese personal letter.

1. opening word or phrase, such as 拝啓 (はいけい)
2. preliminary remarks: reference to the weather or season, inquiry about the addressee's health (often followed by reference to the writer's health), etc.
3. main body
4. concluding remarks: best wishes for the addressee's health, regards to the addressee's family, etc.
5. closing word or phrase such as 敬具 (けいぐ)
6. date
7. sender's full name
8. addressee's full name (with the title 様 (さま), not さん), is usually used in personal letters
9. postscript: anything sender forgot to include in the main body

When writing a letter, you generally use politer language than when talking directly to the addressee.

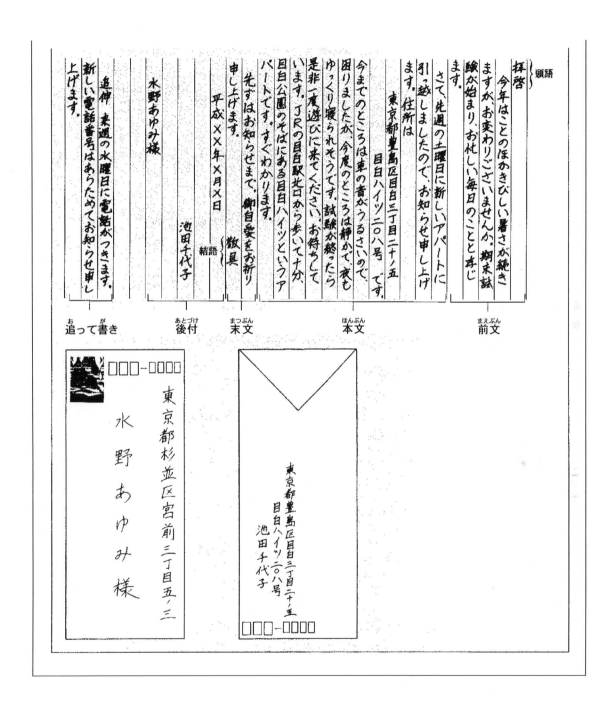

拝啓〈頭語

今年はことのほかきびしい暑さが続き
ますが、お変わりございませんか。期末試
験が始まり、お忙しい毎日のことと存じ
ます。

さて、先週の土曜日に新しいアパートに
引っ越しましたので、お知らせ申し上げ
ます。住所は

　東京都豊島区目白三丁目二十ノ五
　　　　　　　目白ハイツ二〇八号　です。

今までのところは東の音がうるさいので、
困りましたが、今度のところは静かで、夜も
ゆっくり寝られそうです。試験が終わったら
是非一度遊びに来てください。お待ちして
います。JRの目白駅北口から歩いて十分、
目白公園のそばにある目白ハイツというア
パートです。すぐわかります。

先ずはお知らせまで。御自愛をお祈り
申し上げます。

敬具〈結語

　平成××年×月×日

　　　　　　　　　池田千代子

水野あゆみ様

追伸　来週の水曜日に電話がつきます。
新しい電話番号はあらためてお知らせ申し
上げます。

まえぶん 前文	ほんぶん 本文	まつぶん 末文	あとづけ 後付	おって 追って書き

□□□－□□□□

東京都豊島区目白三丁目二十五
目白ハイツ二〇八号
池田千代子
□□□－□□□□

東京都杉並区宮前三丁目五ノ三
水野あゆみ様

二百八十五

Writing 1

Write a short letter to a friend in Japanese. Include the following in your letter.

1. reference to the season or weather
2. inquiry about your friend's health
3. description of your Japanese language study
4. invitation to visit your house next month

Reading 2: トラベル・ガイド：いろは町の気候

Before You Read

You are planning to make a short trip during a school break. You have decided to visit Iroha, a small town near Kyoto. You would like to know the climate there and what clothes you should take, so you consult a travel guidebook. It includes many words you haven't learned, but you can read enough to get the information you need. Before reading the following page from the guidebook, list words relating to each of these topics.

季節　　　雨　　　雪
気温　　　風

Describe in Japanese the kind of weather you associate with these items.

1. オーバー　　　　4. セーター　　　　7. ノースリーブス
2. レインコート　　5. 傘 (umbrella)
3. ショートパンツ　6. T-シャツ

Now Read It!

いろは町の気候

春は昼間は暖かいが、朝夕はまだ寒い。セーターがいる。雨はほとんど降らない。4月は桜がきれいだ。山も美しくて、多くの人がハイキングを楽しむ。

　6月から7月の梅雨の季節は、雨が多い。ちょっと寒い日が多い。傘やレインコートがいる。この季節は、お寺の庭がとても美しい。いろは町の夏はむし暑い。夏の平均気温は28度、平均湿度は90%だ。カジュアルな服がいい。夕方雨がよく降る。傘がいる。

昼間 daytime / まだ still / …がいる one needs…

桜 cherry blossoms / 山 mountain / 美しい beautiful

楽しむ to enjoy

庭 garden

平均 average / 湿度 humidity / カジュアル casual, informal

秋は毎日いい天気が続く。山がとても美しい。秋は一年中で一番美しい季節だ。昼間は15度ぐらいだ。朝夕は涼しいので、セーターやコートがいる。

11月から、寒い北風が吹いて、気温も下がる。いろは町の冬はきびしい。 下がる *to go down*
京都より気温が2〜3度低い。12月から2月まで雪が降る。お寺の庭にも雪が
降って、本当に美しい。お寺や神社には暖房がないので、お寺や神社の中 暖房 *heater*
でもオーバーがいる。

After You Finish Reading

Tell what the weather is like in each season in Iroha.
　　In what season should these people visit Iroha?

1. ギブソン　　雪が好きです。
2. 町田　　　　ハイキングが好きです。
3. 横井先生　　雨の季節のお寺はきれいで、いいですね。
4. 林　　　　　暑い季節が好きです。

京都の夏祭
(*summer festival*):
祇園祭

Writing 2

Write a short description in Japanese of the weather and the four seasons
for some place in your home country.

Language Functions and Situations

Asking Questions About the Japanese Language 🎧

Japanese native speakers are a good source of information about the language. Here are some simple ways to ask someone for help when studying Japanese.

1. Asking about pronunciation

すみません。これはどう発音_{はつおん}しますか。—「とうざいなんぼく」です。

Excuse me. How do you pronounce this? —**Too-zai-nan-boku.** (*East-west-south-north.*)

東西南北

2. Asking how to read **kanji**

すみません。この漢字_{かんじ}はどう読_よみますか。—「あさゆう」です。

Excuse me. How do you read these **kanji**?—**Asayuu.** (*Morning and evening.*)

朝夕

3. Asking about writing

すみません。「あつい」は漢字_{かんじ}でどう書_かきますか。—こう書きます。

Excuse me. How do you write **hot** *in* **kanji**? —*You write it like this.* (*said while writing*)

暑い

4. Asking about meaning

すみません。「湿度_{しつど}」はどういう意味_{いみ}ですか。—空気_{くうき}の中_{なか}の水分_{みずぶん}のことです。英語_{えいご}で *humidity* といいます。

Excuse me. What does **shitsudo** *mean?—It means* **the moisture in the air.** *In English, you say* **humidity.**

Asking for Assistance with **Kanji** 🎧

ギブソン：林_{はやし} さん、ちょっとすみません。日本語を教_{おし}えてください。

林_{はやし}：ええ、いいですよ。何_{なん}ですか。

ギブソン：「ゆき」は漢字_{かんじ}でどう書_かきますか。

林：雨_{あめ}の下_{した}にカタカナの「ヨ」です。

ギブソン：ちょっと書_かいてください。

GIBSON: Mr. Hayashi, excuse me. Can you teach me some Japanese?　HAYASHI: Yes, sure. What can I do for you? (lit., *What is it?*)　GIBSON: How do you write *snow* in **kanji**? HAYASHI: Write a **katakana yo** under the character for *rain*. (lit., *It is a **katakana yo** under **rain**.*)　GIBSON: Please write it for me.

林：こう書きます。
ギブソン：ありがとうございます。

ブラウン：横井先生、質問があるんですが、...
横井：ええ、何ですか。
ブラウン：この漢字は何と読みますか。
横井：「しつど」と読みます。*humidity* のことです。
ブラウン：「温度」とは違いますか。
横井：ええ、違います。
ブラウン：「温度」を書いていただけますか。
横井：こう書きます。
ブラウン：ありがとうございます。

言語ノート

Making Polite Requests

The most common way to make a request is to use the te-form of a verb ＋ください (*please give me the doing of...*).

名前を書いてください。

Please write down your name.

As discussed earlier, どうぞ makes your request more polite.

どうぞ教えてください。

Please tell me.   *or*   **Please teach me.**

More polite forms of request include the following, in increasing order of politeness.

te-form of verb ＋
{
くださいますか
くださいませんか
いただけますか
いただけませんか
}

明日電話してくださいますか。

Would you call me tomorrow?

ブラウンさんと話していただけませんか。

Would you please talk with Ms. Brown?

HAYASHI: You write it like this.   GIBSON: Thank you.

BROWN: Professor Yokoi, I have a question but... (could you help me?)   YOKOI: Yes, what is it?
BROWN: How do you read this **kanji**?   YOKOI: You read it **shitsudo.** It means *humidity*.
BROWN: Is it different from **ondo**?   YOKOI: Yes, it's different.   BROWN: Would you please write
ondo for me?   YOKOI: You write it like this.   BROWN: Thank you very much.

アクティビティー 38

日本人に聞いてください。(*Ask a Japanese.*)

Find a native speaker of Japanese on your campus and ask for the following information.

1. Pronunciation and meaning of these characters
   a. 南西　　　　b. 夕立　　c. 日中
2. How to write these phrases in **kanji**
   a. こうてい　*high and low*
   b. こうてん　*good weather*
   c. だんじょ　*man and woman*

Don't forget to use polite requests when you ask these questions.

Listening Comprehension 🎧

As you listen to the forecast for tomorrow, jot down what the weather will be for each of the following cities: Sapporo, Sendai, Fukushima, Utsunomiya, Tokyo, Nagoya, Wakayama, Hiroshima, Fukuoka, and Miyazaki.

Vocabulary 🎧

Weather

あたたかい	暖かい	warm	たいよう	太陽	sun
あめ	雨	rain	てんき	天気	weather
かぜ	風	wind	てんきず	天気図	weather map
きあつ	気圧	air pressure	てんきよほう	天気予報	weather forecast
きおん	気温	temperature	…ど	…度	…degrees (*counter*)
きこう	気候	climate	はれ	晴れ	clear weather; sunny and clear
くも	雲	cloud	ふく	吹く	to blow (*used with wind*)
くもり		cloudy	ふる	降る	to fall (*used with rain, snow, etc.*)
さむい	寒い	cold	むしあつい	むし暑い	sultry; hot and humid
すずしい	涼しい	cool	ゆき	雪	snow
たいふう	台風	typhoon			

Review: 暑い

Seasons

あき	秋	fall; autumn	なつ	夏	summer
きせつ	季節	season	はる	春	spring
しき	四季	four seasons	ふゆ	冬	winter

Loanword: カレンダー

Adjectives

あかるい	明るい	bright (vs. *dark*)
あだやか(な)		calm (*ocean, personality*); gentle (*breeze*)
おもい	重い	heavy
おもしろい	面白い	interesting; fun
くらい	暗い	dark
スマート(な)		slender (*person*)
たいへん(な)	大変(な)	terrible; awful
つまらない		boring
つよい	強い	strong
ながい	長い	long
にぎやか(な)		lively
はやい	早い; 速い	early; quick; fast
ふまじめ(な)	不まじめ(な)	not serious; lazy (*person*)
へん(な)	変(な)	strange
まじめ(な)		serious (*person*)
みじかい	短い	short
むずかしい		difficult
ゆうめい(な)	有名(な)	famous
よわい	弱い	weak
わかい	若い	young

Loanwords: エレガント(な)、キュート(な)、タフ(な)、ハンサム(な)

Review: 新しい、いい、忙しい、うるさい、(...が) 多い、きたない、きびしい、きれい (な)、元気 (な)、静か (な)、親切 (な)、(...が) 少ない、せまい、高い、低い、暇 (な)、広い、不便 (な)、古い、便利 (な)、やさしい、安い、悪い

Nouns

いなずま	稲妻	lightning	かみなり	雷	thunder
うみ	海	ocean; sea	きた	北	north
おおあめ	大雨	heavy rain	きり	霧	fog

(Continues.)

おおゆき	大雪	heavy snow	こうずい	洪水	flood
かさ	傘	umbrella	そら	空	sky
しも	霜	frost	みなみ	南	south
つり	釣り	fishing	やま	山	mountain
つゆ	露	dew	やまのぼり	山登り	mountain climbing
てがみ	手紙	letter	ゆうだち	夕立	evening shower
にし	西	west			
はなみ	花見	(cherry) blossom viewing			
ひがし	東	east			
ひでり	日照り	drought			
びょうき	病気	sick			
ふぶき	吹雪	snowstorm			
みぞれ		sleet			

Loanwords: キャンプ、コート、サーフィン、スキー、スケート、ハイキング

Verbs

およぐ	泳ぐ	to swim
しぬ	死ぬ	to die
つかう	使う	to use

Other Words

おなじ	同じ	same
ぐらい、くらい		about; approximately
はやく	早く; 速く	early; quickly (*adverb*)

Review: たくさん、よく

Grammar

...でしょう	probably (*conjecture, polite*)	...が、	but (*conjunction*)
...だろう	probably (*conjecture, plain*)	...から、	because (*conjunction*)
...かもしれません	may; might (*conjecture, polite*)	〜てください	please do...
...かもしれない	may; might (*conjecture, plain*)	...けれども	but (*conjunction*)

Kanji

Learn these characters:

天	東	台	少
気	西	番	強
雨	南	春	弱
雪	北	夏	昨
度	高	秋	暑
風	多	冬	寒
			空

チェックリスト

Use this checklist to confirm that you can now:

- Talk about weather reports
- Talk about the four seasons
- Talk about forecasting
- Conjugate adjectives
- Use comparatives and superlatives
- Express plain, nonpast negative and plain past
- Explain reason using 〜ので
- Use the **te**-form of adjectives and verbs
- Express possibility
- Ask questions about the Japanese language

5 Hobbies and Leisure Activities

第五章　趣味_{しゅみ}・余暇_{よか}

趣味_{しゅみ}はお茶_{ちゃ}です。

OBJECTIVES

In this lesson you are going to:

- Talk about hobbies, pastimes, and sports
- Talk about family and learn to introduce family members
- Learn how to express *some, every, none,* and *any*
- Learn how to describe abilities
- Practice using nominalizers こと and の
- Study more uses of the particle も
- Learn how to use the potential form of verbs
- Study the **te**-form of verbs ＋います
- Learn about relative clauses
- Learn how to describe a change in state
- Learn how to respond to compliments

YOOKOSO! MULTIMEDIA

Review and practice grammar and vocabulary from this chapter and watch video clips on the *Yookoso!* Interactive CD-ROM. Visit the *Yookoso!* Online Learning Center at **www.mhhe.com/yookoso3** for additional exercises and resources.

Vocabulary and Grammar 5A

Vocabulary and Oral Activities

Hobbies and Pastimes

Vocabulary: Hobbies and Leisure Activities 🎧

余暇	よか	free time; leisure
趣味	しゅみ	hobby
遊ぶ	あそぶ	to play
楽しむ	たのしむ	to enjoy
特技	とくぎ	special talent; skill
切手集め	きってあつめ	stamp collecting
写真	しゃしん	photography; photograph
園芸	えんげい	gardening
手芸	しゅげい	handicrafts
読書	どくしょ	reading books
絵画	かいが	painting
音楽鑑賞	おんがくかんしょう	music appreciation; listening to music
歌	うた	song
楽器	がっき	musical instrument
茶道	さどう	tea ceremony
コンサート		concert
旅行	りょこう	travel
カルチャーセンター		adult education center
クラブ		club
レジャー		leisure

Review: 映画（えいが）、音楽（おんがく）、スポーツ、釣り（つ）（に行く）、暇（ひま）（な）

アクティビティー **1**

ゴルフはたのしいです。 (*Golf is fun.*)

Associate words in the first column with appropriate words in the second column.

1. 写真
2. 読書
3. 映画
4. 園芸
5. 旅行
6. 手芸
7. 茶道
8. 趣味
9. 切手集め
10. 音楽鑑賞
11. ボーリング
12. 歌

a. ピアノ
b. 電車
c. コンサート
d. 楽しむ
e. フィルム
f. 図書館
g. クラーク・ゲーブル
h. 針と糸 (*needle and thread*)
i. チューリップ
j. 古い手紙
k. 飲み物
l. ボール

アクティビティー **2**

趣味は何ですか。(*What are their hobbies?*)

Various people made these statements. Identify their hobbies.

1. 「マダム・バタフライ」が好きです。
2. 昨日、ジャイアンツの試合を見ました。
3. カメラをいつも持っています。
4. シチューを作るのが上手です。
5. 去年、中国とメキシコとフランスとエジプトへ行きました。

Grammar and Practice Activities

24. Interrogative + か／も／でも 🎧

町田さんと林さんが話しています。

林 ：町田さんは何か趣味がありますか。

町田：そうですね、音楽鑑賞ですね。

林 ：スポーツは何かしますか。

> When asking a social superior about his or her hobbies, use the polite alternate 御趣味. See Language Note on page 327.

Ms. Machida and Mr. Hayashi are talking   HAYASHI: Do you (lit., *Ms. Machida*) have any hobbies?   MACHIDA: Let me see. My hobby is listening to music.   HAYASHI: Do you play any sports?

(*Continues.*)

町田：テニスやバレーボールをします。
　　　林_{はやし}さんの趣味_{しゅみ}は何_{なん}ですか。
　　林：いやあ、何_{なに}もないんですよ。

24.1 By appending the particles か, も, or でも to an interrogative (question word), you can express a whole range of new meanings.

1. An interrogative followed by か yields a word meaning *some…*

2. An interrogative followed by も means *every…* in affirmative sentences; it means *no…* in negative sentences.

3. An interrogative followed by でも means *any.*

These meanings are summarized in the following table. Note the two exceptions where other terms are used instead of the interrogative + も.

> **R**eminder: どれ is used when talking about three or more things. どちら is used when discussing two things.

Interrogative	+ か	+ も **In Affirmative Sentences**	+ も **In Negative Sentences**	+ でも
何_{なに}	何_{なに}か *something*	みんな、みな 全_{すべ}て、全部_{ぜんぶ} *everything*	何_{なに}も *nothing*	何_{なん}でも *anything* (and *everything*), *whatever*
だれ （どなた）	だれか （どなたか） *someone*	みんな、みな （みなさん） *everyone*	だれも （どなたも） *no one*	だれでも （どなたでも） *anyone, whoever*
いつ	いつか *sometime*	いつも *always,* *all the time*	いつも *never*	いつでも *anytime, whenever*
どこ	どこか *somewhere*	どこも *everywhere*	どこも *nowhere*	どこでも *anywhere, wherever*
どれ	どれか *one of them*	どれも *every one,* *everything,* *all of them*	どれも *none of them*	どれでも *any of them,* *whichever one*
どちら	どちらか *either of two*	どちらも *both of them*	どちらも *neither of them*	どちらでも *either of them,* *whichever of the two*

MACHIDA: I play things like tennis and volleyball. What is your hobby, Mr. Hayashi?
HAYASHI: Well, I don't have any.

何か食べますか。—ええ、何でもけっこうです。
Will you eat something? —Yes, anything is fine.
昨日は何か食べましたか。—いいえ、何も食べませんでした。
Did you eat something yesterday?—No, I ate nothing (or No, I didn't eat anything).
だれか来ますか。—いいえ、だれも来ません。
Is someone coming? —No, no one is coming.
いつかそこへ行きましょうか。—ええ、いつでもいいですよ。
Shall we go there someday? —Yes, any time is OK.
三村さんはいつもいませんね。—アルバイトで忙しいんですよ。
Mr. Mimura is never present. —He's busy with his part-time jobs, you know.
この三つの中からどれか選んでください。—じゃ、これをください。
Please choose one of these three. —Well then, please give me this one.
どれがいいでしょうか。—どれでも同じです。
Which one is good? —All of them are the same.
どちらか選んでください。—わたしはどちらでもいいですよ。
Please choose one of these (two). —Either is fine with me.

24.2 When the particles に, へ, から, and まで are part of a sentence containing the interrogative ＋か／も／でも construction, they fall between the interrogative and も or でも.

みんなに会いますか。—いいえ、だれにも会いませんよ。
Will you see everyone? —No, I won't see anyone.
どこかへ行きましたか。—いいえ、どこへも行きませんでした。
Did you go somewhere? —No, I didn't go anywhere.

The particle を is dropped whenever these interrogative-particle combinations are used.

何を見ますか。—何でも見ますよ。
What will you see? —I'm going to see everything.

24.3 Here are some useful expressions formed by combining interrogatives with か.

なぜか *somehow (for some reason)*
なぜか村山さんが好きではありません。
Somehow I don't like Ms. Murayama.

どうか *somehow (often used in requests)*
どうか教えてください。
Please (find a way to) instruct me.

いくつか *some (number of), several*
日本語のことばをいくつか習いました。
I learned some Japanese words.

アクティビティー 3

何_{なん}でも好_すきです。(*I like everything.*)

Fill in each blank with the appropriate interrogative + particle(s) and complete the dialogues.

1. s1: (　　)飲_のみますか。

   s2: ええ、コーラはありますか。

2. s1: (　　)へ行きましょうか。

   s2: そうですね。デパートはどうですか。

3. s1: そこに(　　)いますか。

   s2: ええ、林_{はやし}さんがいます。

4. s1: この映画_{えいが}の中で(　　)を見ましたか。

   s2: いいえ、どれも見ていません。

5. s1: この三冊_{さつ}の本の中のどれがいいですか。

   s2: (　　)いいですよ。

6. s1: 今年の夏_{なつ}はどこへ旅行_{りょこう}しましょうか。

   s2: わたしは(　　)いいですよ。

7. s1: この問題_{もんだい}はやさしいですね。

   s2: ええ、(　　)簡単_{かんたん}に (*easily*) できますね。

8. s1: 土曜日_{どようび}がいいですか、日曜日_{にちようび}がいいですか。

   s2: (　　)いいですよ。

9. s1: あそこにだれがいましたか。

   s2: (　　)いませんでした。

10. s1: (　　)へ行きましょうか。

    s2: いいえ、家_{いえ}にいましょう。今日は(　　)こんでいます (こんでいる *to be crowded*)。

> 冊 is a counter for books.

アクティビティー 4

いつもやさしいです。 (*She's always kind.*)

Answer these questions. Use interrogatives +か, も, or でも as appropriate.

1. 先週_{せんしゅう}の日曜日_{にちようび}、どこかへ行きましたか。

2. 何_{なに}を食べますか。

3. いつか映画_{えいが}を見ませんか。

4. このコンピュータはどれも同_{おな}じですか。

三百

5. コーラとジュースとビールのどれがいいですか。

6. 今日の午後、何もしないんですか。

7. あの先生はいつもやさしいですか。

8. だれもこの練習ができないんですか。

アクティビティー 5

この週末何をしますか。(*What are they going to do this weekend?*)

Using the following table, discuss what hobby each person has and what he or she is going to do this weekend.

[例] s1: 町田さんは何か趣味がありますか。
   s2: クラシック音楽です。
   s1: 週末は何かしますか。
   s2: 日曜日、コンサートへ行きます。

名前	趣味	土曜日	日曜日
ジョン・カワムラ (21歳、大学生)	映画	映画を見る	ジョギングをする
町田ひとみ (20歳、大学生)	クラシック音楽	ステレオを聞く	コンサートへ行く
林 正男 (19歳、大学生)	ない	一日中寝る	テレビを見る
山本 さゆり (18歳、ウエートレス)	買い物	デパートへ行く	ブティックへ行く
高田洋一 (26歳、会社員)	ない	仕事をする	仕事をする
山口 健次 (54歳、会社員)	釣り	仕事をする	釣りに行く
ヘザー・ギブソン (20歳、大学生)	スポーツ	エアロビクスをする	スキーに行く

会社員 *company employee*

VOCABULARY LIBRARY 🎧

More Hobbies

ART

絵をかく	えをかく	to draw a picture
墨絵	すみえ	sumi ink painting
生花	いけばな	flower arranging
書道	しょどう	brush calligraphy

MUSIC AND PERFORMING ARTS

バイオリン		violin
琴	こと	koto (*Japanese zither*)
三味線	しゃみせん	samisen (*Japanese banjo-like instrument*)
日本舞踊	にほんぶよう	Japanese traditional dancing
弾く	ひく	to play (*string instruments*)
吹く	ふく	to play (*wind instruments*)
歌(を歌う)	うた(をうたう)	(to sing) a song
演奏する	えんそうする	to play; to perform on (*a musical instrument*)
クラシック音楽	クラシックおんがく	classical music
演劇	えんげき	(*theatrical*) play

Loanwords: オペラ、ギター、ジャズ、ダンス、ピアノ、ミュージカル、ラップ、ロック

GAMES

テレビゲーム		video game
トランプ(をする)		(to play) cards
碁	ご	go (*a board game*)
将棋	しょうぎ	shogi (*a board game*)
マージャン		mah-jongg
パチンコ		pachinko (*Japanese pinball*)

Loanwords: コンピュータゲーム、チェス

PHOTOGRAPHY

写真(を撮る)	しゃしん(をとる)	(to take) a photo
白黒写真	しろくろしゃしん	black-and-white photo(graphy)
カラー写真	カラーしゃしん	color photo(graphy)

Loanwords: アルバム、カメラ、ビデオカメラ、フィルム

OTHER HOBBIES

骨董品	こっとうひん	antiques
刺繍	ししゅう	embroidery
編物	あみもの	knitting; crochet
手品	てじな	sleight-of-hand; magic
盆栽	ぼんさい	bonsai
ペット(を飼う)	ペット(をかう)	(to keep; to raise) a pet
犬	いぬ	dog
猫	ねこ	cat
鳥	とり	bird
金魚	きんぎょ	goldfish

Loanwords: コンピュータ、ハンティング、ヨガ

アクティビティー **6**

どんな趣味・スポーツをすすめますか。(*What hobby or sport do you recommend?*)

Your partner is a hobby critic. Ask him or her what hobby or sport he or she recommends for the following people. The critic must give one or two reasons why he or she thinks a particular hobby or sport is most appropriate.

1. 話すのが好きな人
2. 花が好きな人
3. 音楽が好きな人
4. 日本文化について知りたい人
5. 海のそばに住んでいる人
6. お金がたくさんある人
7. 時間があまりない人

文化ノート

CULTURE NOTE: 碁、将棋、マージャン、パチンコ

Four popular Japanese games are **go, shogi, mah-jongg,** and **pachinko.** The first two, **go** and **shogi,** both originally from China, are portable board games, but **pachinko** must be played in a **pachinko** parlor equipped with **pachinko** machines. **Mah-jongg** may be played either at home or at a **mah-jongg** parlor where refreshments are served and high-tech devices "shuffle" and deal the game pieces for you.

Go is a two-player game of sophisticated strategy. Each player in turn places a black or white stone on one of the 361 intersections of a 19 × 19 grid board with the aim of surrounding and capturing territories and the opponent's stones.

チーン、ジャラジャラ！パチンコ屋の中はいつもにぎやかです。

(*Continues.*)

Shogi is a two-player board game similar to chess. Each player manipulates 20 pieces headed by a king. More than 500 Japanese make their living as professional **go** and **shogi** players, and the results of their competitions are reported regularly in the newspapers.

Mah-jongg is played by four people using 136 tiles (resembling dominoes) to make strategic combinations. This game is extremely popular among college students, especially male students who may stay up all night playing, often at **mah-jongg** parlors in commercial districts near their universities.

Pachinko is a Japanese version of pinball that began its rise to phenomenal popularity in the late 1940s. With a flipper or knob, the player sends small steel balls into the vertically oriented pinball machine, aiming at specific holes. Depending on which hole a ball enters, varying quantities of steel balls are discharged at the bottom of the machine as the player's winnings. These balls can be reinserted into the machine for extended play or exchanged for money or merchandise such as cigarettes and candy. Minors are not allowed to play **pachinko.**

言語ノート

Nominal Verbs

Countless new verbs can be formed by appending the verb する (*to do*) to certain foreign loanwords and compound nouns (those composed of two or more characters) of Chinese origin. These are called *nominal verbs*. Add する to 旅行 (りょこう) (*travel*) and you get 旅行する (*to travel*). Here are some more nominal verbs you already know.

勉強する、運動する、料理する

ドライブする、ジョギングする、スポーツする

You cannot make verbs this way out of all loanwords and Chinese-origin compound nouns. For instance, you cannot say 銀行 (ぎんこう) する (*to bank*); a completely different verb is required. Nor can you say 会議 (かいぎ) する; you have to say 会議 (かいぎ) をする (*to have a meeting*). Most (but not all) nouns that can be turned into nominal verbs can also be used as the direct object of する.

勉強をする、運動をする、料理をする

ドライブをする、ジョギングをする、スポーツをする

アクティビティー **7**

レジャーをどのように過ごしますか。(*How do you spend your leisure time?*)

Here is how Japanese spend their free time. The activities are listed in decreasing order of popularity. Answer the questions that follow the table.

順位	女性	%*	男性	%
1	ショッピングをする	46.0	テレビを見る	49.0
2	旅行をする	45.9	寝る	34.8
3	手芸・編物をする	45.9	音楽を聞く	34.7
4	テレビを見る	41.1	旅行をする	32.7
5	読書をする	33.4	スポーツをする	30.3
6	友だちと話す	33.2	読書をする	27.8
7	音楽を聞く	30.8	釣りをする	24.8
8	映画を見る	30.2	映画を見る	24.3
9	レストランへ行く	23.4	マージャンをする	23.5
10	スポーツをする	20.6	パチンコをする	21.7

1. 女性に一番人気がある (*popular*) ことは何ですか。
2. 男性に一番人気があることは何ですか。
3. 女性と男性とどちらがスポーツをするのが好きですか。
4. 女性が7番目に好きなことは何ですか。
5. 男性が7番目に好きなことは何ですか。
6. 男性がして、女性がしないことは何ですか。
7. 女性がして、男性がしないことは何ですか。
8. アメリカ人があまりしないことは何ですか。

Make your own questions to ask your classmates.

順位 *rank* 女性 *women* (formal) 男性 *men* (formal) 〜番目 is a counter for ordinal numbers (first, second, third, etc.)

に of 女性に means *among* in this context.

Decimal point is 点 in Japanese. Thus, 45.9% is read 四十五点九 パーセント. 49.0% is read 四十九点ゼロ (or 零) パーセント.

三百五

Vocabulary and Grammar 5B

Vocabulary and Oral Activities
Sports

Vocabulary: Sports 🎧

スポーツ		sports
試合	しあい	game
ジョギング		jogging
マラソン		marathon; long-distance running
野球	やきゅう	baseball
バスケットボール		basketball
バレーボール		volleyball
テニス		tennis
ゴルフ		golf
フットボール		football
サッカー		soccer
水泳	すいえい	swimming
ダイビング		diving
プール		(*swimming*) pool
ヨット		yacht
キャンピング		camping
エアロビクス		aerobics
サイクリング		bicycling

Review: 泳ぐ、ハイキング、山登り

アクティビティー 8

私の好きなスポーツ (*Sports I like*)

Describe your favorite sports to a classmate in Japanese. Substitute different sports and facilities or equipment for the underlined portions.

私はテニスをするのが好きです。テニスは小さいボールとラケットを使います。私は野球を見るのが好きです。週末はテレビで野球を見ます。

アクティビティー 9

一人でしますか。 (*Do you do it alone?*)

Tell what sports satisfy each of the following conditions.

...人で as...person / people

1. 一人でします。
2. 二人でします。
3. 三人以上でします。
4. ボールを使います。
5. 外 (*outdoors*) でします。
6. 海でします。
7. オリンピックの種目 (*event*) です。
8. 冬のスポーツです。
9. 危険な (*dangerous*) スポーツです。

> ...以上 means ... *or more*. Thus, 三人以上 means *three people or more.*
> ...以下 means *less than* ...
> 三人以下 means *three people or less* (that is, zero, one, two, or three people).

Vocabulary: Skills		
上手(な)	じょうず(な)	good at; skillful at
下手(な)	へた(な)	bad at; unskillful at
だめ(な)		no good
得意(な)	とくい(な)	good at and fond of something
苦手(な)	にがて(な)	bad at and dislike something
できる		to be able to do
できない		cannot do

三百七

Grammar and Practice Activities

25. Describing Abilities 🎧

カワムラ：町田さんはピンポンが上手ですね。

町田：いいえ、そんなに上手じゃありませんが、大好きです。

カワムラ：一度一緒にしませんか。

町田：ええ、いいですね。

林：町田さんは何か外国語ができますか。

町田：ええ、フランス語がちょっとできます。

林：それはすごいですね。

町田：林さんは。

林：わたしは外国語がぜんぜんダメです。

> **N**ote the similarity between these expressions and those for stating likes and dislikes (**Grammar 10**, Chapter 2).

25.1 Here is how to express skills and abilities in Japanese.

$$
\begin{array}{l}
\text{A} + \text{は} + \text{B} + \text{が} \\
\text{(person)} \quad\quad \text{(noun)}
\end{array}
\left\{
\begin{array}{l}
\text{上手} \\
\text{下手} \\
\text{得意} \\
\text{苦手} \\
\end{array}
\right\}
\text{です（だ）}
\begin{array}{l}
\text{A is good at B} \\
\text{A is poor at B} \\
\text{A is good at and} \\
\quad\text{likes B} \\
\text{A is poor at and} \\
\quad\text{dislikes B} \\
\end{array}
$$

できます（できる）　A can do B

ブラウンさんはダンスが上手ですね。
Ms. Brown, you are good at dancing, aren't you?

歌が下手で、いつもこまる。
I am poor at singing, and that always gives me trouble.

ギブソンさんはスケートが得意だ。
Ms. Gibson is quite a skater (lit., *is good at and likes skating*).

KAWAMURA: You're good at playing table tennis!　MACHIDA: No, I'm not that good at it, but I love it.　KAWAMURA: How about playing together sometime (lit., *once*)?　MACHIDA: Yes, that would be good.

HAYASHI: Can you speak any foreign languages?　MACHIDA: Yes, I can speak French a little bit.　HAYASHI: That's great.　MACHIDA: How about you?　HAYASHI: I am totally bad at foreign languages.

わたしはフランス語が苦手だ。

I am poor at French (lit., *and dislike it*).

チンさんは水泳ができますか。

Ms. Chin, can you swim (lit., *can you do swimming*)?

25.2 上手 and 下手 are **na-**adjectives. 得意 and 苦手 are **na-**adjectives that may also be used as nouns. When used as a noun 得意 means *special skill* or *specialty* and 苦手 means *weakness* or *weak point*.

得意な外国語はスペイン語です。

My best foreign language is Spanish. (lit., *The foreign language I'm good at and like is Spanish.*)

歌が上手な人はだれですか。

Who is (a person who is) good at singing?

料理が下手な人はたくさんいます。

There are many people who are bad cooks (lit., *poor at cooking*).

私の得意はオムレツです。（得意 *used as noun*）

My special dish is omelettes.

苦手な課目は数学です。

The class I am poor at (*and don't like*) *is math.*

魚料理は苦手です。（苦手 *used as noun*）

Cooking fish is my weak point.

25.3 できます (dictionary form できる) is a Class 2 verb meaning *can do, is possible* and conjugates as such.

兄は楽器ができません。

My older brother cannot play (lit., *do*) *musical instruments.*

雨が降って、ハイキングができなかった。

It rained, and (so) we couldn't go hiking.

25.4 In these expressions notice that the direct object (B in the **Grammar 25.1** chart) is marked with the particle が, not を. This is an exception to the rule that direct object nouns and pronouns are marked with the particle を. You already studied two similar exceptions: the **na-**adjectives 好き and 嫌い. In addition to the **na-**adjectives and verb （できます）in the chart, this rule also applies to the verb わかります (*to understand;* dictionary form わかる).

兄はドイツ語がわかります。

My older brother understands German.

その答え (*answer*) がわからなかった。

I didn't understand that answer.

アクティビティー 10

日本語が上手ですか。(*Are you good at Japanese?*)

Following the example, make complete sentences.

[例] (山口さん)(ダンス)(得意) → 山口さんはダンスが得意です。

1. (山口さんの奥さん)(ボーリング)(上手)
2. (林さん)(バスケットボール)(下手)
3. (シュミットさん)(日本語)(上手ではない)
4. (佐野さん)(あみもの)(得意)
5. (カワムラさん)(フランス語)(苦手)
6. (ギブソンさん)(スキー)(得意)
7. (私)(料理)(できない)
8. (村山さん)(イタリア語)(わかる)

アクティビティー 11

ダンスはできません。(*I can't dance.*)

Make dialogues, following the example.

[例] (バレー／できる)(できない) →
—_____さんはバレーができますか。
—いいえ、できません。

1. (スポーツ／得意)(苦手)
2. (ロシア語／上手)(下手)
3. (バイオリン／上手)(まあまあ)
4. (ピンポン／できる)(できる)
5. (タガログ語／わかる)(わからない)

アクティビティー 12

バスの運転が上手ですか。(*Are you good at driving a bus?*)

Answer these questions truthfully.

1. 車の運転 (driving) が上手ですか。
2. どんな料理が一番得意ですか。
3. 日本語が上手ですか。
4. ご家族 (family) は日本語ができますか。
5. どんなスポーツが上手ですか。
6. どんな楽器が上手ですか。
7. 食べ物の中で何が一番きらいですか。
8. 苦手な食べ物は何ですか。
9. どんな外国語ができますか。
10. ショッピングが上手ですか。

アクティビティー 13

ダイアログ：野球が上手ですね。 (*You are good at baseball.*)

カワムラ：三村さんは野球が上手ですね。
三村：いいえ、野球は好きですが、下手です。

カワムラ：そんなことありませんよ。

三村：いいえ、ぜんぜんダメですよ。

Selecting from the following sports, answer the questions.

Sports: バスケットボール、バレーボール、空手、テニス、ピンポン、
ゴルフ、スキー、野球、ソフトボール、サッカー

1. どのスポーツが好きですか。

(*Choose as many as you like and rank them in order of preference.*)

2. どのスポーツができますか。

(*Rank the sports you can play in order of your skill level.*)

Now compare your answers with your classmates'.

1. みんな、どのスポーツが好きですか。
2. みんなが上手なスポーツは何ですか。

KAWAMURA: You (lit., *Mr. Mimura*) sure are good at baseball.　MIMURA: No, I like baseball,
but I'm no good at it.　KAWAMURA: That's not true. (lit., *No, there isn't such a case.*)
MIMURA: Yes it is. (lit., *No, I am no good at all.*)

CULTURE NOTE: When You Are Praised

It is usually difficult for Japanese to say no, but there are a few situations where Japanese say no immediately. One of those situations is receiving praise. When praised, whether for one's skills, a possession, a family member, or another in-group person, a Japanese first denies the praise or mentions something negative. *No, I'm still learning, No, it's a cheap item, No, my son is not talented.* It is considered rude and unsophisticated to accept praise right away or to boast about one's own skills or talent (or that of an in-group member), even if that skill is self-evident. Predictably, the person making the compliment offers further praise, which is again denied. After two or three exchanges of this kind, the person being praised finally accepts the praise somewhat reluctantly. See **Language Functions and Situations** in this chapter for more examples of how to respond to compliments.

VOCABULARY LIBRARY

More Sports Terms

投げる	なげる	to throw
受ける	うける	to catch (a ball)
打つ	うつ	to hit
ピンポン、卓球	たっきゅう	table tennis; Ping-Pong
プロ		professional
アマ		amateur
体操	たいそう	gymnastics
乗馬	じょうば	horseback riding
射撃	しゃげき	shooting
空手	からて	karate
柔道	じゅうどう	judo
剣道	けんどう	kendo (*Japanese fencing*)
相撲	すもう	sumo wrestling
陸上競技	りくじょうきょうぎ	track and field
選手	せんしゅ	athlete

Loanwords: ウエイト・リフティング、ジム、バドミントン、ボート、ボーリング、ボクシング、ラケット、ラグビー、ランニング、ロッククライミング、レスリング

CULTURE NOTE: 日本のスポーツ *Japanese Sports*

Sumo, a form of wrestling, is considered the Japanese national sport. It started some 2,000 years ago as a religious ritual and is still surrounded in ceremony today. Two sumo wrestlers compete in a dirt ring 4.55 meters in diameter. The object is to force one's opponent out of the ring or to force any part of his body but the soles of his feet to touch the ground. Professional sumo tournaments, each lasting fifteen days, are held six times a year and are televised nationwide. Top-ranked sumo wrestlers attain hero status, including a few non-Japanese who have excelled as professional sumo wrestlers over the years.

すもうは日本の国技 (*national sport*) です。

Most Japanese train in at least one martial art, most commonly judo or kendo, during their secondary schooling. Judo is now practiced worldwide and is an Olympic event.

Karate originated in China and was further developed in Okinawa. It has become popular in many countries.While judo focuses on balance, karate relies on kicks, thrusts, and strikes to best one's opponent.

Kendo, swordfighting with bamboo staffs, developed from the swordsmanship of samurai. Of the various martial arts, judo and kendo in particular place emphasis on moral and spiritual training as well as physical training.

Although interest in soccer and football has been growing, especially since Japan and South Korea co-hosted the soccer World Cup in 2002, the most popular team sport by far is baseball. Japanese professional baseball consists of twelve teams divided into two leagues, the Pacific League and the Central League. Since the teams are owned by corporations, they sport such names as the Nippon Ham Fighters, Chunichi Dragons, Yakult Swallows, and Yomiuri Giants. Baseball is popular as an amateur sport, too, and the annual nationwide competition among high school baseball teams commands the nation's attention for several days when the playoffs are televised.

Japanese participate in and avidly follow many other sports as well, including golf, tennis, marathon running, rugby, and skiing.

26. Nominalizers: こと and の

高田：日本語は得意ですか。

カワムラ：話すのは下手ですが、好きです。

(Continues.)

TAKADA: Are you good at Japanese?   KAWAMURA: I am poor at speaking it, but I like it.

Vocabulary and Grammar 5B

三百十三

高田：書くのはどうですか。

カワムラ：むずかしいです。でも、漢字を書くのはおもしろいです。

A：高田さんはいますか。

B：ええ。でも、高田さんと今話すことは無理です。

A：無理なことはわかりますが、どうか…

B：ダメです。高田さんは今忙しいんです。

In written Japanese, emphasis may be added to a word by writing it in **katakana**, even if the word is not a foreign loanword or a sound word. *だめ* is written in **katakana** in this dialogue for this reason.

Nominalizers are grammatical elements that change verbs, adjectives, etc., into nouns or noun phrases. In English, for instance, by adding *-ing* to the end of a verb, you form the gerund or noun form. (For example: *see → seeing* in *Seeing is believing*.) Thus, *-ing* can be considered a nominalizer in English.

26.1 Generally speaking, only nouns, pronouns, noun phrases, and noun-like elements can be in the subject and object positions of a sentence. When you would like to use verbs and adjectives in those positions, you must change them into noun phrases. In Japanese, こと and の are used to nominalize verbs and adjectives (change them into noun phrases). These two elements are called *nominalizers*. Add one of them to the *plain* form of a verb or adjective to form a noun phrase.

plain form of verb, **i**-adjective, or **na**-adjective + こと or の

Here are some examples of each.

1. Plain form of verb + nominalizer

読むこと	読んだこと	読まないの
読まないこと	読むの	読んだの

2. Plain form of **i**-adjective + nominalizer

大きいこと	大きいの
大きくなかったこと	大きくなかったの

3. Plain form of **na**-adjective + nominalizer

きれいなこと	きれいなの
きれいではないこと	きれいではないの
（きれいじゃないこと）	（きれいじゃないの）
きれいだったこと	きれいだったの
きれいではなかったこと	きれいではなかったの
（きれいじゃなかったこと）	（きれいじゃなかったの）

TAKADA: How about writing it?   KAWAMURA: It's difficult, but it's fun to write Chinese characters.

A: Is Mr. Takada in?   B: Yes, but it's impossible for you to talk to him now.
A: I know it's impossible, but please… (let me see him).   B: No way. Mr. Takada is busy now.

You can use these noun phrases in the subject or object position of a sentence.

日本語を読むのはやさしいです。
Reading Japanese is easy.
SFを読むことが好きです。　　　　　　　　　　　　　　　SF（エスエフ）*science fiction*
I like reading science fiction.
その町がきれいなことは有名です。
その町がきれいなのは有名です。
It's well known that that town is pretty. (lit., *The fact that that town is pretty is famous.*)

Note that the plain, nonpast of a **na**-adjective takes its **na**-form before こと and の, just as it does before any other noun.

26.2 Although both こと and の can be used to nominalize verbs, adjectives, and sentences, there is some difference in nuance between the two. の is used in sentences that express something subjective (i.e., something directly related to the speaker or something perceived or experienced by the speaker). こと is used when talking more generally or objectively. For example,

日本語を話すのはやさしいです。
日本語を話すことはやさしいです。
Speaking Japanese is easy.

The implication of the first sentence is that the speaker is basing the observation on personal experience. The second sentence does not imply a personal opinion, but rather simply makes a generally known observation that Japanese is easy to speak (compared, say, to writing it). For this reason, こと sometimes sounds a bit formal or bookish. Note the difference in meaning between these two sentences.

ブラウンさんが日本語で話すのを聞いた。
I heard Ms. Brown speak in Japanese.
ブラウンさんがいつも日本語で話すことを聞いて、感心した。
I heard that Ms. Brown always speaks in Japanese, and I was impressed.

In many contexts, you can use either こと or の with little difference in meaning other than the implication just explained. In some contexts, however, only こと or の can be used. For instance

わたしは父がお酒を飲むのを見ていた。
I was watching my father drink sake.

In this sentence, の must be used, because the statement involves the speaker's direct perception.

見ることは信じることだ。
Seeing is believing.

This sentence expresses a general fact, so only こと can be used.

アクティビティー 14

この練習をするのはやさしいです。(*It's easy to do this exercise.*)

Complete each sentence, choosing an appropriate phrase from the right-hand column. (More than one alternative is possible.)

1. 日本語を話すのは   a. おもしろい

2. 料理をすることは   b. やさしい

3. テニスをすることは   c. むずかしい

4. 音楽を聞くことは   d. おかしい (*strange*)

5. 山田さんが来たのは   e. 体にいい (*good for one's health*)

アクティビティー 15

テニスをするのはたのしいです。(*Playing tennis is fun.*)

Following the example, complete each sentence.

[例]　（ブラウンさん）（料理を作ります）（好き）
　　　→ ブラウンさんは料理を作るのが好きです。

1. （カワムラさん）（バスケットボールをします）（好き）

2. （林さん）（運動をします）（きらい）

3. （ギブソンさん）（日本語を話します）（上手）

4. （チンさん）（歌を歌います）（きらい）

5. （町田さん）（ピアノをひきます）（得意）

6. （三村さん）（英語を書きます）（苦手）

アクティビティー 16

わたしはゴルフをするのがきらいです。(*I dislike playing golf.*)

Complete the following sentences using こと or の.

1. わたしは…が好きです。

2. …はむずかしいです。

3. …はやさしいです。

4. …はおもしろいです。

5. わたしは…が得意です。

6. わたしは…が苦手です。

7. わたしの日本語の先生は…が上手です。

8. わたしは…が下手です。

9. …はつまらないです。

10. わたしは…がきらいです。

27. More Uses of the Particle も 🎧

ブラウン：山本さん、週末はどうでしたか。

山本：土曜日も日曜日も仕事がありました。

ブラウン：それはたいへんでしたね。こんどの休みはいつですか。

山本：今週も来週も休みはありません。

ブラウン：本当ですか。2週間も休みがないんですか。

カワムラ：山口さんの趣味は何ですか。

山口：写真を撮ることです。

カワムラ：カメラは何台ありますか。

山口：今は5台です。

カワムラ：へえ、5台もあるんですか。

台 *is a counter for cameras*

27.1 A も B も means *both A and B* or *A as well as B* in affirmative sentences, and *(n)either A (n) or B* in negative sentences.

カワムラさんもブラウンさんもアメリカ人です。
Both Mr. Kawamura and Ms. Brown are American.
クラシック音楽もロックもあまり好きじゃありません。
I don't like either classical music or rock music very much.
I like neither classical music nor rock music very much.
ここは春も夏も秋も雨がたくさん降る。
Here it rains a lot in spring, summer, and fall as well.

27.2 Numeral + counter + も means *as much as* or *as many as* the stated quantity; in other words, the number is higher than the speaker expected or more than usual. When this form is used in negative sentences, the implication is the opposite: the number is smaller than expected, *not even the stated quantity.*

うちから駅まで2時間もかかりました。
It took as much as two hours to get from home to the station.
先週のパーティーには300人も来た。
As many as 300 people came to last week's party.

(Continues.)

BROWN: Ms. Yamamoto, how was your weekend? YAMAMOTO: I had to work on both Saturday and Sunday. BROWN: That must have been awful. When is your next day off? YAMAMOTO: I don't have a day off this week or next week. BROWN: Really? You don't have a day off for two whole weeks?

KAWAMURA: What is your (lit., *Mr. Yamaguchi's*) hobby? YAMAGUCHI: My hobby is taking photos. KAWAMURA: How many cameras do you have? YAMAGUCHI: Now I have five. KAWAMURA: Wow, you have *five*?

今日のクラスは学生が 5 人もいない。
There aren't even five students in today's class.
わたしは 学校を 1 日も 休みませんでした。
I didn't miss even one day of school.

アクティビティー **17**

わたしはスキーもテニスも 好きです。(*I like both skiing and tennis.*)

Following the example, complete these sentences using ...も...も.

[例]　カワムラさんはビールが 好きです。
　　　カワムラさんはワインが 好きです。→
　　　カワムラさんはビールもワインも 好きです。

1. チンさんはパーティーに 来ました。
　 林 さんはパーティーに 来ました。
2. 机 の上にペンがあります。
　 机 の上にえんぴつがあります。
3. 林 さんはブロッコリーがきらいです。
　 林 さんはアスパラガスがきらいです。
4. 17 日、雨が 降りました。
　 18 日、雨が 降りました。
5. 三村さんはテニスが 上 手です。
　 三村さんはピンポンが 上 手です。

アクティビティー **18**

どのぐらいしましたか。(*How long did he do it?*)

Following the example, make a dialogue for each exercise item.

[例]　日本語を 勉 強する／5 年 →
　　　—日本語を何年勉 強したんですか。
　　　—5 年です。
　　　—5 年も勉 強したんですか。

1. 寝る／12 時間
2. 旅行する／3 週 間
3. ハンバーガーを 食べる／6 つ
4. 本を 読む／3 冊
5. ワインを 飲む／グラスで 7 杯
6. ボーイフレンドがいる／3 人

> **R**eview counters in Chapter 2. 冊 is a *counter for books,* 杯 is a *counter for glassfuls.*

アクティビティー **19**

ダイアログ：見るのは好きです。(*I like watching it.*)

カワムラ：林さんはフットボールが好きですか。

　　林：見るのは好きですが、するのはちょっと...

　　　　カワムラさんは。

カワムラ：わたしは見るのも、するのも大好きです。

　　林：上手ですか。

カワムラ：まあまあです。

28. Potential Form of Verbs

> ブラウン：林さん、明日、学校へ早く来ることができますか。
>
> 　　林：何時ですか。
>
> ブラウン：6時です。
>
> 　　林：すみませんが、そんなに*早く起きることはできません。
>
> カワムラ：町田さんはフランス語ができますか。
>
> 　　町田：話せませんが、ちょっと読めます。
>
> カワムラ：書けますか。
>
> 　　町田：ええ、やさしい文は書けます。
>
> ブラウン：町田さんは、一人で着物を着られますか。
>
> 　　町田：いいえ、着物を着るのはたいへんです。一人ではちょっと...
>
> ブラウン：じゃあ、どうするんですか。
>
> 　　町田：近くの美容院に行きます。

(Continues.)

KAWAMURA: Do you (lit., *Mr. Hayashi*) like football?　HAYASHI: I like watching it, but I don't like playing it. (lit., *I like watching it, but playing it is a bit...*) How about you?　KAWAMURA: I like both watching and playing it very much.　HAYASHI: Are you good at it?　KAWAMURA: I'm so-so.

BROWN: Mr. Hayashi, can you come to school early tomorrow?　HAYASHI: At what time?　BROWN: Six o'clock.　HAYASHI: I am sorry, but I cannot get up that early.

KAWAMURA: Do you know French? (lit., *Can you, Ms. Machida, do French?*)　MACHIDA: I can't speak it, but I can read a little.　KAWAMURA: Can you write it?　MACHIDA: Yes, I can write easy sentences.

BROWN: Ms. Machida, can you put on a kimono by yourself?　MACHIDA: No. It's difficult to put on a kimono. To do that myself is... (impossible).　BROWN: Then, what do you do?　MACHIDA: I go to a nearby beauty salon.

---

*そんな, one of the **ko-so-a-do** words, means *that kind of*. そんなに means *like that, that much*.

Grammatical constructions expressing abilities, such as *I can swim* and *he is able to come tomorrow* are called *potential expressions* or *potentials*.

28.1 In Japanese, there are two different ways to express abilities or potential. Both correspond to the English auxiliary verb *can*.

28.2 The first potential structure is a combination of the dictionary form (nonpast, plain, affirmative form) of a verb and ことができる.

Dictionary form of verb　＋　ことができる

> **N**ote that in this sentence structure you cannot use の in place of こと.

できる is a Class 2 verb, used here to mean *can* or *is able to do*. The entire structure literally means *the doing of* (verb) *is possible*.

山口さんは2キロ泳ぐことができる。
Mr. Yamaguchi can swim two kilometers.
明日、6時に来ることができますか。
Can you come at 6:00 tomorrow?
昨日、ブラウンさんに会うことができましたか。
Were you able to see Ms. Brown yesterday?

As you can see from these examples, tense, negativity, and formality are expressed in the conjugation of できる; the dictionary form of the preceding verb remains unchanged.

28.3 You can also express abilities and possibilities by conjugating a verb. The conjugated verb forms expressing abilities and possibilities are called the potential forms of a verb and are formed in the following way.

	Class 1	**Class 2**	**Class 3**
Rules	root + e-column hiragana corresponding to the dictionary ending +る	root + られる	irregular
Examples	書く→書ける 読む→読める 会う→会える 話す→話せる 待つ→待てる	食べる→食べられる 見る　→見られる 着る　→着られる	来る→来られる する→できる

These potential forms all end in 〜る (the ending of the dictionary form of Class 2 verbs), and indeed, they conjugate like Class 2 verbs, whether they are derived from Class 1, 2, or 3 verbs. For example,

CLASS 1	CLASS 2	CLASS 3	CLASS 3
書ける	食べられる	できる	来られる
書けない	食べられない	できない	来られない
書けた	食べられた	できた	来られた
書けます	食べられます	できます	来られます

```
u-column → e-column
く  → け
む  → め
う  → え
す  → せ
つ  → て
```

漢字が上手に書けます。
*I can write **kanji** well.*
父はすしが食べられない。
My father cannot eat sushi.
わたしの子どもはまだ話せません。
My child still cannot speak.
ピンポンができますか。
Can you play table tennis?
山口さんは昨日来られなかった。
Mr. Yamaguchi couldn't come yesterday.

In these potential sentences, direct objects are marked with が. In sentences that use the potential form of verbs, the direct object can be marked with either が or を. Therefore

わたしは漢字が上手に書けます。
わたしは漢字を上手に書けます。

are both grammatically correct. Although the meaning is equivalent whether you use が or を, Japanese speakers tend to prefer が in most contexts.

Although some grammarians consider the root ＋られる to be the only correct potential form of Class 2 verbs, many Japanese speakers use a shortened form: the root ＋れる. In fact, nowadays the shortened form is more widely used than the longer form, especially among the younger generation. For now, learn to produce the traditionally "correct" form and to understand the shortened form.

	-られる FORM (LONG FORM)	-れる FORM (SHORT FORM)
食べる	食べられる	食べれる
見る	見られる	見れる
着る	着られる	着れる

(*Continues.*)

For speakers who use these shortened forms, there is no difference other
than accent pattern between the potential forms of 切る (*to cut*; Class 1 verb)
and 着(き)る (*to wear*; Class 2 verb).

アクティビティー **20**

ダイアログ：泳(およ)げますか。(*Can you swim?*)

カワムラ：チンさんの特技(とくぎ)は何(なん)ですか。

　　チン：水泳(すいえい)です。

カワムラ：どれぐらい泳(およ)げますか。

　　チン：そうですね。10キロぐらい泳(およ)げます。

カワムラ：本当(ほんとう)ですか。それはすごいですね。

Answer these questions.

1. 将棋(しょうぎ)か碁(ご)ができますか。
2. マージャンをすることができますか。
3. 上手(じょうず)に写真(しゃしん)が撮(と)れますか。
4. 手芸(しゅげい)ができますか。
5. 絵(え)が上手(じょうず)に描(か)けますか。
6. 編物(あみもの)ができますか。
7. 何(なに)か楽器(がっき)が弾(ひ)けますか。
8. 日本料理(りょうり)が作(つく)れますか。
9. 日本語が上手(じょうず)に話(はな)せますか。
10. 漢字(かんじ)が上手(じょうず)に書(か)けますか。

> See the Language Note on page 324 for an explanation of this use of particle か.

アクティビティー **21**

ここで手紙(てがみ)を出(だ)すことができます。(*You can mail letters here.*)

Following the example, complete each sentence using ことができます.

[例]　（土曜日(どようび)に来(こ)られます）→ 土曜日(どようび)に来(く)ることができます。

1. 午後(ごご)図書館(としょかん)へ行(い)けます。
2. 今日(きょう)の午後(ごご)、林(はやし)さんに会(あ)えます。
3. 10キロ走(はし)れます。
4. 駅(えき)まで歩(ある)けます。
5. ここで泳(およ)げますか。
6. 今(いま)、ブラウンさんと話(はな)せます。
7. 母(はは)に電話(でんわ)できます。

KAWAMURA: What is your special talent?　CHIN: It's swimming.　KAWAMURA: How far can you
swim?　CHIN: Let me see. I can swim about ten kilometers.　KAWAMURA: Really? That's terrific!

三百二十二

322   Hobbies and Leisure Activities

アクティビティー **22**

今日_{きょうこ}来られません。 (*He can't come today.*)

Make dialogues using the potential form of each verb.

Useful word: 走る_{はし} *to run*

[例] (play the guitar) →

—チンさんはギターが弾_ひけますか。

—はい、弾_ひけます。（いいえ、弾_ひけません。）

1. (play tennis)
2. (sing Japanese songs)
3. (run fast)
4. (draw pictures well)
5. (go to a concert with me)

6. (ski)
7. (watch TV with me this afternoon)
8. (read books together with me)
9. (swim in the ocean)
10. (come to my home)

アクティビティー **23**

わたしはスペイン語_ごを話せます。 (*I can speak Spanish.*)

Answer the following questions.

1. あなたはピアノが弾_ひけますか。
2. あなたは上手_{じょうず}に写真_{しゃしん}が撮_とれますか。
3. あなたは自転車_{じてんしゃ} (*bicycle*) に乗_のれますか。
4. あなたはバレーボールができますか。
5. あなたはフランス語_ごで歌_{うた}えますか。
6. あなたは1キロ泳_{およ}げますか。
7. あなたは10キロ走_{はし}れますか。
8. あなたの家族_{かぞく}は日本語_ごが話_{はな}せますか。
9. 明日、映画_{えいが}へ行_いけますか。
10. 土曜日_{どようび}、大学へ来_こられますか。

アクティビティー **24**

インタビュー：できますか。 (*Can you do it?*)

Ask one of the following questions of ten students in your class. Then report to the class how many students responded yes and how many said no.

(*Continues.*)

1. 日本語の歌が歌えますか。
2. 100メートル泳げますか。
3. スケートができますか。
4. 刺繍 (*embroidery*) ができますか。
5. スペイン語が話せますか。
6. 自転車 (*bicycle*) に乗れますか。
7. テニスができますか。
8. 柔道か空手ができますか。

言語ノート

か *or*

The particle **か**, used between two nouns, means *or*.

将棋か碁ができますか。
Can you play *shogi* or *go*?

ジュースかコーラを飲みませんか。
Would you like some (*lit.*, won't you drink) juice or cola?

ブラウンさんかカワムラさんが行きます。
Ms. Brown or Mr. Kawamura will go.

You may add another **か** after the second noun with no change in meaning.

ブラウンさんかカワムラさんが行きます。
柔道か空手ができますか。
Can you do judo or karate?

はい、柔道ができます。
Yes, I can do judo.

はい、両方できます。
Yes, I can do both.

はい、どちらもできます。
Yes, I can do both.

いいえ、どちらもできません。
No, I can't do either.

Both 両方 and どちらも mean *both (or either)* of two.

Vocabulary and Grammar 5C

Vocabulary and Oral Activities
Family

Vocabulary: Family		
家族	かぞく	family
両親	りょうしん	parents
父	ちち	father
母	はは	mother
子供	こども	child; children
息子	むすこ	son
娘	むすめ	daughter
兄弟	きょうだい	siblings
兄	あに	older brother
姉	あね	older sister
弟	おとうと	younger brother
妹	いもうと	younger sister
祖父	そふ	grandfather
祖母	そぼ	grandmother
孫	まご	grandchild; grandchildren
夫婦	ふうふ	husband and wife
夫	おっと	husband
主人*	しゅじん	husband
妻	つま	wife
家内*	かない	wife
おじ		uncle
おば		aunt
親戚	しんせき	relative

Important note: These words are used to refer only to your own family members and relatives. You will study another set of family terms for referring to other people's family members and relatives later in this chapter.

---

* Although in common use, these words are spurned by some Japanese for their sexist implications. 主人 literally means *master* and 家内, *one inside the home.*

アクティビティー **25**

ダイアログ：<ruby>父<rt>ちち</rt></ruby>です。(*This is my father.*)

<ruby>町田<rt>まちだ</rt></ruby>さんとブラウンさんが<ruby>写真<rt>しゃしん</rt></ruby>を見ています。

ブラウン：これは<ruby>私<rt>わたし</rt></ruby>の<ruby>家族<rt>かぞく</rt></ruby>の<ruby>写真<rt>しゃしん</rt></ruby>です。

<ruby>町田<rt>まちだ</rt></ruby>：<u>ブラウンさんの<ruby>右<rt>みぎ</rt></ruby>の<ruby>男<rt>おとこ</rt></ruby>の<ruby>方<rt>かた</rt></ruby></u>はどなたですか。

ブラウン：<u><ruby>父<rt>ちち</rt></ruby></u>です。

町田：この<u><ruby>女<rt>おんな</rt></ruby>の<ruby>子<rt>こ</rt></ruby></u>はだれですか。

ブラウン：<u><ruby>妹<rt>いもうと</rt></ruby></u>です。

Practice the dialogue, substituting the following for the underlined parts.

1. ブラウンさんの<ruby>左<rt>ひだり</rt></ruby>の<ruby>女<rt>おんな</rt></ruby>の<ruby>方<rt>かた</rt></ruby>　　　<ruby>母<rt>はは</rt></ruby>
   <ruby>水玉<rt>みずたま</rt></ruby> (*polka-dot*) のブラウスの<ruby>女<rt>おんな</rt></ruby>の<ruby>方<rt>かた</rt></ruby>　<ruby>姉<rt>あね</rt></ruby>
2. ブラウンさんの<ruby>後<rt>うし</rt></ruby>ろの<ruby>男<rt>おとこ</rt></ruby>の<ruby>方<rt>かた</rt></ruby>　　　<ruby>兄<rt>あに</rt></ruby>
   ストライプ (*stripes*) のシャツの<ruby>男<rt>おとこ</rt></ruby>の<ruby>子<rt>こ</rt></ruby>　<ruby>弟<rt>おとうと</rt></ruby>
3. <ruby>白<rt>しろ</rt></ruby>いブラウスの<ruby>女<rt>おんな</rt></ruby>の<ruby>方<rt>かた</rt></ruby>　　　<ruby>祖母<rt>そぼ</rt></ruby>
   サングラスの<ruby>男<rt>おとこ</rt></ruby>の<ruby>方<rt>かた</rt></ruby>　　　<ruby>祖父<rt>そふ</rt></ruby>

> **N**ote the use of the polite 方 and どなた to refer to an older person in contrast to the neutral 子 and だれ for a child.

Ms. Machida and Ms. Brown are looking at a photo　BROWN: This is a photograph of my family.　MACHIDA: Who is the man on your (lit., *Ms. Brown's*) right?　BROWN: My father. MACHIDA: Who is this girl?　BROWN: My younger sister.

Vocabulary: People

男	おとこ	male
女	おんな	female
人	ひと	person
方	かた	person (*polite*)
子*	こ	child
男の子	おとこのこ	boy
女の子	おんなのこ	girl

Note: While grammatically correct, referring to people as その男 or その女 is rude. You should say その男の人、あの女の人 or, more politely, その男の方、あの女の方。女性 and 男性 are also increasingly common, although they are somewhat more formal.

言語ノート

Words Expressing Respect and Politeness

Japanese has a wide range of expressions and structures to convey different levels of speakers' or writers' feeling of respect and politeness.

(These expressions and structures are generally called honorifics (敬語), which will be introduced gradually, beginning here. Let's take, for example, words meaning *person, people*. In a neutral situation, 人 is used. To show respect, 方 is used.

The prefixes お or 御 are often added to a word to express respect or politeness. For instance, お年寄 is the honorific counterpart of 年寄 (*elderly person*). 御趣味 is the honorific counterpart of 趣味 (*hobbies*), and it is used to refer to the hobbies of socially superior people. However, you cannot arbitrarily attach お and 御 to any Japanese word. You need to learn the customary usages for each word.

アクティビティー 26

私は 林 正男です。(*I am Masao Hayashi.*)

Masao Hayashi is describing his family. Are his statements accurate? Correct any that are wrong.

(Continues.)

---

*子 and 子供 both mean *child* or *children*. 子 must be used with modifiers—for example, その子、うちの子、男の子—but 子供 can be used alone as well as with modifiers.

1. 林俊男は私の父です。
2. 林やすとは私の弟です。
3. 林すみ子は私の姉です。
4. 林くみ子は私の母です。
5. 林太郎は私の祖母です。
6. 林よし子は私のおばです。
7. 林はなは私のおじです。

Now look at Masao Hayashi's family from another perspective, as your own family.

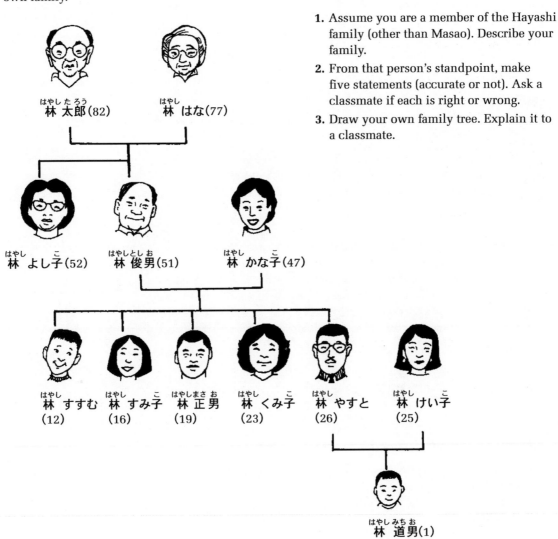

1. Assume you are a member of the Hayashi family (other than Masao). Describe your family.
2. From that person's standpoint, make five statements (accurate or not). Ask a classmate if each is right or wrong.
3. Draw your own family tree. Explain it to a classmate.

林太郎(82)　　林はな(77)

林よし子(52)　林俊男(51)　林かな子(47)

林すすむ(12)　林すみ子(16)　林正男(19)　林くみ子(23)　林やすと(26)　林けい子(25)

林道男(1)

CULTURE NOTE: The Japanese Family

Unlike the prewar years, when families were large and several generations lived under one roof, the average Japanese household today consists of a single nuclear family—two parents with one or two children. There is strong social pressure to marry by age thirty if not earlier. The typical couple has their first child within one to three years of marriage, whereupon the wife is expected to quit her job to take care of the child (unless she already quit her job to get married).

Women are also in charge of running the home—managing the family budget, the children's education, and the family's social schedule—while husbands are occupied with their jobs, often long commutes, and after-hours business socializing. As more and more women enter the workforce, these gender-based social roles have begun to change, especially among the younger generation. But married women, even those who have part-time or full-time jobs, still bear the greatest responsibility for managing the household, even after the children have left the nest.

As women have gained more economic independence through increased job opportunities, the divorce rate has risen. The number of single-parent families is increasing, and a noticeable percentage of young Japanese women are defying social pressures to get married before the age of thirty.

Family life in Japan usually revolves around the children, and their education is the central focus of their parents. Even if the father is transferred to a different city or country, the rest of the family may stay behind for years, so the children can complete their education without disruption. While some Japanese lament the dissolution of the extended and even nuclear family in Japan, blaming it on Western influence, others welcome the options offered by more than one socially acceptable lifestyle. Despite the changes, the family (not the individual) is still seen as the vital social unit in modern Japan.

何を見ているの？

Vocabulary: Other People's Families

御家族	ごかぞく	family
御両親	ごりょうしん	parents
お父さん	おとうさん	father
お母さん	おかあさん	mother
お子さん	おこさん	child; children
息子さん	むすこさん	son
娘さん	むすめさん	daughter
お嬢さん	おじょうさん	daughter
御兄弟	ごきょうだい	siblings
お兄さん	おにいさん	older brother
お姉さん	おねえさん	older sister
弟さん	おとうとさん	younger brother
妹さん	いもうとさん	younger sister
おじいさん		grandfather
おばあさん		grandmother
お孫さん	おまごさん	grandchild; grandchildren
御夫婦	ごふうふ	husband and wife
御主人	ごしゅじん	husband
奥さん	おくさん	wife
おじさん		uncle
おばさん		aunt
御親戚	ごしんせき	relative

Important note: These terms are used when referring to someone else's family members or relatives. These words are respectful in contrast to the humble terms for your own family; be careful not to confuse the two sets of terms.

言語ノート

My Father, Your Father

In Japanese, there are at least two words for identifying each family member or relative, one word for identifying your own family member or relative and another for identifying someone else's. For exmple, 父^{ちち} refers to the speaker's own father, and お父^{とう}さん refers to someone else's father. (You will study some exceptions later.) The former is humble, while the latter is respectful. (Did you recognize the honorific prefix お and honorific suffix さん?) You would never call someone else's father 父^{ちち}, so it is redundant to say わたしの父 (*my father*). Similarly, when asking someone about his or her father, just use お父さん; in that context it would mean *your father*. These two sets of terms for family members reflect the careful distinction between in-group and out-group in Japanese language and society.

アクティビティー **27**

ギブソンさんのお父さんは51歳です。(*Ms. Gibson's father is 51 years old.*)

Now Masao Hayashi is describing Heather Gibson's family. Are the following statements true or false?

1. ギブソンさんのお父さんは49歳です。
2. ギブソンさんのお母さんの名前はマリアンです。
3. ギブソンさんのお兄さんは28歳です。
4. ギブソンさんのお姉さんはコンピュータ・プログラマーです。
5. ギブソンさんのおじいさんは70歳です。
6. ギブソンさんのおばあさんの名前はジュリーです。
7. ギブソンさんの妹さんは20歳です。

モーリス(72)　　キャサリン(70)

ジョン(51)　　マリアン(49)
エンジニア　インテリア・デザイナー

Now try some other family descriptions.

1. Describe the Gibson family, using a family member other than Heather as a point of comparison.

[例]　ジョン・ギブソンさんの奥さんの名前はマリアンです。
　　　ジョン・ギブソンさんにはお子さんが四人います。

2. Now assume you are that person and from that person's standpoint, make five statements (accurate or not) about your family. Ask a classmate if each statement is true or false.

ジュリー　　　ヘザー　　　ジーン　　　ロジャー
(18)　　　　(20)　　　　(28)　　　　(30)
学生　　　　学生　　コンピュータ・　メカニック
　　　　　　　　　　プログラマー

VOCABULARY LIBRARY

More Family Terms

義理の(母)*	ぎりの(はは)	(mother)-in-law
養子	ようし	adopted child
独身者	どくしんしゃ	single (*not married*) person

HUMBLE FORM		RESPECTFUL FORM		
長男	ちょうなん	御長男	ごちょうなん	oldest son
長女	ちょうじょ	御長女	ごちょうじょ	oldest daughter
甥	おい	おいごさん		nephew
姪	めい	めいごさん		niece
いとこ		おいとこさん		cousin

アクティビティー **28**

お姉さんの趣味は何ですか。(*What are your older sister's hobbies?*)

This chart summarizes your family's hobbies and interests. Work with a partner, and answer your classmate's questions about each family member.

[例]　—お姉さんの趣味は何ですか。
　　　—姉の趣味は音楽です。ピアノが得意です。

家族	趣味	注 (Note)
父	仕事	土曜日、日曜日も働く
母	生花	園芸が好き
兄	音楽を聞く	クラシック音楽が大好き
姉	音楽	ピアノが得意
わたし	読書	いつもフランス語の本を読む
弟	テレビを見る	12時までテレビを見る
妹	スポーツ	空手が好き

*Replace the parenthetical family term with its respectful alternate to refer respectfully to someone else's in-law. Thus, 義理のお母さん (*your/his*) *mother-in-law.*

Grammar and Practice Activities

29. The **te**-Form of Verbs + います 🎧

> A： すみません。高田さんはいますか。
>
> B： ええ、でも、電話をしています。
>
> A： そうですか。じゃ、ここで待ちます。
>
> B： ブラウンさんも高田さんを待っていますよ。
>
> A： あの人はいつもすてきな服を着ていますね。
>
> B： 今日はデザイナーズ・ブランドを着ていますよ。
>
> A： ええ。いいドレスですよね。
>
> B： あのドレスは駅の前のブティックで売っていましたよ。

29.1 The **te**-form of a verb + the auxiliary verb います (いる) can be used to express these two meanings.

1. A continuing action at a certain point in time (like the English progressive tense: *I am reading, He was jogging, They will be eating*, etc.)

2. A state or condition that was created by a previous action or event and that is still maintained at a certain point in time.

Whether this construction has the first or second meaning depends on the nature of the verb being used.

29.2 If the verb indicates an action that can continue once started, such as 食べる or 話す, it has the first meaning. Thus, 食べている = *I am eating*. Other verbs of this kind are 飲む, 歩く, 走る, 歌う, 泳ぐ, 書く, 見る, 使う, 作る, 休む, 勉強する, 会う. Typically, they are actions that could theoretically be continued indefinitely.

> 山口さんはうちでビールを飲んでいた。
> *Mr. Yamaguchi was drinking beer at home.*

(*Continues.*)

> Auxiliary verbs are used with main verbs to express a variety of meanings, such as tense. The following verbs cannot be used with the auxiliary verb います: ある *to exist*, いる *to exist*, いる *to need*, できる *can*. While the *can do* meaning of できる does not allow 〜ている, the combination できている does occur with the meaning of *is finished*.

A: Excuse me. Is Mr. Takada in?   B: Yes, but he is on the phone.   A: I see. Then, I will wait here.   B: Ms. Brown is also waiting for him, you know.

A: She always wears nice clothes.   B: She's wearing a designer brand today.   A: Yes. It's really a fine dress.   B: They sell that dress at the boutique in front of the station, you know.

学生が先生と話している。

A student is speaking with the teacher.

母は今、テニスをしています。

My mother is playing tennis now.

29.3 When the verb indicates an action that is noncontinuous, such as 知る (*to come to know*) or 晴れる (*to clear up*), it has the second meaning. Thus, 知っている = I know (that is, *I came to know and I am still in that state*). Other verbs of this type include 死ぬ, 忘れる, 立つ, 座る, 起きる, 言う, 乗る, 着く, 寝る.

あの人を知っていますか。

Do you know that person?

クラスは始まっています。

The class has already started. or *The class is in progress.* (*That is, the class started and is still in that state.*)

母は起きていた。

My mother was up. (*That is, she got up and was still up.*)

今日、空は晴れています。

The sky's clear today. (*That is, the sky cleared up, and it's still in that state.*)

> The affirmative answer to this question is はい、知っています *Yes, I know him.* The negative answer is いいえ、知りません *No, I don't know him.*

When such movement verbs as 行く (*to go*), 来る (*to come*), 帰る (*to return*), 入る (*to enter*), and 出る (*to go out*) appear in this construction, the second meaning is expressed.

ギブソンさんが来ています。

Ms. Gibson is here (*she came and is still here now*).

父はトイレに入っている。

My father is in the bathroom (*he entered the bathroom and is still there*).

> ～ています is often shortened to ～てます in conversations. (That is, い is dropped.)

29.4 In some cases, either meaning (1) or (2) is possible, as shown in the following two examples. Verbs in this category include 着る, 取る, and おぼえる.

カーティスさんはセーターを着ています。

Mr. Curtis is putting on a sweater. (1)

Mr. Curtis is wearing a sweater. (*That is, he put it on, and it's still on.*) (2)

その学生は日本語の単語を覚えています。

Those students are memorizing Japanese words (*now*). (1)

Those students know Japanese words. (*That is, they memorized them and still remember them.*) (2)

CAUTION: The **いる** of the **te-いる** construction and the **いる** you learned meaning *to exist* are identical in form, but grammatically they are completely different. In the **te**-form verb + **いる** construction, *only* **いる** is used whether or not the subject is animate.

29.5 Sometimes, this construction is used to express a habitual action, one that takes place repeatedly.

わたしは毎朝ジョギングをしています。
I jog every morning.

山口さんは田中さんと毎日デートをしています。
Ms. Yamaguchi has a date with Mr. Tanaka every day.

The difference between these sentences and regular nonpast sentences is that these emphasize the habitual nature of the actions more than do regular nonpast sentences. For example

カワムラさんは毎日ジョギングをします。
カワムラさんは毎日ジョギングをしています。
Mr. Kawamura jogs every day.

The first example simply states the fact that John Kawamura jogs every day. The second example, on the other hand, points out that he makes jogging part of his daily activities.

言語ノート

Have You Already Eaten?

When you are asked whether you have finished doing something and you have not done so, you will answer using the **te-いる** form. For example,

昼ごはんをもう食べましたか。
Have you already eaten lunch?
–いいえ、まだ食べていません。
–No, I haven't eaten yet.
–いいえ、まだです。
–No, not yet.

When you have already eaten, you answer using the regular past tense form.

–はい、もう食べました。
–Yes, I already ate.

言語ノート

Some Time Expressions

Here are several expressions for indicating how long or since when an action or event has been taking place.

1. Point in time ＋ **から** = since...

先_{せんしゅう}週からカルチャーセンターへ行っています。

Since last week, I have been going to (study at) a cultural center.

去_{きょねん}年からスペイン語を勉_{べんきょう}強している。

Since last year, I have been studying Spanish.

2. Time expression ＋ 前_{まえ}から = since...ago

五_{いつ}日_か前_{まえ}から電_{でんしゃ}車で学_{がっこう}校へ行っています。

I have been commuting to school by train since five days ago.

三年前_{まえ}から山口さんを知_しっています。

I have known Mr. Yamaguchi since three years ago.

二時間前_{まえ}からここにいます。

I have been here since two hours ago.

You can reword the last sentence as follows.

二時間ここにいます。

I have been here for two hours.

アクティビティー **29**

ダイアログ：何_{なに}をしていますか。(*What is he doing?*)

電_{でん わ}話で

山口_{やまぐち}：もしもし、山口_{やまぐち}です。

ブラウン：もしもし、ブラウンです。カワムラさんはいますか。

山口：ええ、今_{いま}、テレビを見ています。

ブラウン：ちょっとお願_{ねが}いします。

On the phone YAMAGUCHI: Hello. This is Yamaguchi speaking.   BROWN: Hello. This is Brown. Is Mr. Kawamura there?   YAMAGUCHI: Yes, he is watching TV now.   BROWN: May I talk to him?

Practice the dialogue, substituting the following activities for the underlined phrase.

1. 料理をする
2. ステレオで音楽を聞く
3. コンピュータ・ゲームをする
4. 写真を撮る
5. 犬と遊ぶ

アクティビティー **30**

誰が何をしていますか。(*Who is doing what?*)

Using the following illustration, make dialogues.

[例]　—ギブソンさんは今何をしていますか。
　　　—新聞を読んでいます。

アクティビティー 31

いつからしていますか。(*Since when has she been doing it?*)

Rewrite these sentences using the model as an example.

[例]　山口さんは11時に寝ました。→ 山口さんは11時から寝ています。

1. わたしはブラウンさんを2年前に知りました。
2. カワムラさんは30分前にお風呂に入りました。
3. 山口さんの奥さんは3時にデパートに行きました。
4. カーティスさんは去年、日本に来ました。
5. さとみさんは先週、キャンプに出かけました。

> **R**eminder: The particle に following a time expression means *at* (*a certain point in time*). In the same position, the particle から means *from* or *since* (*a certain point in time*).

アクティビティー 32

どんなクラスを取っていますか。(*What classes are you taking?*)

Answer the following questions.

1. 今クラスをいくつ取っていますか。どんなクラスを取っていますか。
   (取る *to take*)
2. いつから日本語を勉強していますか。
3. 毎日、日本語を勉強していますか。
4. 漢字をいくつ知っていますか。
5. 日本語の辞書を持っていますか。
6. あなたはだれか日本人を知っていますか。
7. 今雨が降っていますか。
8. あなたは今ボールペンを使っていますか。
   えんぴつを使っていますか。
9. あなたは今何を着ていますか。
10. あなたは今、立っていますか。すわっていますか。
11. あなたはどこに住んでいますか。(住む *to live*)

30. Relative Clauses 🎧

横井：明日のハイキングに行く人はいますか。

ブラウン：はい、カワムラさんと私です。

横井：ハイキングに行く人のミーティングが1時にあります。
来てください。

ブラウン：わかりました。

カワムラ：山口さんの趣味は何ですか。

山口：テニスです。

カワムラ：よくしますか。

山口：いいえ、まわりにテニスができる人があまりいないんです。

30.1 You have already learned that adjectives modifying nouns precede
the noun.

おもしろいクラス   *interesting class; fun class*

きれいな部屋   *clean room*

In the examples above, a word modifies another word. When a whole
clause modifies a noun, the clause usually takes the form of a relative
clause. In English, the relative clause follows the noun it modifies.

the person who came here yesterday

the person whom I saw yesterday

the hamburger that I ate three days ago

a house where I lived for ten years

In English a relative clause (sometimes also called sentential modifiers) is
introduced with a relative pronoun or adverb such as *who, whom, which,
and where.*

30.2 Japanese relative clauses, like their English counterparts, modify
nouns. However, there are some striking differences between the
two languages.

1. Relative clauses in Japanese *precede* nouns that they modify.

2. There are no relative pronouns or adverbs required in Japanese. Relative
clauses *directly* precede the nouns they modify.

(Continues.)

YOKOI: Is anyone here going on tomorrow's hike?   BROWN: Yes. Mr. Kawamura and I are going.
YOKOI: There's a meeting at one o'clock for those who are going hiking. Please come.
BROWN: OK. (lit., *I understand.*)
KAWAMURA: What is your hobby?   YAMAGUCHI: It's tennis.   KAWAMURA: Do you play often?
YAMAGUCHI: No. There aren't many people I know (lit., *around*) who can play.

三百三十九

わたしが昨日食べた *I ate yesterday*	ピザ *pizza → the pizza I ate yesterday*
あなたが会った *you met*	人 *person → the person you met*
山田さんと話している *is talking with Yamada*	男の人 *man → the man who is talking with* *Mr. Yamada*
わたしが勉強した *I studied*	ところ *place → the place where I studied*

As you see from the examples, to form a relative clause in Japanese you simply position a clause before a noun.

30.3 Note that verb forms used in relative clauses must be plain forms.

> カワムラさんがいつも勉強する時間
> *the time when Mr. Kawamura always studies*
>
> カワムラさんが見ないテレビの番組
> *the TV programs Mr. Kawamura doesn't watch*
>
> 父が買ったステレオ
> *the stereo my father bought*
>
> その話を聞かなかった学生
> *the students who didn't listen to that story*

Polite forms are not used in relative clauses. A noun modified by a relative clause (double-underlined) is a noun clause (single-underlined), and may be used in a sentence anywhere a noun can be used.

> 昨日食べたピザはおいしかったですか。
> *Was the pizza you ate yesterday delicious?*
>
> 父が買ったステレオを見ますか。
> *Do you want to* (lit., *will you*) *look at the stereo my father bought?*

30.4 The possessive marker の is often substituted for the subject particle が in relative clauses and other noun-modifying clauses.

> 父の買ったステレオ
> *the stereo that my father bought*
>
> 母の好きだった本
> *the book that my mother liked*

The topic particle は is not used within relative clauses.

アクティビティー **33**

プログラマーはプログラミングをする人です。(*A programmer is someone who does programming.*)

Complete these sentences using a phrase chosen from the list following the exercise items.

［例］（　　　）はゴルフをする人です。→
（ゴルファー）はゴルフをする人です。(*A golfer is a person who golfs.*)

1. （　　　）はギャンブルをする人です。
2. （　　　）はレスリングをする人です。
3. （　　　）は勉強するところです。
4. （　　　）は本がたくさんあるところです。
5. （　　　）は写真をとる機械 (*machine*) です。
6. （　　　）はひまな時間です。
7. （　　　）は日本人が話す言葉 (*language*) です。
8. （　　　）は映画を見るところです。
9. （　　　）は水泳をするところです。

学校、図書館、プール、カメラ、ギャンブラー、レスラー、日本語、
余暇、映画館

アクティビティー **34**

わたしが先週見た映画はスピルバーグのです。(*The movie I saw last week was a Spielberg movie.*)

Combine these sentences by using a relative clause. In this practice, use the second sentence as the main clause of the resultant sentence. In other words, make sentences in which the predicate of the second sentence comes at the end.

［例］　わたしは昨日公園へ行きました。
その公園はきれいでした。→ わたしが昨日行った公園はきれいでした。
わたしは先週映画を見ました。
その映画はアメリカのです。→ わたしが先週見た映画はアメリカのです。

1. 父は昨日カメラを買いました。
そのカメラは高かったです。

Note that while わたし is marked with が in the resultant sentence, わたし is the topic of the relative clause, not of the sentence. The topic of the first example is 公園 and is marked with は. The が can be replaced by の as explained in Grammar 30.4.

(Continues.)

2. わたしは毎日プールで泳ぎます。

   そのプールはうちのそばにあります。

3. 昨晩CDを聞きました。

   そのCDは町田さんのCDです。

4. カルチャーセンターで先生がヨガを教えています。（教える *to teach*）

   その先生はインドから来ました。

5. わたしはいつも近くのレストランへ行きます。

   そのレストランは安くて、おいしいです。

6. ブラウンさんは中野に住んでいます。

   中野は静かで、便利です。

アクティビティー 35

忙しい人たち (*Busy people*)

Using the illustration from アクティビティー 30, make sentences containing a relative clause.

［例］ 新聞を読んでいる女の人はギブソンさんです。

アクティビティー 36

生花を教えている先生 (*The teacher who teaches flower arranging*)

Complete the sentences using relative clauses.

［例］ あの方は（　　）先生ですか。 → あの方は（日本語を教えている）先生ですか。

1. （　　）パーティーはどうでしたか。

2. あなたは（　　）本を読みましたか。

3. （　　）写真はあまりよくありません。

4. （　　）レストランは大学の北にあります。

5. これは（　　）CDです。

6. これは（　　）学生の部屋です。

7. （　　）女の人は中国人です。

8. （　　）人をマラソン・ランナーといいます。

アクティビティー **37**

教^{おし}えてください。 (*Please tell us.*)

Answer these questions.

1. 日本語を上^{ご じょうず}手に話せる外国人^{がいこくじん}を知^しっていますか。

2. あなたの家^{いえ}のそばにボーリングができるところがありますか。

3. あなたの家^{いえ}のそばに24時間^{じ かん}あいているスーパーはありますか。
（あく: *to become open*）

4. あなたの学校に安^{やす}く昼^{ひる}ごはんを食べられるところがたくさんありますか。

5. あなたの学校の中にはコンサートができるところがありますか。

6. あなたの町^{まち}のそばにスキーができるところがありますか。

7. あなたはマージャンができる人を知^しっていますか。

8. あなたはいいステレオを持^もっている人を知^しっていますか。

9. あなたは趣味^{しゅ み}を楽^{たの}しむ時間^{じ かん}がありますか。

10. あなたがいつも飲^のんでいる飲^のみ物^{もの}は何^{なん}ですか。

アクティビティー **38**

テレビゲームをしている男^{おとこ}の人はだれですか。(*Who is the man who is playing video games?*)

(Continues.)

Using the accompanying illustrations, answer these questions.

1. ブラウンさんと話している女の人はだれですか。

2. テレビゲームをしている男の人はだれですか。

3. 手紙を書いている男の人はだれですか。

4. エアロビクスをしている女の人はだれですか。

5. カーティスさんが読んでいる本は何ですか。

6. Tシャツを着ている男の人はだれですか。

7. 三村さんが飲んでいるもの (thing) は何ですか。

Now describe each illustration.

アクティビティー 39

フランス語が話せる人はだれですか。 (*Who is the person who can speak French?*)

Walk around the classroom interviewing your classmates to find out who satisfies which of the following conditions. Report your results to the class.

1. 空手のできる人

2. カメラを持っている人

3. ピアノが弾ける人

4. 歌が上手に歌える人

5. 昨日ジョギングをした人

6. 先週、映画を見た人

7. 暇がない人

8. 泳げない人

アクティビティー 40

たくさんお金のかかる趣味 (*Hobbies requiring a lot of money*)

List hobbies, games, and sports that satisfy each of the following conditions. Later, compare your list with your classmates' lists.

1. たくさんお金のかかる趣味

2. あまりお金のかからない趣味

3. 4人でするゲーム

4. カードを使うゲーム

5. とても疲れる趣味、スポーツ (*hobbies and sports that tire you*)

6. 家の中でできる趣味

7. アメリカ人がよくするスポーツ

8. 冬、よくするスポーツ

31. Describing a Change in State: なる 🎧

カワムラ：林 さんのアパートは便利ですか。
　　林 ：前は不便でした。でも、近くにスーパーができたので、
　　　　　便利になりました。

カワムラ：それはよかったですね。
　　林 ：それに、最近、地下鉄の駅ができたので、
　　　　　もっと便利になりました。

　　高田：山田さんの娘 さんはおいくつですか。
　　山田：先月6歳になりました。

　　高田：もうそんなに大きくなったんですか。
　　山田：ええ、いつの間にか。

> できる here means *to be constructed, to be completed.*

The verb なる (Class 1) means *to become, to turn into.*

noun + に
na-adjective + に　⎫
root of **i**-adjective + く　⎬ + なります(なる)

来年、大学生になります。
I will be (lit., *become*) *a college student next year.*
夜になって、静かになりました。
After night fell, it became quiet. (lit., *It became night, and it became quiet.*)
お酒を飲んだので、顔が赤くなった。
Because I drank sake, my face turned red.

KAWAMURA: Is your apartment convenient?　HAYASHI: It was inconvenient before, but since a supermarket opened nearby it has become convenient.　KAWAMURA: That was lucky (lit., *good*).　HAYASHI: In addition, a subway station was built (nearby) recently, so it has become more convenient.

TAKADA: How old is your daughter, Mr. Yamada?　YAMADA: She turned six last month. TAKADA: She's already gotten that old (lit., *big*)?　YAMADA: Yes, before you know it… (these things happen).

三百四十五

アクティビティー **41**

選^{えら}んでください。(*Please choose.*)

Fill in the blanks with appropriate adjectives from the list that follows.

Adjectives: 少^{すく}ない、多^{おお}い、長^{なが}い、暇^{ひま}(な)、上手^{じょうず}(な)、赤^{あか}い、安^{やす}い、大きい、暖^{あたた}かい、便利^{べんり}(な)、好^すき(な)、きれい(な)、白^{しろ}い (*white*)

1. 息子^{むすこ}は8歳^{さい}になって、体^{からだ} (*body*) も (　　　) なりました。
2. 理髪店^{りはつてん} (*barber shop*) へ行かなかったので、髪^{かみ}が (　　　) なった。
3. となりに銀行^{ぎんこう}ができて、とても (　　　) なりました。
4. 夏^{なつ}になって、仕事^{しごと}は (　　　) なった。
5. ピアノを毎日練習^{まいにちれんしゅう}しているので、(　　　) なった。
6. 秋^{あき}になって、葉^は (*leaves*) が (　　　) なりました。
7. セールなので、なんでも (　　　) なりました。
8. 春^{はる}になって、(　　　) なった。
9. 6月に入^{はい}って、雨^{あめ}の日が (　　　) なった。
10. 年^{とし}をとって (*getting older*)、髪^{かみ}が (　　　) なった。
11. 掃除^{そうじ}をしたので、部屋^{へや}が (　　　) なった。
12. 最近^{さいきん} (*recently*)、すしが (　　　) なりました。

アクティビティー **42**

わたしは下手^{へた}なので… (*Because I'm not so good at it…*)

Using the model as an example, complete the sentences.

[例] （ピアノが上手^{じょうず}だ）（ピアニスト） →
　　　ピアノが上手^{じょうず}なので、ピアニストになりました。

1. （エアロビクスが好^すきだ）（エアロビクスのインストラクター）
2. （英語^{えいご}が話せる）（英語^{えいご}の先生）
3. （車^{くるま}が好^すきだ）（カー・レーサー）
4. （プログラミングができる）（プログラマー）
5. （体^{からだ}が大きくて、強^{つよ}い）（ボディーガード）

アクティビティー **43**

好_すきになりました。(*I've come to like it.*)

Following the example, explain how each person has changed.

[例]　ゴルフがきらいでした。でも、今_{いま}は好_すきです。→
　　　ゴルフが好きになりました。

1. ピアノが下手_{へた}でした。でも、今_{いま}は上手_{じょうず}です。
2. ブロッコリーがきらいでした。でも、今_{いま}は好_すきです。
3. 読書_{どくしょ}が好_すきでした。でも、今_{いま}はきらいです。
4. 中国語_{ちゅうごく}が苦手_{にがて}でした。でも、今_{いま}は得意_{とくい}です。
5. スピーチが苦手_{にがて}でした。でも、今_{いま}は得意_{とくい}です。
6. ドイツ語が上手_{じょうず}でした。でも、今_{いま}は下手_{へた}です。
7. 料理_{りょうり}が得意_{とくい}でした。でも、今_{いま}は苦手_{にがて}です。

Language Skills

Reading and Writing
Reading 1　サンライズ・カルチャーセンターのお知_しらせ

Before You Read

Suppose you have decided to take a class at a local culture center. What information would you like to know about the class? Here are headings from the class schedule for a culture center in Tokyo. Does it include all the information you would need?

クラスの名前_{なまえ}　　先生　　曜日_{ようび}　　時間　　クラス　　授業料_{じゅぎょうりょう}

What do you think 授業料_{じゅぎょうりょう} means?

(Continues.)

三百四十七

Association: What words from the list below are related to each of the following: 外国語, 手紙 (*letter*), 料理, and ワイン? You may use the same word more than once.

書く、飲む、食べる、フランス語、紙 (*paper*)、ペン、エプロン、コルク、キッチン、話す、練習、作る、夕ごはん、スペイン語、ランゲージ・ラボ、読む、ことば (*word*)、朝ごはん、グラス、辞書、郵便局、シェフ

Now Read It!

サンライズ・カルチャーセンター
春学期のクラスのお知らせ
サンライズ・カルチャーセンターの春学期のクラスは4月1日から始まります。春学期のクラスをいくつか紹介しましょう。

■ 英文レター　入門
「英語は話せるが、書くのは苦手だ。」
「英語で手紙を書くのはむずかしい。」
「英語で手紙が書けない。」
このクラスでは、英語で手紙を書くことを練習します。先生は東京外国語大学の吉田京子先生です。クラスは毎週火曜日、木曜日午後6時から8時までです。授業料は3万5千円です。クラスは東ビル1304号室。

■ ワイン・テイスティング
ワインが大好きな方！ワイン・テイスティングを楽しみましょう。このクラスでは、フランス、ドイツ、イタリア、スペイン、ポルトガル、アメリカのカリフォルニアの赤ワイン、白ワインを楽しみます。先生はオーシャン・ホテルの川口はじめさんです。クラスは毎週金曜日午後7時から9時までです。授業料は4万6千円です。クラスは南ビル2415号室。
学生は20歳以上の方に限ります。

■ 中国語　入門
中国語は世界で一番多くの人が話していることばです。あなたも中国語を勉強しませんか。春学期のおわりには、簡単な会話をすることができます。
先生は日本で20年中国語を教えているリン・ホンミン先生です。クラスは毎週月曜日、水曜日、金曜日5時から7時までです。授業料は4万円です。クラスは月曜日と水曜日は北ビル320号室です。金曜日は南ビル140号室のランゲージ・ラボです。

学期 *semester, quarter* / お知らせ *notice, announcement*

始まる *to start* / いくつか *some, several* / 紹介する *to introduce*
英文 *English writing* / …入門 *introduction to…*

練習する *to practice*

授業料 *tuition* / …号室 *room number.*

楽しむ *enjoy*

…以上 *more than (compare …以下 less than)* / 限る *to be limited to*

世界 *world* / ことば *language*

おわり *end* / 簡単(な) *simple* / 会話 *conversation*

■ 男性のためのクッキング・クラス

食べるのは好きだが、料理をするのは苦手な男性はいませんか。この
クラスでは男性でもできる簡単な料理を習います。先生はテレビや
ラジオでも有名な土井森男先生です。クラスは毎週土曜日午前9時半
から12時までです。昼ごはんにはクラスで作ったものをみんなで食べます。
授業料は2万8千5百円です。クラスは西ビル654号室です。エプロンを
忘れないで下さい。

他に、スペイン語、フランス語、モダン・ダンス、イラスト、生花、ヨガ、
書道、ピアノ、フルート、ゴルフ、ピンポンなどのクラスがあります。

男性 *male* / …のため *for (the sake of)…*

作る *to make*

忘れないでください *please don't forget (from* 忘れる *to forget)*
他に *in addition* / イラスト *illustration*
など *etc.*

After You Finish Reading

The preceding passage describes four classes offered by the Sunrise Culture Center during this coming spring semester. List the name, instructor, dates, times, and tuition for each class in English.

Check your answers with a classmate by using the following dialogue.

s1: すみません。＿＿＿のクラスは何曜日の何時からですか。

s2: ＿＿＿です。

s1: 先生はどなたですか。

s2: ＿＿＿先生です。

s1: 授業料はいくらですか。

s2: ＿＿＿円です。

Which class would you recommend to each of the following people?

1. わたしは来年ペキンとシャンハイへ行きます。
2. わたしは商社 (*trading company*) で働いています。アメリカの会社
   (*company*) によく手紙を書きますが、英語はちょっと…
3. 去年20歳になって、はじめてお酒を飲みました。お酒の中ではワイン
   が一番好きです。
4. ぼくは、中野のアパートに一人で住んでいます。夕ごはんはいつも
   レストランか食堂で食べますが、高くてこまります (*have difficulty*)。

Now study the reading more closely for the following exercises.

1. Find the nominalizers (の and こと) in the description of the English letter-writing class.
2. Find the relative clauses used in the descriptions of the Chinese language and cooking classes.

Writing 1

1. You have decided to enroll in one of the courses offered by the Sunrise
   Culture Center. Complete the application form (申込書) on page 351
   in Japanese.

サークル名	開催週	時 間	受 講 料
指圧でリラックス	1・3	10:30～12:00	9,300円 (3ヵ月)
辰巳流日本舞踊	2・4	10:15～12:00	9,300円 (3ヵ月)
ヨーロピアン・フォークアート	2・4	10:30～12:30	9,300円 (3ヵ月)
フィットネスフラダンス	毎週	12:30～13:30	12,400円 (2ヵ月)
作詞入門	1・3	13:00～14:30	12,400円 (3ヵ月)
シャンソンを楽しく	2・4	15:30～17:00	12,400円 (3ヵ月)
真向法	毎週	15:30～16:30	12,400円 (2ヵ月)
郷土の日本史探訪	2	10:30～12:30	12,400円 (6ヵ月)
彫金	1・3	10:30～12:30	9,300円 (3ヵ月)
デンマークラグメーキング	2・4	10:30～12:30	9,300円 (3ヵ月)
手まり手芸	1・3	13:00～15:00	9,300円 (3ヵ月)
"書"を学ぶ	1・3	13:00～15:00	9,300円 (3ヵ月)
暮らしに生かすインテリア	2・4	13:00～14:30	12,400円 (3ヵ月)
短歌に親しむ	2・4	15:30～17:30	9,300円 (3ヵ月)
パッチワークキルト(初級)	2・4	10:30～12:30	9,300円 (3ヵ月)
ペン習字	毎週	10:30～12:30	12,400円 (2ヵ月)
話し方と朗読	1・3	13:00～14:30	9,300円 (3ヵ月)
スウェーデン刺繍	1・3	13:00～15:00	9,300円 (3ヵ月)
日本画入門	2・4	13:00～15:00	9,300円 (3ヵ月)
万葉集を読む	1・3	15:30～17:00	9,300円 (3ヵ月)
エッセイの書き方 (入門)	2・4	15:30～17:30	9,300円 (3ヵ月)
キーボードを楽しむ	1・3	10:30～12:00	9,300円 (3ヵ月)
美容気功	毎週	11:00～12:00	12,400円 (2ヵ月)
木版画を楽しむ	1・3	13:00～15:00	12,400円 (3ヵ月)
俳画	2	13:00～15:00	9,300円 (6ヵ月)
三味線の手ほどき	毎週	13:00～15:00	12,400円 (2ヵ月)
エッグクラフト	2・4	13:00～15:00	9,300円 (3ヵ月)
般若心経を読む	2・4	15:30～17:30	9,300円 (3ヵ月)
日本の庭園とその歴史	1・3	10:30～12:00	12,400円 (3ヵ月)
レザー工芸	1・3	10:30～12:30	9,300円 (3ヵ月)
童話を書く	2・4	10:30～12:00	9,300円 (3ヵ月)
ブラッシュアップ英会話	毎週	10:30～12:00	12,400円 (2ヵ月)
茶道の歴史と日本文化	2	13:00～15:00	12,400円 (6ヵ月)
インテリジェンス・チェス	2・4	13:00～15:00	9,300円 (3ヵ月)
英会話 (初級)	毎週	13:00～15:00	12,400円 (2ヵ月)
洞東流 書道	4	15:00～16:00	13,500円 (3ヵ月) (材料費込)
フォトレッスン	1・3	15:30～17:30	9,300円 (3ヵ月)
コミュニケーション手話	2・4	15:30～17:30	9,300円 (3ヵ月)
40'sビクス	毎週	11:00～12:15	12,400円 (2ヵ月)
中国語入門	毎週	13:00～14:30	12,400円 (2ヵ月)
リフレッシュ体操	毎週	13:30～15:00	12,400円 (2ヵ月)
カードマジック	4	15:30～17:30	9,300円 (6ヵ月)

**Class schedule from an adult education center
in Tokyo**

```
┌─────────────────────────────────────────────┐
│         サンライズ・カルチャーセンター          │
│           クラス受講申込書                     │
│  ─────────────────────────────────────────  │
│                                              │
│   名前                                        │
│                                              │
│   男・女                                       │
│                                              │
│   電話番号                                     │
│                                              │
│                                              │
│   クラスの名前                                 │
│                                              │
│   学期    春・夏・秋・冬                        │
│                                              │
│   曜日・時間                                    │
│                                              │
│   場所                                         │
│                                              │
│                                              │
│   授業料                                       │
│                                              │
│  ─── ─── ─── ─── ─── ─── ─── ─── ───         │
│                                              │
│              領収書                            │
│                                              │
│  平成   年   月   日   _____  様          │
│                                              │
│  ¥                                            │
│  但し             クラスの授業料として          │
│      サンライズ・カルチャー・センター校長         │
│              山中一男          印               │
│                                              │
└─────────────────────────────────────────────┘
```

クラス受講申込書
（じゅこうもうしこみしょ）
class attendance application form

領収書 （りょうしゅうしょ）
receipt
平成 *Heisei (era)*

但し *conditions* / ...として *as...*
校長 *school principal*
印 *seal*

2. You have been hired by the Sunrise Culture Center to teach a class. What special skill do you have that you could teach? Write your own course description in Japanese. What days of the week will your class meet? At what time? How much will you charge for tuition?

Reading 2　学生とサラリーマンの余暇 調査

Before You Read

If you had some free time, how would you most like to spend it? Rank the following activities in order of preference.

ゴロゴロする (*to loaf around*)

(*Continues.*)

コンサートへ行く

テレビを見る

スポーツをする

友_{とも}だちと話す

旅行_{りょこう}する

Compare your ranking with those of your classmates.

Which of the following do you think are worthwhile activities? Rank them in order of most to least worthwhile.

映画_{えいが}を見る

旅行_{りょこう}する

ステレオで音楽_{おんがく}を聞く

読書_{どくしょ}をする

友_{とも}だちとレストランへ行く

スポーツをする

Compare your ranking with those of your classmates.

Now Read It!

学生とサラリーマンの余暇調査_{よかちょうさ}

日本の学生は余暇_{よか}に何_{なに}をしているのか。学生500人にこの質問_{しつもん}をした。

テレビを見ている学生が一番多_{いちばんおお}かった。2位_いは「家_{いえ}でゴロゴロする」、3位_いは「スポーツをする」、4位_いは「喫茶店_{きっさてん}へ行_いく」、5位_いは「友_{とも}だちとレストランへ行_いく」だった。テレビを見ている時間は女子学生よりも男子_{じょし}_{だんし}学生のほうが長_{なが}い。

では、サラリーマンはどうだろうか。同_{おな}じ質問_{しつもん}をサラリーマン500人にした。旅行_{りょこう}をするサラリーマンが一番多_{ばんおお}い。2位_いは「スポーツをする」、3位_いは「映画_{えいが}を見る」、4位_いは「読書_{どくしょ}をする」、5位_いは「コンサートへ行_いく」だった。この調査_{ちょうさ}から、サラリーマンは映画_{えいが}、読書_{どくしょ}、コンサートなど、教養_{きょうよう}を深_{ふか}める活動_{かつどう}をしていることがわかる。一方_{いっぽう}、学生は余暇_{よか}をあまり有効_{ゆうこう}に使_{つか}っていないことがわかる。

サラリーマン *company worker* / 調査 *survey*
質問 *question*

…位 *number… (rank)*

女子 *female* / 男子 *male*

教養 *knowledge*

深める *to deepen, increase*
活動 *activity* / 一方 *on the other hand* / 有効に *profitably*

After You Finish Reading

Using the information from the preceding passage, list, in English, the favorite activities of both students and company workers in order.

Do you agree with the claim that company workers spend their free time more productively than students?

List all the relative clauses used in the passage.

Writing 2

Conduct a survey in your class on what your classmates do during their free time. Using your survey results, write a short report in Japanese. Follow the format used in the reading.

Useful expression: 余暇に何をしていますか。 *What do you usually do during your free time?*

Sound Words

言語ノート

Japanese has a vast number of words that represent sounds. One category of such words, called 擬声語 (*onomatopoeia*) includes those that imitate natural sounds: for example, the sound of a cat's cry is *meow* in English, ニャー in Japanese. A second category, called 擬態語, is composed of sound words that represent the manner of an action, a situation, or an image, as if the sound expressed those states. *Zigzag* is one of the few such words found in English. Japanese contains an enormous number of these 擬態語. Some examples are ゴロゴロ ([the *"sound"* of someone] rattling around—i.e., being idle), シーン ([the *"sound"* of] dead silence), and キラキラ ([the *"sound"* of] shining). Note that these sound words are written in **katakana**. Entire dictionaries are devoted to these sound words in Japanese. You will learn more of them as you proceed through this textbook.

Language Functions and Situations
Responding to Compliments 🎧

カワムラ：これは山口さんがかいた絵ですか。

　山口：ええ、そうです。

カワムラ：山口さんは絵が上手ですね。

　山口：いやあ、まったくダメなんですよ。

カワムラ：いいえ、そんなことありませんよ。

　山口：そうですか。

(Continues.)

KAWAMURA: Is this the picture you drew, Ms. Yamaguchi?　YAMAGUCHI: Yes, that's right.
KAWAMURA: You are skilled at drawing, aren't you?　YAMAGUCHI: Oh, no. I am no good at all.
KAWAMURA: No, that's not true.　YAMAGUCHI: Do you think so?

三百五十三

ギブソン：町田さん、きれいなブラウスですね。高かったでしょう。

町田：いいえ、安かったんですよ。

ギブソン：え、本当ですか。よく似合いますよ。

町田：そうですか。

How would you respond to the following compliments?

1. スペイン語を話すのが上手ですね。

2. ファッションのセンスがいいですね。

3. わあ、新しい車ですか。カッコイイですね。(*It looks great.*)

4. ハンサムなボーイフレンドですね。

5. テニスが上手ですね。

Role Play

Work in pairs. One person praises the other for the following. The person complimented responds using the patterns in the dialogues.

Useful word: ヘアースタイル *hairstyle*

1. being good at speaking Japanese

2. being good at cooking

3. his or her **kanji** writing is good

4. his or her hairstyle is nice

5. his or her younger sister is pretty

Introducing a Family Member 🎧

山口：ああ、ブラウンさん、おひさしぶりですね。

ブラウン：ああ、山口さん。お元気ですか。

山口：ええ、まあ、何とか。あっ、紹介します。兄の大助です。

大助：山口大助です。妹がいつもお世話になっております。

どうぞよろしく。

ブラウン：妹さんにはいつもお世話になっております。どうぞよろしく。

GIBSON: Ms. Machida, that's a pretty blouse. It must have been expensive.   MACHIDA: No, it was cheap.   GIBSON: Was it really? It suits you well.   MACHIDA: Do you think so?

YAMAGUCHI: Oh, Ms. Brown. I haven't seen you for a long time.   BROWN: Oh, Ms. Yamaguchi. How are you?   YAMAGUCHI: Oh, I'm getting along. (lit., *Yes, well, somehow…*) Let me introduce someone to you. This is my older brother, Daisuke.   DAISUKE: I am Daisuke Yamaguchi. Thank you very much for taking care of my younger sister all the time. Nice meeting you. BROWN: I am always taken care of by your younger sister. Nice meeting you.

言語ノート

お世話(せわ)になっております。

When you are introduced by an acquaintance (Mr. X) to one of his family members or colleagues or someone else from his in-group, you may say to the person introduced, X さんにいつもお世話になっております (*I am always taken care of by Mr. X* or *I am always indebted to Mr. X*). This expression indicates that you and Mr. X are very close and have a good relationship. Also, the compliment makes Mr. X feel good in front of his in-group member. The other party may say, いいえ、X がいつもお世話になっております (*No, X is always taken care of by **you*** or *No, X is always indebted to **you***) or X からいつもうかがっております (*I always hear about you from X*). Either statement now makes you feel good. The latter statement indicates that you are such an important person in X's life that he always talks about you. Alternatively, the other party may say, X がいつもご迷惑をおかけしています (*X is always giving you trouble*). This means *Thank you very much for tolerating X's behavior and forgiving him for it*. These expressions are commonly used in such introductions, whether or not your acquaintance really is taking care of you, and whether or not he really gives you much trouble. Think of them as formalities. The point here is that the distinction between in-group and out-group plays a crucial role in the language behavior of Japanese people.

町田：お母さん、こちらは大学のカワムラさん。

母：まあ、ようこそ、カワムラさん。娘からいつもうかがっております。

カワムラ：ジョン・カワムラです。はじめまして。ひとみさんにはいつもお世話になっております。

母：いいえ、娘がいつもご迷惑をおかけしております。

MACHIDA: Mother, this is Mr. Kawamura from school (lit., *the university*). MOTHER: Oh, welcome, Mr. Kawamura. I often hear about you from my daughter. KAWAMURA: I'm John Kawamura. How do you do. Hitomi is always a great help to me. MOTHER: Oh, no. My daughter is always troubling you.

言語ノート

How to Address Family Members

Japanese family members may address one another by their first names, but they also use terms that define their relationships.

Naturally enough, Japanese children address their father as お父さん (*father*) and their mother as お母さん (*mother*). パパ *papa* and ママ *mama* are terms of address commonly used by young children. (Other variations also exist.) A husband addresses his wife by her first name (without さん) or おまえ *you* (vulgar) or calls her with おい *hey.* A wife calls her husband by his first name (with さん) or as あなた *you.* おまえ and あなた are the closest everyday Japanese comes to *dear* or *honey.* When a couple has a child, they may call each other by the same terms their child would use: お父さん／パパ and お母さん／ママ. Parents call their child by his or her first name (without any title)—for example, 太郎 (*a boy*) or 裕子 (*a girl*)—or they may append the diminutive title suffix ～ちゃん to a young child's name—太郎ちゃん, 裕子ちゃん. Adding ～ちゃん to a name is like making Tommy out of Thomas or Tom. To boys' names ～君 (a familiar title suffix appended to male names of equals or inferiors) may be added; thus, 太郎君. When a family has more than one child, the terms of address are determined by the youngest child. That child is called by his or her first name. An older brother or sister is called お兄ちゃん *older brother* or お姉ちゃん *older sister* (affectionate forms of お兄さん and お姉さん) by other family members. This helps the youngest member of the family understand his or her relationship to the other family members.

Role Play

Practice the following situations with your classmates.

1. You are at home, and a good friend stops by for a few minutes. Introduce him or her to your family. Tell something about him or her. The friend greets the family members and talks about what you are doing at school.

2. You are shopping with your father or mother at a department store. You happen to run into a classmate from school. Introduce your parents and your classmate.

Listening Comprehension

1. You will hear descriptions of the pastimes of four people: Sasaki, Motoyoshi, Kuramoto, and Tamamura. Jot down their hobbies in English and write a brief account of what each person will do this weekend.

2. You will hear an advertisement for a culture center. Write a brief summary in English of the courses offered, the teachers, class times and places, and any other information, such as tuition charged.

Vocabulary 🎧

Hobbies and Pastimes		
あそぶ	遊ぶ	to play
あつめる	集める	to collect
いけばな	生花	flower arranging
え	絵	picture
えんげい	園芸	gardening
えんそうする	演奏する	to play (*a musical instrument*)
かいが	絵画	painting
かく		to draw (*a picture*)
がっき	楽器	musical instrument
カルチャーセンター		adult education center
きって	切手	stamp
きってあつめ	切手集め	stamp collecting
さどう	茶道	tea ceremony
しゃしん	写真	photography; photograph
しゅげい	手芸	handicrafts
しゅみ	趣味	hobby
たのしむ	楽しむ	to enjoy
とくぎ	特技	special talent
どくしょ	読書	reading (*books*)
とる	取る、撮る	to take (*a class*); to take (*a photo*)
よか	余暇	free time
りょうり	料理	cooking
りょこう	旅行	travel

Loanwords: クラブ、コンサート、ダンス、ドライブ、ヨガ、レジャー
Review: 映画、音楽、スポーツ、釣り、暇(な)、練習する

Sports		
しあい	試合	game
すいえい	水泳	swimming
たっきゅう	卓球	table tennis; Ping-Pong
やきゅう	野球	baseball

Loanwords: エアロビクス、キャンピング、ゴルフ、サイクリング、サッカー、ジョギング、ダイビング、テニス、ハイキング、バスケットボール、バドミントン、バレーボール、ピンポン、プール、フットボール、ボート、ボーリング、マラソン、ヨット、ラグビー、ランニング
Review: 運動、泳ぐ、スキー、スケート、スポーツ、山登り

(*Continues.*)

三百五十七

Family Terms

かぞく	家族	family
あに	兄	older brother
あね	姉	older sister
いもうと	妹	younger sister
いもうとさん	妹さん	younger sister (*respectful*)
おかあさん	お母さん	mother (*respectful*)
おくさん	奥さん	wife (*respectful*)
おこさん	お子さん	child (*respectful*)
おじ		uncle
おじいさん		grandfather (*respectful*)
おじさん		uncle (*respectful*)
おじょうさん	お嬢さん	daughter (*respectful*)
おっと	夫	husband
おとうさん	お父さん	father (*respectful*)
おとうと	弟	younger brother
おとうとさん	弟さん	younger brother (*respectful*)
おにいさん	お兄さん	older brother (*respectful*)
おねえさん	お姉さん	older sister (*respectful*)
おば		aunt
おばあさん		grandmother (*respectful*)
おばさん		aunt (*respectful*)
おまごさん	お孫さん	grandchild (*respectful*)
かない	家内	wife
きょうだい	兄弟	siblings; brothers
ごかぞく	御家族	family (*respectful*)
ごきょうだい	御兄弟	siblings; brothers (*respectful*)
ごしゅじん	御主人	husband (*respectful*)
ごしんせき	御親戚	relative (*respectful*)
こども	子供	child
ごふうふ	御夫婦	married couple (*respectful*)
ごりょうしん	御両親	parents (*respectful*)
しゅじん	主人	husband
しんせき	親戚	relative
そふ	祖父	grandfather
そぼ	祖母	grandmother
ちち	父	father
つま	妻	wife
はは	母	mother
ふうふ	夫婦	married couple
まご	孫	grandchild
むすこ	息子	son
むすこさん	息子さん	son (*respectful*)
むすめ	娘	daughter
むすめさん	娘さん	daughter (*respectful*)
りょうしん	両親	parents

Nouns

おとこ	男	male; man	かた	方	person (*polite*)
おとこのこ	男の子	boy	こ	子	child
おとこのひと	男の人	man	ひと	人	person
おんな	女	female; woman	みな		all; everyone
おんなのこ	女の子	girl	みんな		all; everyone
おんなのひと	女の人	woman	もんだい	問題	question; issue; problem

na-Adjectives

じょうず（な）	上手（な）	good at; skilled at
とくい（な）	得意（な）	good at and like; forte
にがて（な）	苦手（な）	bad at and dislike; weak point
へた（な）	下手（な）	poor at

Adverbs

いっしょに	一緒に	together
とくに	特に	especially
まったく	全く	totally

Verbs and Verb Forms

できる	to be able to do	〜れる	(*shorten form of potential*)
なる	to become; to turn into	〜ている	(*progressive*)
わかる	to understand; to be clear	〜られる	(*potential*)

Words Formed From Interrogatives

いつか		sometime; someday	だれも	everyone; no one
いくつか		some; several	どうか	somehow
いつでも		anytime	どこか	somewhere
いつも		always	どこでも	anywhere
すべて	全て	all	どこも	everywhere; nowhere
ぜんぶ	全部	all	どちらか	either
だれか		someone	どちらでも	whichever
だれでも		anyone	どちらも	both; neither

(Continues.)

三百五十九

どなたか	someone (*polite*)	どれも		all of them; none of them
どなたでも	anyone (*polite*)	なぜか		somehow; for some reason
どなたも	everyone (*polite*)	なにか	何か	something
どれか	one of them	なにも	何も	everything; nothing
どれでも	any of them	なんでも	何でも	anything

Kanji

Learn these characters:

手	勉
家	道
族	書
男	使
女	国
子	作
父	音
母	楽
兄	全
姉	部
弟	運
妹	動

チェックリスト

Use this checklist to confirm that you can now:

- Talk about hobbies, pastimes, and sports
- Talk about family and introduce family members
- Express *some, every, none,* and *any*
- Describe abilities
- Use nominalizers こと and の
- Use the particle も in a new way
- Use the potential form of verbs
- Use the **te**-form of verbs ＋います
- Make relative clauses
- Describe a change in state
- Respond to compliments

Appendix 1: Verb Conjugation

	Class 1						
Dictionary Form	会う	書く	話す	立つ	死ぬ*	読む	乗る
Root	会 (わ)	書	話	立	死	読	乗
Plain, Nonpast, Negative	会わない	書かない	話さない	立たない	死なない	読まない	乗らない
Polite, Nonpast, Affirmative	会います	書きます	話します	立ちます	死にます	読みます	乗ります
ましょう Form (Polite Volitional)	会いましょう	書きましょう	話しましょう	立ちましょう	死にましょう	読みましょう	乗りましょう
たい Form	会いたい	書きたい	話したい	立ちたい	死にたい	読みたい	乗りたい
Polite Command	会いなさい	書きなさい	話しなさい	立ちなさい	死になさい	読みなさい	乗りなさい

---

*死ぬ is the only verb whose dictionary form ends in ぬ.

	Class 1		Class 2		Class 3	
Dictionary Form	泳^{およ}ぐ	呼^よぶ	How to create forms	食^たべる	する	来^くる
Root	泳	呼	Drop る ending	食べ	Irregular	Irregular
Plain, Nonpast, Negative	泳がない	呼ばない	Root + ない	食べない	しない	来^こない
Polite, Nonpast, Affirmative	泳ぎます	呼びます	Root + ます	食べます	します	来^きます
ましょう Form (Polite Volitional)	泳ぎましょう	呼びましょう	Root + ましょう	食べましょう	しましょう	来^きましょう
たい Form	泳ぎたい	呼びたい	Root + たい	食べたい	したい	来^きたい
Polite Command	泳ぎなさい	呼びなさい	Root +なさい	食べなさい	しなさい	来^きなさい

四百八十九

	Class 1						
Dictionary Form	会う	書く	話す	立つ	死ぬ	読む	乗る
Potential	会える	書ける	話せる	立てる	死ねる	読める	乗れる
Imperative	会え	書け	話せ	立て	死ね	読め	乗れ
ば Conditional	会えば	書けば	話せば	立てば	死ねば	読めば	乗れば
Volitional	会おう	書こう	話そう	立とう	死のう	読もう	乗ろう
ta-Form	会った	書いた	話した	立った	死んだ	読んだ	乗った
te-Form	会って	書いて	話して	立って	死んで	読んで	乗って
Other Verbs	洗う 使う 歌う 買う 手伝う 笑う 言う 習う	聞く 行く* 磨く 働く はく 歩く	探す 直す	持つ 勝つ 待つ		飲む 休む 住む 楽しむ	帰る 入る 知る 降りる 走る 泊まる 止まる 取る 切る 終わる 始まる

* The **ta**-form and **te**-form of 行く are 行った and 行って, respectively.

	Class 1			Class 2	Class 3	
Dictionary Form	泳^{およ}ぐ	呼^よぶ		食^たべる	する	来^くる
Potential	泳げる	呼べる	Root ＋られる	食べられる	できる	来^こられる
Imperative	泳げ	呼べ	Root ＋ろ	食べろ	しろ	来^こい
ば Conditional	泳げば	呼べば	Root ＋れば	食べれば	すれば	来^くれば
Volitional	泳ごう	呼ぼう	Root ＋よう	食べよう	しよう	来^こよう
ta-Form	泳いだ	呼んだ	Root ＋た	食べた	した	来^きた
te-Form	泳いで	呼んで	Root ＋て	食べて	して	来^きて
Other Verbs	脱^ぬぐ 急^{いそ}ぐ	飛^とぶ 遊^{あそ}ぶ		見^みる 起^おきる 寝^ねる 出^でかける 出^でる 着^きる 教^{おし}える All potential verb forms	Nominal verbs （勉 強^{べん きょう}する、 洗 濯^{せんたく}する）	連^つれてくる 持^もってくる

Yookoso! An Invitation to Contemporary Japanese, Third Edition

365

Appendix 2: Adjective and Copula Conjugation

Adjectives

	Dictionary Form	Prenominal	Predicate			
			Plain			
			Non-past		Past	
			Affirmative	**Negative**	**Affirmative**	**Negative**
i-Adjectives	赤^{あか}い	赤い	赤い	赤くない	赤かった	赤くなかった
	いい	いい	いい	よくない	よかった	よくなかった
na-Adjectives	静^{しず}か	静かな	静かだ	静かではない／静かじゃない	静かだった	静かではなかった／静かじゃなかった

Copula

Dictionary Form	Prenominal	Predicate			
		Plain			
		Non-past		Past	
		Affirmative	**Negative**	**Affirmative**	**Negative**
だ	の／である	だ／である	ではない／じゃない	だった	ではなかった／じゃなかった

	Predicate						Adverbial
	Polite				*te*-Form	Conditional	
	Non-past		**Past**				
	Affirmative	**Negative**	**Affirmative**	**Negative**			
i-Adjectives	赤いです	赤くありません／赤くないです	赤かったです	赤くありませんでした／赤くなかったです	赤くて	赤ければ	赤く
	いいです	よくありません／よくないです	よかったです	よくありませんでした／よくなかったです	よくて	よければ	よく
na-Adjectives	静かです	静かではありません／静かじゃありません	静かでした	静かではありませんでした／静かじゃありませんでした	静かで	静かならば／静かであれば	静かに

Predicate						Adverbial
Polite				*te*-Form	Conditional	
Non-past		**Past**				
Affirmative	**Negative**	**Affirmative**	**Negative**			
です	ではありません／じゃありません	でした	ではありませんでした／じゃありませんでした	で	なら（ば）／であれば	N/A

Yookoso! An Invitation to Contemporary Japanese, Third Edition

367

Appendix 3: Numbers

Native Japanese System	Sino-Japanese System				
1 ひと 一つ	1 いち 一	11 じゅういち 十一			
2 ふた 二つ	2 に 二	12 じゅうに 十二		200 に ひゃく 二百	2,000 に せん 二千
3 みっ 三つ	3 さん 三	13 じゅうさん 十三	30 さんじゅう 三十	300 さんびゃく 三百	3,000 さんぜん 三千
4 よっ 四つ	4 し、よん 四	14 じゅうし、じゅうよん 十四	40 よんじゅう 四十	400 よんひゃく 四百	4,000 よんせん 四千
5 いつ 五つ	5 ご 五	15 じゅうご 十五	50 ごじゅう 五十	500 ご ひゃく 五百	5,000 ご せん 五千
6 むっ 六つ	6 ろく 六	16 じゅうろく 十六	60 ろくじゅう 六十	600 ろっぴゃく 六百	6,000 ろくせん 六千
7 なな 七つ	7 しち 、なな 七	17 じゅうしち、じゅうなな 十七	70 ななじゅう、しちじゅう 七十	700 ななひゃく 七百	7,000 ななせん 七千
8 やっ 八つ	8 はち 八	18 じゅうはち 十八	80 はち じゅう 八十	800 はっぴゃく 八百	8,000 はっせん 八千
9 ここの 九つ	9 く、きゅう 九	19 じゅうく、じゅうきゅう 十九	90 きゅうじゅう 九十	900 きゅうひゃく 九百	9,000 きゅうせん 九千
10 とお 十	10 じゅう 十	20 に じゅう 二十	100 ひゃく 百	1,000 （いっ）せん （一）千	10,000 いちまん 一万

Large Numbers

	100,000	十万 (じゅうまん)
(*one million*)	1,000,000	百万 (ひゃくまん)
	10,000,000	（一）千万 (（いっ）せんまん)
	100,000,000	一億 (いちおく)
(*one billion*)	1,000,000,000	十億 (じゅうおく)
	10,000,000,000	百億 (ひゃくおく)
	100,000,000,000	（一）千億 (（いっ）せんおく)
(*one trillion*)	1,000,000,000,000	一兆 (いっちょう)

Notes

1. Zero is 零 (れい) or ゼロ.

2. 0.314 is read 零点三一四 (れいてんさんいちよん). 2.236 is read 二点二三六 (にてんにさんろくてん). (点 = point)

3. The native Japanese system exists for 1 through 10 only. After 11, only the Sino-Japanese system can be used.

4. Some people read 1,000, 10,000,000, and 100,000,000,000 as 一千 (いっせん)、一千万 (いっせんまん)、and 一千億 (いっせんおく), respectively.

Appendix 4: Counters

The following chart lists common counters (suffixes appended to numbers for counting or naming things), most of which are introduced in this book. Notice the phonological changes that occur when some numbers and counters are joined. The first column (〜番) represents the simplest case: the Sino-Japanese number is followed by the counter with no phonological changes. In other columns, phonological changes occur in some cases. Such variations are marked with an asterisk (*). Where two pronunciations are provided, either may be used, although a particular pronunciation may predominate in a given situation. (For example, *seven o'clock* is usually pronounced しちじ, except over train station public address systems where ななじ is often used to prevent confusion with *one o'clock* いちじ.) Counters that name something are so indicated; all others are used to count. Each chart groups together counters that vary in similar ways. For more on counters, see **Grammar 9,** Chapter 2.

Counters	〜番 (ばん)	〜時 (じ)	〜月 (がつ)	〜回 (かい)
What Is Being Counted or Named	**Serial Numbers** (*Number...*)	**Hours of the Day (Name)** (*... o'clock*)	**Months (Name)**	**Occurrences** (*...times*)
1	いち ばん 一番	いち じ 一時	いち がつ 一月	いっ かい 一回*
2	に ばん 二番	に じ 二時	に がつ 二月	に かい 二回
3	さん ばん 三番	さん じ 三時	さん がつ 三月	さん かい 三回
4	よん ばん 四番	よ じ 四時*	し がつ 四月*	よん かい 四回
5	ご ばん 五番	ご じ 五時	ご がつ 五月	ご かい 五回
6	ろく ばん 六番	ろく じ 六時	ろく がつ 六月	ろっ かい 六回*
7	なな ばん、しちばん 七番	しち じ、ななじ 七時	しち がつ 七月*	なな かい、しちかい 七回
8	はち ばん 八番	はち じ 八時	はち がつ 八月	はっかい 八回*
9	きゅうばん 九番	く じ 九時*	く がつ 九月*	きゅうかい 九回
10	じゅうばん 十番	じゅう じ 十時	じゅうがつ 十月	じっ かい、じゅっかい* 十回
Other Counters with Same Pattern of Variation	〜枚 (まい) thin, flat. objects 〜度 (ど) ...degrees (temperature) ...times (occurrences) 〜倍 (ばい) ...times (magnifications)	〜時間 (じかん) hours, 〜年 (ねん) years (number and name)		〜個 (こ) pieces 〜ヶ月 (かげつ) months 〜課 (か) lessons

Counters	かい 〜階	ほん、ぼん、ぽん 〜本	ふん 〜分	さつ 〜冊
What Is Being Counted or Named	**Floors (of a Building) (Number and Name)**	**Long, Cylindrical Objects**	**Minutes (Number and Name)**	**Books, Bound Volumes**
1	いっ かい 一 階*	いっ ぽん 一 本*	いっ ぷん 一 分*	いっ さつ 一 冊*
2	に かい 二階	に ほん 二本	に ふん 二 分	に さつ 二 冊
3	さん かい、さんがい* 三 階	さん ぼん 三 本*	さん ぷん 三 分*	さん さつ 三 冊
4	よん かい 四 階	よん ほん 四 本	よん ふん 四 分	よん さつ 四 冊
5	ご かい 五階	ご ほん 五本	ご ふん 五 分	ご さつ 五 冊
6	ろっ かい* 六 階*	ろっ ぽん 六 本*	ろっ ぷん 六 分*	ろく さつ 六 冊
7	なな かい、しちかい 七 階	なな ほん、しちほん 七 本	なな ふん、しちふん 七 分	なな さつ、しちさつ 七 冊
8	はっ かい* 八 階*	はっ ぽん 八 本*	はっ ぷん 八 分*	はっ さつ* 八 冊*
9	きゅうかい 九 階	きゅうほん 九 本	きゅうふん 九 分	きゅうさつ 九 冊
10	じっかい、じゅっかい* 十階	じっぽん、じゅっぽん* 十本	じっぷん、じゅっぷん* 十 分	じっさつ、じゅっさつ* 十 冊
Other Counters with Same Pattern of Variation		はい 〜杯 glass(ful)s cup(ful)s ひき 〜匹 small animals	はく 〜泊 overnight stays	しょう 〜章 chapters

Yookoso! An Invitation to Contemporary Japanese, Third Edition

371

Counters	〜足 そく	〜ページ	〜頭 とう	〜人 にん
What Is Being Counted or Named	**Pairs of Footwear (Shoes, Socks, etc.)**	**Pages (Number and Name)**	**Large Animals**	**People**
1	一足* いっ そく	一ページ* いっ	一頭* いっ とう	一人* ひと り
2	二足 に そく	二ページ に	二頭 に とう	二人* ふた り
3	三足* さん ぞく	三ページ さん	三頭 さん とう	三人 さん にん
4	四足 よん そく	四ページ よん	四頭 よん とう	四人* よ にん
5	五足 ご そく	五ページ ご	五頭 ご とう	五人 ご にん
6	六足 ろく そく	六ページ* ろっ	六頭 ろく とう	六人 ろく にん
7	七足 なな そく、しちそく	七ページ なな 、しち	七頭 なな とう、しちとう	七人 しち にん、ななにん
8	八足* はっ そく	八ページ* はっ	八頭 はっ とう	八人 はち にん
9	九足 きゅうそく	九ページ きゅう	九頭* きゅうとう	九人 きゅうにん、くにん
10	十足、じゅっそく* じっ そく	十ページ* じっ、じゅっ	十頭、じゅっとう* じっとう	十人 じゅうにん
Others Counters with Same Pattern of Variation		〜ポンド pounds	〜通 letters つう (i.e., pieces of correspondence) 〜トン tons 〜点 points てん (e.g., in games, grades) 〜滴 drops of liquid てき	

Counters	～日 (ひ)	～日 (にち)	～晩 (ばん)	～歳 (さい)
What Is Being Counted or Named	**Days of the Month (Name)**	**Days (Number)**	**Nights**	**Age (... years old)**
1	一日 (ついたち)*	一日 (いちにち)	一晩 (ひとばん)*	一歳 (いっさい)、一つ (ひと)*
2	二日 (ふつか)*	二日 (ふつか)*	二晩 (ふたばん)*	二歳 (にさい)、二つ (ふた)*
3	三日 (みっか)*	三日 (みっか)*	三晩 (みばん)*	三歳 (さんさい)、三つ (みっ)*
4	四日 (よっか)*	四日 (よっか)*	四晩 (よばん)*	四歳 (よんさい)、四つ (よっ)*
5	五日 (いつか)*	五日 (ごにち、いつか)*	五晩 (ごばん)	五歳 (ごさい)、五つ (いつ)*
6	六日 (むいか)*	六日 (ろくにち、むいか)*	六晩 (ろくばん)	六歳 (ろくさい)、六つ (むっ)*
7	七日 (なのか)*	七日 (しちにち、なのか)*	七晩 (ななばん)	七歳 (ななさい)、七つ (なな)*
8	八日 (ようか)*	八日 (はちにち、ようか)*	八晩 (はちばん)	八歳 (はっさい)、八つ (やっ)*
9	九日 (ここのか)*	九日 (くにち、ここのか)*	九晩 (きゅうばん)	九歳 (きゅうさい)、九つ (ここの)*
10	十日 (とおか)*	十日 (とおか)	十晩 (じゅうばん)	十歳 (じっさい、じゅっさい)、十 (とお)*
Other Irregular Pronunciations of Numbers and Counters	十四日 (じゅうよっか)* 二十日 (はつか)* 二十四日 (にじゅうよっか)*	十四日 (じゅうよっか)* 二十日 (はつか)* 二十四日 (にじゅうよっか)*		二十歳 (はたち)*

Suffixes for Ordinal Numbers	～目 (Used with Japanese Numbers) (*the first, the second*, etc.)	～番目 (Used with Sino-Japanese Numbers)
1	ひと 一つ目	いち ばん め 一番目
2	ふた 二つ目	に ばんめ 二番目
3	みっ め 三つ目	さん ばんめ 三番目
4	よっ め 四つ目	よん ばんめ 四番目
5	いつ め 五つ目	ご ばんめ 五番目
6	むっ め 六つ目	ろく ばんめ 六番目
7	なな め 七つ目	なな ばんめ、しちばんめ 七番目
8	やっ め 八つ目	はち ばんめ 八番目
9	ここの め 九つ目	きゅうばんめ、くばんめ 九番目
10	—	じゅうばんめ 十番目

How to Form Ordinal Numbers

Note: Another way to make ordinal numbers is to add the prefix 第…
(Number …) to the Sino-Japanese numbers (第一、第二、第三、第四、第五、第六、第七、第八、第九、第十、and so on). This prefix may be used in combination with some counter suffixes to name ordered things. Examples are 第三章 (*Chapter Three*) and 第五課 (*Lesson Five*).

The suffix ～目 is commonly used in combination with counters to indicate *the …th*. For example, 九回目 (*the ninth time*), 三日目 (*the third day*), 五足目 (*the fifth pair of footwear*), 二人目 (*the second person*), and so on.

When indicating items having no assigned counter or when you are unsure of the counter, you can usually use the general terms above for *the first* (one), *the second* (one), and so on.

五百

Appendix 5: Time, Days, Months, and Years

Telling Time

		A.M. ごぜん 午前	**P.M.** ごご 午後		
1:00 いち じ 一 時	2:00 に じ 二 時	3:00 さん じ 三 時	4:00 よ じ 四 時	5:00 ご じ 五 時	6:00 ろく じ 六 時
7:00 しち じ、なな じ 七 時	8:00 はち じ 八 時	9:00 く じ 九 時	10:00 じゅう じ 十 時	11:00 じゅういち じ 十 一 時	12:00 じゅう に じ 十 二 時

いっ ぷん 一 分	に ふん 二 分	さん ぷん 三 分	よん ぷん 四 分	ご ふん 五 分	ろっ ぷん 六 分	なな ふん、しちふん 七 分	はっ ぷん 八 分	きゅうふん 九 分	じっぷん、じゅっぷん 十 分

(and so on through 59 minutes)

[例] ごぜん ご じ にじゅうろく ぷん
午前 五 時 二 十 六 分 5:26 A.M.   ごご はち じ よんじゅうなな ふん
午後 八 時 四 十 七 分 8:47 P.M.

Days of the Week

しゅうまつ 週 末 **Weekend**	平 日 へいじつ **Weekday**					しゅうまつ 週 末 **Weekend**
にちよう び 日曜日 *Sunday*	げつよう び 月曜日 *Monday*	か よう び 火曜日 *Tuesday*	すい よう び 水 曜日 *Wednesday*	もくよう び 木 曜日 *Thursday*	きん よう び 金 曜日 *Friday*	ど よう び 土曜日 *Saturday*

Days of the Month

1 ついたち 一 日	2 ふつ か 二 日	3 みっ か 三 日	4 よっ か 四 日	5 いつ か 五 日	6 むい か 六 日	7 なの か 七 日
8 よう か 八 日	9 ここの か 九 日	10 とお か 十 日	11 じゅういち にち 十 一 日	12 じゅう に にち 十 二 日	13 じゅうさんにち 十 三 日	14 じゅうよっ か 十 四 日
15 じゅう ご にち 十 五 日	16 じゅうろく にち 十 六 日	17 じゅうしち にち 十 七 日	18 じゅうはち にち 十 八 日	19 じゅう く にち 十 九 日	20 はつ か 二 十 日	21 にじゅういちにち 二 十 一 日
22 にじゅう に にち 二 十 二 日	23 にじゅうさん にち 二 十 三 日	24 にじゅうよっ か 二 十 四 日	25 にじゅう ご にち 二 十 五 日	26 にじゅうろく にち 二 十 六 日	27 にじゅうしち にち 二 十 七 日	28 にじゅうはちにち 二 十 八 日
29 にじゅう く にち 二 十 九 日	30 さんじゅうにち 三 十 日	31 さんじゅういち にち 三 十 一 日				

Yookoso! An Invitation to Contemporary Japanese, Third Edition

375

Months

いち がつ 一 月 *January*	に がつ 二 月 *February*	さん がつ 三 月 *March*	し がつ 四月 *April*	ご がつ 五 月 *May*	ろく がつ 六 月 *June*
しち がつ 七 月 *July*	はち がつ 八 月 *August*	く がつ 九 月 *September*	じゅうがつ 十 月 *October*	じゅう いち がつ 十 一 月 *November*	じゅう に がつ 十 二 月 *December*

Years

Western year	1988年^{ねん}	1989年	1990年	. . .	2000年	2001年	2002年	2003年
Era	しょう わ 昭 和 *	へいせい 平 成						
Japanese year	六十三年	一年 *or* がんねん 元 年	二年	. . .	十二年	十三年	十四年	十五年

*The **Showa** era began in 1926 and ended when the **Heisei** era began on January 8, 1989.
Technically, the first days of 1989 fall in the **Showa** era, so events that occurred within those
days (such as someone's birth) are often dated **Showa 64.**

Relative Time Expressions

Days	おととい *the day before yesterday*	きのう (さくじつ) 昨日 *yesterday*	きょう 今日 *today*	あした (あす) 明日 *tomorrow*	あさって *the day after tomorrow*
Weeks	せんせんしゅう 先々 週 *the week before last*	せんしゅう 先 週 *last week*	こんしゅう 今 週 *this week*	らいしゅう 来 週 *next week*	さ らい しゅう 再来 週 *the week after next*
Months	せんせん げつ 先々 月 *the month before last*	せん げつ 先 月 *last month*	こん げつ 今 月 *this month*	らいげつ 来 月 *next month*	さ らい げつ 再来 月 *the month after next*
Years	いっ さく ねん 一 昨 年 *the year before last*	きょ ねん さく ねん 去 年 *or* 昨 年 *last year*	こ とし 今年 *this year*	らい ねん 来 年 *next year*	さ らい ねん 再来 年 *the year after next*

五百二

Time Durations

	何分(間) minutes	何時間 hours	何日(間) days	何週間 weeks	何ヶ月 months	何年(間) years
1	一分(間)	一時間	一日(間)	一週間	一ヶ月	一年(間)
2	二分(間)	二時間	二日(間)	二週間	二ヶ月	二年(間)
3	三分(間)	三時間	三日(間)	三週間	三ヶ月	三年(間)
4	四分(間)	四時間	四日(間)	四週間	四ヶ月	四年(間)
5	五分(間)	五時間	五日(間)	五週間	五ヶ月	五年(間)
6	六分(間)	六時間	六日(間)	六週間	六ヶ月	六年(間)
7	七分(間)	七時間	七日(間)	七週間	七ヶ月	七年(間)
8	八分(間)	八時間	八日(間)	八週間	八ヶ月	八年(間)
9	九分(間)	九時間	九日(間)	九週間	九ヶ月	九年(間)
10	十分(間)	十時間	十日(間)	十週間	十ヶ月	十年(間)
14	十四分(間)	十四時間	十四日(間)	十四週間	十四ヶ月	十四年(間)
20	二十分(間)	二十時間	二十日間	二十週間	二十ヶ月	二十年(間)
24	二十四分(間)	二十四時間	二十四日(間)	二十四週間	二十四ヶ月	二十四年(間)

Appendix 6: **Ko-so-a-do** Words

	こ-Series (this)	そ-Series (that)	あ-Series (that over there)	ど-Series (which, what, etc.)
Demonstrative Pronoun (this one, that one, that one over there, which one, etc.)	これ	それ	あれ	どれ
Demonstrative Adjective (this, that, that over there, which, etc.)	この	その	あの	どの
Location (here, there, over there, where)	ここ	そこ	あそこ	どこ
Direction* (polite) (this way, that way, yonder, which way)	こちら	そちら	あちら	どちら
Direction* (informal) (this way, that way, yonder, which way)	こっち	そっち	あっち	どっち
Kind or Type (this kind of, that kind of, that kind of [far away], what kind of)	こんな	そんな	あんな	どんな
Extent (to this extent, to that extent, to that [far] extent, to what extent)	こんなに	そんなに	あんなに	どんなに
Manner ([in a manner] like this/that/ that over there, in what manner)	こう	そう	ああ	どう

*These **ko-so-a-do** words can also be used to refer to people, things, and locations. Here are some examples.

こちらは横井先生 です。
This is Professor Yokoi.

あっちのセーターは9千円 ですよ。
That sweater over there is 9,000 yen.

カーティスさんはそちらにいますか。
Is Mr. Curtis there (lit., *at that place*)?

Appendix 7: Japanese Accent

Basic Rules

1. In standard Japanese speech, a syllable is pronounced with high pitch or low pitch. Pitch is relative; high or low pitch means higher or lower pitch than that of other syllables in a given word or utterance.

2. In standard Japanese, the pitch of the first syllable of a word is always different from that of the second syllable. Thus, if the first syllable has high pitch, the second one has low pitch, and vice versa.

3. Within a single word, once the pitch falls, it doesn't rise again.

Symbols

In many accent dictionaries published in Japan, accent is indicated with two symbols: ⎯ and ⌐. A horizontal bar over a syllable means that this syllable is pronounced with high pitch. A syllable with no bar over it is pronounced with low pitch. A downturn at the end of a bar ⌐ indicates a fall in pitch—that is, the syllable after the downturn is pronounced with low pitch. Here are some examples.

$$\text{o ma wa ri sa n} \qquad \text{inu} \qquad \text{ushi}$$

In the word **o-mawarisan** (*police officer*), the first syllable is pronouced with low pitch, the second and third syllables are pronounced with high pitch, and the last three syllables are pronounced with low pitch. The two words **inu** (*dog*) and **ushi** (*cow*) have the same accent pattern low-high when pronounced independently. However, the difference in notations indicates that the pitch of, for examle, particles (**wa, ga, o,** etc.) following these words will differ. Note that the particles do not have fixed pitch; rather, their pitch (high or low) is determined by the preceding word.

$$\text{inu ga} \qquad \text{ushi ga}$$

Accent Patterns of Words

The following chart shows the possible accent patterns of one- to four-syllable words in standard Japanese speech. Also shown is the accent of one-syllable particles when they follow words with these accent patterns. ○ represents a syllable in a given word, and ● denotes a particle.

Yookoso! An Invitation to Contemporary Japanese, Third Edition

379

One Syllable	Two Syllables	Three Syllables	Four Syllables
き (木; tree)	ねこ (猫; cat)	いのち (命; life)	こんばん (今晩; tonight)
	いぬ (犬; dog)	こころ (心; heart)	やまやま (山々; mountains)
		おんな (女; female)	かがりび (かがり火; bonfire)
き (気; spirit)	うし (牛; cow)	さくら (桜; cherry tree)	ともだち (友だち; friend)

Recently it has become common, especially among young people, to also say

こころ,

keeping the last syllable raised instead of dropping it.

Appendix 8: *Kanji* List

The following are **kanji** presented for active acquisition in *Yookoso!* In **kanji** dictionaries, **kanji** are listed according to their basic components, or radicals. Within each group sharing the same radical, the **kanji** are further classified in terms of the number of strokes beyond those which make up the radical. For instance, 本, which has five strokes, is listed below the radical 木, which has four strokes. Thus, you can find 本 in the one-stroke section under the radical 木. A more complex example is 楽, which contains nine strokes outside the radical and is therefore found in the nine-stroke section. The following list indicates the number of strokes for each **kanji** and the radical under which it is listed in *most* **kanji** dictionaries. The numbers following the radicals are the number of strokes remaining after subtracting the stroke-count of the radical. Note that some characters, such as 木、日、and 人, are themselves radicals.

Kanji	Total Number of Strokes	Radical	Name of Radical	Number of Strokes Beyond the Radical

Chapter 1

Kanji	Total Number of Strokes	Radical	Name of Radical	Number of Strokes Beyond the Radical
日	4	日	（ひ）	0
本	5	木	（き）	1
学	8	子	（こ）	5
生	5	生	（うまれる）	0
名	6	口	（くち）	3
年	6	干	（たてかん）	3
何	7	イ	（にんべん）	5
月	4	月	（つき）	0
人	2	人	（ひと）	0
一	1	一	（いち）	0
二	2	二	（に）	0
三	3	一	（いち）	2
四	5	口	（くにがまえ）	2
五	4	二	（に）	2
六	4	八	（はち）	2
七	2	一	（いち）	1
八	2	八	（はち）	0
九	2	乙	（おつ）	1
十	2	十	（じゅう）	0
百	6	白	（しろ）	1
先	6	兄	（にんにょう）	4
話	13	言	（ごんべん）	6
語	14	言	（ごんべん）	7
大	3	大	（だい）	0

五百七

Kanji	Total Number of Strokes	Radical	Name of Radical	Number of Strokes Beyond the Radical
Chapter 2				
間	12	門	（もん）	4
半	5	十	（じゅう）	3
上	3	一	（いち）	2
下	3	一	（いち）	2
分	4	刀	（かたな）	2
小	3	小	（しょう）	0
好	6	女	（おんな）	3
町	7	田	（た）	2
左	5	工	（え）	2
右	5	口	（くち）	2
中	4	丨	（ぼう）	3
外	5	夕	（ゆうべ）	2
前	9	刂	（りっとう）	7
後	9	彳	（ぎょうにんべん）	6
時	10	日	（ひ）	6
山	3	山	（やま）	0
口	3	口	（くち）	0
千	3	十	（じゅう）	1
万	3	一	（いち）	2
方	4	方	（ほう）	0
近	7	辶	（しんにゅう）	4
遠	13	辶	（しんにゅう）	10
有	6	月	（つき）	2
Chapter 3				
朝	12	月	（つき）	8
明	8	日	（ひ）	4
午	4	十	（じゅう）	2
昼	9	日	（ひ）	5
来	7	木	（き）	3
行	6	行	（いく）	0
聞	14	耳	（みみ）	8
食	9	食	（しょく）	0
出	5	凵	（うけばこ）	3
飲	12	食	（しょく）	4
入	2	入	（いる）	0
休	6	亻	（にんべん）	4
夕	3	夕	（ゆうべ）	0
今	4	人	（ひとやね）	2
週	11	辶	（しんにゅう）	8
曜	18	日	（ひ）	14
毎	6	毋	（なかれ）	2
回	6	口	（くにがまえ）	3

Kanji	Total Number of Strokes	Radical	Name of Radical	Number of Strokes Beyond the Radical
Chapter 3 (cont.)				
見	7	見	(みる)	0
起	10	走	(はしる)	3
読	14	言	(ごんべん)	7
火	4	火	(ひ)	0
水	4	水	(みず)	0
木	4	木	(き)	0
金	8	金	(かね)	0
土	3	土	(つち)	0
会	6	人	(ひとやね)	4
Chapter 4				
天	4	大	(だい)	1
気	6	气	(きがまえ)	2
雨	8	雨	(あめ)	0
雪	11	雨	(あめ)	3
度	9	广	(まだれ)	6
風	9	風	(かぜ)	0
台	5	口	(くち)	2
番	12	田	(た)	7
春	9	日	(ひ)	5
夏	10	夂	(すいにょう)	7
秋	9	禾	(のぎへん)	4
冬	5	冫	(にすい)	3
東	8	木	(き)	4
西	6	西	(にし)	0
南	9	十	(じゅう)	7
北	5	匕	(ひ)	3
高	10	高	(たかい)	0
多	6	夕	(ゆうべ)	3
少	4	小	(しょう)	1
強	11	弓	(ゆみ)	8
弱	10	弓	(ゆみ)	7
昨	9	日	(ひ)	5
暑	12	日	(ひ)	8
寒	12	宀	(うかんむり)	9
空	8	宀	(うかんむり)	5
Chapter 5				
手	4	手	(て)	0
家	10	宀	(うかんむり)	7
男	7	田	(た)	2
女	3	女	(おんな)	0
子	3	子	(こ)	0
母	5	母	(はは)	1
父	4	父	(ちち)	0

Kanji	Total Number of Strokes	Radical	Name of Radical	Number of Strokes Beyond the Radical
Chapter 5 (cont.)				
兄	5	兄	(にんにょう)	3
弟	7	弓	(ゆみ)	4
姉	8	女	(おんな)	5
妹	8	女	(おんな)	5
作	7	イ	(にんべん)	5
族	11	方	(ほう)	7
勉	10	力	(ちから)	8
道	12	辶	(しんにゅう)	9
使	8	イ	(にんべん)	6
国	8	口	(くにがまえ)	5
音	9	音	(おと)	0
楽	13	木	(き)	9
全	6	人	(ひとやね)	4
部	11	都	(おおざと)	8
運	12	辶	(しんにゅう)	9
動	11	力	(ちから)	9
Chapter 6				
思	9	心	(こころ)	5
終	11	糸	(いと)	5
始	8	女	(おんな)	5
物	8	牛	(うし)	4
肉	6	肉	(にく)	0
事	8	亅	(はねぼう)	7
茶	9	艹	(くさかんむり)	6
酒	10	氵	(みず)	7
牛	4	牛	(うし)	0
鳥	11	鳥	(とり)	0
湯	12	水	(みず)	9
野	11	里	(さと)	4
魚	11	魚	(さかな)	0
味	8	口	(くち)	5
悪	11	心	(こころ)	7
料	10	斗	(とます)	6
理	11	玉	(たま)	7
米	6	米	(こめ)	0
品	9	口	(くち)	6
和	8	口	(くち)	5
洋	9	氵	(みず)	6
夜	7	夕	(ゆうべ)	5
言	7	言	(ごんべん)	0
貝	7	貝	(かい)	0

Kanji	Total Number of Strokes	Radical	Name of Radical	Number of Strokes Beyond the Radical

Chapter 7

Kanji	Total Number of Strokes	Radical	Name of Radical	Number of Strokes Beyond the Radical
同	6	口	(くち)	3
長	8	長	(ながい)	0
場	12	土	(つち)	9
市	5	巾	(はば)	2
主	5	、	(てん)	4
電	13	雨	(あめ)	5
売	7	士	(さむらい)	4
切	4	刀	(かたな)	2
店	8	广	(まだれ)	5
引	4	弓	(ゆみ)	1
白	5	白	(しろ)	0
屋	9	尸	(しかばね)	6
黒	11	黒	(くろ)	0
色	6	色	(いろ)	0
買	12	貝	(かい)	5
青	8	青	(あお)	0
赤	7	赤	(あか)	0
服	8	月	(つき)	4
返	7	辶	(しんにゅう)	4
花	7	艹	(くさかんむり)	4
黄	11	黄	(き)	0
員	10	口	(くち)	7
暗	13	日	(ひ)	9
円	4	門	(どうがまえ)	2

Japanese-English Glossary

This glossary lists all Japanese words presented in this book with the exception of lesser known place names, some proper nouns, conjugated forms, compound words, and foreign loanwords that are very similar to the source language word in pronunciation and meaning.

Entries are arranged in a-i-u-e-o Japanese alphabetical order. As in Japanese dictionaries, each word is presented in **hiragana** or **katakana**, followed by the **kanji** transcription, if appropriate.

Verbs and adjectives are cited in their dictionary form except for a few special cases. The classification is provided for each verb: Class 1, 2, or 3.

Nominal verbs are followed by (する). I-adjectives are unmarked, but **na**-adjectives are followed by (な).

English translations for nouns are given in the singular; plural is an alternate gloss in most cases. Only the most commonly used polite variants are included.

Finally, remember that these translations are not equivalents but reminders of the meanings you have learned in class. Only real-life context and native usage can be relied on to define the full range of meaning and nuance for each word.

The following abbreviations are used:

adv.	word or phrase that functions as an adverb
C1	Class 1 verb
C2	Class 2 verb
C3	Class 3 verb
coll.	colloquial
conj.	conjunction
dem. adj.	demonstrative adjective
dem. pron.	demonstrative pronoun
dem. adv.	demonstrative adverb
f.	female speech (word used primarily by females)
i-adj.	i-adjective
inf.	informal
interj.	interjection
intr.	intransitive verb
m.	male speech (word used primarily by males)
na-adj.	**na**-adjective
n.v.	noun that can be made into a nominal verb by appending する (both its nominal meaning and verbal meaning are given)
part.	particle
pl.	plural
p.n.	proper noun
pol.	polite
pron.	pronoun
s.	singular
tr.	transitive verb

あ／ア

ああ　*interj.*　oh, ahh (*exclamation of surprise and pleasure*)　(2)

ああ　*dem. adv.*　like that　(6)

あい　（愛）love　(7)

あいいろ　（藍色）dark blue　(7)

あいさつ（する）（挨拶［する］）*n.v.*　greeting; to greet　(3)

アイス　ice　(GS5)

アイスクリーム　ice cream　(GS5)

アイスティー　ice tea　(GS2)

アイスミルク　cold milk　(GS3)

あいだ　（間）between;　AとBの間に　between A and B　(2)

アイロン　iron;　アイロンをかける　to iron　(7)

あう　（会う）*C1, intr.*　to see, meet (a person)　(GS3)

あお　（青）blue;　（青い）*i-adj.*　blue　(7)

あか　（赤）red　(7);　（赤い）*i-adj.*　red　(2)

あかるい　（明るい）*i-adj.*　bright (*vs. dark*), well-lighted; cheerful (*personality*)　(4)

あかワイン　（赤ワイン）red wine　(5)

あき　（秋）fall, autumn;　あきさめ　（秋雨）autumn rain　(4)

あきる　（飽きる）*C2, intr.*　to become bored, get tired of　(6)

アクションえいが　（アクション映画）action movie　(2)

アクセサリー　accessory, jewelry　(7)

あける　（開ける）*C2, tr.*　to open　(GS1)

あげる　（揚げる）*C2, tr.*　to deep-fry　(6)

あさ　（朝）morning　(GS2)

あさごはん　（朝ごはん）breakfast　(GS2)

あさって　the day after tomorrow　(4)

あざやか（な）（鮮やか［な］）*na-adj.*　vivid　(7)

あさゆう　（朝夕）morning and evening　(4)

あじ　（味）taste, flavor;　あじがいい　（味がいい）to taste good;　あじがない　（味がない）to have no taste;　あじがわるい（味がわるい）to taste bad;　あじみ（する）（味見［する］）*n.v.*　tasting of a sample; to taste a sample;　あじわう　（味わう）*C1, tr.*　to taste　(6)

あした　（明日）tomorrow　(3)

アスパラガス　asparagus　(5)

アスピリン　aspirin　(7)

あそ　（阿蘇）*p.n.*　Aso (*a place in Kyushu*)　(2)

あそこ　*dem. pron.*　over there　(1)

あそぶ　（遊ぶ）*C1, intr.*　to play　(5)

あたし　*pron., inf., f.*　I;　あたしたち　*pron., inf., f., pl.*　we　(1)

あたたかい　（暖かい）*i-adj.*　warm　(GS4)

あたま　（頭）head　(7)

あたらしい　（新しい）*i-adj.*　new　(2)

あちら　*dem. pron., pol.*　over there　(1)

あつい　（厚い）*i-adj.*　thick　(2)

あつい　（暑い）*i-adj.*　hot (*temperature*)　(GS4)

アップルパイ　apple pie　(7)

あつめる　（集める）*C2, tr.*　to collect, gather　(5)

あと（で）（後［で］）after…; later　(3)

あなた　*pron., s.*　you;　あなたたち　*pron., pl.*　you　(1)

あに　（兄）older brother　(5)

あね　（姉）older sister　(5)

あの　*dem. adj.*　that　(1)

あのう　excuse me, well　(1)

アパート　apartment　(GS3)

あびる　（浴びる）*C2, tr.*　to bathe　(GS3)

あぶらえ　（油絵）oil painting　(5)

アフリカ　*p.n.*　Africa　(6)

アマ　amateur　(5)

あまい　（甘い）*i-adj.*　sweet　(2)

あまり、あんまり　*adv.*　(*with negative*) not very much　(2)

あみもの　（編み物）knitting, crocheting　(5)

あむ　（編む）*C1, tr.*　to knit, crochet　(7)

あめ　（雨）rain　(GS1)

アメリカ　*p.n.*　America　(GS1);　アメリカじん　（アメリカ人）American　(1)

あらう　（洗う）*C1, tr.*　to wash　(3)

あらし　（嵐）storm　(4)

アラビアご　（アラビア語）Arabic language　(4)

あられ　hail　(4)

ありがとう　thank you　(GS1)

ある　*C1, intr.*　there is/there are (inanimate things)　(2)

あるく　（歩く）*C1, intr.*　to walk　(GS1)

アルバイト　part-time job, side job　(3)

アルバム　photo album　(5)

あれ　*dem. pron.*　that thing over there　(GS1)

あんぜん（な）（安全［な］）*na-adj.*　safe　(2)

い／イ

いい　*i-adj.*　good　(GS1)

いいえ　no　(GS1)

いう　（言う）*C1, tr.*　to say　(GS1)

いえ　（家）house　(1)

いか　（烏賊）cuttlefish　(6)

いかが　how about　(GS5)

イギリス　*p.n.*　England;　イギリスじん　（イギリス人）English person　(1)

いく　（行く）*C1, intr.*　to go　(GS3)

いくつ　how much, how old　(1)

いくつか　some, several　(5)

いくら　how much, however much…　(GS3)

いけばな　（生け花）flower arranging　(5)

〜いじょう　（〜以上）more than…　(5)

いじわる（な）（意地悪［な］）*na-adj.*　mean　(4)

いす　（椅子）chair　(GS1)

いそがしい　（忙しい）*i-adj.*　busy　(2)

いたい　（痛い）*i-adj.*　painful　(7)

いたす　（致す）*C1, tr., pol.*　to do　(4)

いただきます　I will eat now (*said before eating*)　(6)

いただく　*C1, tr., pol.*　to receive, partake (*humble*)　(4)

いためる　（炒める）*C2, tr.*　to stir-fry　(6)

イタリア　*p.n.*　Italy;　イタリアご　（イタリア語）Italian language;　イタリアじん　（イタリア人）Italian person　(1)

いち　（一）one　(GS2)

いちがつ　（一月）January　(1)

いちご　（苺）strawberry　(6)

いちど　（一度）once, one time　(GS1);　いちども　（一度も）never　(6)

いちにちじゅう　（一日中）all day long　(GS3)

いちば　（市場）market　(7)

いちばん　（一番）number one, best, most　(4)

いちぶ　（一部）part　(7)

いちわり　（一割）ten percent　(7)

いつ　when　(GS4)

いつか　*adv.*　sometime, someday;　いつでも　anytime　(5);　いつも　always　(2)

五百十三

いつのまにか （いつの間にか） without knowing it　(5)
いつか （五日） fifth day　(3)
いっしょに （一緒に） *adv.* together　(GS1)
いつつ （五つ） five　(2)
いと （糸） thread　(7)
いとこ cousin　(5)
いない　not to exist, not there (animate things)　(2)
いなびかり（稲光）；いなずま（稲妻） lightning　(4)
いぬ （犬） dog　(2)
いふく （衣服） clothes　(7)
いま （今） *adv.* now　(GS2)
いみ （意味） meaning　(4)
いも （薯） sweet potato, yam　(6)
いもうと （妹） younger sister；いもうとさん（妹さん） *pol.* younger sister　(5)
いや（な）（嫌［な］） *na-adj.* disgusting, repelling　(4)
イヤリング earring　(7)
いる　*C1, intr.* to exist (*animate things*)　(2)
いる （要る） *C1, tr.* to need, want　(4)
いれる （入れる） *C2, tr.* to put something in; to turn on (a switch)　(3)
いろ （色） color　(7)
いろいろ（な）（色々［な］） *na-adj.* various　(2)
インキ ink　(7)
いんき（な）（陰気［な］） *na-adj.* gloomy　(4)
インスタント・フード instant food　(6)
インスタント・ラーメン instant ramen　(6)
インスタントしょくひん （インスタント食品） instant foodstuffs　(6)
インタビュー（する） *n.v.* interview; to interview　(6)

う／ウ

ウイスキー whiskey　(GS2)
ウール wool　(7)
うえ （上） on, over, up, top　(2)
ウエート・リフティング weight lifting　(5)
ウエートレス waitress；ウエーター waiter　(2)
うえの （上野） *p.n.* Ueno (*a part of Tokyo*)　(2)
うかがう （伺う） *C1, tr., pol.* to inquire, ask; to visit; to hear　(5)
うけつけ （受け付け） receptionist; reception　(1)
うける （受ける） *C2, tr.* to receive　(5)
うしろ （後ろ） behind, back　(2)
うすい （薄い） *i-adj.* thin; light (*in color*), pale　(7)
うそ （嘘） lie　(3)
うた （歌） song；うたをうたう（歌を歌う）to sing a song　(5)；うたう（歌う） *C1, tr.* to sing　(3)
うち　house, (*my*) home; inside　(GS3)
うつ （打つ） *C1, tr.* to hit　(5)
うつくしい （美しい） *i-adj.* beautiful　(4)
うどん udon (*thick, flat wheat noodles*)　(6)
うまれる （生まれる） *C2, intr.* to be born　(1)
うみ （海） ocean, sea　(4)；うみのひ（海の日）Marine Day　(3)
うりだし （売り出し） clearance sale　(7)
うる （売る） *C1, tr.* to sell　(7)
うるさい　*i-adj.* noisy, annoying　(2)
うわぎ （上着） jacket, suit coat　(7)
うんうん　*interj.* I see, I see; yes, yes　(2)
うんてん（する）（運転［する］） *n.v.* drive; to drive　(3)
うんどう（する）（運動［する］） *n.v.* exercise; to exercise　(GS2)

え／エ

え （絵） picture；えをかく（絵を描く）to draw a picture　(5)
エアロビクス aerobics　(3)
えいが （映画） movie；えいがかん（映画館） movie theater　(GS2)
えいぎょうじかん （営業時間） business hours　(6)
えいご （英語） English language　(1)；えいぶん（英文） English writing　(5)
えいよう （栄養） nutrition；えいようし（栄養士） dietician　(6)
ええ　*interj.* yes　(GS1)
えき （駅） station　(2)
エスエフ　science fiction　(5)；エスエフえいが （エスエフ映画） science fiction movie　(2)
エッグサラダ egg salad　(6)
えはがき （絵はがき） picture postcard　(7)
エプロン apron　(5)
えび shrimp　(6)
えらぶ （選ぶ） *C1, tr.* to choose　(5)
エレガント（な） *na-adj.* elegant　(2)
エレベーター elevator　(1)
えん （円） yen　(GS3)
えんげい （園芸） gardening　(5)
えんげき （演劇） theatrical play　(5)
エンジニア engineer　(1)
えんそう（する）（演奏［する］） *n.v.* performing, playing (musical instrument); to perform, play (musical instrument)　(5)
えんぴつ （鉛筆） pencil　(GS1)

お／オ

お honorific prefix　(5)
おい （甥） nephew；おいごさん *pol.* nephew　(5)
おいしい *i-adj.* delicious, tasty　(3)
おいとこさん *pol.* cousin　(5)
おおあめ （大雨） heavy rain　(4)
おおい （多い） *i-adj.* many, much, a lot　(2)
おおきい （大きい） *i-adj.* large, big　(2)
オーストラリア *p.n.* Australia　(GS2)
オーバー overcoat　(4)
オーブン oven　(6)
おおゆき （大雪） heavy snow　(4)
おかあさん （お母さん） *pol.* mother　(5)
おかげさまで thanks to you　(GS1)
おかし （お菓子） sweets (*cake and confections*)　(6)；おかしや（お菓子屋） confectionery shop　(7)
おかしい *i-adj.* funny, strange　(2)；おかし（な） *na-adj.* funny, strange　(6)
おかね （お金） money　(2)
おきゃくさん （お客さん） customer, passenger, guest　(2)
おきる （起きる） *C2, intr.* to get up, rise, wake up　(GS3)
おく （億） hundred million　(2)
おくさん （奥さん） *pol.* wife　(5)
おくりがな （送り仮名） okurigana　(3)
おくる （送る） *C1, tr.* to send; to see someone off　(7)
おくれる （遅れる） *C2, intr.* to be late　(4)
おこさん （お子さん） *pol.* child　(5)
おさけ （お酒） liquor, sake　(GS1)
おじ　uncle；おじさん *pol.* uncle　(5)
おじいさん *pol.* grandfather　(5)

おしえる（教える）*C2, tr.* to teach （3）
おしゃべり（な）*na-adj.* talkative （4）
おじょうさん（お嬢さん）*pol.* daughter, girl （5）
おすすめひん（おすすめ品）recommended item （6）
おそい（遅い）*i-adj.* late, slow （3）
おそく（遅く）*adv.* late （3）
おそらく *adv.* perhaps, maybe （4）
おだやか（な）*na-adj.* calm (ocean, personality); gentle (breeze) （4）
おちゃ（お茶）green tea （GS3）
おっと（夫）husband （5）
おつり（お釣り）change (money) （7）
おてら（お寺）(Buddhist) temple （2）
おでん oden (*Japanese stew*) （6）
おと（音）sound （7）
おとうさん（お父さん）*pol.* father （5）
おとうと（弟）younger brother; おとうとさん（弟さん）*pol.* younger brother （5）
おとこ（男）man （2）; おとこのかた（男の方）*pol.* man; おとこのこ（男の子）boy; おとこのひと（男の人）man （5）
おとす（落とす）*C1, tr.* to drop （6）
おととい the day before yesterday （GS4）
おととし the year before last （7）
おとな（大人）adult （6）
おどる（踊る）*C1, tr.* to dance （3）
おなか stomach （3）
おなかがすく to get hungry （3）
おなじ（同じ）same （4）
おにいさん（お兄さん）*pol.* older brother （5）
おねえさん（お姉さん）*pol.* older sister （5）
おねがい（お願い）request （GS5）
おば aunt; おばさん *pol.* aunt （5）
おばあさん *pol.* grandmother （5）
おはよう good morning （GS1）
オフィス office （1）
おふろ（お風呂）bath; おふろにはいる（お風呂に入る）to take a bath （3）
オペラ opera （5）
おぼえる（憶える）*C2, tr.* to remember, memorize （7）
おまごさん（お孫さん）*pol.* grandchild （5）
おまわりさん *coll.* police officer （2）
おみやげ souvenir （4）
オムレツ omelet （GS3）
おもい（重い）*i-adj.* heavy （2）
おもう（思う）*C1, tr., intr.* to think; おもいだす（思い出す）*C1, tr.* to remember （6）
おもしろい（面白い）*i-adj.* interesting, fun （2）
おもちゃ（おもちゃ屋）toy store （7）
おやすみなさい good night （GS1）
おやつ snack （6）
おゆ（お湯）hot water, boiling water （6）
およぐ（泳ぐ）*C1, intr.* to swim （3）
オランダ *p.n.* Holland （2）
おりる（降りる）*C2, intr.* to get off, get down （3）
オリンピック Olympics （5）
オレンジ orange; オレンジいろ（オレンジ色）orange color （6）; オレンジ・ジュース orange juice （GS3）
おろす *C1, tr.* to withdraw (money) （7）
おわる（終わる）*C1, intr.* to end, finish （3）
おわん（お椀）soup or rice bowl （6）
おんがく（音楽）music （GS3）; おんがくかんしょう（音楽鑑賞）listening to music, music appreciation （5）

おんな（女）woman （2）; おんなのかた（女の方）*pol.* woman; おんなのこ（女の子）girl （5）; おんなのひと（女の人）woman （2）

か／カ

か *part.* question marker; or （1）
〜か（〜課）counter for lessons （2）
が *part.* subject marker （1）; *conj.* but （3）
カーテン curtain （GS1）
カード card （5）
カーネーション carnation （7）
ガールフレンド girlfriend （1）
〜かい（〜階）counter for floors of a building （1）; （〜回）counter for frequency （GS3）
かい（貝）shellfish （6）
かいが（絵画）painting （5）
かいぎ（会議）meeting, conference; （会議をする）to have a meeting （5）
がいこくご（外国語）foreign language(s) （1）
かいしゃ（会社）company （3）; かいしゃいん（会社員）company worker, employee （5）
がいしょく（する）（外食［する］）*n.v.* dining out; to dine out （6）
ガイドブック guidebook （7）
かいもの（する）（買い物［する］）*n.v.* shopping; to shop （GS2）
かいわ（会話）conversation （5）
かう（買う）*C1, tr.* to buy （3）
かう（飼う）*C1, tr.* to keep, raise (a pet) （5）
かえす（返す）*C1, tr.* to return, give back （7）
かえる（帰る）*C1, intr.* to return, go back （GS3）
かえる（変える）*C2, tr.* to change （5）
かお（顔）face; かおをあらう（顔を洗う）to wash one's face （3）
かかく（価格）price （7）
かがく（化学）chemistry （1）
かかる *C1, intr.* to take (time, money), cost （3）
かぎ（鍵）key, lock; かぎをかける（鍵をかける）to lock （7）
かぎる（限る）*C1, tr.* to limit （5）
かく（書く）*C1, tr.* to write （GS1）
かく（描く）*C1, tr.* to draw （5）
かぐや（家具屋）furniture store （7）
がくせい（学生）student; がくせいしょう（学生証）student ID （1）
カクテル cocktail （GS2）
がくねん（学年）year in school; school year （1）
がくぶ（学部）academic department （1）
かけいぼ（家計簿）household finances book （7）
〜かげつ（〜ヶ月）counter for months （1）
かける（掛ける）*C2, tr.* to multiply （GS2）; to make a phone call （3）; to put on (glasses, etc.) （7）
かさ（傘）umbrella （GS3）; かさをさす（傘をさす）to put up an umbrella （7）
かし（華氏）Fahrenheit （4）
かしこまりました certainly, at your service （6）
カジュアル（な）*na-adj.* casual （7）
かす（貸す）*C1, tr.* to lend; rent out （7）
かぜ（風）wind; かぜがふく（風が吹く）wind blows （4）
かぜ（風邪）cold, flu; （風邪をひく）to catch a cold （4）
かぞく（家族）family （5）
ガソリン・スタンド gas station （2）

五百十五

かた（方）*pol.* person （1）

カタカナ katakana （GS2）

かたくるしい（堅苦しい）*i-adj.* formal, ceremonious, stiff （7）

カタログ catalogue （7）

がっか（学科）academic subject （2）

がっき（楽器）musical instrument （5）

がっこう（学校）school （GS3）

かっこういい *i-adj.* good-looking, stylish （5）

かつどう（する）（活動［する］）*n.v.* activity; to engage in activity, be active （5）

かていきょうし（家庭教師）tutor （3）

かど（角）corner （6）

～かどうか whether or not （7）

かない（家内）wife （5）

カナダ *p.n.* Canada （GS2）; カナダじん（カナダ人）Canadian （1）

かなものや（金物屋）hardware store （7）

かね（金）money （5）

かのじょ（彼女）*pron.* she; かのじょたち（彼女たち）*pron. pl.* they (female); かのじょら（彼女ら）*pron. pl.* they (female) （1）

かばん（鞄）bag （GS1）

カフェテリア cafeteria （1）

かぶる *C1, tr.* to wear; to put on (the head) （7）

かべ（壁）wall （GS1）

かみ（紙）paper （GS1）

かみ（髪）hair （3）

かみなり（雷）thunder （4）

カメラ camera （GS3）; カメラてん／カメラや（カメラ店／カメラ屋）camera shop （7）

～かもしれない it might…; perhaps… (*conjecture*) （4）

かよう（通う）*C1, intr.* to commute, frequent （6）

かようび（火曜日）Tuesday （GS4）

から *part.* from; because （1）

カラーしゃしん（カラー写真）color photo(graphy) （5）

からい（辛い）*i-adj.* hot, spicy; salty （6）

カラオケ karaoke (singing to recorded accompaniment) （5）

からだ（体）body （4）

からて（空手）karate （5）

かり（狩り）hunting （5）

かりる（借りる）*C2, tr.* to borrow; to rent （7）

かるい（軽い）*i-adj.* light, not heavy （2）

カルタ Japanese card game （5）

カルチャーセンター adult education center （5）

かれ（彼）*pron.* he; （彼たち）*pron. pl.* they (male); （彼ら）*pron. pl.* they (male or mixed gender) （1）

カレー curry （6）; カレーライス curry and rice （2）

カレンダー calendar （4）

かわいい *i-adj.* cute, pretty （5）

かんがえ（考え）thought, idea （6）; （考える）*C2, intr.* to think （3）

かんきり（缶切り）can opener （6）

かんこく（韓国）*p.n.* South Korea; かんこくご（韓国語）Korean language; かんこくじん（韓国人）South Korean person （1）

かんじ（漢字）kanji （2）

がんじつ（元日）New Year's Day （3）

かんじょう（する）（勘定［する］）*n.v.* tally, calculation, check; to tally, count （6）

かんたん（な）（簡単［な］）*na-adj.* simple, easy （5）

かんづめ（缶詰）canned food （6）

カントリーウエスタン country and western music （2）

がんねん（元年）first year (in era) （3）

き／キ

き（木）tree, wood （2）

きあつ（気圧）air pressure （4）

きいろ（黄色）yellow （6）; きいろい（黄色い）*i-adj.* yellow （7）

きおん（気温）temperature （4）

きかい（機械）machine （2）

きがえる（着替える）*C2, tr.* to change clothes （3）

きく（聞く）*C1, tr.* to listen, hear, ask （GS1）

きけん（な）（危険［な］）*na-adj.* dangerous （5）

きご（季語）seasonal word (*in literature*) （4）

きこう（気候）climate （4）

きこえる（聞こえる）*C2, intr.* can be heard （5）

キス（する）*n.v.* kiss; to kiss （5）

ぎせいご（擬声語）onomatopoeia （5）

きせつ（季節）season （4）

きた（北）north （2）; きたかぜ（北風）north wind （4）

ギター guitar （5）

ぎたいご（擬態語）onomatopoeia （5）

きたない（汚い）*i-adj.* dirty, filthy （2）

きつい *i-adj.* tough, tight （3）

きっさてん（喫茶店）coffee shop （2）

キッチン kitchen （6）

きって（切手）stamp; きってをあつめる（切手を集める）to collect stamps （5）

きっと *adv.* certainly, surely （4）

きぬ（絹）silk （7）

きねん（する）（記念［する］）*n.v.* commemoration, memory; to commemorate （7）

きのう（昨日）yesterday （GS3）

きびしい（厳しい）*i-adj.* strict （2）

ギフト gift, present （3）

きもの（着物）kimono （7）

きゃく（客）customer, passenger （7）

キャベツ cabbage （7）

キャンパス campus （1）

キャンプ（する）*n.v.* camping; to go camping （4）

ギャンブル（する）*n.v.* gamble; to gamble （5）

きゅう（九）nine （GS2）; きゅうじゅう（九十）ninety （GS5）

きゅうか（休暇）day off; vacation; きゅうじつ（休日）day off （3）

きゅうしゅう（九州）*p.n.* Kyushu （1）

キュート（な）*na-adj.* cute （2）

ぎゅうにく（牛肉）beef （6）

ぎゅうにゅう（牛乳）milk （6）

きゅうり cucumber （6）

きょう（今日）today （3）

きよう（な）（器用［な］）*na-adj.* skillful （2）

きょういくがく（教育学）education (*academic subject*) （1）

きょうかい（教会）church （2）

きょうかしょ（教科書）textbook （GS1）

きょうしつ（教室）classroom （GS1）

きょうだい（兄弟）siblings; brothers （5）

きょうと（京都）*p.n.* Kyoto （1）

きょうよう（教養）education; culture; liberal arts （5）; きょうようかもく（教養科目）general education subject （1）

きょねん（去年）last year （3）

きらい（な）（嫌い［な］）*na-adj.* dislike, hate （GS2）

きり（霧）fog （4）

ぎりの（義理の）in-law （5）

きる（着る）*C2, tr.* to wear; to put on (*torso*) (3)
きる（切る）*C1, tr.* to cut (3)
きれい（な）*na-adj.* attractive, pretty; clean (2)
キロ kilometer; kilogram (5)
きをつける（気をつける）to be careful (4)
きんいろ（金色）gold color (7)
ぎんいろ（銀色）silver color (7)
きんがく（金額）price; amount of money (7)
きんぎょ（金魚）goldfish (5)
ぎんこう（銀行）bank (GS2)
ぎんざ（銀座）*p.n.* Ginza (1)
きんじょ（近所）neighborhood (2)
きんようび（金曜日）Friday (GS4)
きんろうかんしゃのひ （勤労感謝の日）Labor Thanksgiving
  Day (3)

く／ク

く（九）nine (GS2); くがつ（九月）September (1)
く（区）city ward (2)
くすりや（薬屋）drugstore, pharmacy (7)
〜ください please; give me (GS2)
くだもの（果物）fruit (GS1); くだものや（果物屋）fruit
  store (7)
くつ（靴）shoe(s); くつした（靴下）socks (GS3);
  くつや（靴屋）shoe store (7)
クッキング・オイル cooking oil (6)
クッキング・スクール cooking school (6)
くに（国）country (1)
くみあわせる（組み合わせる）*C2, tr.* to combine (7)
くも（雲）cloud (4)
くもり（曇り）cloudy; くもる（曇る）*C1, intr.*
  to become cloudy (4)
〜くらい、〜ぐらい about, approximately (4)
くらい（暗い）*i-adj.* dark (4)
クラシックおんがく（クラシック音楽）classical
  music (5)
クラス class (GS2); クラスメート classmate (1)
クラブ club (5)
クリーニングや（クリーニング屋）dry cleaner (7)
クリーム cream, lotion (6)
クリームいろ（クリーム色）cream color (7)
グリーン green (7)
くりかえす（繰り返す）*C1, tr.* to repeat (GS1)
くる（来る）*C3, intr.* to come (3)
くるま（車）car (1)
グレー gray (7)
グレープ grape (GS5)
クレジット・カード credit card (2)
くろ（黒）black; くろい（黒い）*i-adj.* black (7)
クロワッサン croissant (7)

け／ケ

けいぐ（敬具）sincerely (*used in a letter*) (4)
けいざいがく（経済学）economics (1)
けいさんき（計算機）calculator (7)
けいしょく（軽食）light meal, snack (6)
けいたいでんわ（携帯電話）cell (mobile) phone (2)
けいろうのひ（敬老の日）Respect-for-the-Aged
  Day (3)
ケーキ cake (6); ケーキや（ケーキ屋）cake shop (7)
ケース case (7)
けがわ（毛皮）fur (7)

けさ（今朝）this morning (2)
けしき（景色）scenery (6)
けしゴム（消しゴム）eraser (GS1)
けしょうひん（化粧品）cosmetics; けしょうひんてん
  （化粧品店）cosmetics store (7)
けち（な）*na-adj.* miserly (4)
ケチャップ ketchup (6)
〜げつかん（〜月間）counter for duration in months (3)
けっこう（な）（結構[な]）*na-adj.* good, satisfactory (GS5)
げつようび（月曜日）Monday (GS4)
けど *conj. coll.* although, but; けれども *conj.* although,
  but (7)
〜けん（〜軒）counter for houses, buildings (2)
げんき（な）（元気[な]）*na-adj.* healthy, energetic (4)
けんきゅうしつ（研究室）professor's office; research
  office (1)
げんきん（現金）cash (7)
けんこう（な）（健康[な]）*na-adj.* healthy (2)
げんごがく（言語学）linguistics (1)
けんこくきねんび（建国記念日）National Foundation
  Day (3)
けんどう（剣道）Japanese swordmanship, fencing (5)
けんぽうきねんび（憲法記念日）Constitution Day (3)

こ／コ

こ（子）child (4)
ご（碁）go (*Japanese board game*) (5)
ご（五）five (GS2); ごがつ（五月）May (1);
  ごじゅう（五十）fifty (GS5)
ご（御）honorific prefix (5)
こい（濃い）dark (*in color*) (7)
コインランドリー laundromat (3)
こう *dem. adv.* like this (4)
〜ごう（〜号）number... (*room, apartment*) (2)
こうえん（公園）park (2)
こうがい（郊外）suburbs (2)
こうがく（工学）engineering (1)
こうがくぶ（工学部）engineering department (1)
こうきゅう（な）（高級[な]）*na-adj.* first-class (7)
こうこく（広告）advertisement (7)
〜ごうしつ（〜号室）room number... (5)
こうずい（洪水）flood (4)
こうすいりょう（降水量）precipitation (4)
こうちゃ（紅茶）black tea (6)
こうばん（交番）police box (2)
コート coat (4)
コーヒー coffee (GS2)
コーヒーメーカー coffeemaker (6)
コーラ cola (GS2)
ごかぞく（御家族）*pol.* family (5)
ごきょうだい（御兄弟）*pol.* siblings; brothers (5)
こくせき（国籍）nationality (1)
こくばん（黒板）chalkboard (GS1); こくばんけし
  （黒板消し）chalkboard eraser (GS1)
こくみん（国民）citizen(s), the people (3)
ここ *dem. pron.* here (1)
ごご（午後）afternoon, P.M. (GS2)
ここのか（九日）ninth day (3)
ここのつ（九つ）nine (2)
こさめ（小雨）light rain (4)
ごしゅじん（御主人）*pol.* husband (5)
こしょう（胡椒）pepper (6)
ごしんせき（ご親戚）*pol.* relative (5)

ゴスペル gospel music (2)

ごぜん（午前）morning, A.M. (GS2); ごぜんちゅう（午前中） all morning (3)

こたえ（答）response, answer (5); こたえる （答える）C2, intr. to respond (3)

ごちそう（御馳走）treat (food) (3); ごちそうさまでした（御馳走様でした）pol. thank you for the food (said after meal) (6)

こちら dem. pron. here (1); こちらがわ（こちら側）this side (2)

コック cook, chef (6)

こっとうひん（骨董品）antique (5)

コットン cotton (1)

コップ glass, cup (6)

こと（琴）koto (Japanese lute) (5)

こと thing, matter, fact; nominalizer (5)

ことができる to be able to do…, can do… (5)

ことし（今年）this year (3)

ことば（言葉）word, language (4)

こども（子供）child (5); こどものひ（子供の日） Children's Day (3)

この dem. pron. this (1)

ごはん（御飯）meal, cooked rice (3)

ごふくや（呉服屋）kimono store (7)

こまる C1, intr. be in difficulty, have trouble (4)

こむ（混む）C1, intr. to get crowded (5)

こめ（米）rice (uncooked) (6); こめや（米屋）rice dealer (7)

コメディ comedy (2)

ごらく（娯楽）entertainment; pastime (5)

ゴルフ golf (4)

これ dem. pron. this thing (GS1)

これまでに until now, by now (6)

ころ、ごろ（頃）around, approximately (GS3)

ゴロゴロする C3, intr. to loaf, idle one's time away (5)

コロンビア p.n. Colombia (6)

こわれる（壊れる）C2, intr. to get broken (7)

こん（紺）navy blue (7)

こんげつ（今月）this month (1)

コンサート concert (5)

こんしゅう（今週）this week (3)

コンセント plug outlet (6)

コンソメ consommé (6)

こんど（今度）this time (3)

こんにちは good afternoon (GS1)

こんばん（今晩）tonight (3); こんや（今夜） tonight (7); こんばんは good evening (greeting) (GS1)

コンビニ convenience store (7)

コンピュータ・サイエンス computer science (1); コンピューターゲーム computer game (5)

さ／サ

さあ interj. Lets's begin; well, I don't know… (2)

サークル circle, club, activity group (5)

サービス（する）n.v. service, something given for free; to give (do) for free (7)

サーフィン（する）n.v. surfing; to surf (6)

～さい（～歳）counter for age (1)

さいきん（最近）adv. recently (5)

サイクリング（する）n.v. cycling; to cycle (5)

さいしょ（最初）adv. first (7)

サイズ size (7)

さいふ（財布）wallet (2)

ざいりょう（材料）ingredient (6)

サイン（する）n.v. signature; to sign (3)

さがす（探す）C1, tr. to look for (1)

さかな（魚）fish (GS2); さかなや（魚屋）fish store (7); さかなをつる（魚を釣る）to catch fish (5)

さかや（酒屋）liquor store (7)

さく（咲く）C1, intr. to bloom (4)

さくねん（昨年）last year (3)

さくら（桜）cherry blossom (4)

さけ（鮭）salmon (6)

さす C1, tr. to put up (umbrella) (7)

さそう（誘う）C1, tr. to invite (7)

～さつ（～冊）counter for books, notes (2)

サッカー soccer (5)

ざっし（雑誌）magazine (GS3)

さて conj. by the way; well… (4)

さとう（砂糖）sugar (6)

さどう（茶道）tea ceremony (5)

さびしい（寂しい）i-adj. lonely (7)

～さま（～様）pol. Mr., Mrs., Ms., Miss, etc. (4)

さみだれ（五月雨）early summer rain (4)

さむい（寒い）i-adj. cold (GS4)

さよ（う）なら good-bye (GS1)

さら（皿）plate, dish (6)

サラダ salad (GS3); サラダドレッシング salad dressing (6)

サラリーマン salaried worker, white-collar worker (5)

さわる（触る）C1, intr. to touch (3)

～さん Mr., Mrs. Ms., Miss, etc. (GS1)

さん（三）three (GS2)

さんがつ（三月）March (1)

サングラス sunglasses (7)

さんじゅう（三十）thirty (GS5)

サンダル sandal (7)

サンドイッチ sandwich (6)

ざんねん（な）（残念[な]）na-adj. sorry; too bad (GS4)

さんぽ（する）（散歩[する]）n.v. walk, stroll; to take a walk/stroll (GS2)

し／シ

し（四）four (GS2); しがつ（四月）April (1)

し（市）city (2)

～し and (emphatic) (7)

～じ（～時）…o'clock (GS2)

しあい（する）（試合[する]）n.v. game, match (5)

しいたけ shiitake mushroom (6)

シーディー CD (compact disk) (7)

ジーパン jeans; ジーンズ jeans (7)

シーフード seafood (6)

ジェイアール JR (Japan Railways) (2)

シェフ chef (6)

しお（塩）salt; しおからい（塩辛い）i-adj. salty (6)

～しか only (with negative) (7)

しかし conj. but, however (3)

じかん（時間）time; counter for hours (2)

じかんわり（時間割）timetable (1)

しき（四季）four seasons (4)

しぐれ（時雨）drizzle (4)

しけん（する）（試験[する]）n.v. examination; to examine (3)

じこしょうかい（する）（自己紹介[する]）n.v. self-introduction; to introduce oneself (1)

しごと（する）（仕事［する］）*n.v.* job, work; to work (*GS3*)

ししゅう（する）（刺繍［する］）*n.v.* embroidery; to do embroidery (5)

じしょ（辞書）dictionary (*GS1*)

しずか（な）（静か［な］）*na-adj.* quiet, peaceful (2)

した（下）below, under, down (2)

したぎ（下着）underwear (7)

しち（七）seven (*GS2*); しちがつ（七月）July (1); しちじゅう（七十）seventy (*GS5*)

しちゃくしつ（試着室）fitting room (7)

シチュー stew (5)

じっけんしつ（実験室）laboratory (1)

しつど（湿度）humidity (4)

しっと（する）（嫉妬［する］）*n.v.* envy, jealousy; to be jealous (7)

しつもん（する）（質問［する］）*n.v.* question; to ask a question (*GS1*)

しつれい（する）（失礼［する］）*n.v.* discourtesy; be discourteous; excuse oneself (*GS1*)

じてんしゃ（自転車）bicycle (2)

シトシト drizzle (*weather*) (4)

しなぎれ（品切れ）out of stock, sold out (7)

しぬ（死ぬ）*C1, intr.* to die (4)

しばらく it's been a long time (*greeting*); *adv.* a little while (*GS1*)

しぶい（渋い）*i-adj.* astringent (6)

じぶん（自分）oneself, self;（自分で）by oneself (6)

しま（縞）stripe (7)

～しまう *C1, tr.* to finish… (6)

じみ（な）（地味［な］）*na-adj.* quiet (*in color*), plain (7)

ジム gym (5)

じむしつ（事務室）administration office (*inside a building*) (1)

しめる（閉める）*C2, tr.* to close (*door, window, etc.*) (3)

しも（霜）frost (4)

じゃあ *interj.* well, then… (*GS1*)

シャープペンシル mechanical pencil (*GS1*)

～じゃありません *coll.* negative of です (1)

しゃかいがく（社会学）sociology (1)

じゃがいも potato (6)

しゃげき（する）（射撃［する］）*n.v.* shooting; to shoot (5)

ジャケット jacket (7)

しゃしん（写真）photography, photograph (1); しゃしんをとる（写真を撮る）to take a photo (5)

ジャズ jazz (*GS2*)

シャツ shirt (7)

しゃみせん（三味線）shamisen (*Japanese musical instrument*) (5)

シャワー shower; シャワーをあびる（シャワーを浴びる）to take a shower (3)

シャンペン champagne (6)

じゅう（十）ten (*GS2*); じゅうがつ（十月）October (1); じゅうまん（十万）hundred thousand (2)

じゅういちがつ（十一月）November (1); じゅういちにち（十一日）eleventh day (3)

～しゅうかん（～週間）counter for weeks (3)

じゅうごにち（十五日）fifteenth day (3)

じゅうさんにち（十三日）thirteenth day (3)

じゅうしょ（住所）address (1)

ジュース juice (*GS2*)

じゅうどう（柔道）judo (5)

じゅうにがつ（十二月）December (1); じゅうににち（十二日）twelfth day (3)

しゅうぶんのひ（秋分の日）Autumnal Equinox Day (3)

しゅうまつ（週末）weekend (3)

じゅうよっか（十四日）fourteenth day (3)

じゅぎょうりょう（授業料）tuition (5)

しゅくじつ（祝日）national holiday (3)

しゅくだい（宿題）homework (4)

しゅげい（手芸）handicrafts (5)

しゅじん（主人）husband; shop owner (5)

しゅっしん（出身）hometown; origin (1)

しゅみ（趣味）hobby (5)

しゅもく（種目）event; item (5)

しゅるい（種類）kind, type (6)

じゅんい（順位）rank, ranking (5)

じゅんび（する）（準備［する］）*n.v.* preparation; to prepare (3)

しゅんぶんのひ（春分の日）Vernal Equinox Day (3)

しょうかい（する）（紹介［する］）*n.v.* introduction; to introduce (1)

しょうぎ（将棋）shogi (*Japanese board game*) (5)

しょうしゃ（商社）trading company (5)

じょうず（な）（上手［な］）*na-adj.* good at, skilled at (5); じょうずに（上手に）*adv.* skillfully (4)

じょうだん（冗談）joke (7)

しょうてんがい（商店街）shopping mall, shopping street (7)

じょうねつ（情熱）passion (7)

じょうば（乗馬）horseback riding (5)

しょうひん（商品）goods, merchandise (7)

じょうぶ（な）（丈夫［な］）*na-adj.* robust, strong, tough (7)

しょうゆ（醤油）soy sauce (6)

しょうわ（昭和）Showa era (3)

ショーウインドー show window (6)

ショートパンツ shorts (4)

ジョギング（する）*n.v.* jogging; to jog (5)

しょくじ（する）（食事［する］）*n.v.* meal; to eat a meal (6); しょくどう（食堂）dining hall; informal restaurant (2); しょくりょうひん（食料品）foodstuffs (6); しょくりょうひんてん（食料品店）grocery store (7)

じょしがくせい（女子学生）female student (5)

じょせい（女性）woman (5)

ショッピング（する）*n.v.* shopping; to shop (7)

しょどう（書道）brush calligraphy (5)

しらせ（知らせ）notice, announcement (5)

しる（知る）*C1, tr.* to know (3)

しろ（白）white (7);（白い）*i-adj.* white (2)

しろくろしゃしん（白黒写真）black-and-white photo(graphy) (5)

しろワイン（白ワイン）white wine (5)

シンガポール *p.n.* Singapore; シンガポールじん（シンガポール人）Singaporean (1)

しんかんせん（新幹線）bullet train (3)

じんこう（人口）population (2)

じんじゃ（神社）Shinto shrine (2)

しんじる（信じる）*C2, tr.* to believe, trust (3)

しんせき（親戚）relative (5)

しんせつ（な）（親切［な］）kind (2)

シンプル（な）*na-adj.* simple (7)

しんぶん（新聞）newspaper (*GS3*)

じんるいがく（人類学）anthropology (1)

す／ス

す（酢）vinegar (6)

すいえい（水泳）swimming (*GS2*)

すいさいが（水彩画）watercolor (5)

すいようび（水曜日）Wednesday　(*GS4*)
すうがく（数学）mathematics　(*1*)
スーパー　supermarket　(*2*)
スープ　soup　(*GS3*)
スカート　skirt　(*7*)
すき（な）（好き[な]）*na-adj.*　like, favor　(*2*)
スキー　ski　(*GS2*)；スキーをする　to ski　(*4*)
すきやき　sukiyaki　(*GS1*)
〜すぎる（〜過ぎる）*C2, intr.*　to do…excessively (*with conjunctive form of verbs*)　(*6*)
すぐ（に）*adv.*　immediately　(*6*)
すくない（少ない）*i-adj.*　few, little　(*2*)；（少なく）*adv.* few, little　(*6*)
スケート　skate；スケートをする　to skate　(*4*)
スケジュール　schedule　(*3*)
すごい　*i-adj.*　awesome; terrible; very　(*5*)
すこし（少し）*adv.*　a little, a bit　(*3*)
すごす（過ごす）*C1, tr.*　to spend, pass (*time*)　(*5*)
すし（寿司）sushi　(*GS1*)；すしや（寿司屋）sushi restaurant　(*6*)
すずしい（涼しい）*i-adj.*　cool　(*GS4*)
スチュワーデス　stewardess　(*5*)
すっかり　*adv.*　totally　(*7*)
ずっと　*adv.*　all the way　(*4*)
すっぱい（酸っぱい）*i-adj.*　sour　(*6*)
ステーキ　steak　(*GS3*)
ステレオ　stereo　(*5*)
ストーブ　space heater　(*4*)
ストッキング　stockings　(*7*)
ストライプ　stripe　(*5*)
ストロベリー　strawberry　(*6*)
スナック　snack　(*6*)
スニーカー　sneaker　(*4*)
スノーブーツ　snow boots　(*7*)
スパゲッティー　spaghetti　(*6*)
スピーチ　speech　(*4*)
スプーン　spoon　(*6*)
スペイン　*p.n.*　Spain；スペインご（スペイン語）Spanish language；スペインじん（スペイン人）Spaniard　(*1*)
すべて（全て）all　(*5*)
スポーツ　sports　(*GS2*)；スポーツ・カー　sports car；スポーツウエア　sportswear　(*7*)；スポーツせんしゅ athlete　(*5*)
ズボン　trousers　(*7*)
スマート（な）*na-adj.*　slender (*person*)　(*2*)
すまい（住まい）housing, residence　(*1*)
すみえ（墨絵）India ink painting　(*5*)
すみません　excuse me, I'm sorry　(*GS1*)
すむ（住む）*C1, intr.*　to reside, live　(*3*)
すもう（相撲）sumo wrestling　(*5*)
スリッパ　slipper　(*7*)
する　*C3, tr.*　to do　(*GS3*)

せ／セ

〜せい（〜製）made in…　(*7*)
せいきゅうしょ（請求書）bill, invoice　(*7*)
せいじがく（政治学）political science　(*1*)
せいじんのひ（成人の日）Coming-of-Age Day　(*3*)
せいねんがっぴ（生年月日）birth date　(*1*)
せいふく（制服）uniform　(*7*)
せいぶつがく（生物学）biology　(*1*)
セーター　sweater　(*GS3*)
セール　bargain sale　(*7*)

せっし（摂氏）centigrade　(*4*)
せびろ（背広）suit　(*7*)
セブンイレブン（7-イレブン）*p.n.*　7-Eleven store　(*2*)
せまい（狭い）*i-adj.*　narrow, not spacious　(*2*)
ゼロ　zero　(*GS2*)
せわ（する）（世話[する]）*n.v.*　care; to take care of, help　(*5*)
せん（千）thousand　(*GS3*)
ぜん〜（全〜）all；ぜんてん（全店）all store(s)；ぜんぴん（全品）all items　(*7*)；ぜんぶ（全部）all　(*5*)；ぜんぶで（全部で）*adv.*　in total　(*2*)
せんげつ（先月）last month　(*3*)
せんこう（する）（専攻[する]）*n.v.*　academic major; major in　(*1*)
ぜんさい（前菜）appetizer　(*6*)
せんしゅう（先週）last week；せんせんしゅう（先々週）the week before last　(*GS4*)
せんせい（先生）teacher, professor　(*GS1*)
ぜんぜん（全然）not at all (*with negative*)　(*3*)
せんたく（する）（洗濯[する]）*n.v.*　laundry; to do laundry　(*3*)
せんぬき（栓抜き）bottle opener　(*6*)
せんもんかもく（専門科目）specialized subject　(*1*)
せんもんてん（専門店）specialty store　(*7*)

そ／ソ

そう　*dem. adv.*　like that; that way　(*GS1*)
そうです　that's right, that's so　(*GS1*)
そうですね　well, let me see　(*GS2*)
そうじ（する）（掃除[する]）*n.v.*　cleaning; to clean (*house, room*)　(*3*)
〜そうだ　they say… (*with plain form of verb*)　(*7*)
ソース　Worcestershire-type sauce　(*6*)
ソーセージ　sausage　(*6*)
〜そく（〜足）counter for shoes, socks　(*2*)
そこ、そちら　*dem. pron.*　there　(*1*)
そして　*conj.*　and then　(*3*)
そと（外）outside　(*2*)
その　*dem. adj.*　that thing　(*1*)
そのあと（その後）after that　(*3*)
そば　near　(*2*)
そば（蕎麦）soba (*buckwheat noodles*)；そばや（蕎麦屋）soba restaurant　(*6*)
そふ（祖父）grandfather　(*5*)
ソファー　sofa, couch　(*7*)
ソフト（ウエア）software　(*3*)
そぼ（祖母）grandmother　(*5*)
そら（空）sky　(*4*)
そる（剃る）*C1, tr.*　to shave　(*3*)
それ　*dem. pron.*　that　(*1*)
それから　and then　(*3*)
それで　therefore; then; and so　(*3*)
そんな　*dem. adj.*　that kind of …　(*4*)
そんなに　*dem. adv.*　that much, that many　(*5*)

た／タ

〜だ　to be　(*3*)
ダークブルー　dark blue　(*7*)
〜たい　*i-adj.*　to want to do … (*with conjunctive form of verb*)　(*6*)
〜だい（〜台）counter for machines　(*2*)
たいいくかん（体育館）gym　(*1*)
たいいくのひ（体育の日）Health-Sports Day　(*3*)

ダイエット diet (6)

だいがく（大学）university; だいがくせい（大学生）university student; だいがくいんせい（大学院生）graduate student (1)

だいきらい（な）（大嫌い[な]）na-adj. hated, disliked intensely (2)

たいしょう（大正）Taisho era (3)

だいじょうぶ（な）（大丈夫[な]）na-adj. OK, good enough (GS4)

だいすき（な）（大好き[な]）na-adj. favorite, well-liked (2)

たいそう（体操）gymnastics (5)

だいどころ（台所）kitchen (6)

ダイバー diver (7); ダイビング（する）n.v. diving; to dive (5)

タイプ（する）n.v. typing; to type (6)

たいふう（台風）typhoon (4)

たいへん（な）（大変[な]）na-adj. terrible, awful, impressive (4)

ダイヤ diamond (6)

たいよう（太陽）sun (4)

たいわん（台湾）p.n. Taiwan; たいわんじん（台湾人）Taiwanese person (1)

たかい（高い）i-adj. expensive, high (2)

だから conj. therefore, and so (4)

〜たがる C1, intr. to want to do... (with conjunctive form of verb) (6)

たくさん much, many, a lot (2)

タクシー taxi (2)

〜だけ only... (7)

たこ octopus (6)

たす（足す）C1, tr. to add (GS2)

だす（出す）C1, tr. to take out, put out; to mail, send (GS1)

〜たち（〜達）pl. suffix for humans (1)

たつ（立つ）C1, intr. to stand (GS1)

たっきゅう（卓球）table tennis, ping pong (5)

たてもの（建物）building (2)

たてる C2, tr. to set up (a plan), build (7)

たのしい（楽しい）i-adj. fun (2); たのしむ（楽しむ）C1, tr. to enjoy (5)

たのむ（頼む）C1, tr. to request, ask (6)

タフ（な）na-adj. strong, tough (2)

たぶん（多分）adv. perhaps, probably (4)

たべる（食べる）C2, tr. to eat (GS3); たべもの（食べ物）food; たべものや（食べ物屋）food store (6)

たまご（卵）egg; たまごりょうり（卵料理）egg dish (6)

たまに adv. once in a while (3)

たまねぎ（玉葱）onion (6)

ダメ（な）na-adj. not good (5)

ためし（試し）test, trial run (6); ためす（試す）C1, tr. to try (7)

〜たら if, when (7)

だれ（誰）who (GS4); だれか（誰か）someone; だれでも（誰でも）anyone; だれも（誰も）everyone, no one (5)

〜だろう probably... (with plain form of verb) (4)

だんしがくせい（男子学生）male student (5)

たんじょうび（誕生日）birthday (3)

ダンス dance; to dance (5)

だんせい（男性）man (5)

ち／チ

ちいさい（小さい）i-adj. small (2)

チーズ cheese; チーズケーキ cheesecake (6); チーズバーガー cheeseburger (GS5)

チェス chess (5)

チェック check (pattern) (7)

ちか（地下）underground; ちかい（地階）underground floor (GS3); ちかてつ（地下鉄）subway (2)

ちかい（近い）i-adj. near, close (GS3); （近く）adv. near, close (3)

ちがう（違う）C1, intr. to differ (GS1)

チキン・ヌードル chicken noodle (6)

チケット ticket (5)

ちず（地図）map (2)

ちち（父）father (5)

ちゃいろ（茶色）brown; ちゃいろい（茶色い）i-adj. brown (7)

〜ちゃく（〜着）counter for jackets, clothes (2)

ちゃわん（茶碗）teacup, rice bowl (6)

ちゅうかりょうり（中華料理）Chinese food (6)

ちゅうごく（中国）p.n. China; ちゅうごくご（中国語）Chinese language; ちゅうごくじん（中国人）Chinese person; ちゅうごくりょうり（中国料理）Chinese dish (1)

ちゅうしゃじょう（駐車場）parking lot (2)

ちゅうしょく（昼食）lunch (6)

ちゅうもん（する）（注文[する]）n.v. order; to order (7)

チューリップ tulip (7)

ちょう（兆）trillion (2)

ちょうさ（する）（調査[する]）n.v. investigation, survey; to investigate, take a poll (5)

ちょうじょ（長女）oldest daughter (5)

ちょうしょく（朝食）breakfast (6)

ちょうなん（長男）oldest son (5)

〜ちょうみりょう（調味料）seasoning (6)

〜ちょうめ（〜丁目）district number in address (2)

チョーク chalk (GS1)

ちょきん（する）（貯金[する]）n.v. deposit (money), savings; to deposit, save (7)

チョコレート chocolate (GS5)

ちょっと adv. a little, a bit (GS1)

つ／ツ

ついたち（一日）first of the month (3)

つかう（使う）C1, tr. to use (GS1)

つかれる（疲れる）C2, intr. to become tired (3)

つぎ（の）（次[の]）next (GS1)

つくえ（机）desk (GS1)

つくる（作る）C1, tr. to make; to cook (GS1)

つくろう（繕う）C1, tr. to mend (7)

つけもの（漬物）pickle (6)

つける C2, tr. to wear, put on (7)

つたえる（伝える）C2, tr. to tell, convey (6)

つづく（続く）C1, intr. to continue (4)

つつむ（包む）C1, tr. to wrap; つつみがみ（包み紙）wrapping paper (7)

ツナサラダ tuna salad (6)

つま（妻）wife (5)

つまらない i-adj. boring (2)

〜つもりだ to intend to do... (with nonpast, plain form of verb) (6)

つゆ（梅雨）rainy season (June and July) (4)

つゆ（露）dew (4)

つよい（強い）i-adj. strong, powerful (4)

つり（釣り）fishing (4)

つれていく（連れていく）to take, accompany (2)

て／テ

で　*part.*　with; at; by means of　(2)
〜ていく　to do and leave　(6)
〜ている　to be …ing　(4)
〜てください　please do…　(2)
〜てしまう　to complete…　(6)
Tシャツ　T-shirt　(5)
ディスコ　disco　(3)
ていりゅうじょ（停留所）bus stop　(2)
テークアウト　take out food　(6)
デート(する)　*n.v.*　date; to go on a date　(GS2)
テープ　tape　(GS1);　テープ・レコーダー　tape recorder　(7)
テーブル　table　(GS1)
でかける（出かける）*C2, intr.*　to go out, leave　(3)
てがみ（手紙）letter　(GS3)
できる（出来る）*C2, intr.*　to be able to, can; to be completed　(5)
でございます　polite form of です　(7)
デザート　dessert　(6)
デザイン(する)　*n. v.*　design; to design;　デザイナー designer;　デザイナー・ブランド　designer brand　(7)
てじな（手品）magic, sleight of hand　(5)
でしょう　*pol.*　probably　(4)
です　*pol.*　to be　(1)
てつがく（哲学）philosophy　(1)
てつだう（手伝う）*C1, tr.*　to help, assist　(3)
テニス　tennis　(GS2)
では　*conj.*　then　(GS1)
ではありません　negative of です　(1)
デパート　department store　(GS2)
てぶくろ（手袋）glove(s)　(7)
〜てみる　to try to do…　(6)
でも　*conj.*　but　(4)
でる（出る）*C2, intr.*　to leave, go out　(3)
テレビ　TV　(GS3);　テレビゲーム　video game　(5)
てんいん（店員）store clerk　(7)
てんき（天気）weather;　てんきず（天気図）weather map;　てんきよほう（天気予報）weather forecast　(4)
でんき（電気）electric light, electricity　(GS1);　でんきこう（電気工）electrician;　でんきてん（電気店）electric appliance store　(7)
でんごん(する)（伝言[する]）*n.v.*　message; to leave a message　(3)
でんしゃ（電車）electric train　(2)
てんじょう（天井）ceiling　(GS1)
でんたく（電卓）calculator　(GS1)
てんのう（天皇）emperor;　てんのうたんじょうび（天皇誕生日）emperor's birthday　(3)
てんぷら（天麩羅）tempura;　てんぷらや（天麩羅屋）tempura restaurant　(6)
でんわ(する)（電話[する]）*n.v.*　telephone; to make a phone call　(GS2);　でんわばんごう（電話番号）telephone number　(1)

と／ト

と　*part.*　with; and　(GS3)
と　quotation marker　(6)
〜ど（〜度）counter for temperature　(4);　counter for frequency　(2)
ドア　door　(GS1)
〜という（〜と言う）to say that…;　(A)という(B) (B) called (A)　(6)

ドイツ　*p.n.*　Germany;　ドイツご（ドイツ語）German language;　ドイツじん（ドイツ人）German person　(1)
トイレ　rest room, bathroom, toilet　(2)
〜とう（〜頭）counter for large animals　(2)
どう　*dem. adv.*　how　(1)
どういたしまして　you're welcome　(GS1)
どうか　somehow　(5)
とうきょう（東京）*p.n.*　Tokyo　(3)
どうして　how; why　(1)
どうぞ　please, go ahead　(GS1)
とうふ（豆腐）tofu (*bean curd*)　(6)
とうめい(な)（透明[な]）*na-adj.*　transparent　(7)
どうも　*inf.*　indeed; thanks　(GS1)
とお（十）ten　(2);　とおか（十日）tenth day　(3)
とおい（遠い）*i-adj.*　far away　(GS3)
〜とおもう（〜と思う）to think that …　(6)
とおり（通り）avenue　(2)
とかす　*C1, tr.*　to comb　(3)
〜とき（〜時）when…　(7)
ときどき（時々）*adv.*　sometimes　(3)
とくい(な)（得意[な]）*na-adj.*　good at and like; forte　(5)
とくぎ（特技）special talent　(5)
どくしょ(する)（読書[する]）*n.v.*　reading books; to read　(5)
どくしん（独身）single, unmarried person　(5)
とくに（特に）*adv.*　especially　(GS2)
とけい（時計）clock, watch　(GS3);　とけいてん／とけいや（時計店／時計屋）watch shop　(7)
どこ　*dem. pron.*　where　(GS3)
どこか　somewhere　(5)
どこでも　anywhere, everywhere　(5)
どこも　everywhere; nowhere (*with negative*)　(5)
とこや（床屋）barbershop　(5)
とし（年）age　(1)
どしゃぶり（土砂降り）downpour (*of rain*)　(4)
としょかん（図書館）library　(1)
としより（年寄）aged people　(5)
とじる（閉じる）*C2, tr.*　to close (*box, drawer, etc.*)　(GS1)
どちら　*pol.*　where, which (of the two)　(GS4);　どちらか　either;　どちらでも　whichever;　(5)　どちらのほう　which one;　(4)　どちらも　both; neither (*with negative*)　(5)
どっち　*coll.*　which one　(1)
とても　*adv.*　very　(GS3)
どなた　*pol.*　who　(1);　どなたか　*pol.*　someone;　どなたでも　*pol.*　anyone;　どなたも　*pol.*　no one (*with negative*)　(5)
となり（隣）next to; next-door　(2)
どの　*dem. adj.*　which (of more than two)　(1)
とぶ（飛ぶ）*C1, intr.*　to fly　(3)
とほ（徒歩）by walking, on foot　(2)
トマト　tomato　(6)
ともだち（友だち）friend　(GS3)
どようび（土曜日）Saturday　(GS4)
ドライ・クリーニング　dry cleaning　(7)
ドライブ(する)　*n.v.*　drive; to drive　(3)
トランプ　card game　(5)
とり（鳥）bird　(2);　とりにく（鳥肉）chicken meat　(6)
とる（取る）*C1, tr.*　to take　(5)
とる（撮る）*C1, tr.*　to take (a photo)　(7)
どれ　*dem. adj.*　which thing (of more than two)　(GS4);　どれか　one of them;　どれでも　any of them;　どれも　all of them; none of them　(5)

トレードマーク　trademark　(7)
トレーナー　sweatshirt　(7)
ドレス　dress　(7)
どんな　*dem. adj.*　what kind　(GS4)

な／ナ

ない　*i-adj.*　not there, to not exist　(2)
ナイフ　knife　(3)
ナイロン　nylon　(7)
なか　(中)　in, inside　(2)
ながい　(長い)　*i-adj.*　long　(2)
ながそで　(長袖)　long sleeves; long-sleeved　(7)
なかなか　*adv.*　rather, quite　(5)
～ながら　while …ing (*with conjunctive form of verb*)　(6)
なく　(泣く)　*C1, intr.*　to cry　(3)
なげる　(投げる)　*C2, tr.*　to throw　(5)
なし　(梨)　pear　(6)
なぜ　why　(1);　なぜか　somehow　(5)
なつ　(夏)　summer　(4);　なつやすみ　(夏休み)　summer vacation　(6)
など　and so on　(6)
なな　(七)　seven　(GS2);　ななじゅう　(七十)　seventy　(GS5);　ななつ　(七つ)　seven　(2);　なのか　(七日)　seventh day　(3)
なに、なん　(何)　what　(GS4);　なにいろ　(何色)　what color　(1);　なにか　(何か)　something　(5);　なにご　(何語)　what language;　なにじん　(何人)　what nationality　(1);　なにも　(何も)　anything, nothing　(3);　なんかい　(何階)　how many floors　(GS2);　なんがつ　(何月)　what month;　なんさい　(何歳)　how old　(1);　なんじ　(何時)　what time　(GS2);　なんじかん　(何時間)　how many hours　(3);　なんでも　(何でも)　anything　(5);　なんど　(何度)　how many degrees　(4);　なんとか　(何とか)　in some way, somehow　(5);　なんども　(何度も)　many times　(6);　なんにち　(何日)　what day, how many days;　なんねん　(何年)　what year, how many years　(3);　なんねんせい　(何年生)　what year in school　(1);　なんぷん　(何分)　what minute, how many minutes　(3);　なんようび　(何曜日)　what day of the week　(GS4)
ナプキン　napkin　(6)
なべ　(鍋)　pan, pot　(6)
なま(の)　(生[の])　raw　(6)
なまえ　(名前)　name　(GS1)
ならう　(習う)　*C1, tr.*　to learn　(6)
なる　*C1, intr.*　to become, turn into　(4)
なるほど　I see; of course　(4)

に／ニ

に　(二)　two　(GS2);　にがつ　(二月)　February　(1);　にじゅう　(二十)　twenty　(GS2);　にじゅうよっか　(二十四日)　twenty-fourth day　(3)
に　*part.*　(indirect object) at, in　(GS3)
にあう　(似合う)　*C1, intr.*　to be suited, fit　(5)
におい　(臭い)　smell　(6)
にがい　(苦い)　*i-adj.*　bitter　(6)
にがて(な)　(苦手[な])　*na-adj.*　clumsy at and dislike; weak point　(5)
にぎやか(な)　*na-adj.*　lively　(2)
にく　(肉)　meat　(2);　にくや　(肉屋)　butcher shop　(7)
～にくい　*i-adj.*　difficult to… (*with conjunctive form of verb*)　(7)

にし　(西)　west　(4)
～にする　to decide on…　(6)
にちじょうせいかつ　(日常生活)　everyday life　(3)
にちようび　(日曜日)　Sunday　(GS4)
にほん　(日本)　Japan;　にほんご　(日本語)　Japanese language　(GS1);　にほんしゅ　(日本酒)　Japanese saké　(6);　にほんじん　(日本人)　Japanese person　(1);　にほんぶよう　(日本舞踊)　Japanese traditional dance　(5)
～によると　according to…　(7)
ニュース　news　(GS3)
にゅうもん(する)　(入門[する])　*n.v.*　entry level, introduction; to begin　(5)
にる　(煮る)　*C2, tr.*　to boil, stew　(6)
にわかあめ　(にわか雨)　rain shower　(4)
～にん　(～人)　counter for people　(2)
にんき　(人気)　popularity　(5)
にんじん　(人参)　carrot　(6)

ぬ／ヌ

ぬう　(縫う)　*C1, tr.*　to sew　(7)
ぬぐ　(脱ぐ)　*C1, tr.*　to take off clothes　(3)

ね／ネ

ね　*part.*　sentence-final emphatic particle　(GS1)
ねぎる　(値切る)　*C1, tr.*　to bargain, haggle over price　(7)
ネクタイ　necktie　(7)
ネグリジェ　negligee　(7)
ねこ　(猫)　cat　(5)
ねだん　(値段)　price　(7)
ネックレス　necklace　(7)
ねぼう(する)　(寝坊[する])　*n.v.*　oversleeping; to oversleep　(4)
ねむる　(眠る)　*C1, intr.*　to sleep　(3)
ねる　(寝る)　*C1, intr.*　to sleep, go to bed　(GS3)
ねんごう　(年号)　era　(3)
～ねんせい　(～年生)　…year in school　(1)
～ねんまえに　(～年前に)　…years before　(6)
ねんれい　(年齢)　age　(1)

の／ノ

の　*part.*　possessive marker　(GS2);　one (*pronoun*)　(7);　nominalizer　(5)
ノート　notebook　(GS1)
のせる　*C2, tr.*　to put on, place　(6)
～のために　for the sake of, for the purpose of　(6)
～ので　because　(4)
のどがかわく　(咽が乾く)　to be thirsty　(3)
～のはなしでは　(の話では)　according to…　(7)
のべる　(述べる)　*C2, tr.*　to state　(6)
のむ　(飲む)　*C1, tr.*　to drink　(GS3);　のみほうだい　(飲み放題)　all you can drink　(6);　のみもの　(飲み物)　beverage　(GS3)
のり　(海苔)　laver (a kind of seaweed)　(1)
のる　(乗る)　*C1, intr.*　to ride　(3)

は／ハ

は　*part.*　topic marker (*pronounced* わ)　(1)
は　(歯)　tooth;　はをみがく　(歯を磨く)　to brush teeth　(3)

五百二十三

バーゲンセール　clearance sale　(7)
バースデー・ケーキ　birthday cake　(4);
　　バースデー・プレゼント　birthday gift　(3)
パーティー　party　(GS2)
バーベキュー　BBQ　(6)
パール　pearl　(7)
はい　interj.　yes　(GS1)
〜はい　(〜杯)　counter for glass- or cupfuls　(2)
〜ばい　(〜倍)　counter for multiples　(2)
はいいろ　(灰色)　gray　(7)
バイオリン　violin　(5)
ハイキング(する)　n.v.　hiking; to hike　(4)
バイキングりょうり　(バイキング料理)　all you can
　　eat　(6)
はいけい　(拝啓)　Dear…　(used at the beginning of a
　　letter)　(4)
はいたつ(する)　(配達[する])　n.v.　delivery; to deliver　(7)
パイナップル　pineapple　(6)
ハイヒール　high heels　(7)
はいる(入る)　C1, intr.　to enter　(3)
はく　C1, tr.　to wear; to put on (feet or legs)　(4)
はこ　(箱)　box　(2)
はさみ　(鉄)　scissors　(7)
はし　(箸)　chopsticks　(6)
はじ　edge　(2)
はじまる　(始まる)　C1, intr.　to start　(3)
はじめに　(初めに)　first; first of all　(6)
はじめまして　nice meeting you　(GS1)
はじめる　(始める)　C2, tr.　to start　(GS1)
パジャマ　pajamas　(7)
ばしょ　(場所)　place　(5)
はしる　(走る)　C1, intr.　to run　(GS1)
バス　bus　(2)
バスケットボール　basketball　(5)
はずす　C1, tr.　to take off (glasses, etc.)　(7)
パスタ　pasta　(6)
バスてい　(バス停)　bus stop　(2)
バター　butter　(6)
はたち　(二十歳)　twenty years old　(1)
はたらく　(働く)　C1, intr.　to work　(3)
はち　(八)　eight　(GS2);　はちがつ　(八月)
　　August　(1);　はちじゅう　(八十)　eighty　(GS5)
パチンコ　pachinko (Japanese pinball)　(5)
はつおん(する)　(発音[する])　n.v.　pronunciation; to
　　pronounce　(4)
はつか　(二十日)　twentieth day　(3)
はで(な)　(派手[な])　na-adj.　gaudy; bright; loud
　　(in color)　(2)
バドミントン　badminton　(5)
はな　(花)　flower　(4)
はなし　(話)　story; talk; speech　(2)
はなす　(話す)　C1, tr.　to speak, tell, talk　(GS3)
バナナ　banana　(2)
はなみ　(花見)　(cherry) blossom viewing　(4)
はなや　(花屋)　flower shop　(7)
バニラ　vanilla　(GS5)
はは　(母)　mother　(5);　ははのひ　(母の日)
　　Mother's Day　(7)
パパ　papa　(5)
パパイア　papaya　(6)
ハム　ham　(6)
はめる　C2, tr.　to wear, put on (rings, etc.)　(7)
はやい　(早い／速い)　i-adj.　early, fast, quickly　(GS3);
　　(早く／速く)　adv.　early, fast, quickly　(4)

はらう　(払う)　C1, tr.　to pay　(7)
バランス　balance　(6)
はり　(針)　needle　(7)
はる　(春)　spring　(4);　はるがっき　(春学期)　spring quarter,
　　spring semester　(5);　はるさめ　(春雨)　spring rain　(4)
はれ　(晴れ)　clear skies, sunny weather;　はれる
　　(晴れる)　C2, intr.　to get sunny　(4)
バレーボール　volleyball　(5)
はん　(半)　thirty minutes; half　(GS2);　はんぶん
　　(半分)　half　(7)
〜ばん　(〜番)　number…　(GS2);　〜ばんめ　(〜番目)
　　number…　(5)
パン　bread　(6);　パンや　(パン屋)　bakery　(7)
はんがく　(半額)　half price　(7)
ハンカチ　handkerchief　(7)
ばんぐみ　(番組)　program (TV, radio)　(5)
ばんごう　(番号)　number　(GS2)
ばんごはん　(晩ごはん)　dinner, supper　(GS2)
ハンサム(な)　na-adj.　handsome　(2)
はんそで　(半袖)　short sleeves; short-sleeved　(7)
ばんち　(番地)　number (in address)　(2)
パンツ　briefs　(7)
パンティー　panties;　パンティーストッキング　pantyhose
　　(7)
ハンティング　hunting　(5)
バンドエイド　Band-Aid　(7)
ハンバーガー　hamburger　(GS3)
ハンマー　hammer　(7)

ひ／ヒ

ピアス　pierced earrings　(7)
ピアニスト　pianist;　ピアノ　piano　(5)
ピーマン　green pepper　(6)
ビール　beer　(GS2)
ひがし　(東)　east　(2)
〜ひき　(〜匹)　counter for small animals　(2)
〜びき　(引き)　reduced …%　(7)
ひきにく　(ひき肉)　ground meat　(6)
ひく　(引く)　C1, tr.　to subtract, draw　(GS2)
ひく　(弾く)　C1, tr.　to play (a musical instrument)
　　(5)
ひくい　(低い)　i-adj.　low; short　(2)
ひげ　beard, facial hair;　ひげをそる　C1, tr.　to shave facial
　　hair　(3)
ピザ　pizza　(GS2)
ひさしぶり　it's been a long time; after a long absence
　　(GS1)
ビジネス(する)　n.v.　business; do business　(3)
びじゅつ　(美術)　art　(1);　びじゅつかん　(美術館)　art
　　museum　(2)
ひだり　(左)　left side　(2)
ビデオ　video　(6);　ビデオ・ゲーム　video game;
　　ビデオカメラ　videocamera　(5)
ひでり　(日照り)　drought　(4)
ひと　(人)　person　(1)
ひどい　(i-adj.)　terrible　(GS1)
ひとつ　(一つ)　one　(2)
ひとり　(一人)　one person　(2);　ひとりで　(一人で)
　　by oneself　(5)
ビネガー　vinegar　(6)
ひま(な)　(暇[な])　na-adj.　free, not busy　(3)
ひゃく　(百)　hundred　(GS5);　ひゃくまん　(百万)
　　million　(2)

びょういん （病院） hospital *(2)*
びょういん （美容院） beauty parlor *(7)*
びょうき （病気） sickness, illness *(3)*
ひらがな hiragana *(GS1)*
ひる （昼） noon, noontime *(GS2)*
ビル building *(1)*
ひるごはん （昼ごはん） lunch *(GS2)*
ひるま （昼間） daytime *(4)*
ひろい （広い） *i-adj.* wide, spacious, big *(2)*
ピンク pink *(7)*
ピンポン table tennis, ping pong *(5)*

ふ／フ

ファーストフード fast food　ファーストフード・
　レストラン fast food restaurant *(6)*
ファスナー zipper *(7)*
ファックス fax *(1)*
ファッション fashion *(5)*；ファッション・ショー fashion
　show *(7)*
フィッシュバーガー fishburger *(GS3)*
フィット（する） *n.v.* fit; to fit *(7)*
フィルム film *(5)*
ブーケ bouquet *(7)*
ブーツ boots *(7)*
ふうふ （夫婦） married couple；ごふうふ （御夫婦）
　pol. married couple *(5)*
プール swimming pool *(1)*
ふえる （増える） *C2, intr.* to increase *(6)*
フォーク fork *(3)*
フォーマル（な） *na-adj.* formal *(7)*
ふかめる （深める） *C2, tr.* to deepen *(5)*
ふく （服） clothes *(3)*；ふくそう （服装） clothes, dress;
　appearance *(7)*
ふく （吹く） *C1, intr.* to blow (*wind*) *(4)*；ふく
　（吹く） *C1, tr.* to blow (*musical instrument*) *(5)*
ふじんふくてん （婦人服店） women's wear store *(7)*
ふたつ （二つ） two；ふたり （二人） two people *(2)*
ぶたにく （豚肉） pork *(6)*
ふつう （普通） usual, ordinary *(6)*
ふつか （二日） second day *(3)*
フットボール football *(5)*
ぶつりがく （物理学） physics *(1)*
ブティック boutique *(5)*
ぶどう （葡萄） grape *(6)*
ふとる （太る） *C1, intr.* to get fat *(6)*
ふとんや （布団屋） futon store *(7)*
ふぶき （吹雪） snowstorm *(4)*
ふべん（な） （不便［な］） *na-adj.* inconvenient *(2)*
ふまじめ（な） （不真面目［な］） *na-adj.* not serious, lazy
　(*person*) *(4)*
ふゆ （冬） winter *(4)*；ふゆやすみ （冬休み） winter
　vacation *(6)*
フライパン frying pan *(6)*
ブラウス blouse *(5)*
ブラジャー brassiere *(7)*
ブラジル *p.n.* Brazil；ブラジルじん （ブラジル人）
　Brazilian *(1)*
プラモデル plastic model *(7)*
フランス *p.n.* France *(1)*；フランス・パン French
　bread *(7)*；フランスご （フランス語） French
　language；フランスじん （フランス人） French
　person *(1)*
ブランチ brunch *(3)*

プリン pudding *(6)*
プリント print (*pattern*) *(7)*
ふる （降る） *C1, intr.* to fall (*rain and snow*) *(4)*
ふるい （古い） *i-adj.* old *(2)*
ブルー blue *(7)*
フルーツ・サラダ fruit salad *(6)*
フルート flute *(5)*
ブレザー blazer, jacket *(7)*
ブレスレット bracelet *(7)*
プレゼント present, gift *(3)*
フレンチフライ French fries *(GS3)*
プロ professional *(5)*
ブローチ brooch, pin *(7)*
プログラマ programmer；プログラミング（する） *n.v.*
　programming; to do programming *(5)*；プログラム
　（する） *n.v.* program; to program *(7)*
ブロッコリ broccoli *(GS2)*
プロポーズ（する） *n.v.* proposal; propose
　marriage *(7)*
〜ふん（かん） （〜分［間］） counter for duration in
　minutes *(2)*
ぶんか （文化） culture *(1)*；ぶんかのひ （文化の日）
　Culture Day *(3)*
ぶんがく （文学） literature；ぶんがくぶ （文学部） literature
　department *(1)*
ぶんかつばらい （分割払い） installment payment plan *(7)*
ぶんぼうぐ （文房具） stationery *(GS3)*；
　ぶんぼうぐや （文房具屋） stationery store *(7)*

へ／ヘ

へ *part.* toward, to (*pronounced* え) *(GS3)*
ペア pair *(GS1)*
ヘアースタイル hairstyle *(5)*
へいきん （平均） average *(4)*
へいじつ （平日） weekday *(3)*
へいせい （平成） Heisei era *(3)*
へえ *interj.* oh (*exclamation of surprise*) *(3)*
ベーゲル bagel *(7)*
ペキン *p.n.* Beijing *(4)*
ベジタリアン vegetarian *(GS5)*
へた(な) （下手［な］） *na-adj.* poor at, not skilled
　at *(5)*
ペット pet *(5)*
べつに （別に） *adv.* separately; not particularly
　(*with negative*) *(6)*
へや （部屋） room *(2)*
ベルト belt *(7)*
ヘルメット helmet *(7)*
ペン pen *(GS1)*
へん（な） （変［な］） *na-adj.* strange, weird *(2)*
べんきょう（する） （勉強［する］） *n.v.* study; to study *(GS2)*
ベンチ bench *(2)*
べんとう （弁当） box lunch *(6)*
ペンパル pen pal *(1)*
へんぴん（する） （返品［する］） *n.v.* returning merchandise;
　to return merchandise *(7)*
べんり（な） （便利［な］） *na-adj.* convenient *(2)*

ほ／ホ

ほう direction, way (*used in comparative constructions*) *(4)*
ほうがく （法学） law *(1)*
ぼうし （帽子） cap, hat *(7)*
ほうせきてん （宝石店） jewelry shop *(7)*

ほうちょう（包丁）cleaver, big cutting knife *(6)*
ボーイフレンド boyfriend *(2)*
ポータブル portable *(7)*
ボート boat *(5)*
ボーリング bowling *(5)*
ボール ball *(2)*
ボールペン ball-point pen *(GS1)*
ぼく（僕）*pron., m., inf.* I (male);　ぼくたち（僕たち）*pron., m., inf., pl.* we (male) *(1)*
ボクシング boxing *(GS2)*
ポケット pocket *(7)*
ほしい（欲しい）*i-adj.* to want;　ほしがる（欲しがる）*C1, tr.* to want *(6)*
ボタン button *(7)*
ポップコーン popcorn *(6)*
ポツポツ raining in big, scattered drops *(4)*
ボディーガード bodyguard *(5)*
ポテト potato *(6)*;　ポテトチップ potato chip *(7)*
ホテル hotel *(2)*
〜ほど as much as, about *(3)*
ほとんど *adv.* almost;　ほとんど...ない almost never... *(3)*
ポリエステル polyester *(7)*
ポルトガルご（ポルトガル語）Portuguese language *(1)*
ほん（本）book *(GS1)*;　ほんや（本屋）bookstore *(6)*
〜ほん（〜本）counter for long, often cylindrical, items *(2)*
ホンコン（香港）*p.n.* Hong Kong;　ホンコンじん（香港人）Hong Kong native *(1)*
ぼんさい（盆栽）bonsai *(5)*
ほんとう（本当）real, true *(GS2)*;　（本当に）*adv.* really, truly *(4)*

ま／マ

まあまあ so-so, not bad *(2)*
マーガリン margarine *(6)*
マージャン mah-jongg *(5)*
〜まい（〜枚）counter for thin, flat items *(2)*
まい〜（毎〜）every *(3)*;　まいあさ（毎朝）every morning *(GS3)*;　まいしゅう（毎週）every week;　まいつき（毎月）every month *(3)*;　まいにち（毎日）every day *(GS4)*;　まいばん（毎晩）every night *(3)*
〜まいどり（〜枚撮り）counter for film exposures *(7)*
まえ（前）front *(2)*
まぐろ（鮪）tuna *(6)*
まご（孫）grandchild *(5)*
まさか *interj.* that can't be... *(3)*
まじめ（な）（真面目[な]）*na-adj.* diligent, earnest *(2)*
まず first of all *(3)*
まずい *i-adj.* not tasty, bad *(4)*
また *adv.* again *(GS1)*
まだ *adv.* not yet, still *(3)*
まち（町）town *(2)*
まちがいでんわ（間違い電話）wrong number (telephone) *(3)*
まちがう（間違う）*C1, intr.* to make a mistake *(3)*
まつ（待つ）*C1, tr.* to wait *(GS1)*
まったく（全く）*adv.* totally *(5)*
まで *part.* up to, until *(2)*
まど（窓）window *(GS1)*
マトン mutton *(7)*
マフラー scarf *(7)*
ママ mama *(5)*

まめ（豆）bean, pea *(6)*
まもなく（間もなく）soon, before long *(7)*
マラソン（する）*n.v.* marathon; to run a marathon *(5)*
まるい（丸い／円い）*i-adj.* round *(2)*
まわり（回り）around (*location*) *(2)*
まん（万）ten thousand *(2)*
まんいん（満員）full capacity (*train, etc.*) *(6)*
まんが（漫画）cartoon *(7)*
まんなか（真ん中）middle *(2)*
まんねんひつ（万年筆）fountain pen *(1)*

み／ミ

ミンチ ground meat *(6)*
ミーティング meeting *(GS2)*
みえる（見える）*C2, intr.* can be seen *(5)*
みがく（磨く）*C1, tr.* to brush, polish; to wipe clean *(3)*
みかん mandarin orange *(6)*
みぎ（右）right side *(2)*
みじかい（短い）*i-adj.* short *(4)*
ミシン sewing machine *(7)*
みず（水）water (*unheated*);　おみず（お水）water *pol.* *(6)*
みずぎ（水着）bathing suit, swimwear *(7)*
みずたま（水玉）polka dots *(5)*
ミステリー mystery novel *(3)*
みせ（店）store, shop *(7)*
みせる（見せる）*C2, tr.* to show *(3)*
みそ（味噌）miso;　みそしる（味噌汁）miso soup *(6)*
みぞれ sleet *(4)*
みち（道）street *(2)*
みっか（三日）third day *(3)*;　みっつ（三つ）three *(2)*
みつける（見つける）*C2, tr.* to find, discover *(6)*
みどり（緑）green *(7)*;　みどりのひ（緑の日）Greenery Day *(3)*
みな、みんな（皆）all, everyone;　（皆さん）everyone *(5)*
みなみ（南）south *(1)*;　みなみかぜ（南風）south wind *(4)*
みぶんしょうめいしょ（身分証明書）ID (identification) *(3)*
ミュージカル musical show *(5)*
みりん sweet cooking sake *(6)*
みる（見る）*C2, tr.* to see *(3)*
ミルク milk *(3)*

む／ム

むいか（六日）sixth day *(3)*
むかい（向かい）across from, facing *(2)*
むこうがわ（向こう側）the other side *(2)*
むじ（無地）plain (*no pattern*), solid color *(7)*
むしあつい（むし暑い）*i-adj.* sultry; hot and humid *(4)*
むす（蒸す）*C1, tr.* to steam *(6)*
むずかしい（難しい）*i-adj.* difficult *(2)*
むすこ（息子）son;　むすこさん（息子さん）*pol.* son *(5)*
むすめ（娘）daughter;　むすめさん（娘さん）*pol.* daughter *(5)*
むっつ（六つ）six *(2)*
むら（村）village *(2)*
むらさき（紫）purple *(7)*
むらさめ passing rain *(4)*
むり（な）（無理[な]）*na-adj.* impossible, very difficult *(5)*
むりょう（無料）free of charge *(6)*

め／メ

〜め（〜目）suffix making ordinal numbers …th (2)
めい（姪）niece;　めいごさん（姪ごさん）*pol.* niece (5)
めいし（名刺）name card (GS1)
めいじ（明治）Meiji era (3)
めいわく（な）（迷惑［な］）*na-adj.* annoying;めいわく（する）（迷惑［する］）*n.v.* nuisance, trouble; to cause trouble, bother (5)
メーカー　maker (1)
メーター、メートル　meter (4)
メールオーダー　mail order (7)
めがね（眼鏡）eyeglasses;　めがねてん／めがねや（眼鏡店／眼鏡屋）optician's;　めがねをかける（眼鏡をかける）to put on, wear glasses (7)
メキシコ　*p.n.* Mexico;　メキシコじん（メキシコ人）Mexican person (1)
メニュー　menu (GS2)
メモリー　memory (7)
メロドラマ　soap opera (5)
メロン　melon (6)
めん（綿）cotton cloth (7)
めんせき（面積）area, size, floor space (2)

も／モ

も　*part.* too (3)
もう　*adv.* already; never (*with negative*) (GS1);　*adv.* more (2)
もうしこみしょ（申込書）application form (5)
もうしぶんない（申し分ない）satisfactory, good enough (7)
もうしわけない（申し訳ない）be very sorry (7)
もくようび（木曜日）Thursday (GS4)
もしもし　*interj.* hello (*on the telephone*) (2)
もちろん（勿論）of course (2)
もつ（持つ）*C1, tr.* to have, own, hold (3)
もっと　*adv.* more (4)
モデル　fashion model (7)
もの　thing; item (2)
もよう（模様）pattern (7)
もん（門）gate (3)
もんだい（問題）question; issue, problem (4)

や／ヤ

〜や　*part.* and so on (3)
やおや（八百屋）vegetable store, greengrocer (7)
やきとり（焼き鳥）yakitori (chicken shish kebob) (GS4)
やきゅう（野球）baseball (GS3)
やく（焼く）*C1, tr.* to broil, grill, bake (6)
やさい（野菜）vegetable (GS1);　やさいサラダ（野菜サラダ）vegetable salad (6);　やさいジュース（野菜ジュース）vegetable juice (7)
やさしい　*i-adj.* easy; lenient (2)
やしょく（夜食）evening snack (6)
〜やすい　*i-adj.* easy to… (*with conjunctive form of verb*) (7)
やすい（安い）*i-adj.* inexpensive, cheap (2)
やすみ（休み）day off, rest;　やすみのひ（休みの日）day off;　やすむ（休む）*C1, intr.* to take a rest (3)
やっきょく（薬局）pharmacy, drugstore (7)
やっつ（八つ）eight (2)
やはり　after all (4)

やま（山）mountain;　やまのぼり（山登り）mountain climbing (4)
やめる（止める）*C2, tr.* to stop, quit (3)

ゆ／ユ

ゆうがた（夕方）evening (GS2);　ゆうごはん（夕ごはん）dinner (3);　ゆうしょく（夕食）dinner, supper (6);　ゆうだち（夕立）evening shower (4)
ゆうこうに（有効に）effectively (5)
ゆうびんきょく（郵便局）post office (2)
ゆうめい（な）（有名［な］）*na-adj.* famous (2);　ゆうめいじん（有名人）celebrity (6)
ゆか（床）floor (GS1)
ゆき（雪）snow (4)
ゆっくり　*adv.* slowly (1)
ゆでる　cook in boiling water (6)
ゆびわ（指輪）ring (finger) (7)
ゆめ（夢）dream (7)
ゆるい　*i-adj.* loose (7)

よ／ヨ

よ　*part.* sentence-final particle (*emphasis*) (2)
ようか（八日）eighth day (3)
ようき（な）（陽気［な］）*na-adj.* cheerful, lively (4)
ようし（養子）adopted child (5)
ようじ（用事）errand (3)
ようしょく（洋食）Western cuisine (6)
〜ようとおもう（〜ようと思う）to intend to do… (6)
ようひんてん（洋品店）Western clothing store (7);　ようふう（洋風）Western style (6);　ようふく（洋服）Western clothes (7)
ヨーグルト　yogurt (6)
よか（余暇）free time (5)
ヨガ　yoga (5)
よく　*adv.* often, well (1)
よこ（横）side (2)
よしゅう（する）（予習［する］）*n.v.* preparation for class; to prepare for class (GS1)
よっか（四日）fourth day (3);　よっつ（四つ）four (2)
ヨット　yacht (5)
よてい（する）（予定［する］）*n.v.* plan; to plan, schedule (6)
よぶ（呼ぶ）*C1, tr.* to invite (6)
よむ（読む）*C1, tr.* to read (GS3)
よやく（する）（予約［する］）*n.v.* reservation; to reserve (6)
〜より　more than… (4)
よる（夜）night (GS2)
よろしく　please do as you see fit (GS1)
よわい（弱い）*i-adj.* weak (4)
よん（四）four (GS2);　よんじゅう（四十）forty (GS5)

ら／ラ

ラーメン　ramen (*Chinese-style wheat noodles*) (GS3);　ラーメンや（ラーメン屋）ramen restaurant (6)
らいげつ（来月）next month (3)
らいしゅう（来週）next week (3)
ライス　rice (*cooked*) (6)
ライトブルー　light blue (7)
らいにち（する）（来日［する］）*n.v.* coming to Japan; to come to Japan (7)
らいねん（来年）next year (3)

五百二十七

ラグビー rugby (5)
ラケット racket (5)
ラジオ radio (GS2); ラジカセ radio cassette (1)
ラップ rap (2)
ラップトップ・コンピュータ laptop computer (4)
ラフ（な） na.adj. rough (4)
ラム lamb (6)
ランゲージ・ラボ language lab (1)
ランニング running (5)

り／リ

りくじょうきょうぎ（陸上競技） track and field (5)
リポーター reporter (6)
リボン ribbon (7)
リモコン remote control (7)
りゅうがくせい（留学生） foreign student (7)
りょう（寮） dormitory (1)
りょうしゅうしょ（領収書） receipt (7)
りょうしん（両親） parents; ごりょうしん（御両親）
 pol. parents (5)
りょうり（する）（料理［する］） n.v. cooking, cuisine;
 to cook (GS1)
りょくちゃ（緑茶） green tea (6)
りょこう（する）（旅行［する］） n.v. trip, travel; to travel (5)
りんご apple (6)

れ／レ

れい（零） zero (GS2); れいか（零下） below zero (4)
れいぞうこ（冷蔵庫） refrigerator (6)
れいとうしょくひん（冷凍食品） frozen food (6)
レインコート raincoat (4)
れきしがく（歴史学） history (1)
レジ cash register, cashier (7)
レシート receipt (7)
レシピー recipe (6)
レジャー leisure (5)
レストラン restaurant (2)
レスリング wrestling (5)
レタス lettuce (6)
レバー liver (4)
レモン lemon (6)

レンジ oven, range (6)
れんしゅう（する）（練習［する］） n.v. practice, exercise; to
 practice, to exercise (2)

ろ／ロ

ろく（六） six (GS2); ろくがつ（六月） June (1);
 ろくじゅう（六十） sixty (GS5)
ロシア p.n. Russia; ロシアご（ロシア語） Russian
 language; ロシアじん（ロシア人） Russian person (1)
ロック rock and roll (GS2)
ロッククライミング rock climbing (5)
ロブスター lobster (6)
ロマンス romance (2)

わ／ワ

〜わ（〜羽） counter for birds (2)
わ part., f. sentence-final emphatic particle (4)
わあ interj. wow! (GS3)
ワイシャツ dress shirt (7)
ワイン wine (GS2)
わかい（若い） i-adj. young (2)
わがまま（な） na-adj. selfish, egoistic (5)
わかる C1, intr. to understand (GS1)
わしょく（和食） Japanese cuisine (6)
わすれる（忘れる） C2, tr. to forget (5)
ワセリン Vaseline (7)
わた（綿） cotton tufts, plant (7)
わたし（私） pron. I, me (GS1); わたしたち
 （私たち） pron., pl. we (1); わたしの（私の） pron.
 my (GS1)
わふく（和服） Japanese-style clothes (7)
わらう（笑う） C1, tr. to laugh, smile (3)
わりびき（する）（割引［する］） n.v. discount; to discount (7)
わる（割る） C1, tr. to divide (GS2)
わるい（悪い） intr. bad (2)
ワンピース dress (7)

を

を part. direct-object marker (GS1)

English-Japanese Glossary

Abbreviations used in this glossary are explained at the beginning of the Japanese-English Glossary.

A

about, approximately　～くらい、～ぐらい　(4)
academic major; major in　（専攻[する]）せんこう（する）*n.v.* (1)
academic subject　（学科）がっか　(2)
accessory, jewelry　アクセサリー　(7)
according to...　～によると；（～の話では）～のはなしでは　(7)
across from　（向かい）むかい　(2)
action movie　（アクション映画）アクションえいが　(2)
activity; engage in activity　（活動[する]）かつどう（する）*n.v.* (5)
add　（足す）たす　*C1, tr.* (GS2)
address　（住所）じゅうしょ　(1)
administration office　（事務室）じむしつ　(1)
adopted child　（養子）ようし　(5)
adult　（大人）おとな　(6)
adult education center　カルチャーセンター　(5)
advertisement　（広告）こうこく　(7)
aerobics　エアロビクス　(3)
Africa　アフリカ　*p.n.* (6)
after...　（後）あと；after that（その後）そのあと　(3)
after all　やはり　(4)
afternoon　（午後）ごご　(GS2)
again　また　*adv.* (GS1)
age, year　（年）とし　(1)
age　（年齢）ねんれい　(1)
aged people　（年寄り）としより　(5)
ahh　ああ　*interj.* (2)
air pressure　（気圧）きあつ　(4)
all　（全て）すべて　(5)；（全～）ぜん～　(7)；（全部）ぜんぶ　(5)
all day long　（一日中）いちにちじゅう　(GS3)
all items　（全品）ぜんぴん　(7)
all of them　どれも　(5)
all the way　ずっと　*adv.* (4)
all you can drink　（飲み放題）のみほうだい　(6)
all you can eat　（バイキング料理）バイキングりょうり　(6)
almost　ほとんど　*adv.* (3)
a lot, much, many　たくさん　(2)
already　もう　*adv.* (GS1)
although　けど　*conj. coll.*；けれども　*conj.* (7)
always　いつも　*adv.* (2)
A.M. (morning)　（午前）ごぜん　(GS2)
amateur　アマ　(5)
America　アメリカ　*p.n.*；American（アメリカ人）アメリカじん　(1)
amount of money　（金額）きんがく　(7)
and (*emphatic*)　し　(7)
and　と　*part.* (GS3)
and so on　や　*part.* (3)
and so on, etc.　など　(6)
and, and then　そして　*conj.* (3)
and then, after that　それから　(3)

announcement　（知らせ）しらせ　(5)
annoying　うるさい　*i-adj.* (2)　（迷惑[な]）めいわく（な）*na-adj.* (5)
answer　（答）こたえ　(5)；（答える）こたえる　*C2, intr.* (3)
anthropology　（人類学）じんるいがく　(1)
antique　（骨董品）こっとうひん　(5)
any of them　どれでも　(5)
anyone　だれでも；どなたでも　*pol.* (5)
anything　（何でも）なんでも　(5)
anything, nothing　（何も）なにも　(3)
anytime　いつでも　(5)
anywhere　どこでも　(5)
apartment　アパート　(GS3)
appetizer　（前菜）ぜんさい　(6)
apple　りんご　(6)；apple pie　アップルパイ　(7)
application form　（申込書）もうしこみしょ　(5)
appropriate, as you like it　よろしく　(GS1)
approximately (*amount, extent*)　～くらい、～ぐらい　(4)
approximately (*time*)　（頃）ころ、ごろ　(GS3)
April　（四月）しがつ　(1)
apron　エプロン　(5)
Arabic language　（アラビア語）アラビアご　(4)
area　（面積）めんせき　(2)
around (*location*)　（回り）まわり　(2)
art　（美術）びじゅつ　(1)；art museum（美術館）びじゅつかん　(2)
as much as, about　ほど　(3)
ask; listen　（聞く）きく　*C1, tr.* (GS1)
ask; request　（頼む）たのむ　*C1, tr.* (6)
ask; inquire　（伺う）うかがう　*C1, tr.* (5)
asparagus　アスパラガス　(5)
aspirin　アスピリン　(7)
astringent　（渋い）しぶい　*i-adj.* (6)
at, by　で　*part.* (2)
at, in　に　*part.* (GS3)
athlete　スポーツせんしゅ　(5)
attractive　きれい（な）*na-adj.* (2)
August　（八月）はちがつ　(1)
aunt　おば；おばさん　*pol.* (5)
Australia　オーストラリア　*p.n.* (GS2)
autumn　（秋）あき；autumn rain（秋雨）あきさめ　(4)
avenue　（通り）とおり　(2)
average　（平均）へいきん　(4)
awful, awesome, very　すごい　*i-adj.* (5)

B

back　（後ろ）うしろ　(2)
bad　（悪い）わるい　*i-adj.* (2)
bad at and dislike　（苦手[な]）にがて（な）*na-adj.* (5)
badminton　バドミントン　(5)
bag　（鞄）かばん　(GS1)
bagel　ベーゲル　(7)
bakery　（パン屋）パンや　(7)

balance　バランス　*(6)*
ball　ボール　*(2)*
ball-point pen　ボールペン　*(GS1)*
banana　バナナ　*(2)*
Band-Aid　バンドエイド　*(7)*
bank　（銀行）ぎんこう　*(GS2)*
barbershop　（床屋）とこや　*(5)*
bargain, haggle over price　（値切る）ねぎる　*C1, tr.*　*(7)*
bargain sale　セール、バーゲンセール　*(7)*
baseball　（野球）やきゅう　*(GS3)*
basketball　バスケットボール　*(5)*
bath　（お風呂）おふろ　*(3)*
bathe　（浴びる）あびる　*C2, tr.*　*(GS3)*
bathing suit　（水着）みずぎ　*(7)*
bathroom　トイレ　*(2)*
BBQ　バーベキュー　*(6)*
be (copula, plain)　だ　*(3)*
be (copula, polite)　です　*(1)*
be …ing　いる　*(with te-form of verbs)*　*C1*　*(5)*
be able to, can　（出来る）できる　*C2, intr.*;
　　ことができる　*(with dictionary form of verb)*　*(5)*
bean　（豆）まめ　*(6)*
beard　ひげ　*(5)*
beautiful　（美しい）うつくしい　*i-adj.*　*(4)*
beauty parlor　（美容院）びよういん　*(7)*
because, and so　から　*part.*　*(1)*; ので　*(4)*
become, turn into　なる　*C1, intr.*　*(4)*
beef　（牛肉）ぎゅうにく　*(6)*
beer　ビール　*(GS2)*
before long　（間もなく）まもなく　*(7)*
behind, back　（後ろ）うしろ　*(2)*
Beijing　ペキン　*p.n.*　*(4)*
believe　（信じる）しんじる　*C2, tr.*　*(3)*
belt　ベルト　*(7)*
below　（下）した　*(2)*
bench　ベンチ　*(2)*
best　（一番）いちばん　*(4)*
between　（間）あいだ; between A and B
　　（AとBの間に）　*(2)*
beverage　（飲み物）のみもの　*(GS3)*
bicycle　（自転車）じてんしゃ　*(2)*
bill, invoice　（請求書）せいきゅうしょ　*(7)*
biology　（生物学）せいぶつがく　*(1)*
bird　（鳥）とり　*(2)*
birth date　（生年月日）せいねんがっぴ　*(1)*
birthday　（誕生日）たんじょうび　*(3)*
birthday cake　バースデー・ケーキ　*(4)*; birthday gift
　　バースデー・プレゼント　*(3)*
bit, a bit　（少し）すこし　*adv.*　*(3)*; ちょっと
　　adv.　*(GS1)*
bitter　（苦い）にがい　*i-adj.*　*(6)*
black　（黒）くろ／（黒い）くろい　*i-adj.*　*(7)*
black-and-white photo(graphy)　（白黒写真）
　　しろくろしゃしん　*(5)*
black tea　（紅茶）こうちゃ　*(6)*
blazer, jacket　ブレザー　*(7)*
bloom　（咲く）さく　*C1, intr.*　*(4)*
blouse　ブラウス　*(5)*
blow, play *(wind instrument)*　（吹く）ふく　*C1, tr.*　*(5)*
blow *(wind)*　（吹く）ふく; *C1, intr.*　*(4)*
blue　（青）あお、ブルー;（青い）あおい　*i-adj.*　*(7)*
boat　ボート　*(5)*
body　（体）からだ　*(4)*
bodyguard　ボディーガード　*(5)*

boil　（煮る）にる　*C2, tr.*　*(6)*
bonsai　（盆栽）ぼんさい　*(5)*
book　（本）ほん　*(GS1)*; bookstore　（本屋）
　　ほんや　*(6)*
boot　ブーツ　*(7)*
boring　つまらない　*i-adj.*　*(2)*; become bored, get tired of
　　（飽きる）あきる　*C2, intr.*　*(6)*
born (be born)　（生まれる）うまれる　*C2, intr.*　*(1)*
borrow　（借りる）かりる　*C2, tr.*　*(7)*
both　どちらも　*(5)*
bottle opener　（栓抜き）せんぬき　*(6)*
bouquet　ブーケ　*(7)*
boutique　ブティック　*(5)*
bowling　ボーリング　*(5)*
box　（箱）はこ　*(2)*
boxing　ボクシング　*(GS2)*
box lunch　（弁当）べんとう　*(6)*
boy　（男の子）おとこのこ　*(5)*
boyfriend　ボーイフレンド　*(2)*
bracelet　ブレスレット　*(7)*
brassiere　ブラジャー　*(7)*
Brazil　ブラジル; Brazilian person　（ブラジル人）
　　ブラジルじん　*p.n.*　*(1)*
bread　パン　*(6)*
breakfast　（朝ごはん）あさごはん　*(GS2)*;（朝食）
　　ちょうしょく　*(6)*
briefs　パンツ　*(7)*
bright, well-lighted　（明るい）あかるい　*i-adj.*　*(4)*
broccoli　ブロッコリ　*(GS2)*
broil　（焼く）やく　*C1, tr.*　*(6)*
broken (become broken)　（壊れる）こわれる　*C2, intr.*　*(7)*
brooch, pin　ブローチ　*(7)*
brothers　（兄弟）きょうだい　*(5)*
brown　（茶色）ちゃいろ;（茶色い）ちゃいろい　*i-adj.*　*(7)*
brunch　ブランチ　*(3)*
brush　（磨く）みがく　*C1, tr.*; brush teeth　（歯を磨く）
　　はをみがく　*(3)*
brush calligraphy　（書道）しょどう　*(5)*
building　（建物）たてもの　*(2)*; ビル　*(1)*
bullet train　（新幹線）しんかんせん　*(3)*
bus　バス　*(2)*
bus stop　（停留所）ていりゅうじょ;（バス停）
　　バスてい　*(2)*
business; do business　ビジネス（する）　*n.v.*　*(3)*
business hour　（営業時間）えいぎょうじかん　*(6)*
busy　（忙しい）いそがしい　*i-adj.*　*(2)*
but　しかし　*conj.*　*(3)*
but, and　が　*conj.*　*(3)*
but, even so　でも　*conj.*　*(4)*
butcher shop　（肉屋）にくや　*(7)*
butter　バター　*(6)*
button　ボタン　*(7)*
buy　（買う）かう　*C1, tr.*　*(3)*
by means of, at　で　*part.*　*(2)*
by the way, well…　さて　*conj.*　*(4)*

C

cabbage　キャベツ　*(7)*
cafeteria　カフェテリア　*(1)*
cake　ケーキ　*(6)*; cake shop　（ケーキ屋）ケーキや　*(7)*
calculation, bill; tally, calculate　（勘定[する]）かんじょう
　　（する）　*n.v.*　*(6)*

calculator　（電卓）でんたく　(7)

calendar　カレンダー　(4)

calm (ocean, personality)　おだやか（な）　*na-adj.*　(4)

camera　カメラ　(GS3)；　camera shop
（カメラ店／カメラ屋）カメラてん／カメラや　(7)

camping　キャンピング　(5)；　camp; go camping
キャンプ（する）　*n.v.*　(4)

campus　キャンパス　(1)

can, be able to　ことができる　(*with dictionary form
of verb*)　(5)

can be heard　（聞こえる）きこえる　*C2, intr.*　(5)

can be seen　（見える）みえる　*C2, intr.*　(5)

can opener　（缶切り）かんきり　(6)

Canada　カナダ　*p.n.*　(GS2)；　Canadian　（カナダ人）
カナダじん　(1)

canned food　（缶詰）かんづめ　(6)

cap　（帽子）ぼうし　(7)

car　（車）くるま　(1)

card　カード；　card game　トランプ　(5)

care; take care of　（世話［する］）せわ（する）　*n.v.*　(5)

careful (be careful)　（気をつける）きをつける　(4)

carnation　カーネーション　(7)

carrot　（人参）にんじん　(6)

cartoon　（漫画）まんが　(7)

case　ケース　(7)

cash　（現金）げんきん　(7)

cash register, cashier　レジ　(7)

casual　カジュアル（な）　*na-adj.*　(7)

cat　（猫）ねこ　(5)

catalogue　カタログ　(7)

catch a cold　（風邪をひく）かぜをひく　(4)

CD (compact disk)　シーディー　(7)

ceiling　（天井）てんじょう　(GS1)

celebrity　（有名人）ゆうめいじん　(6)

cell (mobile) phone　（携帯電話）けいたいでんわ　(2)

centigrade　（摂氏）せっし　(4)

certainly, at your service　かしこまりました　(6)

chair　（椅子）いす　(GS1)

chalk　チョーク；　chalkboard　（黒板）こくばん；
chalkboard eraser　（黒板消し）こくばんけし
(GS1)

champagne　シャンペン　(6)

change (money)　（お釣り）おつり　(7)

change　（変える）かえる　*C2, tr.*　(3)

change clothes　（着替える）きがえる　*C2, tr.*　(3)

cheap, inexpensive　（安い）やすい　*i-adj.*　(2)

check (*pattern*)　チェック　(7)

cheerful, bright　（明るい）あかるい　*i-adj.*　(4)

cheerful (*mood*)　（陽気）ようき（な）　(4)

cheese　チーズ　(6)；　cheeseburger　チーズバーガー
(GS5)；　cheesecake　チーズケーキ　(6)

chef　シェフ　(6)

chemistry　（化学）かがく　(1)

cherry blossom　（桜）さくら；　cherry blossom viewing
（花見）はなみ　(4)

chess　チェス　(5)

chicken　（鳥肉）とりにく　(6)

child　（お子さん）おこさん　*pol.*　(5)；　（子）こ　(4)；
（子供）こども　(5)

China　（中国）ちゅうごく　*p.n.*　(1)

Chinese language　（中国語）ちゅうごくご；　Chinese person
（中国人）ちゅうごくじん　(1)

Chinese food　（中華料理）ちゅうかりょうり　(6)

chocolate　チョコレート　(GS5)

choose　（選ぶ）えらぶ　*C1, tr.*　(5)

chopsticks　（箸）はし　(6)

church　（教会）きょうかい　(2)

circle, activity group　サークル　(5)

citizen　（国民）こくみん　(3)

city　（市）し　(2)

class　クラス　(GS2)

classical music　クラシック　(GS2)；　（クラシック音楽）
クラシックおんがく　(5)

classmate　クラスメート　(1)

classroom　（教室）きょうしつ　(GS1)

clean　きれい（な）　*na-adj.*　(2)

cleaning; to clean (*house*)　（掃除［する］）そうじ（する）
n.v.　(3)

clear weather　（晴れ）はれ；　clear up　（晴れる）はれる　*C2,
intr.*　(4)

cleaver, big cutting knife　（包丁）ほうちょう　(6)

climate　（気候）きこう　(4)

clock, watch　（時計）とけい　(GS3)

close (*book, box, etc.*)　（閉じる）とじる　*C2, tr.*
(GS1)

close (*door, window, etc.*)　（閉める）しめる　*C2, tr.*　(3)

close, near　（近い）ちかい　*i-adj.*　(GS3)

clothes　（衣服）いふく　(7)；　（服）ふく　(3)；　（服装）
ふくそう　(7)

cloud　（雲）くも；　cloudy　（曇り）くもり；　become cloudy
（曇る）くもる　*C1, intr.*　(4)

club　クラブ　(5)

coat　コート　(4)

cocktail　カクテル　(GS2)

coffee　コーヒー　(GS2)；　coffeemaker
コーヒーメーカー　(6)

coffee shop　（喫茶店）きっさてん　(2)

cola　コーラ　(GS2)

cold, flu　（風邪）かぜ　(4)

cold　（寒い）さむい　*i-adj.*　(GS4)

collect　（集める）あつめる　*C2, tr.*　(5)

color　（色）いろ　(7)

color photo(graphy)　（カラー写真）カラーしゃしん　(5)

comb　とかす　*C1, tr.*　(3)

combine　（組み合せる）くみあわせる　*C2, tr.*　(7)

come　（来る）くる　*C3, intr.*　(3)；　come to…
（に来る）にくる　(7)

comedy　コメディ　(2)

coming to Japan; come to Japan　（来日［する］）
らいにち（する）　*n.v.*　(7)

commemoration; commemorate　（記念［する］）
きねん（する）　*n.v.*　(7)

commute　（通う）かよう　*C1, intr.*　(6)

company　（会社）かいしゃ　(3)；　company worker
（会社員）かいしゃいん　(5)

complete…　〜てしまう　(6)；　be completed　（出来る）
できる　*C2, intr.*　(5)

computer game　コンピューターゲーム　(5)

computer science　コンピュータ・サイエンス　(1)

concert　コンサート　(5)

confectionery shop　（お菓子屋）おかしや　(7)

consommé　コンソメ　(6)

continue　（続く）つづく　*C1, intr.*　(4)

convenience store　コンビニ　(7)

convenient　（便利［な］）べんり（な）　*na-adj.*　(2)

conversation　（会話）かいわ　(5)

convey　（伝える）つたえる　*C2, tr.*　(6)

cook, make　（作る）つくる　*C1, tr.*　(GS1)

五百三十一

cooking; cook （料理［する］）りょうり（する）
n.v. (GS1)

cook, chef コック (6)

cooking oil クッキング・オイル; cooking school
クッキング・スクール (6)

cool （涼しい）すずしい i-adj. (GS4)

corner （角）かど (6)

cosmetics （化粧品）けしょうひん; cosmetics store
（化粧品店）けしょうひんてん (7)

cost かかる C1, intr. (3)

cotton fabric （綿）めん (7); コットン (1)

cotton plant, tuft （綿）わた (7)

counters for noun categories: number of photos on film
（〜枚取り）〜まいどり (7); age （〜歳）〜さい
(1); birds （〜羽）〜わ; books, notebooks （〜冊）
〜さつ; duration in minutes （〜分）、（〜分間）
〜ふん、〜ふんかん (2); duration in months （〜
月間）〜げつかん (3); flat, thin items （〜枚）〜ま
い (2); floors of a building （〜階）〜かい (1);
frequency （〜回）〜かい (GS3); frequency
（〜度）〜ど; glassfuls or cupfuls （〜杯）〜はい;
hours （〜時間）〜じかん; houses, buildings （〜軒）
〜けん; jackets, clothes （〜着）〜ちゃく; large
animals （〜頭）〜とう; lessons, courses （〜課）
〜か; long and often cylindrical items （〜本）
〜ほん; machines （〜台）〜だい (2); months
（〜ヶ月）〜かげつ (1); multiples (times) （〜倍）
〜ばい; people （〜人）〜にん; shoes, socks
（〜足）〜そく; small animals （〜匹）〜ひき (2);
counter for temperature （〜度）〜ど (4); weeks
（〜週間）〜しゅうかん (3)

country （国）くに (1)

country and western music カントリーウエスタン (2)

cousin いとこ; おいとこさん pol. (5)

cream, lotion クリーム (6)

cream color （クリーム色）クリームいろ (7)

credit card クレジット・カード (2)

croissant クロワッサン (7)

crowded (get crowded) （混む）こむ C1, intr. (5)

cry （泣く）なく C1, intr. (3)

cucumber きゅうり (6)

cuisine （料理）りょうり (GS1)

culture （文化）ぶんか (1)

curry カレー (6); curry and rice カレーライス (2)

curtain カーテン (GS1)

customer, guest （お客さん）おきゃくさん pol. (2);
（客）きゃく (7)

cut （切る）きる C1, tr. (3)

cute, pretty かわいい i-adj. (5)

cute キュート（な）na-adj. (2)

cuttlefish （烏賊）いか (6)

cycling; to cycle サイクリング（する）n.v. (5)

D

dance （踊る）おどる C1, tr. (3); ダンス (5)

dangerous （危険［な］）きけん（な）na-adj. (5)

dark, badly lighted （暗い）くらい i-adj. (4)

dark (color) （濃い）こい (7)

dark blue （藍色）あいいろ; ダークブルー (7)

date; go on a date デート（する）(GS2)

daughter, girl （娘）むすめ; （お嬢さん）おじょうさん
pol.; （娘さん）むすめさん pol. (5)

day after tomorrow あさって (4)

day before yesterday おととい (GS4)

day off （休暇）きゅうか; （休日）きゅうじつ; （休み）
やすみ; （休みの日）やすみのひ (3)

daytime （昼間）ひるま (4)

Dear… (used at the beginning of a letter) （拝啓）
はいけい (4)

December （十二月）じゅうにがつ (1)

decide on… 〜にする (6)

deepen （深める）ふかめる C2, tr. (5)

delicious, tasty おいしい i-adj. (3)

delivery; deliver （配達［する］）はいたつ（する）
n.v. (7)

department (academic) （学部）がくぶ (1)

department store デパート (GS2)

deposit; to deposit （貯金［する］）ちょきん（する）
n.v. (7)

design; to design デザイン（する）n.v.;
designer デザイナー; designer brand
デザイナー・ブランド (7)

desk （机）つくえ (GS1)

dessert デザート (6)

dew （露）つゆ (4)

diamond ダイヤ (6)

dictionary （辞書）じしょ (GS1)

die （死ぬ）しぬ C1, intr. (4)

diet ダイエット (6)

dietician （栄養士）えいようし (6)

differ （違う）ちがう C1, intr. (GS1)

difficult （難しい）むずかしい i-adj. (2); be in difficulty,
have trouble こまる C1, intr. (4)

difficult to… 〜にくい (with conjunctive form of verbs)
i-adj. (7)

dining hall （食堂）しょくどう (2)

dining out; to dine out （外食［する］）がいしょく（する）
n.v. (6)

dinner, evening meal （夕ごはん）ゆうごはん (3);
（夕食）ゆうしょく (6); （晩ごはん）ばんごはん
(GS2)

dirty, filthy （汚い）きたない i-adj. (2)

disco ディスコ (3)

discount; to discount （割引［する］）わりびき（する）
n.v. (7)

discourtesy; be discourteous, excuse oneself
（失礼［する］）しつれい（する）n.v. (GS1)

discover （見つける）みつける C2, tr. (6)

disgusting （嫌［な］）いや（な）na-adj. (4)

dish （皿）さら (6)

dislike （嫌い［な］）きらい（な）na-adj. (GS2)

district number （〜丁目）〜ちょうめ (2)

divide （割る）わる C1, tr. (GS2)

diving; to dive ダイビング（する）n.v. (5); diver
ダイバー (7)

do （致す）いたす C1, tr., pol. (4); する C3, tr. (GS3)

do and come 〜てくる (6)

do and leave 〜ていく (6)

dog （犬）いぬ (2)

door ドア (GS1)

dormitory （寮）りょう (GS5)

down （下）した (2)

downpour of rain （土砂降り）どしゃぶり (4)

draw （描く）かく C1, tr.; draw a picture （絵を描く）
えをかく (5)

dream （夢）ゆめ (7)

dress, clothing （服装）ふくそう (7)

dress　ドレス、ワンピース　(7)
dress shirt　ワイシャツ　(7)
drink　(飲む)　のむ　C1, tr.　(GS3)
driving; drive　(運転[する])　うんてん(する)　n.v.;
　　ドライブ(する)　(3)
drizzle　(時雨)　しぐれ　(4)
drop　(落とす)　おとす　C1, tr.　(6)
drought　(日照り)　ひでり　(4)
drugstore　(薬屋)　くすりや　(7)
dry cleaners　(クリーニング屋)　クリーニングや;
　　dry cleaning　ドライ・クリーニング　(7)

E

early, quick　(早い、速い)　はやい　i-adj.　(GS3);
　　(早く、速く)　はやく　adv.　(4)
early summer rain　(五月雨)　さみだれ　(4)
earring　イヤリング　(7)
east　(東)　ひがし　(2)
easy　(簡単[な])　かんたん(な)　na-adj.　(5);
　　やさしい　i-adj.　(2)
easy to...　～やすい　(with conjunctive form of verb)
　　i-adj.　(7)
eat　(食べる)　たべる　C2, tr.　(GS3);　I will eat now (said
　　before eating)　いただきます　(6)
economics　(経済学)　けいざいがく　(1)
edge　はじ　(2)
education (academic subject)　(教育学)
　　きょういくがく　(1)
education　(教養)　きょうよう　(5)
effectively　(有効に)　ゆうこうに　(5)
egg　(卵)　たまご;　egg dish　(卵料理)　たまごりょうり;
　　egg salad　エッグサラダ　(6)
egoistic　わがまま(な)　na-adj.　(5)
eight　(八)　はち　(GS2);　(八つ)　やっつ　(2)
eighth day　(八日)　ようか　(3)
eighty　(八十)　はちじゅう　(GS5)
either　どちらか　(5)
electric appliance store　(電気店)　でんきてん　(7)
electrician　(電気工)　でんきこう　(7)
electricity　(電気)　でんき　(GS1)
electric train　(電車)　でんしゃ　(2)
elegant　エレガント(な)　na-adj.　(2)
elevator　エレベーター　(1)
eleventh day　(十一日)　じゅういちにち　(3)
embroidery; embroider　(刺繍[する])　ししゅう(する)
　　n.v.　(5)
emperor　(天皇)　てんのう　(3)
end, finish　(終わる)　おわる　C1, intr.　(3)
engineer　エンジニア　(1)
engineering　(工学)　こうがく;　engineering department
　　(工学部)　こうがくぶ　(1)
England　イギリス　p.n.　(1)
English language　(英語)　えいご　(1);　English writing
　　(英文)　えいぶん　(5);　English person　(イギリス人)
　　イギリスじん　(1)
enjoy　(楽しむ)　たのしむ　C1, tr.　(5)
enter　(入る)　はいる　C1, intr.　(3)
entertainment　(娯楽)　ごらく　(5)
entry level; begin　(入門[する])　にゅうもん(する)
　　n.v.　(5)
envy; to envy, be jealous　(嫉妬[する])　しっと(する)　n.v.　(7)
era　(年号)　ねんごう　(3)
eraser　(消しゴム)　けしゴム　(GS1)

errand　(用事)　ようじ　(3)
especially　(特に)　とくに　adv.　(GS2)
evening　(夕方)　ゆうがた　(GS2);　evening shower
　　(夕立)　ゆうだち　(4)
evening snack　(夜食)　やしょく　(6)
event; item　(種目)　しゅもく　(5)
every　(毎～)　まい～;　every day　(毎日)　まいにち
　　(GS4);　every month　(毎月)　まいつき　(3);
　　every morning　(毎朝)　まいあさ　(GS3);　every night
　　(毎晩)　まいばん;　every week　(毎週)　まいしゅう　(3)
everyday life　(日常生活)　にちじょうせいかつ　(3)
everyone　(誰でも)　だれでも、(誰も)　だれも;
　　(皆さん)　みなさん　pol.　(5);　(皆)　みんな、みな　(3)
everywhere　どこでも、どこも　(5)
examination　(試験[する])　しけん(する)　n.v.　(3)
excuse me, well...　あのう...　(1)
excuse me　すみません　(GS1)
exercise; to do exercise　(運動[する])　うんどう(する)
　　n.v.　(GS2)
exist (animate things)　いる　C1, intr.　(2)
expensive, high　(高い)　たかい　i-adj.　(2)
eyeglasses　(眼鏡)　めがね;　put on eyeglasses　(眼鏡をかける)
　　めがねをかける　(7)

F

face　(顔)　かお　(3)
facing　(向かい)　むかい　(2)
fact　こと　(5)
fall (rain and snow)　(降る)　ふる　C1, intr.　(4)
fall, autumn　(秋)　あき　(4)
Fahrenheit　(華氏)　かし　(4)
family　(家族)　かぞく;　(御家族)　ごかぞく　pol.　(5)
famous　(有名[な])　ゆうめい(な)　na-adj.　(2)
far away　(遠い)　とおい　i-adj.　(GS3)
fashion　ファッション　(5);　fashion model　モデル;
　　fashion show　ファッション・ショー　(7)
fast, early　(早い、速い)　はやい　i-adj.　(GS3)
fast food　ファーストフード;　fast-food restaurant
　　ファーストフード・レストラン　(6)
fat (get fat)　(太る)　ふとる　C1, intr.　(6)
father　(お父さん)　おとうさん　pol.;　(父)　ちち　(5)
favorite, greatly liked　(大好き[な])　だいすき(な)
　　na-adj.　(2)
fax　ファックス　(1)
February　(二月)　にがつ　(1)
female student　(女子学生)　じょしがくせい　(5)
few　(少ない)　すくない　i-adj.　(2);　(少なく)
　　すくなく　adv.　(6)
fifteenth day　(十五日)　じゅうごにち　(3)
fifth day　(五日)　いつか　(3)
fifty　(五十)　ごじゅう　(GS5)
film　フィルム　(1)
find　(見つける)　みつける　C2, tr.　(6)
finish, end　(終わる)　おわる　C1, intr.　(3)
finish ...ing　～しまう　(with te-form of verb)　C1, tr.　(6)
first　(最初)　さいしょ　adv.　(7)
first; first of all　(初めに)　はじめに　(6)
first-class　(高級[な])　こうきゅう(な)　na-adj.　(7)
first day　(一日)　ついたち　(3)
first of all, to begin with　まず　(3)
first year (in era)　(元年)　がんねん　(3)
fish　(魚)　さかな　(GS2);　catch fish　(魚を釣る)
　　さかなをつる　(5);　fish store　(魚屋)　さかなや　(7)

fish burger　フィッシュバーガー　(GS3)
fishing　(釣り) つり　(4)
fit; to fit　フィット (する)　n.v.　(7)
fitting room　(試着室) しちゃくしつ　(7)
five　(五つ) いつつ　(2)；(五) ご　(GS2)
flood　(洪水) こうずい　(4)
floor　(床) ゆか　(GS1)
floor space　(面積) めんせき　(2)
flower　(花) はな　(4)；flower arranging　(生け花)
　いけばな　(5)；flower shop　(花屋) はなや　(7)
flute　フルート　(5)
fly　(飛ぶ) とぶ　C1, intr.　(3)
fog　(霧) きり　(4)
food　(食べ物) たべもの；food store　(食べ物屋)
　たべものや；foodstuffs　(食料品) しょくりょうひん　(6)
football　フットボール　(5)
foreign languages　(外国語) がいこくご　(1)
foreign student　(留学生) りゅうがくせい　(7)
forget　(忘れる) わすれる　C2, tr.　(5)
fork　フォーク　(3)
formal, ceremonious, stiff　(堅苦しい) かたくるしい
　i-adj.　(7)
formal　フォーマル (な)　na-adj.　(7)
forty　(四十) よんじゅう　(GS5)
fountain pen　(万年筆) まんねんひつ　(1)
four　(四) し、よん　(GS2)；(四つ) よっつ　(2)
four seasons　(四季) しき　(4)
fourteenth day　(十四日) じゅうよっか　(3)
fourth day　(四日) よっか　(3)
France　フランス　p.n.；French language (フランス語)
　フランスご；French person　(フランス人)
　フランスじん　(1)
free, not busy　(暇[な]) ひま (な)　na-adj.　(3)；free time
　(余暇) よか　(5)
free of charge　(無料) むりょう　(6)
French bread　フランス・パン　(7)
French fries　フレンチフライ　(GS3)
Friday　(金曜日) きんようび　(GS4)
friend　(友だち) ともだち　(GS3)
from　から　part.　(1)
front　(前) まえ　(2)
frost　(霜) しも　(4)
frozen food　(冷凍食品) れいとうしょくひん　(6)
fruit　(果物) くだもの　(GS1)；fruit salad
　フルーツ・サラダ　(6)；fruit store (果物屋)
　くだものや　(7)
fry　(揚げる) あげる　C2, tr.　(6)
frying pan　フライパン　(6)
full capacity　(満員) まんいん　(6)
fun　(面白い) おもしろい　i-adj.；(楽しい)
　たのしい　i-adj.　(2)
funny　おかしい　i-adj.　(2)；おかし (な)　na-adj.　(6)
fur　(毛皮) けがわ　(7)
furniture store　(家具屋) かぐや　(7)
futon store　(布団屋) ふとんや　(7)

G

gambling; gamble　ギャンブル [する]　n.v.　(5)
game, match; play a match　(試合 [する]) しあい [する]
　n.v.　(5)
gardening　(園芸) えんげい　(5)
gas station　ガソリン・スタンド　(2)
gate　(門) もん　(3)

gather　(集める) あつめる　C2, tr.　(5)
gaudy, brightly colored　(派手[な]) はで (な)　na-adj.　(2)
general education subject　(教養科目) きょうようかもく　(1)
gentle (breeze)　おだやか (な)　na-adj.　(4)
Germany　ドイツ　p.n.；German language　(ドイツ語)
　ドイツご；German person　(ドイツ人) ドイツじん　(1)
get off, get down　(降りる) おりる　C2, intr.　(3)
get up　(起きる) おきる　C2, int.　(GS3)
gift　ギフト　(3)
girl　(女の子) おんなのこ　(5)
girlfriend　ガールフレンド　(1)
glass, cup　コップ　(6)
gloomy　(陰気[な]) いんき (な)　na-adj.　(4)
glove　(手袋) てぶくろ　(7)
go　(行く) いく　C1, intr.　(GS3)
go back, return　(帰る) かえる　C1, intr.　(GS3)
go out, come out, leave　(出る) でる　C2, intr.；
　(出かける) でかける　C2, intr.　(3)
go to…　(～に行く) ～にいく　(7)
go to bed　(寝る) ねる　C1, intr.　(GS3)
gold color　(金色) きんいろ　(7)
goldfish　(金魚) きんぎょ　(5)
golf　ゴルフ　(4)
good　いい　i-adj.　(GS1)
good, satisfactory　(結構[な]) けっこう (な)　na-adj.　(GS5)
good afternoon　こんにちは　(GS1)
good at, skillful　(上手[な]) じょうず (な)　na-adj.　(5)
good at and like, forte　(得意[な]) とくい (な)　na-adj.　(5)
good-bye　さよ (う) なら　(GS1)
good enough, OK　(大丈夫[な]) だいじょうぶ (な)
　na-adj.　(GS4)
good evening　こんばんは　(GS1)
good-looking, stylish　かっこういい　i-adj.　(5)
good morning　おはよう　(GS1)
good night　おやすみなさい　(GS1)
goods　(商品) しょうひん　(7)
gospel music　ゴスペル　(2)
graduate student　(大学院生) だいがくいんせい　(1)
grandchild　(お孫さん) おまごさん　pol.；
　(孫) まご　(5)
grandfather　(祖父) そふ；おじいさん　pol.　(5)
grandmother　(祖母) そぼ；おばあさん　pol.　(5)
grape　(葡萄) ぶどう　(6)；グレープ　(GS5)
gray　(灰色) はいいろ；グレー　(7)
green　(緑) みどり；グリーン　(7)
greengrocer　(八百屋) やおや　(7)
green pepper　ピーマン　(6)
green tea　(緑茶) りょくちゃ　(6)
greeting; greet someone　(挨拶[する]) あいさつ [する]
　n.v.　(3)
grill　(焼く) やく　C1, tr.　(6)
grocery store　(食料品店) しょくりょうひんてん　(7)
guest, customer　(お客さん) おきゃくさん　(2)
guidebook　ガイドブック　(7)
guitar　ギター　(5)
gym　(体育館) たいいくかん　(1)；ジム　(5)
gymnastics　(体操) たいそう　(5)

H

hail　あられ　(4)
hair　(髪) かみ　(3)；hairstyle　ヘアースタイル　(5)
half　(半) はん　(GS2)；(半分) はんぶん；half price
　(半額) はんがく　(7)

ham　ハム　(6)

hamburger　ハンバーガー　(GS3)

hammer　ハンマー　(7)

handicrafts　(手芸) しゅげい　(5)

handkerchief　ハンカチ　(7)

handsome　かっこういい　*i-adj.*　(5)；　ハンサム (な) *na-adj.*　(2)

hardware store　(金物屋) かなものや　(7)

hat　(帽子) ぼうし　(7)

hate, dislike intensely　(大嫌い [な]) だいきらい (な) *na-adj.*　(2)

have, hold　(持つ) もつ　*C1, tr.*　(3)

he　(彼) かれ　*pron.*　(1)

head　(頭) あたま　(7)

health　(健康) けんこう；　healthy　(健康 [な]) けんこう (な) *na-adj.*　(2)

healthy, energetic　(元気 [な]) げんき (な) *na-adj.*　(4)

hear, inquire　(伺う) うかがう　*C1, tr., pol.*　(5)

hear, ask　(聞く) きく　*C1, tr.*　(GS1)

heavy　(重い) おもい　*i-adj.*　(2)

hello (*answering the telephone*)　もしもし　*interj.*　(2)

helmet　ヘルメット　(7)

help, assist　(手伝う) てつだう　*C1, tr.*　(3)

here　ここ、こちら　*dem. pron.*　(1)

high heel　ハイヒール　(7)

hiking　ハイキング　(4)

history (*study of*)　(歴史学) れきしがく　(1)

hit　(打つ) うつ　*C1, tr.*　(5)

hobby　(趣味) しゅみ　(5)

Holland　オランダ　*p.n.*　(2)

Hong Kong　(香港) ホンコン　*p.n.*；　Hong Kong native　(香港人) ホンコンじん　(1)

home　うち　(GS5)

hometown, native place　(出身) しゅっしん　(1)

homework　(宿題) しゅくだい　(4)

horseback riding　(乗馬) じょうば　(5)

hospital　(病院) びょういん　(2)

hot (*temperature*)　(暑い) あつい　*i-adj.*　(GS4)

hot, spicy　(辛い) からい　*i-adj.*　(6)

hot water　(お湯) おゆ　(6)

hotel　ホテル　(2)

house　(家) いえ　(1)　うち　(GS5)

household finance book　(家計簿) かけいぼ　(7)

housing, residence　(住まい) すまい　(1)

how　どう　*dem. adv.*；　どうして　(1)

how about　いかが　(GS5)

how many days　(何日) なんにち　(3)；　how many degrees　(何度) なんど　(4)；　how many floors　(何階) なんかい　(GS2)；　how many hours　(何時間) なんじかん　(3)；　how many minutes　(何分) なんぷん　(3)；　how many years　(何年) なんねん　(3)

how much, how many　いくつ　(1)；　いくら (*cost*)　(GS3)

how old　いくつ；　(何歳) なんさい　(1)

however, but　しかし　*conj.*　(3)

however much...　いくら　(GS3)

humidity　(湿度) しつど　(4)

hundred　(百) ひゃく　(GS5)

hundred million　(億) おく　(2)

hundred thousand　(十万) じゅうまん　(2)

hungry (get hungry)　おなかがすく　(3)

hunting　(狩り) かり；　ハンティング　(5)

husband　(夫) おっと；　(御主人) ごしゅじん　*pol.*；　(主人) しゅじん　(5)

I

I　あたし　*pron., inf., f.*；　(僕) ぼく　*pron., inf., m.*　(1)；　(私) わたし　*pron.*　(GS1)

ice　アイス　(GS5)

ice cream　アイスクリーム　(GS5)

ice milk　アイスミルク　(GS3)

ice tea　アイスティー　(GS2)

ID (identification)　(身分証明書) みぶんしょうめいしょ　(3)

idea　(考え) かんがえ　(6)

idle one's time away, loaf　ゴロゴロする　*C3, intr.*　(5)

if　～たら　(7)

immediately　すぐ、すぐに　*adv.*　(6)

impossible　(無理 [な]) むり (な)　*na-adj.*　(5)

in, inside　(中) なか　(2)

in, at, to　に　*part.*　(GS3)

in total　(全部で) ぜんぶで　*adv.*　(2)

in-law　(義理の) ぎりの　(5)

inconvenient　(不便 [な]) ふべん (な)　*na-adj.*　(2)

increase　(増える) ふえる　*C2, intr.*　(6)

indeed, thanks　どうも　(GS1)

ingredient　(材料) ざいりょう　(6)

ink　インキ　(7)

inquire, ask　(伺う) うかがう　*C1, tr.*　(5)

inside　うち　(GS3)

inside, center　(中) なか　(2)

installment payment system　(分割払い) ぶんかつばらい　(7)

instant food　インスタント・フード；　(インスタント食品) インスタントしょくひん　(6)

instant ramen　インスタント・ラーメン　(6)

intend to do...　(～ようと思う) ～ようとおもう　(*with verb root*)　(6)

intention　つもり　(7)

interesting, fun　(面白い) おもしろい　*i-adj.*　(2)

interview; to interview　インタビュー (する)　*n.v.*　(6)

introduction; introduce　(紹介 [する]) しょうかい (する)　*n.v.*；　self-introduction; introduce oneself　(自己紹介 [する]) じこしょうかい (する)　*n.v.*　(1)

introduction; beginning level　(入門) にゅうもん　(5)

investigation; investigate　(調査 [する]) ちょうさ (する)　*n.v.*　(5)

invite　(誘う) さそう　*C1, tr.*　(7)；　(呼ぶ) よぶ　*C1, tr.*　(6)

iron (*appliance*)　アイロン；　use an iron　アイロンをかける　(7)

issue, problem　(問題) もんだい　(4)

Italy　イタリア　*p.m.*；　Italian language　(イタリア語) イタリアご；　Italian person　(イタリア人) イタリアじん　(1)

Item, thing　もの　(2)

J

jacket　ジャケット；　jacket, suit coat　(上着) うわぎ　(7)

January　(一月) いちがつ　(1)

Japan　(日本) にほん　*p.n.*；　Japanese language　(日本語) にほんご　(GS1)；　Japanese cuisine　(和食) わしょく　(6)；　Japanese person　(日本人) にほんじん　(1)；　Japanese card game　カルタ　(5)；　Japanese sake　(日本酒) にほんしゅ　(6)；　Japanese traditional dance　(日本舞踊) にほんぶよう　(5)

Japanese-style clothes　(和服) わふく　(7)

jazz　ジャズ　(GS2)

jealousy; to be jealous （嫉妬[する]）しっと(する) *n.v.* (7)

jeans ジーパン、ジーンズ (7)

jewelry shop （宝石店）ほうせきてん (7)

jogging; jog ジョギング(する) *n.v.* (5)

joke （冗談）じょうだん (7)

juice ジュース (GS2)

July （七月）しちがつ (1)

June （六月）ろくがつ (1)

K

ketchup ケチャップ (6)

key （鍵）かぎ (7)

kilometer, kilogram キロ (5)

kimono （着物）きもの; kimono store （呉服屋）
ごふくや (7)

kind, type （種類）しゅるい (6)

kind, nice （親切[な]）しんせつ(な) (2)

kiss; to kiss キス(する) *n.v.* (5)

kitchen （台所）だいどころ、キッチン (6)

knife ナイフ (3)

knit, crochet （編む）あむ *C1, tr.* (7)

knitting (*object*) （編み物）あみもの (5)

know （知る）しる *C1, tr.* (3)

Korean language （韓国語）かんこくご (1)

L

laboratory （実験室）じっけんしつ (1)

lamb ラム (6)

language （言葉）ことば (4)

language lab ランゲージ・ラボ (1)

laptop computer ラップトップ・コンピュータ (4)

large, big （大きい）おおきい *i-adj.* (2)

last month （先月）せんげつ (3)

last week （先週）せんしゅう (GS4)

last year （去年）きょねん; （昨年）さくねん (3)

late （遅く）おそく *adv.* (3); be late （遅れる）
おくれる *C2, intr.* (4)

late, slow （遅い）おそい *i-adj.* (3)

later （後で）あとで (3)

laugh （笑う）わらう *C1, tr.* (3)

laundromat コインランドリー (3)

laundry （洗濯）せんたく (3)

law （法学）ほうがく (1)

lazy （不真面目[な]）ふまじめ(な) *na-adj.* (4)

learn （習う）ならう *C1, tr.* (6)

leave （出る）でる *C2, intr.* (3)

left side （左）ひだり (2)

leisure レジャー (5)

lemon レモン (6)

lend, rent out （貸す）かす *C1, tr.* (7)

lenient, gentle やさしい *i-adj.* (2)

letter （手紙）てがみ (GS3)

lettuce レタス (6)

liberal arts （教養）きょうよう (5)

library （図書館）としょかん (1)

lie （嘘）うそ (3)

light (*not heavy*) （軽い）かるい *i-adj.* (2)

light (*electric*) （電気）でんき (GS1)

light, pale color （薄い）うすい *i-adj.* (7)

light blue ライトブルー (7)

light meal （軽食）けいしょく (6)

lightning （稲光）いなびかり; （稲妻）いなずま (4)

light rain （小雨）こさめ (4)

like, favor （好き[な]）すき(な) *na-adj.* (2)

like that そう *dem. adv.* (GS1)

like this こう *dem. adv.* (4)

limit （限る）かぎる *C1, tr.* (5)

linguistics （言語学）げんごがく (1)

liquor, sake （お酒）おさけ (GS1); liquor store （酒屋）
さかや (7)

listen, ask （聞く）きく *C1, tr.* (GS1)

literature （文学）ぶんがく; literature department
（文学部）ぶんがくぶ (1)

little, a little （少し）すこし *adv.* (3); ちょっと
adv. (GS1)

live, reside （住む）すむ *C1, intr.* (3)

lively にぎやか(な) *na-adj.* (2); （陽気）ようき(な) (4)

liver レバー (4)

lobster ロブスター (6)

lock, key （鍵）かぎ; lock up （鍵をかける）
かぎをかける (7)

lonely （寂しい）さびしい *i-adj.* (7)

long （長い）ながい *i-adj.* (2)

look for （探す）さがす *C1, tr.* (1)

loose ゆるい *i-adj.* (7)

loud, gaudy （派手[な]）はで(な) *na-adj.* (2)

love （愛）あい (7)

low, short （低い）ひくい *i-adj.* (2)

lunch （昼食）ちゅうしょく (6); （昼ごはん）
ひるごはん (GS2)

M

machine （機械）きかい (2)

made in... （〜製）〜せい (7)

magazine （雑誌）ざっし (GS3)

magic, sleight-of-hand （手品）てじな (5)

mah-jongg マージャン (5)

mail, post （出す）だす; mail a letter （手紙を出す）
てがみをだす *C1, tr.* (7)

mail order メールオーダー (7)

make, fabricate （作る）つくる *C1, tr.* (GS1)

make (*a telephone call*) かける *C2, tr.* (3)

make a mistake （間違う）まちがう *C1, intr.* (3)

maker メーカー (1)

male student （男子学生）だんしがくせい (5)

mama ママ (5)

man （男）おとこ (2); （男の方）おとこのかた *pol.*;
（男の人）おとこのひと; （男性）だんせい (5)

mandarin orange みかん (6)

many （多い）おおい *i-adj.*; たくさん (2)

many times （何度も）なんども (6)

map （地図）ちず (2)

marathon; run a marathon マラソン(する) *n.v.* (5)

March （三月）さんがつ (1)

margarine マーガリン (6)

market （市場）いちば (7)

married couple （御夫婦）ごふうふ *pol.*; （夫婦）
ふうふ (5)

mathematics （数学）すうがく (1)

matter こと (5)

May （五月）ごがつ (1)

meal （御飯）ごはん (3)

meal; to eat a meal （食事[する]）しょくじ(する) *n.v.* (6)

mean, bullying　（意地悪［な］）いじわる（な）
　　na-adj.　*(4)*

meaning　（意味）いみ　*(4)*

meat　（肉）にく　*(2)*;　ground meat　（ひき肉）
　　ひきにく；ミンチ　*(6)*

meet, see (*a person*)　（会う）あう　*C1, intr.*　*(GS3)*

meeting　ミーティング　*(GS2)*

meeting, conference　（会議）かいぎ　*(5)*

melon　メロン　*(6)*

memorize　（憶える）おぼえる　*C2, tr.*　*(7)*

memory　メモリー　*(7)*

mend　（繕う）つくろう　*C1, tr.*　*(7)*

menu　メニュー　*(GS2)*

merchandise　（商品）しょうひん　*(7)*

message; leave a message　（伝言［する］）でんごん（する）
　　n.v.　*(3)*

meter　メーター、メートル　*(4)*

Mexico　メキシコ　*p.n.*;　Mexican person　（メキシコ人）
　　メキシコじん　*(1)*

middle　（真ん中）まんなか　*(2)*

milk　（牛乳）ぎゅうにゅう　*(6)*；ミルク　*(3)*

million　（百万）ひゃくまん　*(2)*

miserly　けち（な）　*na-adj.*　*(4)*

mystery (*novel*)　ミステリー　*(3)*

Monday　（月曜日）げつようび　*(GS4)*

money　（お金）おかね　*(2)*；（金）かね　*(5)*

more　もっと　*adv.*　*(4)*

more than...　～より　*(4)*；（～以上）～いじょう　*(5)*

morning　（朝）あさ　*(GS2)*；（午前中）ごぜんちゅう　*(3)*；
　　A.M.　（午前）ごぜん　*(GS2)*

morning and evening　（朝夕）あさゆう　*(4)*

most, top, best　（一番）いちばん　*(4)*

mother　（お母さん）おかあさん　*pol.*；（母）はは　*(5)*

mountain　（山）やま；mountain climbing　（山登り）
　　やまのぼり　*(4)*

movie　（映画）えいが；movie theater　（映画館）
　　えいがかん　*(GS2)*

Mr., Mrs., Ms.　（～様）～さま　*pol.*　*(4)*；～さん　*(GS1)*

multiply　（掛ける）かける　*C2, tr.*　*(GS2)*

music　（音楽）おんがく　*(GS3)*；listening to music
　　（音楽鑑賞）おんがくかんしょう　*(5)*

music store　（レコード店／レコード屋）
　　レコードてん／レコードや　*(7)*

musical　ミュージカル　*(5)*

musical instrument　（楽器）がっき　*(5)*

mutton　マトン　*(7)*

my　（私の）わたしの　*pron.*　*(GS1)*

N

name　（名前）なまえ　*(GS1)*

name card　（名刺）めいし　*(GS1)*

napkin　ナプキン　*(6)*

narrow, small　（狭い）せまい　*i-adj.*　*(2)*

national holiday　（祝日）しゅくじつ　*(3)*

nationality　（国籍）こくせき　*(1)*

navy blue　（紺）こん　*(7)*

nearby place　そば　*(2)*

near, close to　（近い）ちかい　*i-adj.*　*(GS3)*；（近く）
　　ちかく　*(3)*

necklace　ネックレス　*(7)*

necktie　ネクタイ　*(7)*

need, want　（要る）いる　*C1, tr.*　*(4)*

needle　（針）はり　*(7)*

negligee　ネグリジェ　*(7)*

neighborhood　（近所）きんじょ　*(2)*

neither　どちらも　*(5)*

nephew　（甥）おい；（甥ごさん）おいごさん　*pol.*　*(5)*

never　（一度も）いちども　*(6)*；もう　(*with negative*)
　　adv.　*(GS1)*

new　（新しい）あたらしい　*i-adj.*　*(2)*

news　ニュース　*(GS3)*

newspaper　（新聞）しんぶん　*(GS3)*

New Year's Day　（元日）がんじつ　*(3)*

next　（次）つぎ　*(GS1)*；（次の）つぎの　*(6)*

next-door　（隣）となり　*(2)*

next month　（来月）らいげつ　*(3)*

next to　（隣）となり　*(2)*

next week　（来週）らいしゅう　*(3)*

next year　（来年）らいねん　*(3)*

niece　（姪）めい；（姪ごさん）めいごさん　*pol.*　*(5)*

night　（夜）よる　*(GS2)*

nine　（九）きゅう、く；　*(GS2)*　（九つ）ここのつ　*(2)*

ninth day　（九日）ここのか　*(3)*

ninety　（九十）きゅうじゅう　*(GS5)*

no　いいえ　*(GS1)*

noisy　うるさい　*i-adj.*　*(2)*

none of them　どれも　*(5)*

noon　（昼）ひる　*(GS2)*

no one　（誰も）だれも；どなたも　*pol.*　*(5)*

north　（北）きた　*(2)*；north wind　（北風）きたかぜ　*(4)*

not at all　（全然）ぜんぜん　(*with negative*)　*(3)*

notebook　ノート　*(GS1)*

not good　ダメ（な）　*na-adj.*　*(5)*

notice, announcement　（知らせ）しらせ　*(5)*

not serious　（不真面目［な］）ふまじめ（な）
　　na-adj.　*(4)*

not tasty　まずい　*i-adj.*　*(4)*

not there, not to exist　いない　(*animate nouns*)；
　　ない　*i-adj.*　*(2)*

not very much　あ（ん）まり　(*with negative*)
　　adv.　*(2)*

not yet, still　まだ　*adv.*　*(3)*

November　（十一月）じゅういちがつ　*(1)*

now　（今）いま　*adv.*　*(GS2)*

nowhere　どこも　*(5)*

nuisance; cause trouble　（迷惑［する］）めいわく（する）
　　n.v.　*(5)*

number...　（～番）～ばん　*(GS2)*；（～号）～ごう　*(2)*；
　　（～番目）～ばんめ　*(5)*

number　（番号）ばんごう　*(GS2)*

number (*in address*)　（番地）ばんち　*(2)*

number one; first; best　（一番）いちばん　*(4)*

nutrition　（栄養）えいよう　*(6)*

nylon　ナイロン　*(7)*

O

o'clock　（～時）～じ　*(GS2)*

ocean, sea　（海）うみ　*(4)*

October　（十月）じゅうがつ　*(1)*

octopus　たこ　*(6)*

oden　おでん　*(6)*

of course　（勿論）もちろん　*(2)*

office　オフィス　*(1)*

often　よく　*adv.*　*(1)*

oh...　ああ　*interj.*　*(2)*

oh　(*exclamation of surprise*)　へえ　*interj.*　*(3)*

oil painting （油絵）あぶらえ　(5)
old （古い）ふるい　*i-adj.*　(2)
older brother （兄）あに；（お兄さん）おにいさん
　　pol.　(5)
older sister （姉）あね；（お姉さん）おねえさん
　　pol.　(5)
oldest daughter （長女）ちょうじょ　(5)
oldest son （長男）ちょうなん　(5)
Olympic　オリンピック　(5)
omelet　オムレツ　(GS3)
on （上）うえ　(2)
once （一度）いちど　(GS1)
once in a while　たまに　*adv.*　(3)
one （一）いち　(GS2)；（一つ）ひとつ　(2)
one of them　どれか　(5)
one person （一人）ひとり　(2)
oneself （自分）じぶん；by oneself （自分で）
　　じぶんで　(6)
oneself, alone （一人で）ひとりで　(5)
one time （一度）いちど　(GS1)
onion （玉葱）たまねぎ　(6)
only　～だけ；しか　(7)
onomatopoeia （擬声語）ぎせいご　(5)
open （開ける）あける　*C2, tr.*　(GS1)
opera　オペラ　(5)
optician's （眼鏡店／眼鏡屋）めがねてん／めがねや　(7)
or　か　*part.*　(1)
orange　オレンジ；orange color （オレンジ色）
　　オレンジいろ　(6)；orange juice
　　オレンジ・ジュース　(GS3)
order; to order （注文［する］）ちゅうもん（する）
　　n.v.　(7)
ordinary （普通）ふつう　(6)
origin, hometown （出身）しゅっしん　(1)
other side （向こう側）むこうがわ　(2)
out of stock （品切れ）しなぎれ　(7)
outside （外）そと　(2)
oven　オーブン　(6)
oven, range　レンジ　(6)
over （上）うえ　(2)
overcoat　オーバー　(4)
oversleeping, oversleep （寝坊［する］）ねぼう（する）*n.v.*　(4)
over there　あそこ　*dem. pron.*；あちら　*dem. pron., pol.*　(1)
own （持つ）もつ　*C1, tr.*　(3)

P

painful （痛い）いたい　*i-adj.*　(7)
painting （絵画）かいが　(5)
pair　ペア　(GS1)
pajamas　パジャマ　(7)
pan for cooking （鍋）なべ　(6)
panties　パンティー；pantyhose　パンティーストッキ
　　ング　(7)
papa　パパ　(5)
papaya　パパイア　(6)
paper （髪）かみ　(GS1)
parents （御両親）ごりょうしん　*pol.*；（両親）
　　りょうしん　*pl.*　(5)
park （公園）こうえん　(2)
parking lot （駐車場）ちゅうしゃじょう　(2)
part （一部）いちぶ　(7)
particularly, separately （別に）べつに　*adv.*　(6)
part-time job　アルバイト　(3)

party　パーティー　(GS2)
pass (*time*) （過ごす）すごす　*C1, tr.*　(5)
passenger （お客さん）おきゃくさん　(2)；
　　（客）きゃく　(7)
passion （情熱）じょうねつ　(7)
pasta　パスタ　(6)
pastime （娯楽）ごらく　(5)
pattern, design （模様）もよう　(7)
pay （払う）はらう　*C1, tr.*　(7)
pea, bean （豆）まめ　(6)
peaceful （静か［な］）しずか（な）　*na-adj.*　(2)
pear （梨）なし　(6)
pearl　パール　(7)
pen　ペン　(GS1)
pencil （鉛筆）えんぴつ　(GS1)
pen pal　ペンパル　(1)
pepper （胡椒）こしょう　(6)
perhaps, it seems that　おそらく　*adv.*　(4)
perhaps, probably （多分）たぶん　*adv.*　(4)
perhaps… (*conjecture*)　～かもしれない　(4)
person （方）かた　*pol.*；（人）ひと　(1)
pet　ペット　(5)
pharmacy （薬屋）くすりや；（薬局）
　　やっきょく　(7)
philosophy （哲学）てつがく　(1)
photo album　アルバム　(5)
photograph, photography （写真）しゃしん　(1)
physics （物理学）ぶつりがく　(1)
pianist　ピアニスト　(5)
piano　ピアノ　(5)
pickle （漬物）つけもの　(6)
picture （絵）え　(5)
picture postcard （絵はがき）えはがき　(7)
pierced earrings　ピアス　(7)
pineapple　パイナップル　(6)
ping pong　ピンポン　(5)
pink　ピンク　(7)
pizza　ピザ　(GS2)
place （場所）ばしょ　(5)
place, set on　のせる　*C2, tr.*　(6)
plain （地味［な］）じみ（な）　*na-adj.*　(7)
plain (*no pattern*) （無地）むじ　(7)
plan （予定）よてい　(6)
plastic model　プラモデル　(7)
plate （皿）さら　(6)
play （遊ぶ）あそぶ　*C1, intr.*　(5)
play (a musical instrument) （演奏する）えんそうする；
　　（弾く）ひく　*C1, tr.*　(5)
please (do something)　～てください　(2)
please, go ahead　どうぞ　(GS1)
please, give me…　～ください　(GS2)
plug outlet　コンセント　(6)
P.M. （午後）ごご　(GS2)
pocket　ポケット　(7)
police box （交番）こうばん　(2)
police officer　おまわりさん　*coll.*　(2)
polish （磨く）みがく　*C1, tr.*　(3)
political science （政治学）せいじがく　(1)
polka dots （水玉）みずたま　(7)
polyester　ポリエステル　(7)
poor at, unskillful （下手［な］）へた（な）　*na-adj.*　(5)
popcorn　ポップコーン　(6)
popularity （人気）にんき　(5)
population （人口）じんこう　(2)

pork （豚肉）ぶたにく （6）
portable　ポータブル （7）
Portuguese language （ポルトガル語）ポルトガルご （1）
post office （郵便局）ゆうびんきょく （2）
pot （鍋）なべ （6）
potato （薯）いも、じゃがいも、ポテト （6）
potato chip　ポテトチップ （7）
practice; to practice （練習[する]）れんしゅう（する）
　　n.v. （2）
precipitation （降水量）こうすいりょう （4）
preparation; prepare （準備[する]）じゅんび（する）
　　n.v. （3）
preparation for class; prepare for class （予習[する]）
　　よしゅう（する） n.v. （GS1）
present, gift　プレゼント （3）
pretty　きれい（な） na-adj. （2）
price （価格）かかく；（金額）きんがく；（値段）
　　ねだん （7）
print　プリント （7）
probably　～だろう （with plain form of verb）；
　　～でしょう pol. （4）
problem, question （問題）もんだい （4）
professional　プロ （5）
professor, teacher （先生）せんせい （GS1）
professor's office （研究室）けんきゅうしつ （1）
program (radio, TV) （番組）ばんぐみ （5）
program; to program　プログラム（する） n.v. （7）
programmer　プログラマー；　programming; to do
　　programming　プログラミング（する） n.v. （5）
pronunciation; to pronounce （発音[する]）
　　はつおん（する） n.v. （4）
proposal; propose marriage　プロポーズ（する）
　　n.v. （7）
pudding　プリン （6）
purple （紫）むらさき （7）
purpose, for the sake of　～のために （6）
put on, wear: eyeglasses, etc.　かける C2, tr. （7）；the head
　　かぶる C1, tr. （7）；the torso （着る）きる C2, tr. （3）；
　　つける C2, tr. （7）；the feet or legs　はく C1, tr. （4）；
　　rings, etc.　はめる C2, tr. （7）
put out, eject （出す）だす C1, tr. （GS1）
put something in （入れる）いれる C2, tr. （3）

Q

question; ask a question （質問[する]）しつもん（する）
　　n.v. （GS1）
quick （早い、速い）はやい i-adj. （GS3）；quickly
　　（早く、速く）はやく adv. （4）
quiet （静か[な]）しずか（な） na-adj. （2）
quiet, plain (color) （地味[な]）じみ（な） na-adj. （7）
quit　やめる C2, tr. （3）
quite　なかなか adv. （5）

R

racket　ラケット （5）
radio　ラジオ （GS2）
radio cassette　ラジカセ （1）
rain （雨）あめ （GS1）；heavy rain （大雨）おおあめ （4）
raincoat　レインコート （4）
raise or have a pet （飼う）かう C1, tr. （5）
rank, ranking （順位）じゅんい （5）

rap　ラップ （2）
rarely　ほとんど adv. （3）
rather　なかなか adv. （5）
raw （生）なま；（生の）なまの （6）
read （読む）よむ C1, tr. （GS3）
reading books; read books （読書[する]）
　　どくしょ（する） n.v. （3）
real （本当）ほんとう （GS2）；　really （本当に）
　　ほんとうに adv. （4）
receipt （領収書）りょうしゅうしょ、レシート （7）
receive　いただく (humble) C1, tr., pol. （4）；（受ける）
　　うける C2, tr. （5）
recently （最近）さいきん adv. （5）
reception office （受け付け）うけつけ （1）
recipe　レシピー （6）
recommended item （おすすめ品）おすすめひん （6）
red （赤）あか；（赤い）あかい i-adj. （2）
reduced …%　（～引き）～びき （7）
refrigerator （冷蔵庫）れいぞうこ （6）
relative （ご親戚）ごしんせき pol.；（親戚）
　　しんせき （5）
remember （思い出す）おもいだす C1, tr. （6）
remember, memorize （憶える）おぼえる C2, tr. （7）
remote control　リモコン （7）
rent, lend （貸す）かす C1, tr. （7）
rent, borrow （借りる）かりる C2, tr. （7）
repeat （繰り返す）くりかえす C1, tr. （GS1）
reporter　リポーター （6）
request, ask （お願い）おねがい （GS5）
request （頼む）たのむ C1, tr. （6）
reservation; to reserve （予約[する]）よやく（する）
　　n.v. （6）
reside （住む）すむ C1, intr. （3）
respond （答える）こたえる C2, intr. （3）；　response
　　（答え）こたえ （5）
rest （休む）やすむ C1, intr. （3）
restaurant　レストラン （2）
rest room　トイレ （2）
return, give back （返す）かえす C1, tr. （7）
return, go back （帰る）かえる C1, intr. （GS3）
returning merchandise; return merchandise （返品[する]）
　　へんぴん（する） n.v. （7）
ribbon　リボン （7）
rice (cooked) （御飯）ごはん （3）；　ライス （6）
rice (uncooked) （米）こめ （6）
rice bowl （茶碗）ちゃわん （6）
rice dealer （米屋）こめや （7）
ride （乗る）のる C1, intr. （3）
right side （右）みぎ （2）
ring (finger) （指輪）ゆびわ （7）
rise, get up （起きる）おきる C2, intr. （GS3）
robust （丈夫[な]）じょうぶ（な） na-adj. （7）
rock and roll　ロック （GS2）
rock climbing　ロッククライミング （5）
romance　ロマンス （2）
room （部屋）へや （2）
room number… （～号室）～ごうしつ （5）
rough　ラフ（な） na-adj. （4）
round （丸い、円い）まるい i-adj. （2）
rugby　ラグビー （5）
run （走る）はしる C1, intr. （GS1）
running　ランニング （5）
Russia　ロシア；p.n.；　Russian language （ロシア語）
　　ロシアご；　Russian person （ロシア人）ロシアじん （1）

S

safe　(安全[な])　あんぜん(な)　*na-adj.*　(2)

sake (for the purpose of)　～のために　(6)

saké (*liquor*)　(お酒)　おさけ　(*GS1*)

salad　サラダ　(*GS3*);　salad dressing サラダドレッシング

salaried worker　サラリーマン　(5)

sale　(売り出し)　うりだし　(7)

sales　セールス　(7)

salmon　(鮭)　さけ　(6)

salt　(塩)　しお;　salty　(塩辛い)　しおからい　*i-adj.*; salty, spicy　(辛い)　からい　*i-adj.*　(6)

same　(同じ)　おなじ　(4)

sandal　サンダル　(7)

sandwich　サンドイッチ　(6)

Saturday　(土曜日)　どようび　(*GS4*)

sausage　ソーセージ　(6)

say　(言う)　いう　*C1, intr.*　(6);　*C1, tr.*　(*GS1*)

scenery　(景色)　けしき　(6)

schedule　スケジュール　(3)

school　(学校)　がっこう　(*GS3*);　school year　(学年) がくねん　(1)

science fiction　エスエフ　(5);　science fiction movie (エスエフ映画)　エスエフえいが　(2)

scissors　(鋏)　はさみ　(7)

seafood　シーフード　(6)

season　(季節)　きせつ　(4)

seasonal word　(季語)　きご　(4)

seasoning　(調味料)　ちょうみりょう　(6)

seaweed (*laver*)　(海苔)　のり　(1)

second day　(二日)　ふつか　(3)

see　(見る)　みる　*C2, tr.*　(3)

see, meet (*a person*)　(会う)　あう　*C1, intr.*　(*GS3*)

see someone off　(送る)　おくる　*C1, tr.*　(7)

self　(自分)　じぶん　(6)

selfish　わがまま(な)　*na-adj.*　(5)

sell　(売る)　うる　*C1, tr.*　(7)

send　(出す)　だす　*C1, tr.*　(*GS1*)

sense　センス　(5)

September　(九月)　くがつ　(1)

serious　(真面目[な])　まじめ(な)　*na-adj.*　(2)

service; do gratuitously　サービス(する)　*n.v.*　(7)

set up a plan, build　(建てる)　たてる　*C2, tr.*　(7)

seven　(七)　しち、なな　(*GS2*);　(七つ)　ななつ　(2)

seventh day　(七日)　なのか　(3)

seventy　(七十)　しちじゅう、ななじゅう　(*GS5*)

several　いくつか　(5)

sew　(縫う)　ぬう　*C1, tr.*;　sewing machine ミシン　(7)

shave　(剃る)　そる;　shave facial hair　ひげをそる *C1, tr.*　(3)

she　(彼女)　かのじょ　*pron.*　(1)

shellfish　(貝)　かい　(6)

shirt　シャツ;　long sleeves; long-sleeved　(長袖) ながそで　(7);　short sleeves, short-sleeved　(半袖) はんそで　(7)

shoe　(靴)　くつ　(*GS3*);　shoe store　(靴屋) くつや　(7)

shooting; to shoot　(射撃[する])　しゃげき(する) *n.v.*　(5)

shop owner　(主人)　しゅじん　(5)

shopping; to shop　(買い物[する])　かいもの(する) *n.v.*　(*GS2*);　ショッピング(する)　(7)

shopping district, shopping street　(商店街) しょうてんがい　(7)

short　(短い)　みじかい　*i-adj.*　(4)

shorts　ショートパンツ　(4)

show　(見せる)　みせる　*C2, tr.*　(3)

show window　ショーウインドー　(6)

shower (rain)　(にわか雨)　にわかあめ　(4)

shower　シャワー　(3)

shrimp　えび　(6)

shrine (Shinto)　(神社)　じんじゃ　(2)

siblings　(兄弟)　きょうだい;　siblings, brothers　(御兄弟) ごきょうだい　*pol.*　(5)

sick　(病気)　びょうき　(3)

side　(横)　よこ　(2)

signature; to sign　サイン(する)　*n.v.*　(3)

silk　(絹)　きぬ　(7)

silver color　(銀色)　ぎんいろ　(7)

simple　(簡単[な])　かんたん(な)　*na-adj.*　(5); シンプル(な)　*na-adj.*　(7)

sincerely (*used in a letter*)　(敬具)　けいぐ　(4)

sing　(歌う)　うたう　*C1, tr.*　(3);　sing a song (歌を歌う)　うたをうたう　(5)

Singapore　シンガポール　*p.n.*;　Singaporean (シンガポール人)　シンガポールじん　(1)

single person (not married)　(独身)　どくしん　(5)

six　(六つ)　むっつ　(2);　(六)　ろく　(*GS2*)

sixth day　(六日)　むいか　(3)

sixty　(六十)　ろくじゅう　(*GS5*)

size　サイズ　(7)

skating　スケート;　to skate　スケートをする　(4)

skiing　スキー　(*GS2*);　ski　スキーをする　(4)

skillful　(器用[な])　きよう(な)　*na-adj.*　(2);　skillful (上手[な])　じょうず(な)　*na-adj.*　(5);　skillfully (上手に)　じょうずに　*adv.*　(4)

skirt　スカート　(7)

sky　(空)　そら　(4)

sleep　(眠る)　ねむる　*C1, intr.*　(3);　(寝る)　ねる *C1, intr.*　(*GS3*)

sleet　みぞれ　(4)

slender (person)　スマート(な)　*na-adj.*　(2)

slipper　スリッパ　(7)

slow　(遅い)　おそい　*i-adj.*　(3);　slowly ゆっくり　*adv.*　(1)

small　(小さい)　ちいさい　*i-adj.*　(2)

smell　(臭い)　におい　(6)

snack　おやつ;　(軽食)　けいしょく;　スナック　(6)

sneakers　スニーカー　(4)

snow　(雪)　ゆき;　heavy snow　(大雪)　おおゆき; snowstorm　(吹雪)　ふぶき　(4)

snow boots　スノーブーツ　(7)

so, really　そう　*dem. adv.*　(*GS1*)

so-so, not bad　まあまあ　(2)

soap opera　メロドラマ　(5)

soccer　サッカー　(5)

sociology　(社会学)　しゃかいがく　(1)

socks　(靴下)　くつした　(*GS3*)

sofa, couch　ソファー　(7)

software　ソフト　(ウエア)　(3)

sold out　(品切れ)　しなぎれ　(7)

some　いくつか　(5)

someday　いつか　*adv.*　(5)

somehow　どうか;　(何とか)　なんとか　(5)

someone　(誰か)　だれか;　どなたか　*pol.*　(5)

something　(何か)　なにか　(5)

sometime　いつか　*adv.*　(5)
sometimes　（時々）ときどき　*adv.*　(3)
somewhere　どこか　(5)
son　（息子）むすこ；（息子さん）むすこさん　*pol.*　(5)
song　（歌）うた　(5)
soon　（間もなく）まもなく　(7)
sorry, too bad　（残念[な]）ざんねん（な）　*na-adj.*　(GS4)
sorry, excuse me　すみません　(GS1)
sound　（音）おと　(7)
soup　スープ　(GS3)
soup or rice bowl　（お椀）おわん　(6)
sour　（酸っぱい）すっぱい　*i-adj.*　(6)
south　（南）みなみ　(1)
South Korea　（韓国）かんこく　*p.n.*；South Korean
　　person　（韓国人）かんこくじん　(1)
south wind　（南風）みなみかぜ　(4)
souvenir　おみやげ　(4)
soy sauce　（醤油）しょうゆ　(6)
space heater　ストーブ　(4)
spacious, wide　（広い）ひろい　*i-adj.*　(2)
spaghetti　スパゲッティー　(6)
Spain　スペイン　*p.n.*；Spaniard　（スペイン人）
　　スペインじん；Spanish language　（スペイン語）
　　スペインご　(1)
speak, talk, converse　（話す）はなす　*C1, tr.*　(GS3)
special talent　（特技）とくぎ　(5)
specialized subject　（専門科目）せんもんかもく　(1)
specialty store　（専門店）せんもんてん　(7)
speech　スピーチ　(4)
spend (time)　（過ごす）すごす　*C1, tr.*　(5)
spicy　（辛い）からい　*i-adj.*　(6)
spoon　スプーン　(6)
sports　スポーツ　(GS2)
sports car　スポーツ・カー　(7)
sportswear　スポーツウエア　(7)
spring　（春）はる　(4)
spring rain　（春雨）はるさめ　(4)
spring semester　（春学期）はるがっき　(5)
stamp　（切手）きって；stamp collecting　（切手集め）
　　きってあつめ　(5)
stand　（立つ）たつ　*C1, intr.*　(GS1)
start　（始まる）はじまる　*C1, intr.*　(3)；（始める）
　　はじめる　*C2, tr.*　(GS1)
state, tell　（述べる）のべる　*C2, tr.*　(6)
station　（駅）えき　(2)
stationery　（文房具）ぶんぼうぐ　(GS3)；stationery
　　store　（文房具屋）ぶんぼうぐや　(7)
steak　ステーキ　(GS3)
steam (*in cooking*)　（蒸す）むす　*C1, tr.*　(6)
stereo　ステレオ　(5)
stew　シチュー　(5)
stewardess　スチュワーデス　(5)
stir-fry　（炒める）いためる　*C2, tr.*　(6)
stockings　ストッキング　(7)
stomach　おなか　(3)
stop　やめる　*C2, tr.*　(3)
store, shop　（店）みせ　(7)
store clerk　（店員）てんいん　(7)
storm　（嵐）あらし　(4)
story; talk; speech　（話）はなし　(2)
strange, funny　おかし（な）　*na-adj.*　(6)；おかしい
　　i-adj.　(2)
strange, odd　（変[な]）へん（な）　*na-adj.*　(2)
strawberry　（苺）いちご、ストロベリー　(6)

street　（道）みち　(2)
strict　（厳しい）きびしい　*i-adj.*　(2)
stripe　（縞）しま　(7)；ストライプ　(5)
stroll; to stroll　（散歩[する]）さんぽ（する）　*n.v.*　(GS2)
strong, durable　（丈夫[な]）じょうぶ（な）　*na-adj.*　(7)
strong, powerful　（強い）つよい　*i-adj.*　(4)
strong, tough　タフ（な）　*na-adj.*　(2)
student　（学生）がくせい；student ID　（学生証）
　　がくせいしょう　(1)
study; to study　（勉強[する]）べんきょう（する）　*n.v.*　(GS2)
subtract　（引く）ひく　*C1, tr.*　(GS2)
suburbs　（郊外）こうがい　(2)
subway　（地下鉄）ちかてつ　(2)
such as that　そんな　*dem. adj.*　(4)
sugar　（砂糖）さとう　(6)
suit　（背広）せびろ　(7)
suited (be suited, fit)　（似合う）にあう　*C1, intr.*　(5)
suit coat　（上着）うわぎ　(7)
sultry　（むし暑い）むしあつい　*i-adj.*　(4)
summer　（夏）なつ　(4)；summer vacation　（夏休み）
　　なつやすみ　(6)
sun　（太陽）たいよう　(4)
Sunday　（日曜日）にちようび　(GS4)
sunglasses　サングラス　(7)
sunny　（晴れ）はれ　(4)
supermarket　スーパー　(2)
surely, certainly, undoubtedly　きっと　*adv.*　(4)
sushi restaurant　（寿司屋）すしや　(6)
sweater　セーター　(GS3)
sweatshirt　トレーナー　(7)
sweet　（甘い）あまい　*i-adj.*　(2)
sweets (cake and confections)　（お菓子）おかし　(6)
swim　（泳ぐ）およぐ　*C1, intr.*　(3)
swimming　（水泳）すいえい　(GS2)
swimming pool　プール　(1)
swimwear　（水着）みずぎ　(7)

T

table　テーブル　(GS1)
table tennis　（卓球）たっきゅう　(5)
Taiwan　（台湾）たいわん　*p.n.*；Taiwanese (person)　（台湾人）
　　たいわんじん　(1)
take　（取る）とる　*C1, tr.*　(5)
take, escort　（連れていく）つれていく　(2)
take, require (*money, time*)　かかる　*C1, intr.*　(3)
take a bath　（お風呂に入る）おふろにはいる　(3)
take (a photo)　（撮る）とる　*C1, tr.*　(7)
take out, eject　（出す）だす　*C1, tr.*　(GS1)
take a shower　（シャワーを浴びる）シャワーをあびる　(3)
take care of　（世話する）せわ（する）　*n.v.*　(5)
take off, remove (*glasses, etc.*)　はずす　*C1, tr.*　(7)
take out (*food*)　テークアウト　(6)
talk　（話す）はなす　*C1, tr.*　(GS3)
talkative　おしゃべり（な）　*na-adj.*　(4)
tape　テープ　(GS1)；tape recorder
　　テープ・レコーダー　(4)
taste　（味わう）あじわう　*C1, tr.*　(6)
tasting a sample; taste a sample　（味見[する]）
　　あじみ（する）　*n.v.*　(6)
taste, flavor　（味）あじ；taste good　（味がいい）
　　あじがいい；taste poorly　（味が悪い）あじがわるい；
　　have no taste　（味がない）あじがない　(6)
tasty　おいしい　*i-adj.*　(3)

taxi　タクシー　(2)

tea　（お茶）おちゃ　(GS3)

tea ceremony　（茶道）さどう　(5)

teach　（教える）おしえる　C2, tr.　(3)

teacher, professor　（先生）せんせい　(GS1)

teacup, rice bowl　（茶碗）ちゃわん　(6)

telephone; to make a phone call　（電話［する］）
　でんわ（する）n.v.　(GS2); telephone number
　（電話番号）でんわばんごう　(1)

tell　（話す）はなす　C1, tr.　(GS3)

temperature　（気温）きおん　(4)

temple (Buddhist)　（お寺）おてら　(2)

tempura　（天麩羅）てんぷら;　tempura restaurant
　（天麩羅屋）てんぷらや　(6)

ten　（十）じゅう　(GS2);　とお　(2)

tennis　テニス　(GS2)

ten thousand　（万）まん　(2)

tenth day　（十日）とおか　(3)

terrible　すごい　i-adj.　(5);　（大変［な］）
　たいへん（な）na-adj.　(4);　ひどい　i-adj.　(GS1)

textbook　（教科書）きょうかしょ　(GS1)

thank you　ありがとう　(GS1)

thanks to you　おかげさまで　(GS1)

that　あの　dem. adj.;　それ　dem. pron.　(1)

that much, that many　そんなに　dem. adv.　(5)

that (thing)　その　dem. adj.　(1);　that thing over there あれ
　dem. pron.　(GS1)

theatrical play　（演劇）えんげき　(5)

then, if so　じゃあ　interj.;　では　conj.　(GS1)

then, therefore　それで　(3)

there　そこ、そちら　dem. pron.　(1)

therefore　だから　conj.　(2)

there is/there are (inanimate things)　ある　C1, intr.　(2)

they (female)　（彼女たち）かのじょたち;　（彼女ら）
　かのじょら　pron., pl.　(1)

they (male)　（彼たち）かれたち;　（彼ら）かれら
　pron., pl.　(1)

thick, not thin　（厚い）あつい　i-adj.　(2)

thin　（薄い）うすい　i-adj.　(7)

thing, fact　こと　(5)

thing　もの　(2)

think (opinion)　（思う）おもう　C1, tr., intr.　(6)

think　（考える）かんがえる　C2, intr.　(3)

third day　（三日）みっか　(3)

thirsty (be thirsty)　（咽が乾く）のどがかわく　(3)

thirteenth day　（十三日）じゅうさんにち　(3)

thirty　（三十）さんじゅう　(GS5)

this　この　dem. pron.　(1)

this morning　（今朝）けさ　(2)

this month　（今月）こんげつ　(1)

this side　（こちら側）こちらがわ　(2)

this thing　これ　dem. pron.　(GS1)

this time　（今度）こんど　(3)

this week　（今週）こんしゅう　(3)

this year　（今年）ことし　(3)

though　けど　conj., coll.;　けれども　conj.　(7)

thought　（考え）かんがえ　(6)

thread　（糸）いと　(7)

three　（三）さん　(GS2);　（三つ）みっつ　(2)

throw　（投げる）なげる　C2, tr.　(5)

thunder　（雷）かみなり　(4)

Thursday　（木曜日）もくようび　(GS4)

ticket　チケット　(5)

tight　きつい　i-adj.　(2)

time, counter for hours　（時間）じかん　(2)

timetable　（時間割）じかんわり　(1)

tire, become tired　（疲れる）つかれる　C2, intr.　(3)

today　（今日）きょう　(3)

tofu　（豆腐）とうふ　(6)

together　（一緒に）いっしょに　adv.　(GS1)

toilet　トイレ　(2)

Tokyo　（東京）とうきょう　p.n.　(3)

tomato　トマト　(6)

tomorrow　（明日）あした　(3)

tonight　（今晩）こんばん　(3);　（今夜）こんや　(7)

too　も　part.　(3)

tooth　（歯）は　(3)

top　（上）うえ　(2)

totally　すっかり　adv.　(7);　（全く）まったく
　adv.　(5)

touch　（触る）さわる　C1, intr.　(3)

tough, durable　（丈夫［な］）じょうぶ（な）na-adj.　(7)

tough, strict　きつい　i-adj.　(2)

town　（町）まち　(2)

toy store　（おもちゃ屋）おもちゃや　(7)

track and field　（陸上競技）りくじょうきょうぎ　(5)

trademark　トレードマーク　(7)

trading company　（商社）しょうしゃ　(5)

transparent　（透明［な］）とうめい（な）na-adj.　(7)

travel; to travel　（旅行［する］）りょこう（する）n.v.　(5)

treat to food　（御馳走する）ごちそうする　(3)

tree　（木）き　(2)

trial　（試し）ためし　(6)

trillion　（兆）ちょう　(2)

trouble; cause trouble　（迷惑［する］）めいわく（する）
　n.v.　(5)

trousers　ズボン　(7)

true　（本当）ほんとう　(GS2);　truly　（本当に）
　ほんとうに　adv.　(4)

trust　（信じる）しんじる　C2, tr.　(3)

try　（試す）ためす　C1, tr.　(7)

try to do...　～てみる　(6)

T-shirt　Tシャツ　(5)

Tuesday　（火曜日）かようび　(GS4)

tuition　（授業料）じゅぎょうりょう　(5)

tulip　チューリップ　(7)

tuna　（鮪）まぐろ　(6);　tuna salad　ツナサラダ　(6)

turn into　なる　C1, intr.　(4)

turn on (a switch)　（入れる）いれる　C2, tr.　(3)

tutor　（家庭教師）かていきょうし　(3)

twelfth day　（十二日）じゅうににち　(3)

twentieth day　（二十日）はつか　(3)

twenty　（二十）にじゅう　(GS2)

twenty-fourth day　（二十四日）にじゅうよっか　(3)

twenty years old　（二十歳）はたち　(1)

two　（二）に　(GS2);　（二つ）ふたつ　(2)

two people　（二人）ふたり　(2)

TV　テレビ　(GS3)

type, kind　（種類）しゅるい　(6)

typing; to type　タイプ（する）n.v.　(6)

typhoon　（台風）たいふう　(4)

U

umbrella　（傘）かさ　(GS3);　put up an umbrella
　かさをさす　(7)

uncle　おじ;　おじさん　pol.　(5)

under　（下）した　(2)

underground （地下）ちか （*GS3*）

underground floor （地階）ちかい （*GS3*）

understand わかる *C1, tr.* （*GS1*）

underwear （下着）したぎ （7）

undress （脱ぐ）ぬぐ *C1, tr.* （3）

uniform （制服）せいふく （7）

university （大学）だいがく； university student （大学生）だいがくせい （1）

until now これまでに （6）

up （上）うえ （2）

up to, until まで *part.* （2）

use （使う）つかう *C1, tr.* （*GS1*）

usual （普通）ふつう （6）

V

vacation （休暇）きゅうか （3）

vanilla バニラ （*GS5*）

various （色々[な]）いろいろ(な) *na-adj.* （2）

Vaseline ワセリン （7）

vegetable （野菜）やさい （*GS1*）; vegetable juice （野菜ジュース）やさいジュース （7）; vegetable salad （野菜サラダ）やさいサラダ （6）; vegetable store （八百屋）やおや （7）

vegetarian ベジタリアン （*GS5*）

very とても *adv.* （*GS3*）

very, awful すごい *i-adj.* （5）

very (much) （大変[な]）たいへん(な) *na-adj.* （4）

very sorry （申し訳ない）もうしわけない （7）

video ビデオ （6）

videocamera ビデオカメラ （5）

video game テレビゲーム、ビデオ・ゲーム （5）

village （村）むら （2）

vinegar （酢）す、ビネガー （6）

violin バイオリン （5）

visit; inquire （伺う）うかがう *C1, tr.* （5）

vivid （鮮やか[な]）あざやか(な) *na-adj.* （7）

volleyball バレーボール （5）

W

Wednesday （水曜日）すいようび （*GS4*）

Western clothes （洋服）ようふく （7）

Western clothing store （洋品店）ようひんてん （7）

Western cuisine （洋食）ようしょく （6）

Western-style style （洋風）ようふう （6）

wait （待つ）まつ *C1, tr.* （*GS1*）

waiter ウエター； waitress ウエトレス （2）

wake up （起きる）おきる *C2, intr.* （*GS3*）

walk （歩く）あるく *C1, intr.* （*GS1*）

walking, on foot （徒歩）とほ （2）

wall （壁）かべ （*GS1*）

wallet （財布）さいふ （2）

want （欲しがる）ほしがる *C1, tr.*；（欲しい）ほしい *i-adj.* （6）

want to… ～たがる (*with conjunctive form of verb*) *C1, intr.* （6）

want to… ～たい (*with conjunctive form of verb*) *i-adj.* （6）

ward (*in city*) （区）く （2）

warm （暖かい）あたたかい *i-adj.* （*GS4*）

wash （洗う）あらう *C1, tr.*； wash one's face （顔を洗う）かおをあらう （3）

watch (clock) shop （時計店／時計屋）とけいてん／とけいや （7）

water （お水）おみず；（水）みず （6）

watercolor （水彩画）すいさいが （5）

we (female) あたしたち *pron., inf., f., pl.* （1）

we (male) （僕たち）ぼくたち *pron., m., inf., pl.* （1）

we （私たち）わたしたち *pron., pl.* （1）

weak （弱い）よわい *i-adj.* （4）

weak point （苦手）にがて （5）

wear (see "put on") かぶる *C1, tr.*；つける （7）；はく （4）；（着る）きる （3）

weather （天気）てんき； weather forecast （天気予報）てんきよほう； weather map （天気図）てんきず （4）

week before last （先々週）せんせんしゅう （*GS4*）

weekday （平日）へいじつ （3）

weekend （週末）しゅうまつ （3）

weight lifting ウエート・リフティング （5）

weird （変[な]）へん(な) *na-adj.* （2）

well… あのう… （1）

well, see you じゃあ… *interj.* （*GS1*）

well (done) よく *adv.* （1）

well-lighted （明るい）あかるい *i-adj.* （4）

west （西）にし （4）

what （何）なに、なん （*GS4*）; what （何）なん （*GS1*）; what color （何色）なにいろ （1）; what day （何日）なんにち （3）; what day of the week （何曜日）なんようび; what kind どんな *dem. adj.* （*GS4*）; what language （何語）なにご （1）; what minute （何分）なんぷん （3）; what month （何月）なんがつ; what nationality （何人）なにじん （1）; what time （何時）なんじ （*GS2*）; what year （何年）なんねん （3）; what year in school （何年生）なんねんせい （1）

when (in questions) いつ （*GS4*）

when… （～時）～とき （7）

where どこ *dem. pron.* （*GS3*）; どちら *pol.* （*GS4*）

whether… ～かどうか （7）

which (of two) どちら （*GS4*）; which (of more than two) どの *dem. adj.* （1）

whichever どちらでも （5）

which one どちらのほう （4）; どっち *coll.* （1）

which thing (of more than two) どれ *dem. adj.* （*GS4*）

while… ～ながら (*with conjunctive form of verbs*) （6）

whiskey ウイスキー （*GS2*）

white （白）しろ （7）（白い）しろい *i-adj.* （2）

white-collar worker サラリーマン （5）

who だれ （*GS4*）; どなた *pol.* （1）

why どうして、なぜ （1）

wide （広い）ひろい *i-adj.* （2）

wife （奥さん）おくさん *pol.*；（家内）かない；（妻）つま （5）

wind （風）かぜ； wind blows （風が吹く）かぜがふく （4）

window （窓）まど （*GS1*）

wine ワイン （*GS2*）; red wine （赤ワイン）あかワイン （5） white wine （白ワイン）しろワイン （5）

winter （冬）ふゆ （4）; winter vacation （冬休み）ふゆやすみ （6）

with, by で *part.* （2）

with (together) と *part.* （*GS3*）

withdraw (*money*) おろす *C1, tr.* （7）

without knowing it （いつの間にか）いつのまにか （5）

woman （女）おんな *(2)*;（女の方）おんなのかた *pol.* *(5)*;
　（女の人）おんなのひと *(2)*;（女性）じょせい *(5)*
women's wear store （婦人服店）ふじんふくてん *(7)*
wood （木）き *(2)*
wool ウール *(7)*
word （言葉）ことば *(4)*
work （働く）はたらく *C1, intr.* *(3)*
wow わあ *interj.* *(GS3)*
wrap （包む）つつむ *C1, tr.*; wrapping paper
　（包み紙）つつみがみ *(7)*
wrestling レスリング *(5)*
write （書く）かく *C1, tr.* *(GS1)*
wrong number (*telephone*) （間違い電話）
　まちがいでんわ *(3)*

Y

yacht ヨット *(5)*
year before last おととし *(7)*
year in school （学年）がくねん *(1)*

years before （〜年前に）〜ねんまえに *(6)*
yellow （黄色）きいろ *(6)*;（黄色い）きいろい *i-adj.* *(7)*
yen （円）えん *(GS3)*
yes ええ、はい *interj.* *(GS1)*
yesterday （昨日）きのう *(GS3)*
yoga ヨガ *(5)*
yogurt ヨーグルト *(6)*
you あなたたち *pron., pl.* *(1)*
you あなた *pron., s.* *(1)*
young （若い）わかい *i-adj.* *(2)*
younger brother （弟さん）おとうとさん *pol.*;
　（弟）おとうと *(5)*
younger sister （妹さん）いもうとさん *pol.*
　（妹）いもうと *(5)*
you're welcome どういたしまして *(GS1)*

Z

zero （零）れい、ゼロ *(GS2)*
zipper ファスナー *(7)*